# Brief Contents

# Contents

# Ethics in a Computing Culture

**BO BRINKMAN**
**AND**
**ALTON F. SANDERS**

COURSE TECHNOLOGY
CENGAGE Learning

Australia • Brazil • Japan • Korea • Mexico • Singapore • Spain • United Kingdom • United States

# COURSE TECHNOLOGY
## CENGAGE Learning

**Ethics in a Computing Culture**
Bo Brinkman and Alton F. Sanders

Executive Editor: Marie Lee

Acquisitions Editor: Brandi Shailer

Senior Product Manager: Alyssa Pratt

Development Editor: Ann Shaffer

Editorial Assistant/Associate Product Manager:
  Stephanie Lorenz

Content Project Manager: Jennifer Feltri

Associate Art Director: Faith Brosnan

Associate Marketing Manager: Shanna Shelton

Cover Designer: Wing-ip Ngan, Ink design, inc.

Cover Image Credit: Shutterstock/Csaba Peterdi

Compositor: Integra

For product information and technology assistance, contact us at **Cengage Learning Customer & Sales Support,** www.cengage.com/support

For permission to use material from this text or product, submit all requests online at **cengage.com/permissions**
Further permissions questions can be e-mailed to
**permissionrequest@cengage.com**

Library of Congress Control Number: 2011942866

ISBN-13: 978-1-111-53110-2

ISBN-10: 1-111-53110-2

**Cengage Learning**
20 Channel Center Street
Boston, MA 02210

Cengage Learning is a leading provider of customized learning solutions with office locations around the globe, including Singapore, the United Kingdom, Australia, Mexico, Brazil, and Japan. Locate your local office at: **international.cengage.com/region**.

Cengage Learning products are represented in Canada by Nelson Education, Ltd.

For your lifelong learning solutions, visit **course.cengage.com**
Visit our corporate website at **cengage.com**.

Some of the product names and company names used in this book have been used for identification purposes only and may be trademarks or registered trademarks of their respective manufacturers and sellers.

Any fictional data related to persons or companies or URLs used throughout this book is intended for instructional purposes only. At the time this book was printed, any such data was fictional and not belonging to any real persons or companies.

Course Technology, a part of Cengage Learning, reserves the right to revise this publication and make changes from time to time in its content without notice.

The programs in this book are for instructional purposes only.

They have been tested with care, but are not guaranteed for any particular intent beyond educational purposes. The author and the publisher do not offer any warranties or representations, nor do they accept any liabilities with respect to the programs.

Printed in the United States of America
2 3 4 5 6 7 16

# Preface

This book is intended to be used in a one-semester undergraduate course on computer ethics. Students are expected to have completed college-level composition and literature courses, but coursework in computing is not required for students who use computers in their everyday life. The book has been used successfully with both computer science majors, and with majors from a wide variety of other disciplines.

## APPROACH

Our teaching philosophy is that a computer ethics course serves two main functions: one is to introduce students to important theories from ethical philosophy and related fields, and the other is to help students see how these theories are relevant to computing and to everyday life. In order to do this, we ask students to read, reflect, decide, and explain (in that order).

We try to select case studies that are playful, contemporary, and surprising in an effort to keep students engaged and intrigued. We do not avoid controversy, but instead we often demand that students take a strong position, and defend it. The book is designed to support this style of teaching.

## ORGANIZATION AND COVERAGE

This book has nine chapters. Some chapters (1, 2, and 8) are organized around a particular branch of theory that is helpful for ethical decision makers in computing. Each of the others is organized around a central theme (such as privacy or safety).

**Chapter 1** introduces the fundamentals of moral and ethical reasoning that will be used in the rest of the text. The chapter covers the moral theories most useful for practical reasoning. Like most textbooks on computer ethics, this book covers relativism, consequentualism, deontological theories, virtue theory, and contractarianism. It also covers some theories that appear less frequently in textbooks concerning computer ethics, such as common morality, the ethics of justice, and the ethics of caring. All of the moral theory necessary for working with the material in the later chapters is covered in Chapter 1.

**Chapter 2** introduces professional ethics and professional codes of ethics, which necessarily requires some discussion of professions and professionalism. Although much of the discussion applies to any profession, the emphasis is on the computer professions, to the extent that the word "profession" applies to them. Future computer scientists, future software engineers, and students destined for other related professions have a clear interest in the professional ethics of their vocations. The significance of such material to students with other plans is perhaps less self-evident, but no less real. The decisions of computing professionals will strongly affect many people in all aspects of society. Thus, these topics are of interest to all students.

**Chapter 3** examines in detail the impact of computers and other technology on our expectations and experiences of privacy. Large databases, the Internet, cell phones, and numerous other programs or devices have already altered our multiple notions of privacy. We explore our "right to privacy" in terms of what it should be and what it can be. We look at legal issues concerning privacy as well as moral issues concerning privacy.

**Chapter 4** examines the nature of intellectual and intangible property. We cover issues related to copyrights, patents, trademarks, and plagiarism. Many of the case studies are taken from recent controversial cases involving such matters as file sharing, patenting of software, and copy protection. We also explore the new concept of virtual goods, in which property, and potentially its value, is virtual, in the sense of having a worth expressed in virtual money.

**Chapter 5** looks at the many ways people place their trust in computers and explores when such trust is justified. The chapter includes numerous real cases involving negative consequences of computer failures. The chapter explains the difficulties of preventing such failures and what can be done to mitigate the risks. The chapter also discusses various kinds of maliciousness involving computers, including viruses, intrusions, and theft of information.

**Chapter 6** explores the ways computers and other modern technology change us. Computers affect our safety, our privacy, our communication capabilities, our access to information, and many other aspects of our lives. In so doing, they also affect our attitudes, our expectations, our ways of interacting with our fellow humans, and even our values. In short, they affect who we are. Wikipedia, video games, Facebook, and many other such recent creations are affecting how we act. These issues are examined in this chapter.

**Chapter 7** presents a detailed discussion of freedom of expression, as well as the new problems involved in protecting that freedom in the age of computers and the Internet. It traces the legal principles of free expression as defined by the United States Constitution and also explores problems with the inherent multinational aspect of the Internet.

**Chapter 8** looks at how computing technologies affect vulnerable groups in modern society, such as children and the physically disabled. Technology does not always bestow its benefits on all people equally; in fact, some groups are completely excluded from the advantages of technology. Sometimes technology, such as computers, actually harms people in certain vulnerable groups. This chapter examines in detail all of these issues.

**Chapter 9** addresses the ubiquity of computers. It explores the ways they are becoming more and more a part of our lives, not only as tools employed by humans, but sometimes as substitutes for humans, or for some part of a human. From robot vacuum cleaners to stock-trading software that automatically chooses stocks to buy or sell, computers are performing tasks and making decisions without direct human intervention. This chapter explores the potential benefits and risks of such technology.

## FEATURES OF THE TEXT

Each chapter includes the following pedagogical features:

- **Case Studies**—The plentiful case studies in every chapter provide concrete examples of situations involving moral or ethical questions. Most chapters begin with at least one case study and all chapters include numerous case studies beginning early in the chapter. Frequently a case is presented before all of the principles potentially involved in the case have been discussed. That is intentional. To paraphrase Oliver Wendell Holmes, we think it often useful to decide the questions of the case first and determine the principle afterwards. Moral reasoning, like the law, relies less on logic and more on experience. Obviously, logic is required, but seldom do we decide practical ethical questions from deductive reasoning from first principles.

- **Reflection Questions**—Each section is followed by two to six Reflection Questions. This allows students to pause after each section and spend some time in reflection and writing about what they have just read. The Reflection Questions are meant to serve as prompts to get the students thinking. Many Reflection Questions contain interesting new material, and so they should be required reading, even if the student is not required to answer them as homework. Most of the Reflection Questions require the student to take a position, and justify it, while others require further research. Each Reflection Questions section focuses on a particular aspect of the critical thinking process, and are labeled as follows:

  - **Position**—The main purpose of these questions is to get students to take a position and justify it.

  - **Application**—To answer an Application question, the student has to apply a theory, concept, or definition to a case. This helps the student understand the practical uses of specific concepts.

- **Context**—These questions require the student to pay special attention to the role of context in applying theories or concepts. Often times a Context Question will consist of an earlier Reflection Question that has been slightly altered by changing its context a little. Students will often be surprised by how a slight change in context alters their answers to these questions.

- **Research**—To expand a student's understanding of a topic, Research Questions require outside research of some kind. Some ask the student to find sources on the Web, while others require the student to interview family members or fellow students.

- **Summary**—At the end of each chapter, a bulleted list of main points summarizes the essential topics. In particular, the summaries focus on any important theories or concepts. Each chapter summary also restates important definitions.

- **Chapter Exercises**—In addition to the hundreds of Reflection Questions spread throughout the body of the text, each chapter ends with some Review questions as well as additional Position, Application, Context, and Research questions that ask students to step back and take a look at the larger picture. The Review questions ask for a restatement or review of received knowledge and do not require much depth or time. The other questions are intended to form the basis of major writing assignments.

- **Works Cited**—Bibliographic entries of works that were explicitly cited in the chapter are included at the end of each chapter.

- **Related Readings**—We believe that students should be challenged to engage with journalism, artistic creations, and primary sources, not just the textbook. The related readings section is meant to help the instructor and interested student find other readings related to the chapter. We find that for most of our students it is these related readings that the students still remember three to five years after taking the course. This section includes more than just reading suggestions. A variety of interesting film and television shows are also included.

## FOR THE INSTRUCTOR

It is expected that, for a traditional three-credit college course (meeting three hours per week for fifteen weeks), each chapter will take one to two weeks. Chapters 1 and 2 should be covered first because the tools developed in these chapters are used throughout the rest of the book.

We recommend using this book as a way to prepare students for in-class discussion. We believe that students learn best by reflecting on a dilemma, then making a decision, and then explaining their decisions. Furthermore, we believe that writing is the natural expression of, and tool for, reflection. The book is designed to provide students with ethical dilemmas and prompts for reflection. Students should read a little bit, and write a little bit, every day, outside of class. In-class time is best used to clarify tricky ideas, or to allow students to work in groups (small or large) to explain and question each other's ideas.

## INSTRUCTOR RESOURCES

One of the authors of this book, Bo Brinkman, maintains a Web site and Twitter feed to provide instructors using this textbook with additional discussion prompts, example grading rubrics, and so on.

The authors' blog, *EthicsInAComputingCulture.com*, provides sample course schedules, reading lists, paper assignments (with grading rubrics), in-class exercises, and more. Much of the material on EthicsInAComputingCulture.com is Creative Commons licensed for free reuse, remixing, and republication.

The Twitter feed, @EiaCC (for "Ethics in a Computing Culture") routinely provides links to interesting news stories that can be used in class discussion or as background for writing assignments. The authors read any tweets that mention @EiaCC daily, so this is also a good way to clarify questions about the book, report errata, and engage with other instructors who also use the book.

The following teaching tools are also available to instructors on a single CD-ROM and through the Instructor Companion Site at *login.cengage.com*.

- **Electronic Instructor's Manual**. The Instructor's Manual follows the text chapter-by-chapter to assist in planning and organizing an effective, engaging course. The manual includes learning objectives, chapter overviews, lecture notes, ideas for classroom activities, and additional resources. A **sample course syllabus** is also available.

- **PowerPoint Presentations**. This text provides PowerPoint slides to accompany each chapter. Slides are included to guide classroom presentation, to make available to students for chapter review, or to print as classroom handouts. Instructors may customize the slides to best suit their course with the **complete figure files** from the text.

- **ExamView**®. This textbook is accompanied by ExamView, a powerful testing software package that allows instructors to create and administer printed, LAN-based, and Internet exams. ExamView includes hundreds of questions that correspond directly to the text, enabling students to generate detailed study guides that include page references for further review. The computer-based and Internet testing components allow students to take exams at their computers, and save the instructor time by grading each exam automatically. These test banks are also available in **Blackboard**, **WebCT**, and **Angel** compatible formats.

## ACKNOWLEDGMENTS

The authors wish to acknowledge the heroic efforts of the editors and production staff of Cengage Learning, who worked hard to keep the material focused and the prose clear.

We especially wish to acknowledge the good work and fruitful discussions with our students at Miami University, who have, over the years, provided many useful and insightful perspectives on the material and cases covered in the book.

Finally, a special thanks to our reviewers, who provided invaluable suggestions and critiques of the chapters as we wrote them: Florence Appel, St. Xavier University; Augusto Casas, St. Thomas Aquinas College; Nicole English, University of Missouri—Kansas City; John Sullins, Sonoma State University; and Jay Summet, Georgia Institute of Technology.

# Chapter 1

# Critical Reasoning and Moral Theory

In this chapter we will introduce the basic components of the ethical reasoning that will be used through the rest of the book. In particular, we will focus on the key ideas of eight ethical theories, as well as on the fundamentals of ethical argumentation.

There are ethical decisions for which knowledgeable, well-meaning, rational, human beings cannot agree on the best course of action. When searching for answers on moral issues, we will often ask questions for which there is no one single correct answer. However, that does not mean there are no incorrect answers. For most questions, there are many incorrect answers—in fact, an infinite number of them. Moral theories are useful because they can help you explain why one answer might be better than another. Moral theories can also help you figure out why you might find it difficult to agree with another person about the answer to a moral question.

Throughout this chapter we will discuss a number of case studies that illustrate specific moral questions.

## 1.1 CASE: BORROWING A PASSWORD

Our first case is an extremely simple one. It is offered to introduce our approach to the topic of ethical analysis and decision making. Those readers who have studied programming may think of it as analogous to a "hello world" program, which is a simple program designed to teach a student one or two basic commands in a new programming language.

1

### 1.1.1 Borrowing a Password, Scenario 1

Alice and Josh, two first-year undergraduate students, are good friends. Josh tells Alice that his account on the university's network has been disabled and he needs to complete a paper for his English class. He asks Alice to give him her password so that he can log onto her account and write the paper. Because Alice considers Josh to be a close friend, she provides him with her password. Josh logs onto Alice's account and completes his paper for English. He did not look at the content of any of Alice's files, nor did he delete or modify anything. He simply wrote his paper and logged off the system.

### Reflection Questions

1. POSITION Did anyone in Scenario 1 do anything wrong? Use your intuition to define "wrong" as you deem appropriate for the context of the case. Explain your reasoning.

2. POSITION Explain how you interpreted the word "wrong" in Question 1. Did you consider any other interpretations?

3. CONTEXT How, if at all, would various university policies affect your answer to Question 1? For example, would it make a difference if the university policy explicitly forbade revealing your password to another party or signing onto the system as someone other than yourself?

4. POSITION If Alice's decision to provide Josh with her password was definitely against university policy, would that necessarily mean that sharing the password was wrong?

5. CONTEXT The case did not specify why Josh's account was disabled. Did that hinder your ability to answer Question 1? If so, what sort of facts might have affected your answer?

6. CONTEXT The case specifies that Alice and Josh are both first-year students. Would it make any difference to your answer if they were seniors? Explain why or why not.

7. CONTEXT The case does not specify Alice's or Josh's major subject, age, or experience with computers. Would information on any of those attributes affect your answer to the first question?

Despite the apparent simplicity of this first case, students tend to arrive at surprisingly different conclusions about the rightness or wrongness of sharing the password. The most common response is that both Alice and Josh probably violated university policy, but that it was not wrong to do so in this particular situation.

### 1.1.2 Borrowing a Password, Scenario 2

This scenario is like the previous one with one potentially significant difference. In this case, Josh and Alice are software engineering majors. Josh is a senior and Alice has already graduated. She is working for a software development firm, Alpha Software as a software engineer. Josh asks to use Alice's account at Alpha

Software rather than a university account. As before, Josh completed his paper without looking at anything he was not authorized to see and he didn't do anything other than create a word processing file for his paper.

## Reflection Questions

1. POSITION Did anyone in Scenario 2 do anything wrong? Again, use your intuition to define "wrong" as you deem appropriate for the context of the case. Explain your reasoning.

2. CONTEXT Suppose Josh has accepted a job at Beta Software, a competitor of Alpha Software. He is not currently employed by Beta Software, but will begin working for them thirty days after graduation. Would that information affect your answer to the previous question? Explain.

3. CONTEXT Suppose the terms of Alice's employment required her to protect the confidentiality of corporate information and that Alice was well aware of that requirement. Would that affect any of your previous answers? Explain.

4. CONTEXT Suppose the terms of Alice's employment required her to protect the confidentiality of corporate information, but she didn't read this information in the various documents she had signed and paid little attention in the orientation lectures when she started the job. Hence, she was not actually aware of the requirement to protect the confidentiality of corporate information. Would this affect your previous analysis of the case? Explain.

5. POSITION Suppose Alice had denied Josh's request. Did anyone in the scenario do anything wrong in your view? Explain.

### 1.1.3 Borrowing a Password, Scenario 3

This scenario is like Scenario 2 except for the following significant addition. When Josh completed his paper, he e-mailed the paper to his professor. He then logged off of Alice's account. Alpha Software monitors the e-mail of its employees and it was observed that an e-mail with an attachment of a file in Alice's directory had been sent to a server outside of Alpha Software's network. Alice's boss, Carol, confronted Alice, who readily admitted her transgression of company policy. Carol viewed Alice's actions as a cavalier disregard for company security and fired Alice. Alice was given two weeks' pay and escorted off the premises.

## Reflection Questions

1. POSITION Did anyone in Scenario 3 do anything wrong? As before, use your own interpretation of the appropriate meaning of "wrong." Explain your reasoning.

2. CONTEXT Suppose Alpha Software never told Alice that her e-mail would be monitored. Would that affect your answer to the previous question? Explain.

3. CONTEXT Suppose Carol had once been guilty of doing something similar. She also was caught, but simply received a reprimand. Would that affect your answer to Question 1?

4. CONTEXT Suppose we agree, for the time being, that Carol was justified in firing Alice. We know something that Carol cannot know, namely that Josh did not view any Alpha Software files and did not alter anything belonging to Alpha Software in any way. If, through some mysterious process Carol could know what we know, would she still be justified in firing Alice? Explain.

Upon reading and thinking about these scenarios, most students have little difficulty deciding who, if anyone, did something wrong. However, it is also true that most students have considerable difficulty in articulating just why they think what they think. As you learn more about moral theories, you will gain greater insight into your own moral decision-making processes.

## 1.2  CASE: WARNING OR TICKET?

In Scenarios 2 and 3 in the previous case, Alice's role as a computer professional has important implications for what she ought to do. It is quite likely, however, that you are not familiar with the rights and responsibilities of computer professionals, and hence should not be expected to see these implications right away. (You'll learn more about these rights and responsibilities in Chapter 2.) In order to clarify the importance of one's profession in ethical decision-making, we will now consider a case related to a profession that most people know more about: police officer.

### 1.2.1  Warning or Ticket? Scenario 1

Herman Schmidt is a police officer. One morning he observed a driver, Dolores Delgado, a young working mother, who failed to stop at a stop sign. Dolores and Officer Schmidt have known each other for years, and although they have never been close, they have always been friendly with each other.

When stopped, Dolores readily concedes that she missed the stop sign. She says that she was on her way to drop off her daughter at her day-care center before going to work. A bee had flown through the window, upsetting her daughter, and Dolores had become distracted. As a result, she simply did not notice the stop sign. She appeals to Officer Schmidt to overlook her error and let her be on her way so that she can get her daughter to day care and still get to work on time.

Officer Schmidt has a decision to make. The law in this case permits a certain amount of discretion by the police in the case of a "rolling stop," but that discretion clearly does not apply in this case. Dolores did not even see the stop sign, much less slow down for it.

## Reflection Questions

1. POSITION What should Officer Schmidt do? In particular, should he:
   a. Give Dolores a warning?
   b. Give Dolores a ticket?
   c. Arrest Dolores?

   Note that the question asks what Officer Schmidt should do, not what you think he is likely to do. The latter would be a prediction and might involve matters not under discussion here, such as the resolve and character of the decision maker.

2. CONTEXT Suppose Dolores had been an 18-year-old male whom Officer Schmidt did not know. Should that affect the officer's decision? Explain.

3. CONTEXT Suppose Officer Schmidt and Dolores had had a romantic relationship in the past. Should that affect Officer Schmidt's decision? Explain.

4. CONTEXT Suppose Dolores had been rude and argumentative with Officer Schmidt. Should that affect his decision?

5. POSITION Question 1 offers three, and only three, possible choices for Officer Schmidt. Do you have a definite opinion on the proper course of action? If so, why do you have that opinion? If you don't have a clear opinion, do you think additional information would help form your opinion? If so, what information?

## 1.2.2 Warning or Ticket? Scenario 2

The situation is the same as in Scenario 1 except that, when Dolores ran the stop sign, she struck a pedestrian in the crosswalk, badly injuring him.

## Reflection Questions

1. CONTEXT You still have three choices about Officer Schmidt's proper course of action: give Dolores a warning, cite her, or arrest her. Has the information about the pedestrian changed your opinion from the previous scenario? Why or why not?

2. CONTEXT Suppose the person struck by Dolores happened to be the mayor. Would that affect Officer Schmidt's proper action? Why or why not? Obviously, in the situation described here, there might be considerable reason for Officer Schmidt to do something other than what he deems to be correct.

3. POSITION Suppose Officer Schmidt had stopped Dolores for running the stop sign the previous week and had given her a warning. Was Officer Schmidt wrong to have done that? Explain.

### 1.2.3   No Harm, No Foul

Different people have different responses to these two scenarios. It is common in classroom discussion of this case for some to argue that a police officer is required to uphold the law and that the policy of issuing a ticket for running a stop sign should be the same independent of whether the officer knows the driver and also independent of the consequences of the error.

Students often take the **no harm, no foul** approach, arguing that it is wrong to punish a person for a simple mistake when no harm was done. (The phrase "no harm, no foul" comes from recreational basketball, where one does not usually enforce the rules about fouls unless the fouled player's performance is significantly affected.) If harm was done, however, then we must levy some form of punishment. Hence, it is proper for Officer Schmidt to let Dolores off in the first scenario, but not the second.

Some students find that they change their opinion, depending on how much they know about Dolores's behavior. For example, suppose Dolores had not been distracted by a bee bothering her child, but instead suppose she had been texting while driving. Often students who previously advocated leniency change their view after receiving this information. Because there is no way to refute or verify her story, you cannot know for certain whether Dolores is telling the truth. One way to deal with such uncertainty is to rely on the public policy as reflected by the law.

Notice that the reasons for a particular decision—in this case, whether to warn, ticket, or arrest—give rise to additional questions of a more general nature: is the "no harm, no foul" principle valid? Is the law the most important factor? Do we assume people are telling us the truth unless there is concrete evidence to the contrary?

### Reflection Questions

1. APPLICATION Did the "no harm, no foul" principle affect your initial answers to any of the scenarios of the first case involving Alice and Josh?

2. CONTEXT In Scenario 3 of the first case, it is unlikely that Josh knew that Alice would be fired. One might argue that Josh should have known that there was at least a possibility of Alice getting into trouble if she let him use her account. In your judgment of Josh's actions, do you consider what he should have known as well as what he knew?

3. POSITION Suppose Alice's argument that no harm had come from her bad decision to allow Josh to use her account convinced Carol to let her off with a warning. Would Carol's decision be justified? Explain.

## 1.3   MORALITY AND ETHICS

Traditionally, ethics has referred to the philosophy of morality. Lately, however, the term has also been used more broadly to refer to the ideals and rules of professional groups. For this reason, we will use the following definition of ethics, as given by Michael Davis. He has stated and published the definition in a number of places, but the source we are using is his book, *Profession, Code, and Ethics.*

> **Ethics** is a set of *morally permissible* standards of a *group* that each member of the group (at his/her rational best) wants every other member to follow even if their doing so would mean that he/she must do the same (Davis, 40).

Using this definition as our starting point, we can talk about "the ethics of software developers" or the "ethics of Google," and start to analyze the standards that these groups ought to follow. Note that, according to this definition, the standards must be morally permissible. In other words, they may not be immoral, although they could be morally neutral. Hence, a set of criminal standards, such as the "ethics of thieves," is not really ethics, just as counterfeit money is not really money. Also, the phrase "his or her rational best" refers to the mental state of the person who wants the rules to be followed. The person is assumed to be a rational person whose capacity for reasoning is not diminished through some form of injury, disease, drugs, grief, fear, and so on. A related topic, morality, concerns the standards desired by all humans at their rational best. Morality is the set of ethical rules that apply when the group includes all rational humans. As Davis puts it:

> **Morality** is the set of standards everyone (every rational person at his/her rational best) wants everyone else to follow even if their following them means having to do the same (41).

In this book, our use of "ethical" is not synonymous with "morally good." Instead, we use "ethical" to express consistency with a particular standard. For example, in the United States it is against the ethical standards of physicians to advertise prices for their services. There is nothing inherently moral or immoral about advertising prices, so the prohibition on advertising prices is morally permissible. In other words, an action might be unethical, but morally permissible.

We have already seen two examples of where a person is clearly faced with an ethical decision that is also a moral decision. Alice was employed as a software engineering professional in scenarios two and three of Case 1.1. Her ethical decision was an unusual one for a software engineering professional and she was new at her profession, but she made the decision as a software engineering professional. Helping a friend is a desirable action and is generally morally permissible. Maintaining the security of her company's network was an ethical obligation. She needed to weigh the two issues.

More typical is the situation of Officer Schmidt in Case 1.2. Officer Schmidt was faced with a decision that police officers confront routinely. As part of a larger group of law enforcement officers, he is subject to certain ethical rules. However, Officer Schmidt is also a member of a much larger group, the human race, and thus is subject to the rules of human morality. Hence, it could happen that one's ethical duty to one's profession conflicts with moral standards. For example, Officer Schmidt, as a police officer, is ethically obligated to follow the orders of his superiors. That is a morally permissible rule. If, however, that superior gave him an order to do something immoral, Officer

Schmidt's duty to follow the rule would conflict with morality. Many German soldiers during World War II were faced with exactly that dilemma. In such cases, the moral obligation outweighs the ethical rule.

Our working definition of morality, as given by Davis, may not match your notion of what morality is. We shall address this issue in greater detail in the next section, where we address various definitions of "morality." First, however, we should ask if Davis's definition is meaningful. Are there any standards that everyone wants everyone else to follow? If there are no such standards, then we are faced with a vacuous definition.

As it happens, yes, such standards seem to exist, although their precise formulation is elusive. Just as language appears to be universal with respect to human social groups, so too does morality. The same basic rules regarding killing, stealing, lying, and so on, seem to be enforced in all human groups. However, rules regarding human behavior are complex, with many exceptions. Reasoning about such matters is often tricky. For example, suppose you promise your son that you will be home in time to take him to the zoo. Clearly, in this case, if you were to break your promise in order to play poker with your friends, you would have violated a common moral rule. However, if you broke your promise in order to rush a heart attack victim to the hospital, you would not be guilty of breaking the moral rule, because protecting and preserving human life trumps keeping the promise to your son.

In the rest of this chapter, we look at various approaches to systematizing and clarifying the complexities of such decisions by some of the great thinkers on the subject.

### Reflection Questions

1. CONTEXT In Scenario 1 of Case 1.1, Alice and Josh are first-year students. In your view, is there a set of ethical rules for students? Explain.

2. CONTEXT In Scenarios 2 and 3 of Case 1.1, Alice is a professional and has an ethical code to follow. Josh is still a student and so he does not have that same code. How, if at all, do you think that should affect your evaluations of their actions? Explain.

## 1.4  MORAL THEORY

A **moral theory** is a way of defining morality. As we said earlier, our working definition of "morality" is not necessarily the same definition accepted by everyone. Distinguishing moral actions from immoral actions, the right from the wrong, the good from the bad, has been a quest of humans throughout history. We can look at the quest for defining morality essentially as an attempt to answer one or both of the following questions:

1.  How do I know that X is good?
2.  Why is X good?

We will look at a few of the important efforts to address such questions. Frequently the various ways of defining morality lead to the same ethical decisions, but sometimes what is morally permissible can vary, depending on how you define the concept. Sometimes the differences are major and can lead to fundamental disagreement. In an ethical discussion, it is important to understand the underlying definition of morality that is being used and the group for which the ethical standards apply. For example, two people may have a fundamental disagreement on the morality of abortion. If those two people are physicians, it is likely that they will have fundamental disagreements on certain ethical decisions within their profession. If they are both software engineers, the moral disagreement over abortion is far less likely to play a role in their ethical decision making.

## 1.4.1 Religious Ethics

The term **religious ethics** refers to a set of ethical standards for the followers of a particular religion. It is natural for a person who adheres to a particular religion to define "doing the right thing" according the dictates of his or her religion. Indeed, all major religions offer their own set of ethics. In that case, the morally permissible standards of the particular group required by our definition of *ethics* would be the standards accepted by the followers of that religion (or a particular sect of that religion). Those standards would be morally permissible according the morality defined by that religion. Because most religions hold that the standards of that religion are appropriate for all humans, the ethical standards for the followers of the religion are generally the same as the moral standards.

Some people think that the teachings of their religion are all they need to make ethical decisions, even in their professional lives. In that case, they are equating *ethical* judgments for their profession with *moral* judgments (that is, ethical judgments that apply to everyone). The first problem with using religious ethics for ethical judgments in a professional context is that the ethical rules for most professions contain rules that are not moral rules. For one example, consider the ethics of IT professionals. It is unlikely that one's religion directly addresses the issue of whether it is moral to postpone installing Microsoft's latest security update until next week. Yet, you might well consider it a breach of ethics if the IT professional in charge of your e-mail server did that, particularly if it resulted in loss of files due to some sort of virus that would otherwise have been prevented.

There is another problem with defining ethics, particularly professional ethics, in terms of religious ethics. We want people to be ethical regardless of their religious beliefs. That is, agnostics, atheists, Buddhists, Christians, Jews, Muslims, and everybody else, should all be ethical—they should follow the standards set forth by their profession. This means our ethical models must provide a way for anyone to do the right thing, to the extent that the right thing can be determined. We don't want people to have to believe that God decreed that murder is bad in order for them to believe that murder is bad. Thus, the methods of ethical decision-making that we will suggest in this book will be generally consistent with, or at least not violate, religious beliefs.

### Reflection Questions

1. **APPLICATION** Is it possible for a person who faithfully follows the rules of his or her religion to be immoral? Explain.

2. **APPLICATION** Is it possible for a person who faithfully follows the rules of his or her religion to be unethical? Explain.

3. **APPLICATION** Is it possible for a person who often violates the rules of his or her religion to be moral? Explain.

4. **APPLICATION** Is it possible for a person who often violates the rules of his or her religion to be ethical? Explain.

### 1.4.2  Divine Command Theory

The **divine command theory** is a moral theory that holds that X is good because God commands it, and for no other reason. This idea dates back to Plato's dialogue *Euthyphro*, written in the fourth century BC. The condensed version of the Euthyphro question goes like this: "Is goodness loved by the gods because it is good, or is it good because it is loved by the gods?" Important theologians have squared off on both sides of the argument. Thomas Aquinas (1225 – 1274 C.E.), for example, believed that things are good in and of themselves, while John Calvin (1509 – 1564) and Martin Luther (1483 – 1546) held no standards for good and evil exist outside of God.

Let's return a moment to the questions raised in the introduction to Section 1.4. With respect to the first question (How do I know that X is good?), in many societies, religious institutions play a major role in teaching children the difference between right and wrong. Most people start life by learning moral rules, but only gradually come to understand the reasons for those rules. Some religious thinkers believe, however, that there is no answer to the "why is X good" question, other than "God commands X." This is what we mean by the divine command theory of morality. We do not presume to know the answer to the Euthyphro question, but for the purposes of this book, we reject the divine command theory. We are concerned primarily with the ethical standards of those who create or sell various kinds of technology, particularly computers and computer software, and by groups that use such technology in ways that affect the public. Hence, we need answers to "Why is X good?" to which people of all the religions represented in our society can agree.

Figure 1.1 summarizes the key ideas of divine command theory.

- God, and only God, decrees what is right and what is wrong.
- God's decrees are communicated to us via all or some of the following:
  - religious texts
  - human messengers of God, such as priests or prophets
  - divine revelation
- God's decrees are all we need to determine the right action in any situation.

**FIGURE 1.1** Key ideas of divine command theory

## Reflection Questions

1. APPLICATION Can a person who is not religious act morally? Why or why not?

2. APPLICATION Can a person who is not religious act ethically? Why or why not?

### 1.4.3  Cultural Relativism

**Cultural relativism** is a moral theory that holds that no valid rational criterion for determining the right thing to do exists. According to this theory, an action is judged good or bad based only on the standards that have been adopted by one's society. Although individuals may be judged by whether they conform to the standards of their culture, different cultures cannot be judged against each other.

Cultural relativism seems attractive, at first, because it appears to promote tolerance of other cultures. **Tolerance** is the willingness to let people do what they wish, as long as there is no overriding justification to do otherwise. Cultural relativism goes beyond tolerance, claiming that there is never any acceptable justification for one culture to override the wishes of another.

This position is difficult to defend. We know, for example, that in early Mesoamerica humans were regularly sacrificed to gods. The numbers and reasons are in dispute, but the evidence suggests that thousands of people per year were sacrificed. We know of the inquisition that was took place in Europe, particularly Spain, beginning in the fifteenth century. For years, extreme torture was used, and thousands were executed. We know of the Nazis creating camps where millions were systematically exterminated. Most of us agree to refer to such acts as atrocities and to condemn the acts as immoral. Cultural relativism would argue that the people committing the acts were acting within the framework of their culture and should not be judged by our standards, but by the standards of their culture. Critics of cultural relativism argue that such acts are immoral in any culture, and that some universal moral standards apply to all cultures.

As mentioned earlier, two attributes of human culture seem to be universal: morality and language. Every culture, whether technologically primitive or advanced, has both a moral structure and a language. Moral structures, like languages, differ substantially in their particulars but, also like languages, share many common elements. In both cases, the rules can be quite complex—too complex to articulate in a few simple statements. However, the fact that we cannot articulate the rules does not mean they do not exist. Native speakers who know nothing of grammar nevertheless are fluent in their speech. Similarly, all human cultures have some form of moral structure and these structures seem to include the same basic concepts. As with language, the rules have exceptions and can be difficult to pin down, but they exist. This "natural morality" is considered by some to be a gift of God and by others a product of evolution. In either case, it appears to be linked to human beings rather than to human culture. If moral relativism can thus be proven untenable, it follows that there are moral universals, just as we believe that there are language universals. Bernard Gert, in his book, *Common Morality,* says the following:

> The existence of a common morality is supported by the widespread agreement of most moral matters by all moral agents. Insofar as they do not use any beliefs that are not shared by all moral agents, they all agree that killing, causing pain or disability, or depriving of freedom or pleasure any other moral agent is immoral unless there is an adequate justification for doing such an action. Similarly, they all agree that deceiving, breaking promises, cheating, breaking the law, and neglecting duties also need justification in order not to be immoral. There are no real doubts about these matters. The claim that there are moral rules prohibiting such actions as killing and deceiving means only that these kinds of actions are immoral unless they can be justified. Given this understanding, all moral agents agree that there are moral rules prohibiting such actions as killing and deceiving. (Gert 2004, 8-9)

As Gert points out, the justifications for such exceptions vary across cultures. Note, however, justifications are not convictions; they are products of reason and interpretation of evidence and are consequently subject to evaluation and comparison. Cultural relativism has been examined by many scholars and the current prevailing view is that the case for cultural relativism is weak. And like divine command theory, cultural relativism does not provide useful guidance in deciding what is right when interacting with people of other cultures.

Figure 1.2 summarizes the key ideas of cultural relativism.

---

- Cultural relativism is based on the following two premises:
    - Morally judging an individual involves comparing the individual's behavior to the standards of his or her culture.
    - There is no rational way to compare cultures with respect to morality.
- From those premises, it follows that there can therefore be no universal human morality.
- Critics of cultural relativism argue that moral standards exist for human beings independent of culture. Hence, both of the premises of cultural relativism are false.

---

**F I G U R E  1.2**   Key ideas of cultural relativism

### Reflection Questions

1. APPLICATION Could a person be a cultural relativist and still be a moral person according to your notion of morality?

2. APPLICATION One problem with cultural relativism is defining the boundaries of a culture. Clearly, anyone living in the United States today is living in a different culture than someone living in the society of the ancient Aztecs. But how about a man who as of today has lived all of his forty years in rural Alabama verses a woman who has lived all of her twenty years in New York City? Are they members of the same culture?

Do students residing in university housing belong to the same culture as professors working at that same university? How about an African American living in Columbus, Ohio versus a Native American of the Miami Tribe living in Oklahoma? Give a collection of plausible heuristic rules for determining whether two people belong to the same culture.

3.  RESEARCH If we differentiate different cultures so finely that each person defines his or her own culture, we could wind up with a new moral theory: subjectivism. Research the different kinds of subjectivism and present the arguments for and against this theory.

## 1.4.4   Virtue Theory

**Virtue theory** is a moral theory that, as the name implies, concerns the nature of virtue and what it means to have virtue. Virtue focuses more on the nature of the person making a decision, rather than the decision itself. Virtue theory has a long history. It was introduced by Plato (c. 428 – c. 348 B. C.) in ancient Greece in fourth century, but was developed primarily by Aristotle (384-322 B. C.). In particular, it answers two questions:

- What does it mean to be "good?"
- How does one become good?

Aristotle's approach to the question "What does it mean to be good?" was to try to list the **virtues**, which are the characteristics of a good person, including courage, friendliness, and modesty. Each virtue is an **ideal mean** between two extremes of a human characteristic. An ideal mean in this context means that it is the half-way point when one considers all relevant factors. For example, courage is the ideal between cowardice and recklessness. To have no fear of anything is foolish and to be afraid of everything is cowardly. However, a courageous person is not necessarily merely half afraid and half fearless. The degree of bravery depends on the context. Climbing a cliff for the thrill of doing it is not equal to climbing a cliff in order to rescue another person. The virtuous person's courage would allow for greater risk in the second case than in the first.

Aristotle also answers, in part, the question, "How does one become good?" He says that there are two kinds of virtues: intellectual virtues and character virtues. One acquires intellectual virtues through education, whereas one develops a good character by habitually acting according to the virtues. According to him, we are not born virtuous but must learn it over time. It takes time and experience to absorb the teaching needed to develop intellectual virtues. We learn to be virtuous in character by mimicking virtuous behavior, until it becomes habitual. For example, if one wants to become generous, then she ought to make a habit of doing acts that appear generous: give alms to the poor, help a friend move, donate time to a local charity, and so on. Eventually acting generously will become a habit that she does not have to think about.

According to this way of thinking, moral decision-making boils down to a basic question, "What would a good person do in this situation?" Ethical decision-making based on a virtue theory model of morality would be "What would a virtuous member of this group do in this situation?"

For example, suppose you are a software engineer who has been directed by your boss to release a product that you believe to be insufficiently tested. Suppose further that the software is used in an automobile and could affect the safety of the passengers. Clearly refusing to comply with your boss's command could have consequences that you fear. Nevertheless, a virtuous person who is convinced that such an action is wrong would have the courage to refuse because it is the courageous thing to do. Our example is, of course, incomplete here because the decision process for determining the wrongness of the action is not addressed here. We will look more extensively into such matters later in the book.

The number of virtues varies according to how you count. For example, Aristotle considered courage to be the ideal mean of both fear and confidence: "In fear and confidence, courage is the mean. Of those who exceed it, the person who exceeds in fearlessness has no name (many cases lack names), while the one who exceeds in confidence is rash. He who exceeds in being afraid and is deficient in confidence is a coward" (32).

We could therefore consider courage to be two different virtues which happen to have the same name or one virtue that is ideal along two dimensions of character. Our list of the virtues is in Table 1.1. Extremes marked with asterisks are names we created and are not attributed to Aristotle.

**TABLE 1.1     Aristotle's virtues and vices**

| virtue | domain | extremes [vices] | |
|---|---|---|---|
| | | deficit | excess |
| courage | fearlessness | cowardly | reckless* |
| | confidence | cowardly | rash |
| temperance | pleasure and pain | insensible | intemperate |
| generosity | giving and taking money | stingy | wasteful |
| magnificence | giving and taking money | petty* | tasteless and vulgar |
| greatness of soul | honor and dishonor | small of soul | vain |
| even tempered | anger | slow-tempered | quick-tempered |
| truthfulness | self assessment* | self-deprecating | boastful |
| wittiness | amusement | boorish | clownish |
| friendliness | relationship to others | quarrelsome | obsequious |
| properly disposed to shame | shame | shameless | shameful |
| appropriate indignation | empathy* | spiteful | envious |

In the first scenario of Case 1.2, if Officer Schmidt did not give Dolores a ticket, would he be acting virtuously? The virtues of friendliness, truthfulness, and good temper are all related to the case, but the most closely related virtue is righteous indignation. **Righteous indignation** is the anger we feel at someone's undeserved good or bad fortune. According to this way of thinking, Dolores deserves to get a ticket, because she broke the law, and also because her behavior might have endangered others. The virtuous person, while desiring to please Dolores, would most likely still give her the ticket that she deserved.

Figure 1.3 summarizes the key ideas of virtue ethics.

- Virtue Ethics is agent-centered as opposed to act-centered. That is, it focuses more on the character of the person making the decision rather than on the decision itself.
- A person becomes virtuous by repeatedly doing virtuous acts until they become habitual.

**F I G U R E  1.3**  Key ideas of virtue ethics

## Reflection Questions

1. APPLICATION Think of two people you know very well and who are, according to your current perception of virtue, truly virtuous people. Suppose both are presented with an ethical decision. Will both of these virtuous people make the same decision?

2. APPLICATION Some professions use an apprenticeship system for becoming a professional. For example, physicians must learn much through formal training, but must also serve a kind of apprenticeship working for a senior physician. Thus, the young physician develops the proper habits of being a physician. Explain why such training is consistent with the childhood training of a virtuous person according to virtue theory.

### 1.4.5  Utilitarianism and Consequentialism

In 1958, the philosopher G. E. M. Anscombe introduced the term **consequentialism** to denote any theory of ethics that holds that the consequence of an action, not the motivation behind the action, makes the action good or bad. **Utilitarianism** is a consequentialist moral theory that says that the right decision is the one that causes the most happiness.

The philosopher Jeremy Bentham (1748-1832) is usually regarded as the father of utilitarianism, with John Stuart Mill (1806-1873) regarded as its strongest proponent. The principle of utilitarianism says that one ought to do that which causes the greatest utility. **Utility** in this case means maximizing happiness in the world. According to Bentham, utilitarianism is motivated by the "greatest happiness principle." But how do we define happiness? According to Mill, "happiness is…pleasure and the absence of pain," whereas unhappiness means "pain and the absence of pleasure." It is important to understand that the pleasure referred to in utilitarianism is not simply physical pleasure. Mental and emotional pleasure in the sense of satisfaction of accomplishment, appreciation of an interesting idea, aesthetic pleasure of a poem or sonata, or the pleasure in helping others are equally significant in the calculation of the utility.

The moral act, according to utilitarianism, is the one that maximizes happiness. Because that maximization of happiness will occur in the future as a consequence of the act, the nature of utilitarianism is necessarily predictive. That means that our ability to predict the consequences of a decision determines to a significant degree the morality of our actions.

Utilitarianism comes in a variety of forms. Broadly, we divide the many types into two major categories: act utilitarianism and rule utilitarianism. In **act utilitarianism**, each ethical choice is evaluated according to whether or not the action taken maximizes happiness, compared to the other options. In **rule utilitarianism**, we select a set of rules, and each act is evaluated as to whether it conforms to them. The rules are selected so as to maximize happiness if followed faithfully. Notice that some acts that are allowed under rule utilitarianism could, in principle, cause unhappiness, and hence be contrary to act utilitarianism. However, the aggregate of acts that follows the rules maximizes happiness, even if not entirely uniformly. We will explore the details of these two theories further in the next two sections.

**1.4.5.1 Act Utilitarianism**    Act utilitarianism is conceptually easy to understand. When we have an ethical decision to make, we make it so as to maximize the total amount of happiness in the world. As mentioned earlier, Bentham referred to this as the greatest happiness principle, which is often phrased as "the greatest good for the greatest number." The process of calculating which action will lead to the greatest happiness is sometimes called the **utilitarian calculus**. In act utilitarianism, the calculations must be done frequently and by ordinary persons.

In simple examples, act utilitarianism seems very useful. For example, imagine your friend asks you, "How do I look?" You could lie and say, "Fantastic!" Or, you could be truthful and list the things you don't like about your friend's appearance. But in this case, being truthful is likely to be hurtful, while telling a white lie does not seem to harm anyone. An act utilitarian calculation indicates that telling the white lie maximizes utility, and so it is the right thing to do. This helps explain why most of us are comfortable with these types of untruths. Note, however, that this does not show that it is always okay to lie. The act utilitarian analysis depended heavily on the fact that no harm would come from this particular lie.

The utilitarian calculus can, at times, be tricky. Some factors that complicate the calculation are as follows:

- Some pleasures are different from others in quality, and so count either more or less than others.
- It is hard to know whether a particular action will actually make another person happier or not.
- Many decisions affect thousands or millions of people for dozens or hundreds of years, which makes their impact on total happiness very hard to estimate.

For example, suppose you have the power to confiscate the entire fortune of a massively rich person, with a net worth of, say, 30 billion dollars. Hence, if you took all of the billionaire's money, you could give each of the 300 million people in the United States approximately 100 dollars. It is true that the ex-billionaire would be very unhappy, but the rest of the people would be somewhat happier. Hence, when presented in this very simplistic way, confiscating the money seems to be the moral thing to do.

It is unlikely that you accept this reasoning. The problem is that our calculation was too simplistic. We assumed that everyone would be happy to get 100 dollars. But surely most of us would feel guilty about getting 100 dollars at the expense of someone else. Furthermore, we might worry that the same thing that happened to the ex-billionaire might happen to us, which also decreases our happiness. It is highly plausible that an overwhelming majority of people receiving a 100-dollar bonus by the theft of someone else's money would actually be less happy. Two utilitarians might end up disagreeing about this case because they disagree about whether or not the recipients of the money would be happy, and because they disagree about how to weigh the ex-billionaire's extreme unhappiness against the mild increase in happiness for millions of people. In other words, the determination of what maximizes happiness should take into account the depth of the unhappiness or happiness as well as the quality of it.

When we attempt to calculate the happiness or unhappiness of everybody, there is still more to consider beyond the depth and quality of the emotions. For example, the way in which the happiness and unhappiness is distributed should be taken into account. Many people being a little happier does not necessarily balance with one person being extremely unhappy. Finally, variations over time should be considered. For example, giving all school children candy for lunch may make them happier in the short run, but ultimately candy for lunch would diminish overall happiness.

Another case that highlights the difficulty of the utilitarian calculus involves someone who is profoundly unhappy. Suppose this person has no close friends and no family to mourn him if he were to die. Is it then, according to utilitarianism, morally right to kill this person so that the unhappiness in the world will be diminished? Again, it is unlikely that any reader would accept such an argument, but an act utilitarian analysis supports the idea. As we will see later in this chapter, rule utilitarianism helps resolve some of these difficulties.

**1.4.5.2 An Application of Act Utilitarianism**   Let us do a careful analysis of Officer Schmidt's case using act utilitarianism. He might reason as follows: "If I let Dolores go, I will not have to write the ticket, and I will not have to waste my time testifying in court. I certainly will be happier. Dolores will certainly be much happier since she did not get a ticket. So, overall, there is definitely an increase in happiness."

According to this line of reasoning, what could decrease happiness? One of the main reasons for giving tickets is to deter drivers from taking chances and from not concentrating on their driving. If Dolores later committed the same offense because she was not sufficiently motivated to be more careful, that might result in injury or death, which would greatly increase pain and suffering.

Officer Schmidt, however, has read studies that indicate that mothers driving with their children in the car are statistically the least dangerous drivers on the road. Moreover, he knows Dolores to be a responsible person, probably especially so with her child in the car. He concludes that the deterrent factor is not significant. There are some other remote possibilities of increasing unhappiness. For example, perhaps the act of violating his ethical duty as a police officer is habit forming and would, in a sense, corrupt Officer Schmidt. He dismisses that notion as far-fetched and can find no other such hazards. He concludes then, quite correctly, that in this particular case the act utilitarian analysis indicates that letting Dolores off would be the morally correct thing to do, despite its conflict with his ethical duty.

Notice that Officer Schmidt's knowledge of the statistical studies of driver profiles had an impact on his decision. Acceptance of act utilitarianism as a definition of morality necessarily suggests that the officer had a duty to attempt to make himself aware of such information. If acting morally requires you to make such predictions, then it would follow that acting morally would require you to prepare yourself for that as best you can. However, even if you try to be as capable as you can with such calculations, it is still very difficult to do so and making such calculations can lead to error. That was, in large part, the reason rule utilitarianism was introduced.

## Reflection Questions

1. APPLICATION Suppose your friend has a valuable antique. She does not know it is valuable and throws it away. Would you then be at liberty to take it from her trash can? After all, to do so would not decrease her happiness because she has no knowledge of the article's value. Support your answer using an act utilitarian argument.

2. POSITION In Section 1.1 we mentioned the "no harm, no foul" principle. Does being a utilitarian imply that one must accept the "no harm, no foul" principle? Explain why or why not.

**1.4.5.3 Rule Utilitarianism**   The basic premise of rule utilitarianism is that easy-to-follow rules will lead to fewer calculations. The rules can be examined at length by experts, and thus will increase utility (happiness) better than act utilitarianism despite the fact that in some cases individual acts may decrease utility.

A simple analogy can explain this possibly confusing notion. Suppose you are required to move through a maze that is a labyrinth of interconnected chambers. The walls are smooth and the light is bad and so it is very difficult to predict at a particular fork the merits of taking one path over another. However, a simple rule will get you through the maze successfully: as you enter the maze, put your right hand on the right hand wall, and then move forward, without ever backing up or taking your hand off the wall. In this way, you will always find your way through the maze. It will not necessarily be the shortest path; in fact, it could be the longest. But you will get through.

Compare this approach to either randomly wandering the maze or attempting to remember where you have been in the maze. The random approach will cause you to wander around in circles. Remembering where you have been will be too difficult in a large maze, leading you to make mistakes, which again leads to going around in circles.

The logic of rule utilitarianism is similar. If you have a good set of rules and reason to believe they maximize utility, then following them is better than acting randomly, and you'll be much less error-prone than attempting to evaluate individual acts as advocated by act utilitarianism. According to rule utilitarianism, we should adopt a set of rules and then violate them only in the case where compelling evidence indicates that utility is increased by such a violation. To continue with the maze analogy, if you can see the exit, then you can take your hand off of the wall and exit the maze.

In the case of the maze, the rule is a very simple one and its usefulness is clear. Deciding on a set of rules to maximize happiness is a much more daunting task. We shall certainly not pretend that we know an optimal set of utilitarian rules. We can however present a plausible working set adequate for the analysis of our cases. Although not originally presented as a set of utilitarian rules, the rules of common morality as presented by Bernard Gert will serve well for our purposes. Gert's rules are as follows:

1. Do not kill.
2. Do not cause pain.
3. Do not disable.
4. Do not deprive of freedom.
5. Do not deprive of pleasure.
6. Do not deceive.
7. Keep your promises.
8. Do not cheat.
9. Obey the law.
10. Do your duty.

In Gert's model, there is no need for a separate "Do not steal" rule because it is covered by a combination of rules, although primarily by rule 4. Recall that these are rules that you must follow unless you can justify breaking one in a particular situation. Justification, in the context of rule utilitarianism, is a compelling reason to believe that breaking the rule would result in greater utility. The default obligation then is to follow the rule. Only when there is a compelling case that utility will be enhanced is there justification for breaking the rule.

**1.4.5.4 An Application of Rule Utilitarianism**    Returning yet again to Officer Schmidt, we can examine our reasoning to see if a rule utilitarian argument will justify letting Dolores off. The previous argument does not work here. Remember that the argument needs to be compelling. The decision under act utilitarianism relied upon a statistical study and Officer Schmidt's opinion about Dolores's sense of responsibility while driving. Those were adequate to tip the scales between two equal alternatives, but here the choices are not equal. There needs to be conclusive evidence (a compelling case) to overturn rule 10. The case is good but not compelling and hence Officer Schmidt must do his duty and give Dolores a ticket. Figure 1.4 summarizes the key ideas of utilitarianism.

- Happiness is the only moral good.
- Morality is the maximization of total happiness.
- The consequences of an action are more important than the motivation behind the action when evaluating whether or not the action was morally correct.
- Pleasure should not be interpreted necessarily as physical pleasure. Mental pleasure and emotional pleasure are included.
- There are two major kinds of utilitarianism:
    - Act Utilitarianism: Each act is to be evaluated morally according to the degree to which it increases or decreases overall human happiness. The moral act is the one that maximizes happiness.
    - Rule Utilitarianism: Rules are established that when followed by everyone will result in maximizing happiness. Although a particular act, when done according to a rule, may not maximize happiness, the overall result, when the rules are followed will maximize happiness.

**F I G U R E  1.4**   Key ideas of act utilitarianism

### Reflection Questions

1. ⃞APPLICATION⃞ Give an example of a situation where rule utilitarianism, using the rules we suggested, would lead to a different decision than act utilitarianism.

2. ⃞APPLICATION⃞ Suppose you are in a lifeboat with several other act utilitarians. The lifeboat is overloaded and so the heaviest people in boat are thrown overboard until the lifeboat is no longer overloaded. Was that a moral act? Explain.

### 1.4.6   Deontological Ethics

Deontological ethical theories differ sharply from utilitarianism and other consequentialist theories in that, for many decisions, the reasons become more important than the ends. A **deontological** ethical theory focuses on rights, duties, obligations, and rules. Hence, according to these theories, some rules must be followed, even if following a particular rule would result in a bad end. Instead of cataloging the many types of deontological ethics, we will focus on one example, expressed in the moral theories of the German philosopher, Immanuel Kant (1724-1804). This makes sense because virtually all deontological theories owe something to Kant.

It is easiest to understand Kant's position by comparing it to utilitarianism. Utilitarians hold that happiness is the only thing that is always inherently good. Kant, on the other hand, says "Nothing … [can] be called 'good' without qualification except a *good will*" [our emphasis]. A **good will** in Kant's terminology is the will of a person to act solely according to a code of morality based purely in reason. Every act is thus moral or immoral according to whether it is consistent with the good will. Taking the position that every being capable of rational thought ought to follow the same moral rules, he set out to find rules that could be proven correct simply based on reason and logic.

Kant's main contribution to moral philosophy can be summed up in one principle: the categorical imperative. The **categorical imperative** is a rule that must always be followed by all rational beings. "Categorical" means absolute, unconditional, and an end in itself, while "imperative" means a command.

Kant provides several formulations of the categorical imperative. He viewed each formulation as a different way of stating the same imperative. The equivalence of the different formulations is not self-evident, and we will treat them as separate laws without attempting to establish equivalence among the different formulations. Rather than present Kant's philosophy in detail, we focus on two laws that are particularly useful in applied ethics:

1. **Universal law of nature**—Act only according to maxims (principles) that could be adopted as universal laws.
2. **Principle of the end in itself**—Treat humans, both yourself and others, always as ends in themselves, and never merely as a means to an end.

The universal law of nature requires that we are willing to make the subjective principle that determined our decision a universal requirement for all. Only if the principle can be made universal is the act morally correct.

The universal law of nature can be used to construct a mathematical-like proof that a maxim is not morally acceptable. For example, let's start with the maxim "It is always morally acceptable to steal anything that you want." A Kantian might argue as follows:

- If it is okay to steal, then we should not expect to have any personal property.
- If there is no such thing as personal property, then there is no such thing as "stealing."
- Hence, the maxim is logically invalid; either there is no such thing as stealing (so the maxim is invalid), or stealing is wrong (so the maxim is invalid).

Hence, in this analysis, the claim that stealing is morally wrong is based purely on a logical argument. The rule "it is okay to steal" has been proved to be nonsensical, and all rational beings have a duty to recognize this fact.

In some cases it is not possible to prove that a maxim is logically inconsistent. In this case one might use the universal law of nature to show that if the maxim were a universal law, it would lead to some other bad outcome. For example, consider the following maxim: it is okay for me to dump my garbage in my yard, rather than subscribing to trash pickup. If this were made a universal law, it would lead to negative consequences such as decreases in home values, the spread of disease, and so on, but it does not necessarily lead to a logical inconsistency.

The universal law of nature is most useful for proving a particular proposed moral rule is incorrect. It is much more difficult to use it in real cases, because it is hard to figure out which maxim we ought to be analyzing. Let's again consider Scenario 1 of the Officer Schmidt case. If Officer Schmidt lets Dolores off, what is the maxim by which he makes that decision? Officer Schmidt's decision would start with the premise that he, as a police officer, can overrule the law. The argument, similar to that above, would be:

- An officer's primary job is to enforce the law.
- If a police officer can overrule the law, then there is no law beyond the opinions of police officers.
- If there is no law, there is nothing to enforce and hence no police (they would have nothing to do).
- Hence the rule is invalid. Either police officers cannot overrule the law, in which case the maxim is invalid, or there is no law to enforce (and hence no officers to enforce it) and so the maxim is invalid.

It is less obvious, but also true, that Officer Schmidt would violate the principle of the end in itself by letting Dolores off. Dolores's act of asking Officer Schmidt to let her off was manipulative, even if that had not been her conscious intent. Hence Dolores was attempting to use Officer Schmidt as a means, and thus violated the principle of the end in itself. Now Officer Schmidt, if he cooperates with this, is treating himself as a means rather than an end. Hence, he too will violate the principle of the end in itself.

What if Officer Schmidt does not realize that he is being manipulated? According to the categorical imperative, Officer Schmidt has a duty to avoid using any human being as a means rather than an end. Even if it were not Dolores's intent to manipulate Officer Schmidt, his shirking of his duty would be such a violation in and of itself.

As with consequentialism, deontological ethics can lead us into a number of moral quandaries. The lack of exceptions to the rules is a particular problem with deontological ethics. One of the most cited examples is that of a woman who comes to your door and asks to hide from a killer who is pursuing her. You allow her to hide in your closet and then the killer comes to the door and asks if she is in your house. According to Kant, you may not lie, even in this case. You may refuse to answer, which, in this case, probably is an answer, but you may not deceive the killer. Many of us would consider it acceptable, and in fact mandatory, to lie in this extreme situation. A common view expressed about that kind of situation is that the value of a human life must take precedence over telling the truth and it is necessary to deceive the killer, assuming that capturing or disabling the killer is not feasible. The categorical imperative would not allow for that, which is viewed by some as a serious flaw to the model.

There is much more to Kant than is mentioned here and there is more to deontological ethics than Kant. However, this short summary should be enough to help you practice ethical decision-making as it applies to computer ethics in the upcoming chapters.

Figure 1.5 summarizes the key ideas of deontological ethics.

- The only good is the good will.
- Each act is to be evaluated as to whether it is consistent with the good will.
- Consistency with the good will is established by the categorical imperative.
- The categorical imperative has more than one formulation:
  - *Universal law of nature:* Act only according to maxims that could be adopted as universal laws.
  - *Principle of the end in itself:* Treat humans, both yourself and others, always as ends in themselves, and never merely as a means to an end.

**F I G U R E  1.5**  Key ideas of deontological ethics

## Reflection Questions

1. APPLICATION Suppose student A asks to copy student B's paper, and student B agrees. Using the principle of the end in itself, argue that *both* students (not just student A) have acted immorally.

2. APPLICATION Consider the maxim "It is always morally acceptable to lie." In the spirit of the universal law of nature, prove that this maxim cannot be universally adopted. (Hint: If everyone lied whenever it was convenient, would lying still be useful?)

## 1.4.7  Contractarianism

Contractarianism is both a political theory and a moral theory. Some of its attributes can be merged with consequentialist theories or with deontological theories. There are, in fact, contractarian versions of each. Contractarianism stems from the writings of the English philosopher Thomas Hobbes (1588-1579). The premise behind his work is that people are rational beings who wish to promote their own self-interests, and the best way of doing that is to promote the common interests of society.

According to Hobbes, we were all originally in a "state of nature," in which we acted alone (or, in family units) to provide for our worldly needs of food and shelter. In the state of nature, the scarcity of resources naturally leads people into competition with each other, resulting in perpetual violent conflict. As a result, wrote Hobbes, human lives are naturally "solitary, poor, nasty, brutish, and short."

In Hobbes's view, the only way to overcome this natural inclination toward violence is to come together with others for mutual benefit. We enter into contracts in which each party agrees to certain obligations in exchange for other benefits. Although such contracts are often implicit (that is, never explicitly articulated), they are real and enforced by social norms and by political institutions. The claim is that, in this way, a person can serve his or her own self-interest while at the same time acting for the public good.

The obvious question to ask with regard to contractarianism is this: "Is a person's self-interest really maximized by acting for the public good?" This is a difficult question to answer. One well-known approach to this problem uses game theory to show that cooperation is, in the long run, the best policy. **Game theory** is a branch of mathematics in which an individual (a player) makes choices that potentially create points for the player. The number of points a player wins depends on his or her choices and on the choices of other players.

To apply game theory to contractarianism, consider the famous **prisoner's dilemma** in which two people are offered a choice, namely to cooperate or to defect. Each must make the choice without knowing what the other will do. No matter what the other does, defection yields a higher payoff than cooperation. The dilemma is that if both defect, both do worse than if both had cooperated. The prisoner's dilemma has been the subject of much analysis and scholarship. Scholars, especially economists, have great interest in situations in which individual rational actions lead to collective irrational results.

In order to understand this better, let's look at the hypothetical story after which the dilemma is named. There are many different versions and formulations of the prisoner's dilemma. In this version, adapted from Robert Axelrod, two prisoners are being held by police in the investigation of a crime. Each is interrogated individually and given the following choices. If you both testify against the other, your prison sentence will be five years each. If you both remain silent, you will both get six months. If only one testifies, then that prisoner will go free and the other prisoner will get 10 years. In this situation, to cooperate means to help your partner by remaining silent. To defect means to testify against your partner.

If you are one of the prisoners, you might reason as follows: my partner will either testify or not. If she testifies, I will be better off also testifying since serving five years is better than serving ten years. If my partner does not testify, I am again better off testifying since then I won't serve any time at all. Hence, no matter what my partner does, I am better off testifying.

The reasoning is correct, as far as it goes, and does not seem to support the premise that cooperation enhances self-interest. However, if both remain silent, then both will serve only six months, the second best sentence. If both reason in the manner of the previous paragraph, both will serve five years. The issue is, how does one reason so as to remain silent, when there is a danger of being double-crossed and thus serving 10 years?

The problem with using the prisoner's dilemma as a refutation of social contract theory is that it is simply not a satisfactory model of the world. The problem, as presented, is a one-shot decision. A better model is one involving repeated interaction—in other words, an iterated prisoner's dilemma.

Again, there are numerous versions of the iterated prisoner's dilemma. The following has been used in computing tournaments in which programmers compete against each other, using the programming strategy they find most efficient.

In each round, a computer program plays the role of one of the prisoners from the story above. In each round the program can either defect or cooperate. One game between two computers consists of 200 rounds. In each round, each computer program decides simultaneously whether it will defect or cooperate. That is, it chooses one of the two actions that are available to it. Each program then gets points according to its choice and the choice of its opponent.

The points scored for all possible choices for the competing programs in each round are given in Table 1.2. The pairs of numbers indicate the points earned by both programs. The first number is the number of points given to Program 1 and the second number is the number of points awarded to Program 2. For example, in a particular round, if Program 1 chooses the Defect choice and Program 2 chooses the Cooperate choice, then Program 1 will score 5 points and Program 2 will score zero points for that round. After this is done 200 times, the winner is the program with the most total points.

**TABLE  1.2    Points scored for each program in the Iterated Prisoner's Dilemma**

|  | Program 2 cooperates | Program 2 defects |
|---|---|---|
| Program 1 cooperates | 3,3 | 0,5 |
| Program 1 defects | 5,0 | 1,1 |

The best strategy for programs to use when playing this game appeared to be the strategy called "tit for tat", which consists of the following two rules:

1.  Cooperate in the first round.
2.  Thereafter, do whatever the opponent did in the previous round.

The program using the tit-for-tat strategy has consistently won the competition and the extraordinary success of the tit-for-tat strategy in computer competitions suggests that the idea of one's self-interest being served by cooperating with one's peers is at least plausible. Obviously, it does not prove that cooperating with one's fellow humans is the best policy, but it suggests that the long term winners will be those who retaliate when exploited, but otherwise cooperate for the common good, even if they risk personal loss in the short run. Note also, however, that in a "terminal" situation in which one's partner cannot be in a position to retaliate, the original prisoner's dilemma makes it potentially advantageous to break the contract and defect rather than cooperate.

One way to alter the calculations related to the prisoner's dilemma, as well as calculations related to similar problems, is for the contracting parties to mutually agree on a strong third party to enforce the agreement. For example, in the case of the two robbers, the robbers could agree in advance not to betray each other. This could then be enforced by the head of their gang: betrayers are killed. This ensures that both robbers stick to the agreement, and so both end up with the short six-month prison sentence, instead of the longer five-year sentence.

Contractarian moral theories view moral behavior as a type of cooperation that, in the long run, benefits everyone. But contractarians tend to believe that people will not stick to the social contract simply out of self-interest, because problems similar to the prisoner's dilemma abound in real life. Establishing a powerful institution, such as a government or church, to enforce adherence to the moral social contract is necessary to solve these dilemmas.

Figure 1.6 summarizes the key ideas of contractarianism.

- Human beings wish to promote their own self-interest.
- An individual's self-interest is best served by acting for the common good.
- The contract of contractarianism is the agreement to act according to rules that promote the common good.
- Political theories about governments are based on ideas about social contracts, with laws serving as the rules of social contracts, and the police and military enforcing the terms of the contract.

**F I G U R E  1.6**  Key ideas of contractarianism

### Reflection Questions

1.  RESEARCH Go to *www.YouTube.com*, and view the video "Golden Balls – £100,000 Split Or Steal? 14/03/08". Do the behaviors of the contestants confirm or refute Hobbes' claim that humans are naturally selfish? Explain.

2.  APPLICATION We suggested that contractarianism could be merged with a consequentialist theory or deontological theory. Imagine a social contract evolves with one inviolate principle, the categorical imperative. Now imagine a different, social contract in which the one inviolate principle is that the measure of goodness is total human happiness. How would laws concerning perjury, theft, and assault be likely to differ under those two social contracts? Explain.

### 1.4.8   Ethics of Justice

Most ethicists are in search of ethical theories that have two key qualities:

- **Impartiality**—Every person is treated equally and no one is given preferential treatment in the theory.

- **Universality**—A decision reached by applying the theory should be correct for everyone that has a similar decision to make.

These characteristics are usually quite desirable, because they make it clear that we each should live up to the same standards that we hold for other people. Most deontological and consequentialist ethicists hold to these principles.

Impartiality, in particular, is problematic when we try to apply ethical theories to real life problems. Many of our social systems are designed to be intentionally partial to one group or another. Consider the following provoking questions:

- Is it morally permissible to award college scholarships based on academic merit?
- Is it morally permissible to award college scholarships based on financial need?
- Is it morally permissible to tax people who live in cities in order to fund phone lines in rural areas?

These questions concern situations in which impartiality is impossible because they involve shifting financial resources from one group to another. All of these are standard practices in the United States, though some are more controversial than others.

One of the most popular approaches to the problem of impartiality comes from the contractarian John Rawls. In his classic work, *A Theory of Justice*, he explores the basic rules that are necessary to ensure fairness in society as a whole. He argues that all social contract theories of ethics must share a common core, which is that the society should be fair. He argues that two principles of **justice as fairness** underlie all just societies. These two principles are paraphrased as follows:

1. Each person should have as extensive a set of basic freedoms as possible, as long as it does not prevent others from having the same freedoms.
2. Social and economic inequalities are justified only if:
   a. Everyone has a fair chance to obtain the better position.
   b. Such inequalities provide the greatest benefit to the least advantaged; this is known as the **difference principle**.

Furthermore, Rawls says that these principles should be applied in a strict order of precedence. The right to basic liberties comes first, then the right to equal opportunity, then the difference principle.

Rawls's theory can be viewed as a moral theory because it provides some universal principles for what we ought to do. For example, it allows one to argue that it is okay for a person to be rich while others are poor, as long as this state of affairs ultimately benefits the poor. It also claims, however, that this is the *only* justification for economic inequality.

If one accepts Rawls's theory, it is easy to justify need-based college scholarships, because they provide the greatest benefit to the least advantaged. Justifying subsidies for rural phone systems is more difficult. Building a phone system in a rural area is much more expensive than building one in an urban area. It is also unclear whether urban dwellers are more advantaged than people living in the country. So the difference principle does not immediately lead to justification. Supporters of subsidizing rural phone service might still appeal to Rawls by claiming that phone service is a fundamental right and that "every person is entitled to purchase telephone service at an affordable rate." This claim is, obviously, open to debate. But if one agrees with it, then Rawls's first principle provides justification for the difference; it is necessary for urban dwellers to subsidize rural phone systems in order for everyone to have basic liberties.

Is there any reason to accept Rawls's principles? The book in which Rawls justifies his principles is long and complicated. Exploring his reasoning fully is beyond our scope. However, we do want to introduce one of his main ideas, which he calls the **veil of ignorance**. Rawls suggests a thought experiment: What if, before you were born into the world, you got to choose a social contract? What kind of contract would you choose? Rawls further stipulates, however, that you must make this decision in complete ignorance of what qualities you will have once you are born. You do not know how smart you will be, or how rich, or whether you will be healthy. In some sense you will be randomly assigned to a lot in life. He argues that, from behind this veil of ignorance, any rational person's choice of social contract would include his two principles. His principles (he claims) guarantee that, no matter where you start out, you have a fair opportunity to improve your lot in life.

Rawls's theory of justice is not a moral theory for individuals, but rather a way of evaluating various possible social contracts. He would claim that a "just" or "fair" social contract must follow his principles. We include it here, however, because his principles (and especially the difference principle) are often used as the basis for arguments about how technologists should factor the plight of disadvantaged groups into their decision-making.

Figure 1.7 summarizes the key ideas of Rawls's theory of justice.

- Rawls's theory of justice describes a set of minimum conditions a social contract must satisfy in order for rational persons to accept it, which he calls justice as fairness.
- In order for a social contract to be just, it must be the case that:
  - Everyone has as much freedom as possible
  - Everyone has equal opportunity to reach desirable positions in society
  - All socio-economic differences are of the most benefit to the least advantaged (the difference principle)
- The difference principle explains why impartiality is sometimes not desirable.

**FIGURE 1.7** Key ideas of Rawls's theory of justice

## Reflection Questions

1. APPLICATION Use Rawls's principles to evaluate utilitarianism. In other words, if a society truly followed utilitarianism, would it be inherently unjust? Explain your reasoning.

2. APPLICATION Imagine a strange culture where at birth a new baby had his or her education, marriage arrangements, and career decided by a computer program that randomly assigned such things to individuals. Every person earned exactly the same salary and any kind of application for schools or jobs was handled by computers choosing people at random. Would that society be a just society according to Rawls? Explain.

## 1.4.9  Ethics of Caring

The final moral theory that we will use in this book is Nel Noddings's ethics of caring. Noddings is critical of both the utilitarian and Kantian approaches to morality. Both of those approaches are popular, in large part, because they try to *prove* things about moral decisions, using an approach similar to math, science, or logic. Noddings believes that such approaches are not helpful for teaching real people how to actually act morally. She says, of moral philosophy:

> We may present a coherent and enlightening picture without proving
> anything and, indeed, without claiming to present or to seek moral
> knowledge or moral truth. The hand that steadied us as we learned to ride
> our first bicycle did not provide propositional knowledge, but it guided
> and supported us all the same, and we finished up "knowing how" (3).

Noddings claims that morality really boils down to achieving a single moral ideal, a single virtue, which is caring for other individuals. Noddings proposes an **ethics of caring**, which defines goodness in terms of whether or not we take care of the people around us. In Noddings's view, caring is the only inherent good (recall that Kant holds that a "good will" is inherently good, and utilitarians consider happiness to be inherently good). She says that we naturally long to be in caring relationships, and that this impulse is what provides the "motivation for us to be moral." "We want to be *moral* in order to remain in the caring relation and to enhance the ideal of ourselves as one-caring." By **one-caring,** Noddings means someone who fulfills the role of a caregiver in their interactions with others; "one-caring" refers to that role.

In Noddings' view, caring is a natural and perhaps even biological phenomenon. Someone who has never felt moved to care for another person is not just immoral, she claims, but pathological. Following that impulse to care, however, is not always easy. In order to act morally, we need to embrace the ethical ideal of caring, to work to make ourselves one-caring for those with whom we have relations.

For our purposes, four components of Noddings' theory of caring are of particular interest:

- Caring is characterized by a feeling of engrossment in the needs of another person and by acting to care for the person based on their situation, by the one-caring.

- For caring to happen, it is necessary for the cared-for person to be receptive to being cared for.

- While it is possible to "care about" everyone, it is not possible to "care for" everyone. Hence, it is morally acceptable (and in fact necessary) to be partial, to only care for a relatively small number of individuals.

- Because caring involves being engrossed in the specific situation of a specific individual, it does not lead to universal moral rules.

Noddings' theory is, in some ways, completely opposite to Rawls's theory of justice. Rawls focuses on institutions and what a just institution should look like.

He explicitly rejects considering individuals or individual relationships. Noddings, on the other hand, completely rejects any approach to ethics that does *not* focus on individual relationships. For Noddings, how we relate to other particular individuals (loving them, hating them, helping them, hurting them) is our fundamental morality. She claims that to be moral is to care for (and receive caring from) those we relate to.

Of all of the theories presented in this chapter, the ethics of caring is the hardest for most computer professionals to put into practice. Software designers usually work in small groups creating applications that will be used by hundreds, thousands, or millions of users. Most of the users will be people with whom the developer has no direct relationship. Noddings herself indicates that it is not possible to "care for" this many people. Nevertheless, many computer professionals get into technology (particularly medical technology) because they want to help people. Thus, a computer professional can still ask some important questions related to the ethics of caring:

- Does this action enhance the ideal of myself as one-caring, or detract from it?
- Will the product I am creating allow its users to enhance their ideals of themselves as one-caring, or detract from it?
- Is the person I am trying to help actually receptive to my help?
- Is my mental attitude one of engrossment in the cared-for person's needs, or am I mentally distant?

Figure 1.8 summarizes the key ideas of Noddings's ethics of caring.

- The virtue of caring is the supreme moral good.
- Impartiality is rejected because it is impossible to care for everyone. It is only necessary to care for those with whom one has a relationship.
- There is no general or universal way to judge (from the outside) whether an action is right or wrong, because it depends on the context of the relationship between the one-caring and the person being cared for.

**FIGURE 1.8**  Key ideas of Noddings's ethics of caring

## Reflection Questions

1.  APPLICATION  One problem for elderly people, as they become more forgetful, is that they often can't remember whether or not they have taken their medication. Several companies have created computerized pill dispensers that automatically open and give an alarm, when it is time to take pills. Some versions also automatically contact the patient's doctor, telling the doctor whether or not the patient has missed or skipped doses. Would it be morally permissible to *require* an elderly patient to use this technology? Give an answer using Noddings's ethics of caring to support your argument.

2.  CONTEXT Using the technology described in the previous
    application, doctors at the University of Cincinnati recently determined
    that 58% of epileptic children do not take their epilepsy medication
    as prescribed. Under the ethics of caring, should the caregivers of
    these children be punished for not complying with the doctor's
    instructions?

## 1.5   ETHICAL REASONING

As you may recall if you studied geometry, Euclidean geometry consists of a series
of proofs demonstrating that an assertion about a geometric figure is true. Each
proof consists of a series of steps which is either an axiom or a statement derived
from earlier steps. The axioms are the statements you accept as true without proof
because either they are self-evident or they are stipulated to be true. A Euclidean
proof is easy to read and to check for correctness.

The deductive reasoning on which Euclidean geometry is based is called **pure
reason** and its purpose is to establish the truth. In this book, we are more concerned with **practical reason**, which is the reasoning used to make decisions.
Both use proofs of sorts, but the nature of the reasoning is often quite different.

For example, suppose I ask you to justify, or prove, that it is ethical
(or unethical) for Alice to give Josh her password in Scenario 2 of Case 1.1.
Constructing such a proof using practical reason would be quite different from
constructing a proof using pure reason. True, the issues are quite clear cut. Josh
wants Alice to violate the terms of her employer in order to do him a favor.
Even so, we would need to consider a series of possibly mitigating circumstances.
Furthermore, once we have provided our "proof," others are free to dispute it.
Unlike with pure reason, in the realm of practical reason we do not always have
the benefit of common axioms, and the rules of inference are sometimes in dispute as well.

Although Aristotle did not explicitly discuss practical reasoning, he did make
a distinction between deliberation, which is a form of practical reasoning, and
syllogistic reasoning, which is reasoning appropriate for the sciences. In the following discussion we will use a form of Aristotle's deliberation to reason about
ethical issues.

### 1.5.1   Deliberative Critical Discussion

A deliberative critical discussion starts with the premise that intelligent, knowledgeable, well-intended people who think carefully and rationally about an ethical issue may disagree. Often, after thoughtful and informed discussion, people
who disagree will ultimately agree. But sometimes, even the best efforts to come
to a common judgment will fail. Even so, a successful discussion should provide
all parties with greater insight into their own positions as well as those who
disagree.

As you discuss ethical issues, whether in writing or face-to-face with your classmates and instructor, you need to keep the following guidelines in mind:

1. There is no winner of a successful deliberative critical discussion. The goal is not to defeat the other parties in the discussion; the goal is to understand their position and to help them understand yours.

2. Assume that everyone taking part in the discussion is a well-intended, rational person who deserves your respect.

3. Avoid rhetorical devices intended to persuade without a rational substantive basis. In other words, avoid the type of argumentative discussion seen so often on television news shows, in which advocates of opposite extremes compete to convince the audience that their position is the correct one.

    a. In oral discussions, agree to let one person speak at a time, with no interruptions and no filibusters.
    b. Avoid charged language and hyperbole. For example, in Scenario 2 of our case, Dolores ran a stop sign and as a result injured a pedestrian. Referring to those facts as a "reckless disregard for the law, which resulted in an assault on an innocent bystander," cannot be justified from the facts of the case that we have. The phrase, "reckless disregard" and the word "assault" both imply things that are not evident and may well be false.
    c. Avoid *ad hominem* attacks, which are arguments against the person arguing rather than against the statements being made. Attacking an individual as an effort to diminish the strength of his or her argument does not promote understanding.

In a deliberative critical discussion, both parties bring their own knowledge to the discussion. Suppose two persons, Alpha and Beta, are having a discussion. Alpha has impressions and observations of the world, as does Beta. Their experiences are possibly very similar, but may not be. Additionally, each has a set of beliefs. Some of those beliefs are convictions such as "God exists" or "Kindness is good." Some are simply beliefs about the world, which may or not be correct. For example, perhaps Alpha believes Mobile is the capital of Alabama. That belief is wrong, but consulting a map, atlas, or the Web site for Alabama would probably quickly cause Alpha to abandon that belief. If, however, Alpha believes that abortion is wrong, it is unlikely that citing an authority will have an effect on Alpha's belief. If such a belief is the cause of the disagreement, it may be the case that no resolution of the difference in judgments will be possible.

Various reasons might prevent Alpha and Beta from coming to a common resolution:

1. They might disagree about the facts. For example, perhaps Alpha believes that strict law enforcement will reduce accidents whereas Beta believes that strict law enforcement has little effect on accidents. Therefore Alpha argues that Officer Schmidt should definitely give Dolores a ticket, and Beta argues that since that will have little impact on safety, Officer Schmidt should make

his decision on other factors, such as doing a small favor for a friend. If there were a comprehensive study that provided compelling evidence for one position or the other, then Alpha and Beta might come to an agreement. However, if there were no such study that provided convincing evidence to both parties, then Alpha and Beta would continue to disagree.

2.  Alpha and Beta may not agree on each other's reasoning. In most cases, this is due to a reasoning error. Theoretically, a clear demonstration of the error should resolve the matter. However, such a demonstration can be difficult, particularly if one or more of the participants is uninformed about the relevant topic. For example, statistical inference can be difficult, and a person lacking sufficient knowledge of statistics can find it difficult to follow an argument based in statistics. Finally, one party might simply lack the intellectual ability to understand an argument. Note that, for readers of this text, the likelihood of this being the reason for disagreement in a deliberative critical discussion is unlikely unless some special circumstance (such as drugs, alcohol, or illness) is involved.

3.  Alpha and Beta may have different values. For example, Alpha and Beta may agree that strict law enforcement reduces accidents, but Beta, unlike Alpha, believes that maintaining good community relations is far more important than reducing accidents.

## 1.5.2   Ethical Arguments and the Importance of Context

An ethical argument is quite different from an argument about why two angles of a triangle are or are not equal. An ethical argument is similar to a legal argument, in that evidence is presented, arguments are disputed, and exceptions to rules are common. Despite these similarities, the two types of arguments are not the same. Legal arguments relate to a single set of statutes and previous decisions by judges and juries. Ethical arguments sometimes involve interactions among several different moral theories or codes of ethics. Also, keep in mind that, in an ethical argument, a person's position on a particular issue is often based, at least initially, on intuition. Usually, one's intuition of what is right and what is wrong provides a strong heuristic (common sense) guide. Indeed, according to virtue ethics, the truly virtuous person would have the right intuition as a matter of practice.

Context is always important in reasoning, but in ethical arguments it plays a particularly large role. One essential step in analyzing a particular case is to determine what facts are relevant and what facts are not. In practical situations, it is possible for supposedly irrelevant facts to become significant factors. For example, suppose that Dolores is African American and that Officer Schmidt is of German descent, and that, at the time Officer Schmidt stopped Dolores for speeding, the city was in great turmoil over alleged police harassment of African Americans. Suppose further, that Officer Schmidt had previously been accused of improper treatment of African American suspects. Suddenly a normally irrelevant issue such as Dolores's ethnicity becomes a potentially significant factor.

### Reflection Questions

1. [CONTEXT] Earlier, we gave an act utilitarianism analysis in which Officer Schmidt made use of a statistical study indicating that mothers whose children were in the car were the safest drivers. We did not attempt to justify Officer Schmidt's use of that study but, by our silence, implied that it was a sound study. Suppose, however, we had said that Officer Schmidt was aware of a study that African American women were 7% less likely than the general population to have an accident and that Dolores was African American. Would you think Officer Schmidt was justified in using that as part of his utilitarian calculation? Explain.

2. [CONTEXT] Suppose the study mentioned in Question 1 suggested that African American women were 7% more likely than the general population to have an accident and Dolores was African American. Would Officer Schmidt be justified in using that as part of his utilitarian calculation? Explain.

### 1.5.3  Reasoning by Analogy: Casuistry and Circumstantial Reasoning

The *American Heritage Dictionary* defines **casuistry** as "the determination of right and wrong in questions of conduct or conscience by the application of general principles of ethics." That is the second entry for "casuistry" in the dictionary. The first is "Specious or excessively subtle reasoning intended to rationalize or mislead." Casuistry is the technique of argumentation most often used in legal reasoning and can, at times, seem to be a rhetorical technique used for twisting the truth rather than establishing it. The *Cambridge Dictionary of Philosophy* provides a more detailed definition:

> The case-analysis approach to the interpretation of general moral rules. Casuistry starts with paradigm cases of how and when a given general rule should be applied, and then reasons by analogy to cases in which the proper application of the rule is less obvious... (107).

Ethical reasoning, like legal reasoning and other forms of reasoning that deal with highly context-dependent situations, seems to require techniques quite different from those of geometry and similar formal systems. Working from principles and rules frequently makes it extremely difficult to arrive at the best conclusion. Consider the following example from Jonsen and Toulmin:

> If I go next door and borrow a silver soup tureen, it goes without saying that I am expected to return it as soon as my immediate need for it is over: that is not an issue and gives rise to no problem.

> If, however, it is a pistol that I borrow and if, while it is in my possession, the owner becomes violently enraged and threatens to kill one of his other neighbors as soon as he gets back the pistol, I shall find myself in a genuinely problematic situation. I cannot escape from it by lamely invoking the general maxim that borrowed property ought to be returned promptly (7).

For almost any ethical principle, in order to properly account for all of the exceptional circumstances in which the principle might need to be used, we would need a list of conditions and constraints that would be too long to be useful. Indeed, it seems highly unlikely that it is even possible to compile such a list.

That is why we approach ethical problems by looking at various cases and using them as paradigms. Let us not forget, however, the first definition listed in the *American Heritage Dictionary*. Complex issues can sometimes be verbally manipulated by people skillful at winning arguments to confuse the real issues and reach a false conclusion. That is one reason why discussion and constant re-examination of the reasoning process are so important. In this book, ethical arguments are not contests between competing positions. As we take part in deliberative critical discussion throughout this book, arguments will serve as investigations that seek to establish the truth to the extent possible. The following section illustrates one use of that method.

### 1.5.4   Case: To Tell or Not To Tell

Professor Cooper has a rule in his class that students may use laptop computers for taking notes, but only for that purpose. Using a laptop to surf the Web, check e-mail, or work on homework is forbidden. Arnold, a student in Professor Cooper's class, happens to notice that Briana is working on homework for another class. He raises his hand, and when acknowledged, publicly announces that Briana is breaking Professor Cooper's rule for laptops.

#### Reflection Questions

1. APPLICATION Was Arnold's action ethical? Explain.

2. CONTEXT Ethical standards pertain to a specific group. Hence, to determine Arnold's ethical responsibilities, it must be with respect to a specific group to which Arnold belongs. What group containing Arnold did you use to determine the ethical standard for Question 1? Explain.

### 1.5.5   A Sample Deliberative Critical Discussion

The following is an example of deliberative critical discussion that takes place in a fictional classroom where the students all have names that are Greek letters.

PROFESSOR: Was Arnold's action ethical?

ALPHA: I say that Arnold's actions were neither ethical nor unethical. There was no moral issue here. Nor was any code of ethics violated. I don't see an issue at all.

BETA: I disagree. I believe Arnold violated the students' code of ethics. Alpha was certainly correct to say that there was no *explicit* code of ethics violated, but I believe that students constitute a group and that group has norms of behavior. None of us has ever signed a contract agreeing not to rat out our colleagues, but it is a standard that we all understand.

GAMMA: I disagree with Alpha, but I also disagree with Beta. I think surreptitiously breaking the rule concerning laptops is a form of cheating. Professor Cooper has explicitly forbidden using laptops for any purpose other than taking notes. Therefore, we can reasonably expect that breaking that rule could involve a penalty on class participation grade. By hiding what she is doing, Briana is actually cheating. Because cheating is immoral, Arnold is morally obligated to tell.

ALPHA: Well, I cannot accept Gamma's argument. I do think, however, that Beta has a strong point. It is considered poor form to tattle on another student. I even agree with Gamma that a moral obligation would force Arnold to tell Professor Cooper about the violation. I just can't see using your laptop in class as cheating. Even if it were, I don't know that that implies that Arnold is obligated to tell. He may be obligated not to lie about it, but I don't think he is required to volunteer information of that kind.

DELTA: Of course, a few minutes ago, you couldn't see any ethical or moral aspects to this case Alpha. I think you should…

PROFESSOR: Delta, I must interrupt you there. That comment amounts to an *ad hominem* attack and does not contribute to our purpose. What Alpha previously thought does not now affect the validity of his argument. Perhaps you should begin again.

DELTA: Sorry, Professor. Sorry, Alpha. Let me start over. I think that Briana could be cheating, but we don't know for sure. The case does not tell us whether there is a class participation grade. If there is, I think Briana is cheating. I have to agree with Alpha, though. I see no obligation of Arnold to tell. Without an obligation, he is breaking the students' contract and is being unethical.

GAMMA: I see your point. However, I think there could be a different reason that Arnold has an obligation. If Professor Cooper has a class participation grade and if Professor Cooper grades on a curve, then Arnold has an obligation to himself and his colleagues not to let Briana potentially lower their grades. How about it Professor? Does Professor Cooper have a class participation grade? If so, does she grade on a curve?

PROFESSOR: The case does not tell us that. You however have made a clear statement:

- If Professor Cooper has a class participation grade *and*
- If Professor Cooper Grades on a curve

- Then Arnold is behaving ethically because he has an obligation to himself and to his fellow students to report what is, in effect, cheating.
- Otherwise (if either or both of the first two statements are false) Arnold is behaving unethically by breaking the (unwritten) student code.

We can certainly evaluate that statement, even though we don't know the answers to the first two statements from what the case gives us.

ALPHA: I agree with Gamma. Well done, Gamma. That is a nice clear analysis.

BETA: I agree that Gamma has done a nice job, but I still don't agree. Even if there is a curve, why is Arnold required to volunteer that information? That is not his job. It is Professor Cooper's job to grade fairly and to do what is necessary to be sure his grading is fair. Why does Arnold have to do that for her?

GAMMA: So, as I see it, we have a new question. If you know that someone is cheating, and you also know that the cheating might hurt others in the class because the grade is curved, are you morally obligated to tell on that person?

DELTA: I've been thinking about the issue of the curve, and I don't think it is really relevant. More accurately, I think that in a larger sense, every grade is curved in a way. If a person leaves this class with a higher grade than he or she deserves, that reduces the value of the grade I get. For example, if I am the only one to receive an A, people say, "Delta got an A. He was the only one to do that." If another person who does not deserve an A also got one, then my A would be diminished unfairly.

GAMMA: Delta may have a point there, but I prefer that we postpone that issue to focus on what seems to be the main issue here. On what grounds would Arnold be obligated to tell Professor Cooper about the violation of the rule?

BETA: Well, can the rule, "You must tell on a cheater," be made universal? That would tell us whether it's moral according to deontological ethical theory.

ALPHA: Certainly it appears that the utilitarian point of view favors such a rule. As pointed out by Delta, cheaters hurt everybody, maybe even themselves. Clearly then, cheating reduces overall happiness.

GAMMA: That's true, but does telling about the cheating mitigate that loss of happiness?

PROFESSOR: Well that's all our time for today. Continue to think about this case and produce a short free writing exercise for next time with your current position.

## SUMMARY

In this chapter you have learned about the nine moral theories summarized in Table 1.3.

**T A B L E  1.3    Summary of moral theories**

| | | |
|---|---|---|
| Divine command theory | Proponents' arguments | ■ Presents no possible conflict with religious belief. |
| | | ■ Is not assailable via rational argument. |
| | Critics' arguments | ■ Does not directly address questions of modern life that are not spiritually relevant. |
| | | ■ Does not include people outside of the religion. |
| Cultural relativism | Proponents' arguments | ■ No objective way to evaluate cultures; morality must therefore be evaluated relative to a given culture; promotes tolerance. |
| | Critics' arguments | ■ Empirical evidence suggests that universal moral principles exist; does not provide guidance for cross-cultural interaction. |
| Virtue ethics | Proponents' arguments | ■ Acts are committed by people and so the best way to have moral acts is to have moral people. |
| | | ■ No set of rules or principles for action can cover all situations. |
| | Critics' arguments | ■ There is no rational way of deciding the best course of action in a difficult situation. |
| | | ■ The set of virtues seems incomplete and lacks a rational basis. |
| Act utilitarianism | Proponents' arguments | ■ The only way to judge an act is to examine the consequences of that act. |
| | | ■ When examining the consequences of an act, one should use the overall impact on human happiness as the measure of goodness. |
| | Critics' arguments | ■ There are numerous problematic cases in which act utilitarianism conflicts with intuition and/or religious norms. |
| | | ■ Calculating consequences and happiness is complex and highly prone to error. |
| Rule utilitarianism | Proponents' arguments | ■ Rules can make the evaluation of an act much less prone to calculation errors. |
| | | ■ Rigorous compliance with the rules (except for compelling reasons to violate) will maximize happiness providing the rules are selected properly. |
| | Critics' arguments | ■ It is still difficult to determine whether a set of rules will truly maximize overall happiness. |
| Deontological ethics | Proponents' arguments | ■ Categorical imperatives, such as the universal law of nature and the principle of the end in itself, tend to be simple to state and easy to apply. |
| | | ■ Acknowledges the importance of motivation in determining whether an act was good or not. |
| | | ■ Because the principle is categorical, there are no exceptions. |
| | Critics' arguments | ■ Lack of exceptions lead to cases where the consequences are unacceptable according to intuition and/or religious convictions. |

**T A B L E   1.3    Summary of moral theories (Continued)**

| | | |
|---|---|---|
| Contractarianism | Proponents' arguments | ■ A rational theory that an individual's best interest is served by acting for the common good. |
| | | ■ The premise that an individual's interest is best served by acting for the common good is supported by empirical evidence. |
| | Critics' arguments | ■ Major premise that an individual's interest is best served by serving the common good may be incorrect. |
| | | ■ Even if major premise is correct, there will always be a possibility for a greater advantage to an individual for immoral behavior if that individual can avoid retaliation by those wronged by the justice system. |
| Rawls's theory of justice | Proponents' arguments | ■ Makes it easy to understand why we may not necessarily be obligated to do away with all economic inequalities. |
| | | ■ Encourages people to help the least fortunate. |
| | Critics' arguments | ■ The justification for Rawls's claims is much more complicated, and controversial, than those for utilitarianism or Kant's principles. As a result, it is unlikely to ever be widely accepted. |
| Nodding's ethics of caring | Proponents' arguments | ■ Many of our moral heroes, like Mother Teresa, are characterized by their capacity for caring for others, not for their abilities to follow rules or to calculate how their acts will affect others. |
| | | ■ Unlike utilitarianism, it explains why it is okay to focus your energies on caring for those close to you, rather than those in far-away places. |
| | Critics' arguments | ■ Because of its focus on close relationships, the ethics of caring does not easily lead to universal rules or judgments of the kind needed by computing professionals. |

Table 1.4 summarizes some common reasons for disagreement in the ultimate conclusion of a deliberative critical discussion and some strategies for resolving the differences.

**T A B L E   1.4    Summary of differences and possible reconciliations**

| Reasons for the different conclusions | | Reconciliation strategies |
|---|---|---|
| Different perceptions of the world | | ■ New direct observations |
| | | ■ Reports from a mutually trusted source |
| | | ■ No remedy if there is insufficient evidence to establish one perception definitively |
| Different beliefs | Factual | ■ Refutation of false belief |
| | | ■ Appeal to a mutually trusted source |
| | Convictional | ■ Conversion (unlikely) |
| | | ■ No remedy if the disagreement is fundamental |
| Faulty reasoning | Mistake | ■ Demonstration of fallacy |
| | Ignorance | ■ Edification |
| | Insufficient intellect | ■ No remedy; very rare and unlikely ever to occur in this course (although too often individuals will attribute this possibility to a person with an opposing viewpoint) |

## CHAPTER EXERCISES

1. REVIEW Restate Davis's definitions of morality and ethics, and explain the difference between them.

2. REVIEW List the two main problems with relying exclusively on religious ethics to establish the standards of other groups such as engineers, accountants, or teachers.

3. REVIEW Restate the definition of the divine command theory of morality.

4. REVIEW Explain the differences between divine command theory and religious ethics.

5. REVIEW State the two premises of cultural relativism.

6. REVIEW Could one be a proponent of cultural relativism and also of divine command theory? Explain.

7. REVIEW Could a proponent of virtue theory also be a proponent of cultural relativism? Explain.

8. REVIEW Could a person be a proponent of divine command theory and also be a utilitarian? Explain.

9. REVIEW What is the main difference between act utilitarianism and rule utilitarianism?

10. REVIEW List Gert's ten rules of common morality.

11. REVIEW Could a person be a proponent of contractarianism and also be a cultural relativist? Explain.

12. REVIEW Could a person be a proponent of contractarianism and also a proponent of virtue theory? Explain.

13. REVIEW State Rawls's principles for a just society.

14. APPLICATION Three students, Valerie, Karen, and Ursula, are discussing a court case on a recent television show. Valerie is a virtue theorist, Karen a Kantian, and Ursula an act utilitarian. In the show they were discussing, a person who was mentally ill refused his medication and became violent, killing an innocent person. The defense argued that the man should be not guilty by reason of insanity. The prosecution argued that the man was guilty of voluntary manslaughter for refusing his medication when he knew he was ill. The students are not discussing the legal guilt of the man, but rather his moral responsibility. Describe the position that each student would be most likely to hold.

15. APPLICATION Consider the following argument: "If you are a consequentialist, in order to act morally, you need to be able to predict the consequences of a particular act. If you know a lot about human psychology and about probability and statistics, you will be better prepared to correctly predict consequences of many more acts than you would if you did not knows those subjects. Hence, it is immoral for a college student to neglect

taking those subjects." Do you agree with this argument? Explain why it is or is not a valid argument.

16. APPLICATION You are in court after having been caught speeding. You were going 65 mph in a 35-mph zone and received a major fine. Having taken a course in ethics, you explain to the judge that according to the principles of deontological ethics, the golden rule should apply. Surely, if the judge were facing a major fine, she would want the sentence suspended. Because she should do unto others as she would wish for others to do unto her, she should suspend your sentence. Do you think the judge should accept that argument? Explain.

17. APPLICATION A common type of moral question involves runaway trolleys. There are many variants, but the basic premise is that you are on a runaway trolley that is approaching a fork in the tracks, with people further down the line on each set of tracks. These people will be gravely injured or, more likely, killed if they are hit by the run-away trolley. It's up to you to pull the switch that determines which set of tracks the trolley takes. The following is a collection of typical decisions. For each, select one moral theory and determine the action that your chosen moral theory would advise. You may choose the same theory for each of the five decisions, or vary theories as you wish. You will probably find some cases in which the theory conflicts with your own intuition. In that case, identify the source of the conflict.
    a.   The trolley is heading for three children. On the other track is one child. Should you switch tracks?
    b.   The trolley is heading for three children. On the other track is one child. It is your daughter. Should you switch tracks?
    c.   The trolley is heading for your daughter. On the other track are three children. Should you switch tracks? (Note: This is not necessarily the same as choice b above.)
    d.   The trolley is heading for three children. On the other track is a gasoline truck. Should you switch tracks?
    e.   The trolley is heading for three children. On the other track is the President of the United States. Should you switch tracks?

18. RESEARCH A classic paper by Garrett Hardin, "The Tragedy of the Commons," was published in the journal *Science* in 1968. Hardin's thesis is, "The population problem has no technical solution; it requires a fundamental extension in morality." Read Hardin's paper and consider the problem he refers to as "The tragedy of the commons." How is this problem addressed by any of the moral theories we have covered in this chapter? Explain.

19. RESEARCH Isaac Asimov, the well-known science fiction writer, wrote a series of short stories and novels about robots, including the story from the motion picture, *I Robot*. The robots in the stories were all designed with built-in circuitry that required them to operate according to the "three laws

of robotics." Although Asimov did not present the laws as a moral code, one might choose to look at them that way. Read one or more of Asimov's stories (nine of which are collected into the book *I, Robot*) and try to interpret the laws of robotics as a moral code for robots. How do his robots' laws compare with the moral theories we have examined here?

20. RESEARCH Inappropriate analogies are common and are often used to "prove" a point in advertisements, political arguments, and jokes. Find three such bogus arguments in the current media and explain why the analogies are faulty.

## WORKS CITED

American Heritage Dictionary, 3$^{rd}$ Edition. Boston: Houghton Mifflin Company, 1992. Print.

Anscombe, G. E. M. "Modern Moral Philosophy." *Philosophy Vol.* 33.124 (1958): 6-16. Print.

Aristotle. *Nicomachaen Ethics*. Trans. Roger Crisp. Cambridge: Cambridge University Press, 2000. Print.

Asimov, Isaac. *I, Robot*. Garden City: Doubleday, 1950. Print.

Audi, Robert, Ed. *The Cambridge Dictionary of Philosophy*, 2$^{nd}$ Edition. Cambridge: Cambridge University Press, 1999. Print.

Axelrod, Robert. *The Evolution of Cooperation*. Cambridge: Basic Books, 1984. Print.

Davis, Michael. *Profession, Code and Ethics*. Burlington: Ashgate, 2001. Print.

Gert, Bernard. *Common Morality: Deciding What to Do*. Oxford: Oxford University Press, 2004. Print.

Hardin, Garrett. "The Tragedy of the Commons," *Science* 162. 3859 (Dec. 13, 1968): 1243–1248. Print.

Hobbes, Thomas. Leviathan. New York: Oxford University Press USA, 2009. Print.

Jonsen, Albert R. and Stephen Toulmin, *The Abuse of Casuistry*. Berkeley: University of California Press, 1988. Print.

Noddings, Nel. *Caring: A Feminine Approach to Ethics and Moral Education*. Berkeley: University of California Press, 1984. Print.

Rawls, John. *A Theory of Justice: Revised Edition*. Cambridge: Belknap Press of Harvard University Press, 1999. Print.

## RELATED READINGS

The following sections provide information on further reading and some useful resources for research or position papers.

## Concise Summaries

Pojman, Louis P, and James Fieser. *Ethics: Discovering Right and Wrong*. Boston: Wadsworth Cengage Learning, 2009. Print. (Excellent, easy-to-read overview.)

Rachaels, James and Stuart Rachaels. *Elements of Moral Philosophy*, *6th Ed*. Boston: McGraw-Hill, 2009. Print. (A short overview of ethical theory and moral philosophy.)

Scroton, Roger. *Kant: A Very Short Introduction*. Cambridge: Cambridge University Press, 2001. Print. (Covers more than ethics, but includes a concise discussion of the categorical imperative.)

## General References

Rachaels, James and Stuart Rachaels. *The Right Thing to Do: Basic Readings in Moral Philosophy*. Boston: McGraw-Hill, 2009. Print. (An anthology of excerpts from original sources with commentary.)

## Web Resources

Stanford Encyclopedia of Philosophy: *http://plato.stanford.edu*. This is an excellent searchable source. Advice on how to properly cite material from the Encyclopedia can be found at *http://plato.stanford.edu/cite.html*.

Utilitarianism Resources: *www.utilitarianism.com*. Home page of resources for utilitarianism.

# Chapter 2

# Computing Professions and Professional Ethics

We use the term "professional" in many ways. Here are just a few examples:

- In 1913, the legendary Jim Thorpe was brought under scrutiny for having played semi-professional baseball before his extraordinary performance in the 1912 Olympics. Because he had received money for playing baseball, he was ruled a professional. His Olympic gold medals were taken away and his name was removed from the record books. The medals were restored only in 1982, well after Thorpe's death in 1953.

- On a television program, police are investigating a murder. The murder has the earmarks of a planned assassination. The investigator remarks to his colleague, "This was a real professional job."

- An ad in the personals section of a well-known Web site reads, "Single white professional woman, 34, seeks professional man of any race, 30–40, for friendship, conversation, and possible relationship."

Think about these different uses of the term "professional." Frequently, it simply means that the person is getting paid. In the case of Jim Thorpe, that was enough to cost him his amateur standing and therefore his Olympic medals. The detective in the television program used the term differently. True, the murderer may have been paid, but the "real professional job" mentioned by the detective implied the use of considerable know-how and skill rather than the exchange of money.

In the personals ad, the woman placing the ad used the term in still a different way. She was indicating that she held a professional job, one that required education and abilities beyond manual labor and one that involved significant responsibilities and obligations. Hers was, in fact, not merely a job, but a profession. In this chapter, we explore these various meanings of the words "professional" and "profession," particularly as they pertain to computing and the computing professions. We then examine the significance of such issues to both potential professionals and to the general public.

## 2.1  CASE: FIGHTING INJUSTICE

Although this case, like most of the cases in this book, was inspired by real events, the details are made up.

Rachael was a senior computer science major who worked part-time for IT services at her university. As part of her duties, she needed to install a new printer driver on Professor Paige's printer. Professor Paige, while rushing off to teach a class, had said, "Go on in Rachael. Just log me out of my e-mail program and do what you need to do."

Professor Paige was having a bad semester. She had never been the most popular teacher in the Computer Science Department, but this semester she had become a target of the ZTs, a student organization on campus. The name "ZT" is short for ZTBT (Zero Tolerance for Bad Teaching). The ZTs maintain a Web site which publishes accounts of what the students consider to be bad teaching practices. It includes quotes from class, examples of grading errors, and photos. The Web site's main attractions are satirical videos made by students. The videos are often very clever at lampooning the organization's targets and are very popular with the students. That semester the group had been relentlessly making fun of Professor Paige, particularly her clumsiness.

Rachael had taken classes with Professor Paige and found her to be a competent teacher who seemed to take a genuine interest in her students. Rachael was aware that the ZTs had targeted the professor, but she had not done anything beyond watching and enjoying the videos.

However, when she sat down to log Professor Paige out of her e-mail account, she noticed that the professor's Inbox was on the screen. Her eye happened to catch a subject line that read "So sorry about your diagnosis." Instead of logging out of the professor's account, Rachael opened the message and read, to her dismay, that Professor Paige had recently been diagnosed with multiple sclerosis. Suddenly, the videos took on a different complexion in Rachael's eyes.

All day Rachael was distressed at what she now perceived as an injustice. That evening she posted a comment on the ZT Web site revealing that Professor Paige had MS and asking that she be left alone. Rachael's comment was challenged, a number of students asking how she could possibly know that. Rachael explained, in a comment on the Web site, how she had come to read Professor's Paige's e-mail. That comment had immediate consequences.

Rachael's boss, Stacy McFarland, called Rachel in for a conference. Ms. McFarland pointed out that Rachael had violated the privacy policy of IT services. That policy had been explained and emphasized when Rachael took the job. She had signed documents signifying her willingness to follow the policy. She had violated a trust that people on the IT staff rely on to do their jobs properly. As a senior computer science major, she had violated the ethical standards of her job and of her chosen profession. She had behaved unprofessionally. Rachael tried to explain the reasons for her actions, but Ms. McFarland was not interested. Rachael was fired, and there would be no recommendation for future employment.

### Reflection Questions

1. [POSITION] Were Rachael's actions moral? Explain.
2. [POSITION] Were Rachael's actions ethical? Explain.
3. [POSITION] Was Ms. McFarland justified in firing Rachael? Explain.
4. [CONTEXT] Suppose Rachael had not been in Professor Paige's office because of her job with IT services. Suppose she had simply been a student who was in the office for a conference when Professor Paige was temporarily called away for some reason. Would that change either of your first two answers? Explain.
5. [POSITION] Did Professor Paige behave ethically when she asked Rachael to log her off rather than doing it herself? Explain.

## 2.2   CASE: REFUSING TO DO A FAVOR FOR A FRIEND

Greg is a recent graduate of a well-known university. He majored in computer science and is now employed as a software engineer at a large software consulting firm. One Monday he received a call from Michael, a close friend and one of Greg's former housemates, who was still in school as a senior computer science major. Michael was calling on his cell phone from northern Michigan. He went snowmobiling with friends over a long weekend and encountered a snowstorm that closed the roads, preventing him from getting back to campus in time to submit his project on artificial intelligence. He was finished with the project but failed to turn it in earlier because he had expected to be back in time to go over it one more time.

Michael was unable to reach any other friends; his closest friends were snowed in with him in Michigan. The project was due at 5:00 PM that day. In desperation, Michael asked for Greg's help in preventing the severe late penalty called for in his professor's polices. Michael wanted to give Greg his password and have Greg log on to the university network, locate his project, and turn it in for him. Greg would be familiar with the learning management software system used by the department and would have no trouble submitting the project electronically.

Greg refused. He said it would be a clear violation of the university's Code of Student Conduct as well as, in his estimation, a violation of the Software Engineering Code of Ethics. He would be misrepresenting his true identity and would be doing so on his firm's computer. He wanted to help Michael, but he could not do what Michael asked. Professional duty forced him to refuse.

### Reflection Questions

1. POSITION Did Greg do the right thing? Explain.

2. CONTEXT Because Greg is no longer a student, does the university's Code of Student Conduct apply to him? Explain.

3. POSITION Because you have not read the Software Engineering Code of Ethics, you do not know whether Greg is correct in claiming that using a work computer to submit a friend's school assignment would violate it. If you were going to write a code of ethics for software engineers, what would you write about situations like this? Explain.

## 2.3 PROFESSIONS AND CODES

Recall the definition of ethics from Michael Davis, presented in Chapter 1:

A set of *morally permissible* standards of a *group* that each member of the group (at his/her rational best) wants every other member to follow even if their doing so would mean that he/she must do the same.

Davis's definition refers to a set of standards that apply to a particular group. But what do we mean by a set of standards? And what group are we talking about? In this chapter, we'll try to answer both of these questions. We'll start by focusing on the relevant group, people who work in computing professions.

### 2.3.1 Why We Care about Professional Standards of Computing

The privacy, safety, and well-being of the general public are often affected by computers and the software that runs on computers. The public therefore has an understandable interest in the people who write the software, manage the systems, and make computer policies. Following are some examples of how the public can be affected by computers and the people who manage them.

In 1985, Katie Yarborough, a 61-year-old woman, was nearing the end of her radiation treatment for breast cancer at the Kennestone Regional Oncology Center in Marietta, Georgia. The radiation machine, known as the Therac-25, malfunctioned and delivered a radiation burn that went entirely through Katie Yarborough's shoulder. The doctors and technical specialists initially could not believe the event had happened. The Therac-25 was considered completely reliable, and because radiation burns do not manifest their severity immediately, the physical symptoms were misleading. Although Ms. Yarborough had screamed in pain at the moment of the burn, the physical signs immediately afterwards consisted only of a red mark on each side of her shoulder. It would be weeks before it was evident that her shoulder had been terribly injured.

Despite its reputation, however, the machine was actually unreliable. Katie Yarborough was only the first victim, and although her experience was horrible, it was not the worst. Before the full truth was discovered, three people died and three others were terribly wounded.

Among the problems was the manner in which the software for the Therac-25 had been developed. The lack of modern development and testing methods greatly increased the chance of disastrous errors. You will learn more about the famous Therac-25 in greater detail in Chapter 5.

Recently, an incident of a very different nature occurred that involved a private citizen and a computer vendor's help desk. In December 2008, a Sacramento woman called her computer vendor's technical support number to get help locating files on her computer. Among these files were some personal photos. The technical support representative helped the woman find the files. She later discovered the photos posted on a Web site along with slanderous and incorrect information about her sex life. The woman claimed that the technical support person must have been responsible for posting the photos on the Web site. Complicating the story was the fact that the computer vendor's technical support team was located in another country. In response to inquiries from the news media, a spokesperson for the company reported that the company had removed the technical support person from his position so he would no longer be answering calls.

Even more recently, a public problem involving computers and software was a major story in the news media. In March 2010, Toyota recalled 133,000 Prius hybrid automobiles in the United States because of a software problem with the braking system. Many other automobiles were recalled in Europe and elsewhere. There is no reason to believe that Toyota was using an inherently faulty software development process. On the other hand, the error, no matter how it happened, affected many people.

The allegation was levied against Toyota that it had not informed the public of the problem as quickly as it should have. Toyota insisted it acted promptly and in the best interest of its customers. Whatever the validity of the allegations, keep in mind that the allegations were made against Toyota, the corporation. No one argued that the software engineers, programmers, or systems analysts employed by Toyota ought to suffer professional consequences, even if the allegations proved to be valid.

For some activities, we take the performer's professional requirements for granted. If, for example, you consult a surgeon, you are confident that person has credentials indicating that he or she has education and training appropriate for that profession. Moreover, someone other than the surgeon has confirmed those credentials. People who don't have such credentials are not allowed to call themselves surgeons, and more importantly, are not allowed to perform surgery. Even if you have a great deal of ability using a knife and have studied anatomy extensively, you cannot start your own surgery business. We simply do not want a group of do-it-yourself surgeons operating in our society. Moreover, for such occupations, we want each practitioner to be individually responsible for his or her actions. For example, if you are a doctor, it does not matter whether you are in private practice or work for a corporation. If you violate the physicians' code of ethics, it does not matter who pays your salary or what your employer's codes and policies are; it is you who are guilty of a breach of ethics. Even if your company chooses to forgive some transgression, your profession may not.

Physicians play an important role in society, and it makes sense that we hold them to standards of competence and responsibility suitable for that role. It also makes sense for the public to have a say in what standards are deemed to be suitable for that role. That is, although physicians, like lawyers, teachers, engineers, and a variety of other professional occupations, determine among themselves standards that they wish to follow, the general public also has a say in whether those standards are sufficient and appropriate.

Computer professionals are not physicians. They do, however, exercise considerable control over issues that affect society as a whole. Consider the following:

- For every computer system, there is at least one person who has access to all its files. That person, usually called a system administrator, has the authority to move, copy, and delete any or all files on the system. If you were to start your own business and decided to hire a person to manage your computing network, that person would be in a position to wield enormous power over your business. If the system administrator were malicious, files could be intentionally stolen or destroyed. If the system manager were incompetent, key files could be lost or destroyed accidently.

- For every database, there is at least one person who has access to all of the data in the database. Like system administrators, database administrators need to be able to work "under the hood," which requires them to have special privileges.

- For every request for information from the World Wide Web, there is at least one person who has access to all information sent or received. Your information generally passes through many different computers and systems, each one of which is managed by at least one person who has access to everything passing through the system.

- For every trip on a commercial or private vehicle, whether a plane, train, bus, or car, there is at least one person who made decisions that directly affect the safety of the passengers because of the computer hardware and software used by that vehicle.

- For every hospital admission, there is at least one person who makes decisions that strongly affect the patient's comfort and safety. One or more computer professionals designed and implemented computer systems that control life support systems, provide information concerning blood type, allergies, etc., and keep track of billing.

In the following section, we examine what it means to be a professional. We also examine the standards that distinguish occupations from professions, particularly occupations associated with computing. Finally, we examine the impact of professional standards on those within the profession and the members of the general public who are affected by those standards.

### Reflection Questions

1.  APPLICATION List 3 situations in which a computer professional, either directly or indirectly, could strongly affect your life.

2.  CONTEXT People in other professions can also strongly affect your life: teachers, pharmacists, and airline pilots are just three examples. For these three, consider how they compare to computer professionals with respect to: required education, licensing, and level of trust. (Note: This is not a research question. You are being asked to evaluate these professionals according to what you currently know about them.)

## 2.3.2   Defining "Profession"

Law and medicine are the two vocations that everyone agrees are professions. In both cases, considerable education is required, and each plays an important role in society. Lawyers and doctors must conform to rules that pertain only to their respective professions, rules governing not only their competence at their jobs but their conduct as well. That is, they must adhere to the rules of their professional ethics.

How do the computing professions compare to these recognized professions? Should, for example, computer programmers or other IT workers be held to high ethical standards the way doctors are? Should software engineers be licensed the way lawyers are?

No single definition of "profession" is accepted by everyone. However, author and philosopher Michael Bayles has done a thorough examination of various professions and of the literature pertaining to the notion of a profession. According to Bayles (7), the consensus view is that any profession:

-   requires extensive training
-   involves significant intellectual effort
-   provides an important service to society

Bayles then identifies three other features common to most professions:

-   certification or licensing
-   organization of members
-   autonomy in one's work

### Reflection Questions

1.  POSITION In the United States you need a license to practice medicine or law. You also need a license to be an airline pilot, a plumber (in most states), or even to sell liquor. Provide a rationale for requiring a license for each of these vocations.

2.  POSITION In the United States you do not need a license to be a software engineer unless you practice in Texas. Provide a plausible rationale for Texas's requirement. Provide a plausible rationale for the lack of that requirement in other states.

### 2.3.3 The Good Works Project

Wendy Fischman and her colleagues in the Good Works Project at the Harvard Graduate School of Education are involved in a large research project examining how young people deal with ethical problems in their professions. The Good Works Project very broadly defines "profession" as follows:

> One can define "profession" narrowly, including only those careers—such as law or medicine—that require specific training and licensing. The definition used here is much broader. It encompasses any career in which the worker is awarded a degree of autonomy in return for services to the public that are performed at a high level. According to this definition, it is within the power of the individual worker to behave like a professional, should she or he choose to do so (12).

The phrases "services to the public" and "performed at a high level" are similar to the characteristics of a profession identified by Bayles. The definitions do not, however, fully agree; the definition used by the Good Works Project would include a number of occupations that lack Bayles's necessary attributes.

### Reflection Questions

1. APPLICATION Would an occupation that had Bayles's three required attributes plus the three additional attributes Bayles considers common to most professions necessarily be a profession according to the definition used by the Good Works Project? Explain.

2. APPLICATION Is the weather person on the local television station a professional according to either Bayles or the Good Works Project? Explain.

### 2.3.4 Kultgen's Wheel of Attributes of Professions

Author and philosopher John Kultgen, a professor at the University of Missouri, Columbia, presents twenty attributes compiled by sociologist Geoffrey Millerson from twenty-one scholars of sociology as necessary for a vocation to be considered a profession. His paraphrased list is as follows (60):

1. Involves a skill based on a theoretical foundation.

2. Requires extensive education.

3. Requires passing an exam.

4. Is organized and represented by one or more professional organizations.

5. Adheres to a code of conduct.

6. Provides altruistic service.

7. Requires members to assume responsibility for the affairs of others.

8. Is indispensable for the public good.

9. Members are licensed, so their work is sanctioned by the community.

10. Members are independent practitioners, serving individual clients.

11. Members have a fiduciary relationship with their clients.

12. Members do their best to serve their clients impartially without regard to any special relationship.

13. Members are compensated by fees or fixed charges.

14. Members are highly loyal to their colleagues.

15. Members regularly contribute to professional development.

16. Members' prestige is based on guaranteed service.

17. Members use individual judgment in applying their profession.

18. The work is not manual.

19. Profits do not depend on capital.

20. Professional status is widely recognized.

Kultgen considers the first thirteen attributes to be core characteristics, widely accepted as indicating a profession. Furthermore, he envisions a wheel where each spoke represents a particular attribute. The outer rim represents the standard professions of law and medicine, and the center represents those occupations that are never considered professional—jobs such as picking fruit or bussing tables, which are honest occupations, but not professions. Figure 2.1 shows

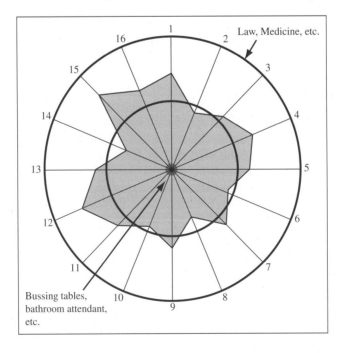

**FIGURE 2.1** An example of Kultgen's wheel

such a wheel, with sixteen spokes representing the first sixteen attributes on Kultgen's list. Inside the wheel, we have plotted the outline of a fictitious occupation, forming a polygon partially within the small, inner circle. The small, inner circle represents the dividing line between professional occupations and nonprofessional ones. We have chosen not to suggest any scale on the spokes, nor to justify the placement of the inner circle. The dividing line is admittedly somewhat arbitrary. The occupation depicted meets the standard for a profession in most, but not all, of the categories.

As suggested by the figure, the word "professional" must be considered fuzzy in the same way we refer to "fuzzy logic"—i.e., the boundaries of its meaning are not clear. Consider the word "tall," for example. We would all agree that Yao Ming, the 7 feet, 6 inch former center for the Houston Rockets, is a tall person. We would also agree that Danny DeVito, the well-known producer, director, and actor with a height of 5 feet, 0 inches, is not a tall person. How about the actors, Geena Davis or Denzel Washington, who each stand six feet even? Most of us would agree that Geena Davis is a tall *woman*, but fewer of us would agree that she is a tall *person*. Likewise, many people would consider Denzel Washington a tall person, but not everyone. Often, our perception of such words as "tall" varies according to the people with whom we are talking. For example, if we were speaking with Yao Ming and his former teammates on the Houston Rockets, Geena Davis and Denzel Washington would be the same height as Aaron Brooks and Kyle Lowry, the two shortest players on the team. On the other hand, if we are talking with the members of a gymnastics team or the bull riders in a rodeo, Geena Davis and Denzel Washington would probably be a lot taller than any of the people with whom we were speaking, since the average height in each of those groups is 5 feet, 6 inches. Hence, basketball players might not call Geena Davis and Denzel Washington tall, but gymnasts and bull riders might.

## Reflection Questions

1.   APPLICATION  Choose an occupation other than law or medicine that you think of as a profession. Which of Kultgen's twenty attributes does it have?

2.   APPLICATION  Does medicine have all of Kultgen's thirteen core attributes?

3.   APPLICATION  Does law have all of Kultgen's thirteen core attributes?

4.   RESEARCH  Name a vocation you do not consider a profession that nevertheless has at least two of Kultgen's thirteen core attributes; list the attributes it has.

5.   APPLICATION  Using Kultgen's wheel, make the argument that software engineering is—or is not—a profession. (Note: This is not a research question. You are expected to answer according to what you currently know about the software engineering occupation.)

### 2.3.5   A Moral Basis for Professions

Michael Davis, the philosopher and author whose definitions we used in Chapter 1, doesn't try to nail down the particular attributes of a profession. Instead, he defines "profession" in terms of moral issues (3):

> A profession is a number of individuals in the same occupation voluntarily organized to earn a living by openly serving a certain moral ideal in a morally permissible way beyond what law, market, and morality would otherwise require.

This definition requires a little explanation. First of all, recall that "morally permissible," defined in the previous chapter, refers to something that is either explicitly moral or morally neutral. Now let's consider the term "moral ideal." According to Davis:

> A **moral ideal** is a state of affairs that, though not morally required, everyone (that is, every rational person at his/her rational best) wants everyone else to approach, all else being equal. Moreover, everyone wants that so much that they are willing to reward, assist, or at least praise such conduct if that is the price for others to do the same (6).

Conversely, anyone violating the moral ideal is disproved of, criticized, and discouraged from such behavior. It must be morally permissible, but not necessarily morally required.

Now let's consider some other points worth noting about Davis's definition. First, a profession is necessarily linked with a code of ethics:

> It is impossible to satisfy the definition of profession without (something like) a code of ethics, impossible to teach "professionalism" without teaching the code (at least implicitly), and indeed impossible to understand professions without understanding them as bound by such a code. Without a code of ethics, there are only (more or less) honest occupations, trade associations, and the like. There are no professions. (1)

Another aspect of Davis's definition is less obvious and does not appear in any of the previous definitions: a professional puts profession first. That is, when a conflict arises between the professional's code and the policy of an employer or perhaps even the law, the professional's code must take precedence. That is why a journalist feels she must choose to go to jail rather than reveal the identity of a source, or why a doctor in a country that does not recognize doctor-patient privilege may do the same if confronted with a choice of violating doctor-patient privilege or going to prison.

Finally, notice that Davis's definition does not require the code of ethics to be enforced by the group or by some other authority. In the case of law and medicine, the rules (or at least some of the rules) are enforced by the law as well as by professional organizations. It is commonly assumed that if there is no mechanism for enforcing a code, the code has no real value. However, having people declare their intention to follow a code—having them promise, in effect—is a well-known mechanism for affecting their behavior. Wedding vows, the Hippocratic Oath, and the oath of office taken by certain government officials are all meaningful, even though the actual conditions included in the declarations are not directly enforced. If you and I sit down to a game of checkers, there is no external authority to appeal to for a rule judgment, yet the rules of the game are important. Similarly, a code of ethics, if accepted by all the members of a profession, can be important independent of an enforcement mechanism.

The occupations associated with computing that we often call professions are not, with the possible exception of software engineering, professions under Davis's definition. They do qualify as professions in the sense put forward by Fischman and her colleagues, but a profession in their model need not follow any specified code of ethical conduct as would be required by Davis. This may change as time goes on. Furthermore, it leaves open the following question: *Should* the computing professions be changed to fall in line with Davis's definition? We explore this issue later in this chapter.

### Reflection Questions

1. APPLICATION When students enter a university, they are commonly presented with the university's requirements for student conduct. Suppose a student argues that (1) the university's requirements define a code of conduct for students, (2) the requirements and hence the code is morally permissible, (3) students enter the university voluntarily, and (4) the students are there in order to become qualified for a job (i.e., to earn a living), therefore the code is, by Davis's definition, a professional code of ethics—and being a university student is a profession. Explain what is wrong with this argument.

2. APPLICATION Does teaching qualify as a profession under any or all of the definitions discussed so far? If so, which definitions, and what attributes of teaching makes it qualify as a profession? If not, what parts of the definitions does teaching not meet?

## 2.4 ETHICAL STANDARDS

We have now considered four views of what makes a profession. Most computing occupations seem to be professions according to Fischman and the Good Works Project but are definitely not professions according to Davis. The degree of professionalism seems to vary considerably when we apply the criteria suggested by either Bayles or Kultgen. It is clear, however, that the standards practiced by the people in the various computing occupations have a strong effect on the general public. Hence, we now address the issue of the standards for computing professionals—what they currently are and what they should be.

Several codes of conduct for computing professionals have been proposed, and some adopted, by certain professional associations in various countries, including the United States. For example, the Association for Computing

Machinery (ACM) has adopted a code of ethics that is included in the appendix. Similarly, a joint effort by the ACM and the Institute of Electrical and Electronic Engineers (IEEE) produced the *ACM/IEEE Software Code of Ethics and Professional Practice*, which is also included in the appendix. Nevertheless, as we shall see, there is still not complete agreement as to what the standards should be.

### 2.4.1   An Example in the Form of a Trick Question

The following question is a variation of an example often given by Michael Davis: Suppose you are a practicing professional, and in the course of discussions with your client, who is a prominent local contractor, you discover that he has been bribing city officials to get inside information on bids for city projects. Should you report your client to the authorities or keep his confidence?

There is only one correct answer to this question: It depends. You don't know the proper course of action because a crucial piece of information was left out—namely, what profession are we talking about? (Hence, this is a trick question.) For example, if you are an engineer, you are ethically bound to report your client to the proper authorities. If, however, you are a practicing attorney, you are ethically bound not to report your client except in certain situations, and if asked, you must refuse to answer. Professional ethical standards vary by profession, and as in this example, may require diametrically opposed actions.

If you are an attorney or a physician, the law recognizes your professional obligation to keep your clients' confidence and will not require you to testify against a client. In fact, the law does not allow you to testify against your client. If you are a reporter and your "client" is a source whose comments you promised to keep off the record, you have an (unwritten) ethical obligation to keep his confidence. Some states recognize your obligation to avoid revealing your sources, but the federal government does not. If a reporter refuses to reveal her source in federal court, she can be, and usually is, found to be in contempt of court, requiring her to spend time in prison and possibly pay a substantial fine. Ethical obligations are usually consistent with the law. Occasionally, however, they are not.

#### Reflection Questions

1.   APPLICATION  Lawyers are required to keep the confidence of their clients. Give the strongest argument you can as to how such a rule could be morally permissible.

2.   APPLICATION  Lawyers are required to keep the confidence of their clients. Give the strongest argument you can as to how such a rule cannot be morally permissible.

### 2.4.2   Specifying the Standard

Suppose you are given the task of providing a set of standards for all computing professionals to follow. You will have a number of problems to solve. You will want your set of rules to be clear and concise. They will need to be simple enough so that everyone in the profession can understand them, yet detailed enough to cover all of the things you expect of a computing professional. Clearly, it is a difficult challenge. In this section, we examine the manner in which standards are stated and how one might go about following a standard.

**2.4.2.1 Form** Ethical standards, according to Davis's model, may take the form of rules, principles, or ideals. The following outline gives examples, based on those used by Davis (40), of each of these categories:

1. **Rules** tell us certain things we must do (obligations) and certain things we must not do (prohibitions). Here are some examples of each taken directly from the *ACM Code of Ethics* or from the *ACM/IEEE Software Engineering Code of Ethics and Professional Practice*:

    a. Obligations (from the *ACM Code of Ethics*)

        i. "As an ACM member, I will honor property rights, including copyrights and patents." (1.5)
        ii. "As an ACM member, I will give proper credit for intellectual property."(1.6)

    b. Prohibitions (from the *ACM/IEEE Software Engineering Code of Ethics and Professional Practice*)

        i. "...software engineers shall, as appropriate, not knowingly use software that is obtained or retained either illegally or unethically." (2.02)
        ii. "...those managing software engineers shall, as appropriate, not punish anyone for expressing ethical concerns about a project." (5.12)

2. **Principles** are truths that are to be consistently maintained unless there is a compelling reason to do otherwise. The *ACM/IEEE Software Engineering Code of Ethics and Professional Practice* specifies eight principles:

    1. PUBLIC—Software engineers shall act consistently with the public interest.
    2. CLIENT AND EMPLOYER—Software engineers shall act in a manner that is in the best interests of their client and employer consistent with the public interest.
    3. PRODUCT—Software engineers shall ensure that their products and related modifications meet the highest professional standards possible.
    4. JUDGMENT—Software engineers shall maintain integrity and independence in their professional judgment.
    5. MANAGEMENT—Software engineering managers and leaders shall subscribe to and promote an ethical approach to the management of software development and maintenance.
    6. PROFESSION—Software engineers shall advance the integrity and reputation of the profession consistent with the public interest.

7.  COLLEAGUES—Software engineers shall be fair to and supportive of their colleagues.

8.  SELF—Software engineers shall participate in lifelong learning regarding the practice of their profession and shall promote an ethical approach to the practice of the profession.

3.  **Ideals** are goals that are inherently good to achieve. However, failure to achieve them is not necessarily wrong. Sometimes an ideal actually cannot be fully achieved, but even then it is good to strive to achieve it. Ideals often express the main reason for a profession's existence: Physicians strive to make people healthy, lawyers strive for justice, engineers strive to harness the powers of nature for the good of humanity, and so on. Other times, ideals express goals that are much less general. Here, for example, is a standard for computer professionals included in a code adopted by three Swedish trade unions: "Computer professionals develop systems that use technology in such a way as to satisfy the interests of the user." (Dahlbam 15)

It is good for a computer professional to develop systems that satisfy users, but sometimes, despite one's best efforts, that's impossible. It is nevertheless good to strive to ensure that all users are satisfied, even if that cannot always be achieved. It is always right to try to reach toward an ideal, but it is not always wrong to fail.

**2.4.2.2 Content**    What rules should you include in a code of ethics? That depends on the function you want the code to serve. For example, the *ACM Code of Ethics* requires ACM members to be honest and trustworthy, but that standard does little to help a professional make an ethical decision. Moreover, it is not evident that it fits Davis's requirement that professional standards go "beyond what law, market, and morality would otherwise require."

However, in addition to spelling out decision-making rules, codes of ethics often specify requirements for the profession. To understand what this means, let's consider an intentionally over-the-top example. Suppose a highly talented software engineer is also a very violent individual who has the unfortunate habit of murdering people who anger him. The authorities correctly identify him as a violent criminal and arrest him on multiple counts of murder. Unfortunately, due to some major errors in procedure on the part of the police and the prosecuting attorneys, the most damning evidence is disallowed and he is acquitted. Thus, officially, he has not violated the law.

If you were a software engineer, would you want this person to be allowed to continue in his profession as a software engineer? His technical competence clearly is not the issue here; he is extremely capable of producing software. Is he in violation of the *ACM Code of Ethics* or the *ACM/IEEE Software Engineering Code of Ethics and Professional Practice*? Obviously, neither code has specific provisions against murdering, but it seems clear that the general moral imperatives of the ACM Code would apply to this kind of behavior. The *ACM/IEEE Software Engineering Code of Ethics and Professional Practice* has no provision that clearly addresses such a case unless the victims were either colleagues or clients.

Fortunately, such extreme cases are rare, and though sometimes helpful for exploring a set of rules' boundaries, they are not particularly useful to the practicing professional. In the next section, we look at a more realistic problem.

## Reflection Questions

1. **POSITION** Can a professional code of ethics be a moral ideal if it does not include such basic moral requirements as honesty and truthfulness? Explain.

2. **APPLICATION** Suppose you are the chief information officer (CIO) for a large hospital and you are considering bids from two different companies. One of the companies is a startup consisting of only five people, all of whom are recent graduates of a well-known engineering college. They have had few previous contracts, but they have done well on the jobs they have done so far. The other company is a well-established major firm. As CIO, you are aware that The Software Engineering Institute, a federally-funded research and development center that evaluates companies' software development processes (referred to as capability maturity models), has assessed the major firm at the highest level. The software system you are accepting bids for is used to schedule room occupancy. This can be quite complex in a hospital. Room assignments can be made simultaneously from various places within the hospital, and many factors have to be considered. Although patients are clearly affected by how well the software functions, there is no evident direct risk to patients in the event of a software failure. Suppose the bid from the small startup company is for $100,000, with a delivery date of six months, and the bid from the major firm is $300,000, with a delivery date of 18 months. Should you choose the larger, presumably more reliable, firm, or go with the faster, cheaper startup company? Justify your answer.

3. **POSITION** Are the issues presented in the previous question primarily economical or ethical? Explain.

4. **CONTEXT** Suppose you are about to have a medical procedure and are considering two hospitals. One of them chose the major firm in deciding which scheduling software to use. The other went with the startup company. Would that make any difference in your decision? Explain.

## 2.4.3  Following the Standards

Following a set of ethical standards would seem to be easy, or at least no harder than acting morally in the general sense. Sometimes, however, the complexities of the situation make it difficult to know which rules apply, and following one rule might even cause you to violate another one.

Isaac Asimov was a well-known science fiction writer who wrote, among many other things, a series of stories about robots. In Asimov's stories, the robots were constructed with three built-in laws that were part of a robot's essential being. A robot simply could not break the laws. The three laws were as follows:

1. A robot may not injure a human being or, through inaction, allow a human being to come to harm.

2. A robot must obey orders given it by human beings except where such orders would conflict with the First Law.

3. A robot must protect its own existence as long as such protection does not conflict with the First or Second Law.

Notice that Asimov gives only three laws and arranges them in terms of priority. Asimov was nevertheless able to construct clever situations in which it was not evident what a robot's action would be, even though the robot had to follow the three rules.

With only three laws of robotics, Asimov was able to illustrate situations in which it was difficult to determine exactly which law should apply. Real codes involve even greater complexity. The *ACM Code of Ethics* contains 24 rules. The *ACM/IEEE Software Engineering Code of Ethics and Professional Practice* contains 80 rules divided into eight categories. Neither code assigns priorities to its rules. Hence, following them consistently may be difficult. Often, one can count on one's intuition being consistent with the code. Sometimes, however, one's intuition is not sufficient, and the professional must work hard to account for all of the factors relevant to the decision.

Sometimes, a rule, though a good rule, should not be obeyed because of the context. One famous case involved a lawyer whose client, a convicted and executed murderer, had told the lawyer where the body of one of his victims was buried. Despite pleas from the victim's family, the lawyer refused to divulge the information to the family on the basis of attorney/client privilege. She continued to refuse to divulge the information even after a waiver was granted from the Ethics Board. The case has been analyzed by a number of ethicists and the most common conclusion is that the lawyer made an ethical decision, but not a moral one. She may have been trying to make the best moral decision, but she seems to have failed. This appears to be one of the relatively rare cases where the ethical decision, as defined by rigorous, even dogmatic, compliance with one's code of ethics, leads to an immoral decision.

## Reflection Questions

1. APPLICATION Let us assume that the lawyer who refused to reveal the site of her client's victim was intending to do the right thing. Make the strongest case you can that her decision was moral.

2. APPLICATION Let us assume that the lawyer who refused to reveal the site of her client's victim was intending to do the right thing. Make the strongest case you can that what her decision was nevertheless immoral.

3.   POSITION Let us assume that the lawyer's decision not to reveal the site of her client's victim was immoral. Let us further assume that she was intending to do the right thing, but was simply wrong. Does the fact that she made a mistake in choosing the immoral act make her an immoral person? Explain.

## 2.4.4   Case: A Better Way

Earlier in this chapter, we looked at the imaginary case of a software engineer who murdered his enemies. We now look at a more realistic case to see how well we can apply the *ACM/IEEE Software Engineering Code of Ethics and Professional Practice*.

Chandler is a recent graduate in computer science and has just been given his first assignment as a software developer for a major corporation. His group develops in-house software applications for the company's scientific research group. His first assignment involves calculations with large sparse matrices (matrices where many of the entries are zero) as inputs. While testing the software, he observes that the program, when run on inputs for which the solution is known, produces imprecise results, implying that the calculations are imprecise. The calculations meet the minimal acceptable degree of precision but not the preferred degree of precision.

Chandler traces the problem to the standard library program that he used for multiplying matrices. After looking more closely at the library program, and doing some research in algorithms, he concludes that a new suite of programs dealing with sparse matrices needs to be programmed in order to meet the project's specifications. His boss informs him that there is neither the time nor the budget for such an auxiliary project and that he should complete his program using the current library suite. Chandler's boss has been with the company for over twenty years and, although he is a good manager and a nice person, he has not been very involved with actual programming for quite some time. Chandler is pretty sure that his boss doesn't really understand the problem. The boss's solution is to include in the documentation a statement that "current technology makes higher degrees of precision impractical." Chandler objects. He says there are very good algorithms for solving this problem today and that implementing those algorithms would not be very difficult.

This case represents a rather common problem encountered by many people, particularly young people, in computing, engineering, or scientific professions. As with most real problems, the correct answer will depend a great deal on context. There is no single rule for arriving at the proper solution, because many factors could potentially influence the decision. As with legal reasoning, in ethical reasoning the key is to know all of the facts of the case.

When considering Chandler's particular problem, you need to keep in mind these key points:

1.   Chandler could meet the minimum acceptable requirements for the application by using the programs already in the standard library. A program that met the minimum requirements would be good enough, even if it is not necessarily the best possible.

2. Chandler is confident that the new programs he wants to create will produce the preferred degrees of precision. It's important to ask why he is so confident. It is natural for new professionals to be eager to do well. It is also natural for new professionals to have fresh perspectives on problems. They are not tied to the old ways of doing things because they never did things that way. Frequently, and perhaps in this case, they find a better way of doing things. They are also inexperienced, however. Sometimes, their inexperience causes them to perceive problems in a naïve way—i.e., not to consider all the relevant factors.

3. Chandler's boss is probably less capable than Chandler technically. All computing professions are constantly changing in terms of both technology and methodology. Some things that were not practical years ago, when the boss was most current, are not even difficult now. People like the boss, with substantial managerial or administrative duties, often find that they are no longer as knowledgeable about the most recent advances as the younger generation of professionals. It is consequently quite plausible that Chandler knows more about technology and techniques than his boss.

4. Chandler's boss is more knowledgeable than Chandler about company issues, including budgets and project priorities.

Several parts of the *ACM/IEEE Software Engineering Code of Ethics and Professional Practice* apply here. We will examine them one at a time.

- CLAUSE 3.01 **"Strive for high quality, acceptable cost, and a reasonable schedule, ensuring significant tradeoffs are clear to and accepted by the employer and the client, and are available for consideration by the user and the public."** This suggests that Chandler should "strive" to make sure the "significant tradeoffs" (e.g., the extra cost vs. the gain in precision) are clear to the company and the client. If Chandler could include more explicit language in the project's documentation, that might address the issues raised by this clause.

- CLAUSE 3.05 **"Ensure an appropriate method is used for any project on which they work or propose to work."** Chandler's argument here is that the method he is proposing is more appropriate. The method demanded by the boss is not inappropriate, however. Hence, this clause cannot justify an attempt by Chandler to overrule his boss.

- CLAUSE 3.11 **"Ensure adequate documentation, including significant problems discovered and solutions adopted, for any project on which they work."** Here, Chandler has a strong argument. Clearly, the statement suggested by the boss does not really meet the requirements of this clause. Chandler should insist upon a more extensive and explicit explanation of the precision issue.

- CLAUSE 4.01 **"Temper all technical judgments by the need to support and maintain human values."** This suggests that Chandler should take into account the affect on his boss of attempting to go over his head.

Tempering one's judgment is not necessarily to change one's judgment, but simply requires all relevant factors, including minor ones, to be considered. Here we have a typical case of tradeoffs that cannot be measured precisely and must to be evaluated by best estimates from experience. His boss might be harmed in terms of reputation and he is quite likely to be annoyed. Neither of these points would necessarily be sufficient to change Chandler's mind, but, with enough other contributing factors, they might tip the scales in one direction or another.

We can reasonably conclude that the code does not support Chandler going to higher authorities to get permission to implement the alternate suite of programs for a new sparse matrix package. The code does support Chandler pushing for more explicit explanations in the documentation, however; it also supports going against his boss, if necessary, to make the truth, as well as it can be determined, clear to all parties.

### Reflection Questions

1. APPLICATION Does the *ACM Code of Ethics* require Chandler to appeal to higher authorities regarding his desire to use the new programs? Explain.

2. APPLICATION Does the *ACM Code of Ethics* allow Chandler to appeal to higher authorities regarding his desire to use the new programs? Explain.

3. APPLICATION Do either the *ACM Code of Ethics* or the *ACM/IEEE Software Engineering Code of Ethics and Professional Practice* prohibit Chandler from appealing to higher authorities regarding his desire to use the new programs? Explain.

## 2.4.5 How Important Are Codes?

Neither the *ACM Code of Ethics* nor the *ACM/IEEE Software Engineering Code of Ethics and Professional Practice* provides the basis of a profession according to Michael Davis's definition. They do not define a moral ideal that is openly and voluntarily followed by those of the would-be profession. In the United States, most computer professionals are not familiar with the particular rules of either code. And some of those who are familiar with the codes do not accept them fully.

The *ACM Code of Ethics* is a code of ethics for members of the Association for Computing Machinery. Although the ACM is a major professional organization for computer scientists, software engineers, and other computing occupations, many who consider themselves computing professionals do not belong to the ACM. Hence, there is no particular reason to accept the ACM Code as the appropriate one for setting standards for all computing professionals. Second, as with most codes for relatively young disciplines, there are significant problems with the parts of the ACM Code. For example, the

ACM Code includes, as one of its general moral imperatives, "Avoid harm to others." The word "harm" is defined in the code as "injury or negative consequences, such as undesirable loss of information, loss of property, property damage, or unwanted environmental impacts." Note that a programmer working on target identification for armed robots or a security specialist working on cyber war strategies would seem to be in violation of this moral imperative. Such a programmer is explicitly in the business of trying to cause injury or an undesirable (to the enemy) loss of information. Should computer professionals be ethically required to refuse to work on such harmful systems?

### Reflection Questions

1. CONTEXT If you believe that computer professionals should be allowed to work on military systems that cause harm, restate the general moral imperative so it speaks to that. Be sure to take into consideration the fact that the code applies to all professionals who belong to the ACM, some of whom are not Americans. If you do not believe that computing professionals should be allowed to work on military systems, explain the likely consequences of the computing profession agreeing with you.

2. CONTEXT Consider the general moral imperative "Respect the privacy of others." Here, also, there are potential situations where the requirement becomes problematic. Identify such a situation and explain why it is problematic.

### 2.4.6   Becoming a Professional

For new physicians and attorneys, a specific event marks one's entry into the profession. In the case of a physician, it occurs when the Hippocratic Oath is administered. In the case of an attorney, it occurs when you pass your state's bar exam. In the case of computing professionals, however, no single event signals entry into the profession. Hence, a computer professional's formal obligations most commonly come in the form of codes of conduct dictated by one's employer. In Case 2.1, Rachael was still a student and would not commonly be considered a professional. Her "professional" obligations came entirely from the policies of her employer, which she agreed to follow when she took the job.

One of the authors of this book, in his youth, had a summer job picking cotton. Picking cotton by hand is, without doubt, very close to the center of our diagram of Kultgen's wheel shown earlier in Figure 2.1. It requires almost no special preparation, and to get the job you just need to apply. It would not be considered a profession by anyone's standards. Nevertheless, specific rules apply, even for that job. The rules are straightforward and anyone should be able to follow them. For one thing, you should never drop the husks from the cotton balls into the bag. That would add to the bag's weight and, therefore, increase your pay;

but, if discovered, it would mark you as a dishonest worker—one who could not be trusted and consequently should not be re-hired.

Informal rules of conduct, like the rule about cotton husks, exist for most, perhaps all, legitimate occupations. But professions generally require a more explicit set of rules and some sort of credentials that indicate that the professional is capable of following those rules. Moreover, at least for those occupations in the outer rings of Kultgen's wheel, there is some sort of rite of passage that establishes one's membership in the profession. Simply declaring oneself as a professional is not sufficient.

At the present time, people who consider themselves computing professionals have no generally recognized credentials, and no rites of passage, that establish them as professionals. When a business for developing software, repairing computers, or troubleshooting home computer systems promises fast, dependable, professional service, the people offering that professional service may or may not have a formal education in the field, may or may not have extensive experience, and may or may not have a commitment to a moral ideal. Becoming a computing professional is seldom so simple as becoming a cotton picker, but there is presently no explicit credential that one can have to establish oneself as a computer professional.

## Reflection Questions

1. APPLICATION Suppose people who pick cotton got together and formed an association, The Professional Cotton Pickers Association. They formulated a set of rules of proper conduct for cotton pickers and made it a requirement that all members of the association must agree to follow the rules. Would those cotton pickers then be professionals according to any or all of the models presented? Explain.

2. POSITION Suppose you had a problem with your computer and so you went to a local business that specialized in troubleshooting computer problems. Suppose further that you were concerned because your computer had some private financial information in some of the files that you would not like to be disclosed. The manager and owner of the business assures you that everyone there is "a true professional," so that you are assured of competent, professional service. Would that be sufficient to convince you that you had nothing to worry about? If so, explain why you think so. If not, suggest what additional information might put your mind at ease.

### 2.4.7    Case: Pornography on a University Computer

Sheila was the system manager for the College of Engineering at a university in the Midwest. The system consisted of a complex network of computers that included many personal workstations and several larger machines that functioned as servers. Sheila's position was subordinate to the Dean of Engineering, who had reported difficulties with his workstation. In particular, the performance on the dean's systems had, in recent weeks, degraded steadily, and he was now suffering what he considered intolerable delays for some important applications.

As the system manager, Sheila was a superuser, meaning she had direct access to all files and directories on the network. She was a highly competent and well-respected system manager and considered herself a professional. She did not, however, belong to any professional organizations. As a member of the university's staff, she had access to the publications of multiple professional societies, so she had allowed her memberships in the ACM and the IEEE to lapse.

Sheila quickly discovered that the performance problem was linked to a full hard disk. The number of files was not so large as to prohibit the computer from operating, but it did degrade the performance for a number of applications. In the process of moving some of the local files to the server, Sheila noticed that a great many files had the ".wmv" filename extension, indicating that they were probably video files. Out of curiosity, she opened one of the files and discovered that it was a pornographic video. Further investigation revealed that many, perhaps all, of the .wmv files were of a similar nature. The dean had filled up most of his hard disk on a university computer with pornographic videos. Sheila was dismayed. She considered the following actions:

a. Confront the dean and demand that he delete the files.
b. Report the matter to the provost.
c. Transfer the files to the server to improve performance of the workstation and say nothing to anyone.

## Reflection Questions

1. **POSITION** What should Sheila do? Explain.

2. **CONTEXT** If the files had been vacation videos of the dean and his family, should Sheila's decision be any different?

3. **POSITION** Should there be a code of conduct for system managers that would help Sheila decide her best course of action? If so, what should that code say?

4. **POSITION** Sheila looked at the dean's files without his permission. If that became known, should Sheila face consequences? In particular, if Sheila confronted the dean and he fired her for looking at his files, would he be justified?

5. **RESEARCH** This case was inspired by an actual set of events reported in the *Boston Globe* on May 19, 1999 and later covered by a number of prominent newspapers, magazines, and journals. The actual case, which was substantially different from the one we presented, involved the resignation of Ronald Thieman, at that time dean of Harvard Divinity School. Research the actual case, as represented in the media, and supply an argument for your position on which of the parties you think behaved ethically and which did not. Where, if at all, did professional obligations play a role for the parties of that case?

## 2.5  PROFESSIONALISM AND THE LAW

Unless you are a lawyer, violating your profession's code is not a legal matter. For most professions, any enforcement mechanisms are associated with and enforced by the relevant professional organization. In many cases, however, no enforcement mechanisms exist. There are, for example, no means of enforcing the *ACM Code of Ethics*. Some professions, such as law, medicine, civil engineering and accounting, require a government license. The government has no interest in whether the people working in these professions are professional according to some abstract concept. The government is, however, interested in the well-being of its citizens. There are activities in society that people depend on, and some of those activities require special training and/or abilities. We do not wish to have amateurs performing surgery, building bridges, or installing sewer systems.

Presently, most computing professionals are not licensed by the government. In the early-1990s, there was an effort in Texas to create standards for licensing software engineers. Initially, both the IEEE and the ACM were involved in defining a suitable body of knowledge and developing exams to test one's mastery of that body of knowledge. The ACM ultimately withdrew from the effort, but the IEEE proceeded. At this time, a small number of professional software engineers are in fact licensed in Texas. However, there is quite a lot of disagreement as to whether the licensing process in Texas is useful with regard to the welfare of the public.

The ACM's position is that software engineering as a discipline is too immature for its body of knowledge to be defined with precision. Hence, an examination would not necessarily test a prospective software engineer's qualifications. The ACM, in fact, suggests that such a license might be counterproductive in that the public could be misled about the ability of licensed software engineers to produce reliable software.

There are generally three components to establishing one's credentials for a profession:

1. education

2. experience

3. examination

With the exception of the licensed software engineers in Texas, today's computing professionals are not required to be qualified under any of those three components. There are various kinds of certifications, some from professional organizations and some from corporations, but a software engineer does not need to be certified in anything in order to be considered a professional. Of course, most computing professionals are employed by a company or a government agency, both of which enforce their own standards.

The lack of licensing does not mean that computing professionals are independent of the law. Any business that involves the sale of software, whether directly as a software product or indirectly as software embedded in some other device such as a microwave, smartphone, or automobile, is subject to a lawsuit brought by a customer harmed as a result of the faulty software. Employers commonly require practices that are considered sound within the profession to prevent such lawsuits.

Often the most critical applications of computing technology are in devices that are scrutinized by various government agencies for other reasons. For example, an embedded computer in a medical device or a passenger plane would be subject to various requirements for testing and inspections by the FDA or FAA, respectively.

### Reflection Questions

1. RESEARCH Look up the ACM's policy statement on licensing software engineers. Do you agree or disagree with that position? Attempt to justify your position.

2. POSITION Not all software engineers work on products that affect public safety. Moreover, not all software development is done by people who are software engineers. Should there be some type of legal regulation on any type of software other than the regulations that already exist? Explain.

## 2.6  CASE: GOING INTO BUSINESS

Antonio was very bright young man who did not do well in school. He managed to graduate from high school, but he had no desire to go to college and would not have been able to get into any of the more selective schools. He was, however, extremely interested in computers and was very knowledgeable about computing systems. Friends and others would often seek his help in solving problems with their personal computers. Someone suggested to Antonio that he try advertising his abilities and help people for a fee. Antonio ran an ad in the local paper and did, in fact, get some takers. His customers were generally satisfied with his work, and gradually he built up a reputation for being good at helping people to solve the routine problems with setting up and troubleshooting computing systems. Over time, he became very successful, and his business expanded to include installation and maintenance of computing systems for local businesses. Antonio then discovered that maintaining computers could provide him with some useful information.

Once, when working on a system for a local plant, he noticed a memo discussing plans to reduce the workforce. As it happened, Antonio had invested in some land in the area that he was holding onto in hopes of an increase in its value. He realized the land was likely to go down in value rather than up as a result of the plant's downsizing, and so he decided to sell it as soon as possible. His analysis was correct, and he was able to sell at a profit before the price went down.

Antonio reasoned that such information might often come his way from his work, and so he made a habit of trying to read his customers' letters, memos, and plans whenever he could. He never did anything illegal with the additional information, and usually his additional knowledge did not yield any actual monetary gain. He did, however, learn a great deal about many people in his town, and occasionally he would find some information that would benefit him. For example, he learned that a local car dealer who owed him a substantial amount of money was in rather deep financial trouble. Antonio decided to propose taking his payment in the form of a used car in order to settle the debt. Again, his timing was good, given that a short time later the dealer went bankrupt.

Antonio was a very successful and respected member of his community. He knew much more about some people's lives than they might have liked, but they never knew of his additional knowledge. He was very careful not to gossip or to reveal to anyone what he learned. He never considered what he was doing as wrong in any sense. He considered himself an honest businessman who remained discreet about his clients' business.

### Reflection Questions

1. APPLICATION Were Antonio's actions (reading his customers' files) moral from an act utilitarian viewpoint? Explain.

2. APPLICATION Were Antonio's actions consistent with the *ACM Code of Ethics*? Explain.

3. APPLICATION Is there any reason to believe that Antonio should adhere to the *ACM Code of Ethics* or, for that matter, any professional code of ethics? Explain.

4. POSITION Is Antonio a professional? If so, what is his profession? Explain.

5. APPLICATION Antonio did not believe his acquisition of his clients' information to be morally wrong. Make the strongest case you can that Antonio's position is valid.

6. APPLICATION Antonio did not believe his acquisition of his client's information to be morally wrong. Make the strongest case you can that Antonio's position is not valid.

## 2.7 MULTICULTURAL PERSPECTIVE: THE NEW ZEALAND COMPUTER SOCIETY'S CODE OF PROFESSIONAL CONDUCT

Computers are technologically advanced machines. It's no surprise, then, that computing professionals are found primarily in technologically advanced societies.

The global computing industry has been largely influenced by computing industry in the United States, particularly in the area of software development. However, many other countries have thriving computer industries. Many countries have adopted or adapted the *ACM/IEEE Software Engineering Code of Ethics*

**F I G U R E  2.2**    The Eight Tenets of the New Zealand Computer Society *Code of Professional Conduct*

1. **Non-Discriminatory** – Members shall treat people with dignity, good faith and equity; without discrimination; and have consideration for the values and cultural sensitivities of all groups within the community affected by their work;

2. **Zeal** – Members shall act in the execution of their profession with integrity, dignity and honour to merit the trust of the community and the profession, and apply honesty, skill, judgement and initiative to contribute positively to the well-being of society;

3. **Community** – Members' responsibility for the welfare and rights of the community shall come before their responsibility to their profession, sectional or private interests or to other members;

4. **Skills** – Members shall apply their skills and knowledge in the interests of their clients or employers for whom they will act without compromising any other of these Tenets;

5. **Continuous Development** – Members shall develop their knowledge, skills and expertise continuously through their careers, contribute to the collective wisdom of the profession, and actively encourage their associates to do likewise;

6. **Outcomes and Consequences** – Members shall take reasonable steps to inform themselves, their clients or employers of the economic, social, environmental or legal consequences which may arise from their actions;

7. **Potential or Real Conflicts of Interest** – Members shall inform their clients or employers of any interest which may be, or may be perceived as being, in conflict with the interests of their clients or employers, or which may affect the quality of service or impartial judgement;

8. **Competence** – Members shall follow recognised professional practice, and provide services and advice carefully and diligently only within their areas of competence.

*and Professional Practice.* Others have created their own codes from scratch, to better reflect the cultural context and values of their country. One such code is the *Code of Professional Conduct* used by the New Zealand Computer Society (NZCS). The eight tenets of this code are presented in Figure 2.2.

There is some overlap between the codes, in that they seem to address some of the same issues. For example, Tenet 5 of the NZCS Code says "Members shall develop their knowledge, skills and expertise continuously through their careers…" This seems very similar to Principle 8 of the *ACM/IEEE Software Engineering Code of Ethics and Professional Practice*, which says "Software engineers shall participate in lifelong learning regarding the practice of their profession…" Clearly both groups think it is important to remind computing professionals to engage in lifelong learning.

On the other hand, some issues are addressed by only one of the two groups. For example, the second half of Tenet 5 of the NZCS Code says "Members shall… contribute to the collective wisdom of the profession, and actively encourage their associates to do likewise." One way to interpret this is that members of the NZCS are encouraged to do research, write articles, publish books, and so on. The *ACM/IEEE Software Engineering Code of Ethics and Professional Practice* also encourages software engineers to do this (through rule 6.03), but it is not covered in the eight principles.

Cultural differences can have a big effect on which principles or ethical standards a computer society chooses to emphasize. Neither the NZCS Code nor the *ACM/IEEE Software Engineering Code of Ethics and Professional Practice* specifically address bribery. This is probably because bribery is not a routine problem in New Zealand or the United States. However, the codes of some countries include prominent prohibitions against bribery, because bribery is routine in those countries and a serious threat to the public. Closely examining codes of ethics from different cultures can help you learn about the values, and problems, of those cultures.

## Reflection Questions

1. CONTEXT Make a copy of the list of Principles from the *ACM/IEEE Software Engineering Code of Ethics and Professional Practice*, and the list of Tenets from the NZCS Code. For each Principle in the *ACM/IEEE Software Engineering Code of Ethics and Professional Practice*, look for a Tenet in the NZCS code that has roughly the same meaning. If you find such a match, underline the two portions and label them so it is easy to find the match again later. After you are done, circle any portion of a Principle or Tenet that does not seem to have a match in the other Code. Keep in mind that, just as we saw with Tenet 5, some of the Principles and Tenets actually contain multiple ideas, and should be sub-divided.

2. POSITION Identify one ethical standard that is contained in one code but not in the other (just considering the Tenets and Principles). Explain why that standard ought (or ought not) to be included in a code of ethics for computing professionals.

3. POSITION In both codes, each principle has a short title, such as "Public," "Colleagues," or "Zeal." Compare the two sets of titles. Which set is preferable? Explain your reasoning.

4. POSITION Compare the "Public" principle of the *ACM/IEEE Software Engineering Code of Ethics and Professional Practice* to the "Community" principle of the NZCS code. Which is more useful in ethical decision-making? Which one makes more stringent demands on the computer professional? Explain your reasoning.

5. POSITION In the *ACM/IEEE Software Engineering Code of Ethics and Professional Practice*, the "Public" principle comes first, but in the NZCS Code "Community" comes third, after "Non-Discriminatory" and "Zeal." Was this a wise choice on the part of the NZCS? Explain your reasoning. (Note: The NZCS Code is 10 years more recent than the *ACM/IEEE Software Engineering Code of Ethics and Professional Practice*, so you can assume that the authors of the NZCS Code were aware of the *ACM/IEEE Software Engineering Code of Ethics and Professional Practice* Code.)

6.  [POSITION] The NZCS Code explicitly bans "potential or real conflicts of interest" as well as discrimination. The *ACM/IEEE Software Engineering Code of Ethics and Professional Practice*, on the other hand, does not explicitly address them. However, you can assume that both are *probably* implied in the *ACM/IEEE Software Engineering Code of Ethics and Professional Practice* by the "Judgment" principle. Do you think it is important to mention both of these explicitly (as the NZCS Code does), or is the approach in the *ACM/IEEE Software Engineering Code of Ethics and Professional Practice* acceptable? Explain your reasoning.

## SUMMARY

The least restrictive definition of "professional" is the definition formulated by the Good Works Project. According to that definition, the only requirement is a degree of autonomy and a high level of service to the public. The definition that includes the most attributes is that of Kultgen and his wheel of attributes. The definition provided by Michael Davis relates most directly to our interest in the ethical responsibilities of professionals. Davis requires that a profession's members voluntarily serve a particular moral ideal, in a morally permissible way, beyond what the law, the market, and morality would otherwise require.

The *ACM/IEEE Software Engineering Code of Ethics and Professional Practice* and the *ACM Code of Ethics* are the best-known codes in the United States. They are the two principle codes for software engineers and computer scientists in the United States. Neither, however, speaks for an entire profession.

Computer professionals are not licensed by law, except for software engineers in Texas. The ACM's policy explicitly opposes the licensing of software engineers.

Around the world, the computing societies from most technologically advanced countries have adopted codes of ethics. The New Zealand Computer Society's Code of Professional Conduct is just one example.

## CHAPTER EXERCISES

1.  [REVIEW] Is journalism a profession if we confine ourselves to the three attributes that Bayles identifies as necessary?

2.  [REVIEW] What are the three properties that Bayles identifies as common to most professions?

3.  [REVIEW] List three occupations that would be professions according to the Good Works Project, but that do not have Bayles's three required attributes.

4.  [REVIEW] Would an occupation with Bayles's three required attributes necessarily be a profession according to the Good Works Project's definition? Explain.

5. REVIEW What is a moral ideal?

6. REVIEW State Davis's definition of a profession.

7. REVIEW Would an occupation that met Davis's definition of a profession necessarily meet the definition of the Good Works Project? Explain.

8. REVIEW Is it possible for an ethical rule to conflict with a moral rule? Explain.

9. REVIEW What is a fuzzy concept?

10. REVIEW Is a professor of computer science a professional according to Davis? Explain.

11. APPLICATION Look at Case 2.2 again. Is Greg right in stating that such an act would violate the *ACM/IEEE Software Engineering Code of Ethics and Professional Practice*?

12. APPLICATION Would Greg have violated the *ACM Code of Ethics* had he helped his friend as asked in Case 2.2? Explain.

13. RESEARCH Look up the details of the Toyota recall of the Prius in 2010 and explain how, if at all, the issues of standards of professional practice in computing could have been involved.

14. POSITION Should computing professionals strive to be a profession in the sense discussed by Michael Davis? Explain.

15. RESEARCH Every American university has a registrar. Learn what a registrar does and decide whether (1) registrars constitute a profession, and (2) registrars *should* be a profession. Explain your reasoning.

16. RESEARCH Is there a profession of school principals? Explain.

17. POSITION We have argued that a code of ethics without an enforcement mechanism can still be useful. Is such a code, in your judgment, adequate for computing professionals? Explain.

18. POSITION One might argue that there is more than one computing profession. Do you think so? Explain.

19. POSITION System administrators and database administrators have special privileges. Should there be special laws concerning the behavior of such people? If you think so, suggest what such laws might require. If you think not, explain why not.

20. CONTEXT The *ACM Code of Ethics* has as one of its general moral imperatives "Honor property rights, including copyrights and patents." If you were an ACM member within the European Union, where no patents for software exist, would you be required by the code to honor a U.S. patent for a particular piece of software? Explain.

21. POSITION Suppose a team of software engineers working for a software firm was negligent, and that the team's faulty software caused a major accident involving loss of life. The company was sued and settled the case. What should happen to the software engineers? In particular, should any punitive action against them be levied by their company, their professional

organization, the civil courts, the criminal courts, or some combination involving more than one of those possibilities? Explain.

## WORKS CITED

Bayles, Michael. *Professional Ethics*. Belmont: Wadsworth Publishing Company, 1984. Print.

Dahlbam, Bo. "A Scandinavian View on the ACM Code of Ethics." *Computers and Society* June 1994: 14-20. Print.

Davis, Michael. *Profession, Code and Ethics*. London: Ashgate Publishing Company, 2002. Print.

Fischman, Wendy, Becca Solomon, Deborah Schutte, Howard Gardner. *Making Good: How Young People Cope with Moral Dilemmas at Work*. Cambridge: Harvard University Press, 2004. Print.

Kultgen, John. *Ethics and Professionalism*. Philadelphia: University of Pennsylvania Press, 1988. Print.

## RELATED READINGS

### Fiction

Asimov, Isaac. *The Complete Robot*. Garden City, New York: Doubleday, 1982. Print. (This is a collection of Asimov's robot stories. Most are short stories, but there are also some mysteries that originally appeared as separate books. Asimov was very good at manufacturing dilemmas from the three rules of robotics; the book provides excellent examples of surprising ways that rules can conflict with one another.)

### Nonfiction

Gardner, Howard, Mihaly Csikszentmihalyi, and William Damon. *Good Work: When Excellence and Ethics Meet*. New York: Basic Books, 2001. Print. (This is another book on the extensive Good Works Project at the Harvard Graduate School of Education. The authors, three psychologists, look at the problems young professionals face in trying to do "good work.")

Holmes, W. Neville. *Computers and People: Essays from the Profession*. Hoboken: Wiley-Interscience, 2006. Print. (The author, a computer scientist and researcher at the University of Tasmania, compiled this collection of articles he wrote for the magazine *Computer*, the house journal of the IEEE Computer Society.)

Russell, J. S. "Taking Umpiring Seriously: How Philosophy Can Help Umpires Make the Right Calls." *Baseball and Philosophy: Thinking Outside the Batter's Box*. Bronson, Eric and Bill Littlefield, eds. Chicago: Open Court, 2004. pp. 87-104. Print. (This is an interesting short essay on interpreting rules.)

# Chapter 3

# Privacy

Computers and computer networks have had a tremendous impact on our expectations and experiences of privacy. For example, it is now much harder to keep dark secrets than it was in the past. Sex offenders can be identified through online databases, plagiarists can be caught by comparing writing to sources on the Internet, and databases of leaked e-mails shine a light on corporate and government wrongdoing. However, these same technologies have also made new, potentially devastating crimes possible. Thieves can steal millions of credit card numbers by hacking computer databases, and hackers can spy on us in our homes. Meanwhile, ordinary people can no longer assume they are going about their business unobserved. For example, if you happen to be planning a big on-campus party via Facebook, you should assume that your school's security officers, the dean's office, and possibly the local police department know about the party, too.

Recognizing and dealing with privacy problems raised by computer systems is complicated by the lack of agreement about how to describe our right to privacy. Dictionaries generally give three definitions of **privacy**: 1) seclusion (which means being set apart or out of view); 2) secrecy or concealment; and 3) freedom from intrusion. These definitions conflict with each other, complicating our attempts to agree about privacy issues.

In this chapter we explore some definitions of privacy, and then use the ideas we develop to analyze some of the privacy challenges created by the Internet and by the computerized collection of data.

## 3.1 CASE: SECURITY CLASS

Professor Blake teaches computer security. In his computer security class, he teaches students how easy it is to intercept e-mail and instant messages (IMs). As an assignment, students are required to intercept e-mails and IMs from the university's network and post them to the class blog.

When Jessica, one of his students, objected to the assignment on the grounds that it was an invasion of privacy, Professor Blake disagreed for two reasons:

- It is very easy to intercept e-mail, so e-mails cannot be considered private.
- The e-mail accounts are on university servers, the contents of which are actually public, so reading them is not a privacy violation.

### Reflection Questions

1. [POSITION] When you write e-mail using your school e-mail account, do you expect it to be private? Why?

2. [CONTEXT] Would your answer be different if it were an e-mail account you received through an employer, instead of through your school? Why or why not?

3. [POSITION] Should Dr. Blake be allowed to continue to use this assignment? Why or why not?

4. [POSITION] Should Dr. Blake be allowed to continue to teach students how to intercept e-mails and IMs, if he does not have students use these skills to actually intercept IMs or e-mails? Why or why not?

## 3.2  CASE: MICHAEL'S ESSAY

Professor Hernandez teaches persuasive writing at a university. Every year she requires students to write an essay defending something they actually oppose. The purpose of the exercise is to help students see that arguments that sound good aren't necessarily the same as arguments that are logical, and also to give students experience in playing devil's advocate.

Michael is a student in Professor Hernandez's class. In his essay, "In Defense of Terrorism: Terrorism as the Only Path from Oppression to Democracy," Michael argued that all modern democratic states were founded by terrorists. He described parallels between George Washington and Osama bin Laden. He finished the paper by advocating strongly that the United States ought to provide financial and logistical support to terrorist groups active in nondemocratic countries as a method for spreading democracy.

Professor Hernandez receives assignments in electronic form. She grades papers by typing comments into the file before assigning the final grade. While grading some class work, she discovered several papers by Michael's classmates that appeared to be plagiarized. After she finished grading, she uploaded the papers to Plagiarism Preventer, a popular Web site that checks papers for plagiarism. It also permanently stores student papers submitted to the service so that they can be used in future plagiarism checks of other papers.

Professor Bobson, who teaches at a different college, also uses Plagiarism Preventer to detect and prevent plagiarism. One of the student papers he submitted to the site matched Michael's paper significantly because they quoted many of the same sources. Because of the high degree of similarity, Plagiarism Preventer provided Professor Bobson with the full text of Michael's paper. This included Professor Hernandez's comments, Michael's full name, and Michael's grade, which was an A+. Professor Hernandez's comments were all very positive: "Nice argument," "Good points," "A useful interpretation of George Washington's role in the revolution."

Unlike Professor Hernandez, Professor Bobson was appalled at the content of the paper. He immediately reposted the full text of the paper (including Michael's name and grade, and Professor Hernandez's comments) on his blog under the title "Terrorist Supporters Set Up Shop at Major University," and included Professor Hernandez's name and the name of her university. The post generated a lot of attention on blogs, social media sites, and cable news channels. Both Michael and Professor Hernandez started to receive angry and threatening phone calls and e-mails, including death threats. Meanwhile, the university received thousands of complaints from concerned alumni and parents.

## Reflection Questions

1. APPLICATION Michael's paper became public through a series of actions performed by other people:

   ▪ Professor Hernandez uploaded his paper to Plagiarism Preventer without his knowledge.

   ▪ Plagiarism Preventer allowed Professor Bobson to download the paper.

   ▪ Professor Bobson posted the paper on the Internet.

   ▪ Various blogs and social media sites drew attention to the paper.

   ▪ Traditional media outlets publicized the controversy widely on TV and in newspapers.

   ▪ Upset people called Michael at home to harass and threaten him.

   Which of the actions in this series violated Michael's privacy? Some of the actions may have violated rights other than privacy, but in this question you should focus on privacy violations only. You may want to explicitly state the definition of privacy you are applying to the case.

2. POSITION Which actions listed in Question 1 were unethical but did not violate Michael's privacy? Explain your answer, again making reference to which definition of privacy you think applies.

3. CONTEXT Which of your answers to the previous two questions would change if Michael's grade had not been included in the paper? What if Michael's name had not been included in the paper? Explain your answers.

4. [APPLICATION] Is it unethical for college professors to use Plagiarism Preventer without student consent? Justify your answer, using one of the ethical theories from Chapter 1.

5. [APPLICATION] Is it unethical for Plagiarism Preventer to give the full text of student works to third parties? Justify your answer, using one of the ethical theories from Chapter 1.

## 3.3  THEORIES AND CONCEPTIONS OF PRIVACY

When people called Michael at his home to harass him (in Case 3.2), the harassment and threats were clearly immoral. But were the harassing callers also violating Michael's privacy? The answer to this question depends on the definition of privacy you have in mind.

People who think of privacy as seclusion or secrecy usually blame the person whose privacy was lost. For example, you might say it's Michael's responsibility to keep his phone number secret, or else unplug his phone, if he wanted to keep his privacy.

People who think of privacy as freedom from intrusion, on the other hand, tend to focus on the expectations and desires of the person whose privacy was lost. The national Do Not Call law, which prohibits telemarketers from calling phone numbers listed on the registry, has been tremendously popular because it stops businesses from intruding into our personal lives to try to sell us things. In this sense, the harassing callers are invading Michael's privacy.

So the first major problem with building a consensus on privacy issues is that the three major dictionary definitions of privacy lead to very different conclusions. The second major problem is that the three definitions of privacy are not broad enough to capture every problem that we think of as a privacy problem.

In Case 3.2, various media outlets widely publicized Michael's paper, and this publicity contributed to the amount of harassment he experienced. It is not clear, however, whether the media was invading Michael's privacy. If you define "privacy" as secrecy, then the media did not violate Michael's privacy because Michael's paper was already publicly available on Professor Bobson's blog. If you define "privacy" as freedom from intrusion, then the reporters did not violate Michael's privacy because they did not have any direct interactions with him. Nevertheless, many people feel that the media should not widely publicize information that makes an innocent person look bad.

The taxonomy of privacy-related problems, presented later in this chapter, will help you analyze issues related to privacy and computing. But first, let's look at the "privacy as freedom from intrusion" and "privacy as secrecy" definitions in more depth.

### 3.3.1  The Right to be Let Alone

Most dictionaries define the **right to privacy** as the "right to be free from intrusion." This definition was popularized by Louis Brandeis (who would go on to be a justice of the Supreme Court of the United States) and Samuel Warren in a famous article in the *Harvard Law Review*, published in 1890. According to Warren and Brandeis:

> Recent inventions and business methods call attention to the next step which must be taken for the protection of the person, and for securing to the individual… the right "to be let alone." Instantaneous photographs and newspaper enterprise have invaded the sacred precincts of private and domestic life; and numerous mechanical devices threaten to make good the prediction that "what is whispered in the closet shall be proclaimed from the house-tops." (195)

This statement is as relevant today as it was when it appeared more than a century ago.

At the time that Warren and Brandeis wrote their article, there was widespread disagreement about whether or not a right to privacy could exist. A **right** is a liberty or entitlement owed to a person simply because he or she is a person. In the United States, for example, the government acknowledges a person's rights to free speech, to free practice of religion, to benefit from one's own labor or investments, and so on.

Opponents of the right to privacy usually try to show that what we call "privacy" actually derives from other rights. For example, consider the claim that we have the right not to be secretly videotaped in a department store dressing room. Opponents of the right to privacy might argue that the department store, when it videotapes you, is violating an implicit contract with you, but not violating a supposed right to privacy. By making private changing rooms available, they have implied that they will protect your seclusion in that space. When they videotape you in the changing room it is not a privacy violation, but a violation of the implicit contract.

As another example, suppose a friend posts an embarrassing picture of you on Facebook and tags it with your name, making it very likely that your employer and family will see it. You could argue that an intellectual property right has been violated and not your privacy. That is, you could argue that you ought to have intellectual property rights to pictures of yourself, and that others should not be able to use a picture of you without your permission.

This was an issue even back in 1890, when cameras were first becoming widespread. At the time, opponents of the right to privacy claimed that there was no such right, and that intellectual property rights and contract law were sufficient to protect people from so-called privacy violations. Warren and Brandeis sought to debunk these ideas.

To demonstrate that intellectual property law cannot be used to protect privacy, they raised the example of private letters published against the wishes of the author. As Warren and Brandeis point out, "Letters not possessing the attributes of literary compositions are not property entitled to [intellectual property] protection."

They also argued that contract law is not sufficient to protect private correspondence. It is true that contract law can, in some cases, prevent the publication of private correspondence by the receiver, because the receiver, by accepting a letter, enters into an implicit contract to keep the letter private. However, Warren and Brandeis argued that contract law cannot protect private correspondence from snooping third parties, because they do not have an established relationship with the sender, something which is usually required for a contract to be valid.

In summary, Warren and Brandeis argue:

> … the [privacy] rights, so protected, whatever their exact nature, are not rights arising from contract or from special trust, but are rights as against the world; and, as above stated, the principle which has been applied to protect these rights is in reality not the principle of private property, unless that word be used in an extended and unusual sense. The principle which protects personal writings and any other productions of the intellect or of the emotions, is the right to privacy, and the law has no new principle to formulate when it extends this protection to the personal appearance, sayings, acts, and to personal relation, domestic or otherwise. (213)

They conclude that a "right to be let alone" already existed and was recognized by the courts, even though it was not explicitly written in the law. As a result, they wrote, "a man's house is his castle, impregnable, often even to [officers of the law.]" They recommended that a person whose privacy is breached should be allowed to sue, except in circumstances where the privacy breach is necessary for public safety or for the functioning of a court of law.

### 3.3.2  Application of Warren and Brandeis

We can apply this conception of privacy as a "right to be let alone" to the case study about Michael's essay. In the "right to be let alone" conception of privacy, we focus on the grievance felt by the harmed party and on actions that directly make them feel harassed, embarrassed, or exposed. Which of the parties in the case are guilty of privacy violations under this definition?

Both Professor Hernandez and Professor Bobson committed breaches of trust, but this is not a privacy problem according to the definition of Warren and Brandeis. They would argue that these are exactly the types of situations that could be handled by contract law. Hernandez broke her trust with Michael. This may have violated an implicit contract with Michael to keep his work confidential. Bobson did not have a relationship with Michael, but he did break his trust with Plagiarism Preventer by publicly posting the materials it provided.

The parties that most clearly violated Michael's right to be let alone are Professor Bobson and the harassing callers. It is easy to see that the harassing callers were intruding on Michael's peace in his home. Professor Bobson, on the other hand, violated Michael's right when he decided to single Michael out, and shame him, by posting his essay for the whole world to see. If Professor Bobson had decided Michael should be "let alone," he would have gone to much greater lengths to protect Michael from harassment. Instead, he seems to have implicitly encouraged the harassment.

## Reflection Questions

1. POSITION When anthropologists and sociologists talk about private life, they typically mean the life of the family and the home, as opposed to public life, which concerns work outside the home and events in the public square. Should the "right to be let alone" apply only to private life, or should it extend to places like the office and public beaches as well? Explain your answer.

2. APPLICATION Some police officers object to being videotaped while they are going about their jobs (for example, writing traffic tickets). If a bystander videotapes a police officer writing a traffic ticket, does this violate the police officer's right to be let alone? Why or why not?

### 3.3.3 Privacy as Concealment

Judge Richard Posner, a former justice of the 7th Court of Appeals and a law professor at the University of Chicago, is one of the most respected legal minds of our age. He believes that there is no fundamental right to privacy and that people are interested in privacy only because they want to conceal their own wrongdoing or prevent embarrassment. In a video interview published on *http://bigthink.com*, Judge Posner says,

> As a social good ... I think privacy is greatly overrated, because privacy basically means concealment. People conceal things in order to fool other people about them. They want to appear healthier than they are, smarter, more honest... [it is] what economists call a superior good; the demand for it rises as people become wealthier. Because it has this instrumental value, you want to control information about yourself; that will enable you to make advantageous transactions personally, professionally, and commercially with other people. (Posner 2008)

Judge Posner argues that, in the future, modern notions of privacy will be obsolete. His argument has three main parts:

- Pre-modern peoples (living in small villages or tribal cultures) had no real ability to conceal anything about themselves, and therefore no privacy. It is perfectly natural for people to live with little or no privacy.

- Contemporary people are willing to give up their private information, and become transparent, in return for very small financial incentives or improvements in convenience. This proves that we do not value individual privacy.

- Concealment is most useful to criminals, and least useful to honest people. Therefore privacy is mostly a social harm that reduces safety, not a social good.

In this book, we call the view articulated by Posner **privacy as concealment**. It often takes the form of the "I have nothing to hide" argument. For example, the USA PATRIOT Act of 2001 gave the government the ability to inspect library records without a warrant. A supporter of this policy might argue: "I do not mind if the government gets access to my library records, because I have nothing to hide."

This "I have nothing to hide" argument says that people are not concerned about privacy because they do not have anything they wish to conceal.

Posner stops short of saying that concealment is always bad. He agrees that everyone has a right to conceal their bodies by wearing clothes, and to conceal embarrassing but necessary behaviors like excretion and hygiene. But he denies that there is a right to conceal personal information except in very limited cases. In fact, Posner argues that we should stop using the word "privacy" altogether, saying, "The word 'privacy' has strongly positive connotations (like 'freedom'), which obscures analysis." (Posner 2005)

### 3.3.4    An Application of Privacy as Concealment

The privacy as concealment definition supports Professor Blake's position in Case 3.1. He might argue that if you want to conceal the contents of your e-mail, then you should learn to use e-mail encryption software or be careful not to send e-mails that you don't want others to see. Either way, he would argue that it is the responsibility of the person sending the e-mail, not the one intercepting it, to maintain any desired level of privacy.

Now let's consider how Posner's view of privacy plays out in Case 3.2. To people who read brief newspaper articles about the situation, Michael, the student who wrote the paper, comes off looking like a terrible person because he compared Osama bin Laden favorably to George Washington. However, if Professor Bobson, the media, and the public had taken the time to understand Michael's paper in the context of the assignment, they would have realized that he believed the exact opposite of the position he argued in his paper. Thus, you might argue that Michael ought to be able to conceal the contents of his paper until he is sure that the audience understands this point. You can probably think of other situations in which it is advisable to conceal information unless or until you can be sure the receiver understands the context. However, this type of concealment is exactly what Posner is arguing against.

### Reflection Questions

1. RESEARCH During the spring and summer of 2010, Facebook users revolted against changes in Facebook's privacy policy. Find news stories about the controversy that provide concrete evidence either supporting or refuting Posner's position. Summarize your findings.

2. POSITION Posner claims that people do not value personal privacy, and that therefore personal privacy is not really important. What is the other option for what to do in response to Posner's claim? That is, if you think personal privacy is important, but you acknowledge that people do not value it, what should be done?

### 3.3.5    Solove's Taxonomy of Privacy Problems

So far we have considered two attempts to define privacy, one in terms of freedom from intrusion and the other in terms of concealment. Daniel Solove, a professor at the George Washington University School of Law in Washington DC, is extremely critical of such attempts to precisely define privacy. He says:

> If we persist in the existing discourse, we will continue down a road that leads to nowhere.... Using the traditional method—seeking to define privacy's essence or core characteristics ... [results in] endless disputes over what falls inside or outside the domain of privacy (39).

Solove's approach is to work bottom-up instead of top-down. That is, instead of starting with a single clear definition, and then discovering that not all privacy problems are covered by the definition, he starts with a list of the common kinds of privacy problems. In Solove's view, this is more likely to be useful in practice and in policy-making. Solove presents his list as a hierarchical Taxonomy of Privacy. Take a moment, now, to read over Figure 3.1, which summarizes his taxonomy and provides brief definitions of each type of privacy problem.

- **Information collection**
  - Surveillance—Monitoring continuously, usually via audio, visual, or computer technology.
  - Interrogation—"Pressuring... individuals to divulge information."
- **Information processing**
  - Aggregation—Collecting many small pieces of information about a person and linking them together, to create new information.
  - Identification—"Connecting information to individuals."
  - Insecurity—Inadequately safeguarding collections of personal data against theft.
  - Secondary use—Using data that people willingly gave for one purpose for some other purpose they did not approve.
  - Exclusion—Failing to notify individuals that their data is being collected, or failing to provide a way for individuals to view or correct such data.
- **Information dissemination**
  - Breach of confidentiality—Breaking a contractual or fiduciary duty to keep someone else's information private.
  - Disclosure—Publishing private, but true, information in a way that damages the reputation of the subject.
  - Exposure—Publicly displaying certain physical or emotional attributes of another that are normally considered private, especially if such display is humiliating or embarrassing.
  - Increased accessibility—Making records that are technically available to the public easier to access.
  - Blackmail—Exerting power over another by threatening to reveal damaging information about that person.
  - Appropriation—Using someone else's identity for one's own ends.
  - Distortion—"Manipulat[ing]... the way a person is perceived and judged by others."
- **Invasion**
  - Intrusion—Communicating with people in a way that disturbs their peace or makes them feel uncomfortable.
  - Decisional interference—Controlling (usually by authority of the government) what one is allowed to do in one's private life.

**F I G U R E 3.1** Solove's taxonomy of privacy problems

A thorough discussion of Solove's taxonomy, with all of the definitions and examples for each category, is beyond the scope of this book. Fortunately, most of Solove's categories are well understood and will not need further discussion (for example, breach of confidentiality, blackmail, and so on). It will be helpful to address a few of the categories that are particularly confusing or controversial.

Some of Solove's categories are controversial because they seem, at least at first glance, not to be privacy problems, but some other kind of problem. Aggregation and increased accessibility are particularly problematic because they both involve processing or disseminating data that is already publicly available. We will focus our discussion on just these two categories.

The growth and success of social networking and the Internet have made aggregation and increased access big business. Google, Facebook, Netflix, and most other successful Internet companies make their money by building dossiers of their users' likes and dislikes. This allows the Web site to carefully select ads that the user is likely to be interested in, maximizing the effectiveness of the ad space.

In the area of information processing, the dangers of aggregation, in particular, are often overlooked. Solove says, "When analyzed, aggregated information can reveal new facts about a person that she did not expect would be known about her when the original, isolated data was collected." One well-known example of this was a site called PleaseRobMe (the site is no longer operating, but you can find reports about it in the media). PleaseRobMe was a Web site that allowed the user to quickly find houses where the owners were away from home. It worked by aggregating a person's social networking status updates (from sites like Twitter, Foursquare, Flickr, and Facebook) and home address information. If you just took a picture in Washington D.C. and you live in Montana, a robber can be fairly confident that your house will be unoccupied for a while.

Solove might argue that the privacy problem in this case is a problem of aggregation. Even though a robber could do this process by individually checking Facebook pages or other social media sites to find people who are away from home, they are unlikely to do so because pulling together all the data and analyzing it is too time consuming when done by hand. By aggregating the data, PleaseRobMe created a much greater privacy threat than the individual social networking sites do in releasing the data.

A similar argument could be made about increased accessibility. When data becomes easier to access, people find new uses for it. For example, under the Civil Rights Act of 1964, it is usually illegal to reject job applicants based solely on their arrest records. In the past, this wouldn't have been a major issue for most people because, although arrest records have always been public information, it was the rare employer who would take the time to search every local newspaper for the past ten years to see if a job applicant appeared in the police blotter. Those bent on violating the Civil Rights Act could theoretically ask law enforcement for arrest records, but because doing so could arouse suspicion, it wouldn't be a smart thing to do. Today, however, the combination of online arrest records, online court records, and Internet search engines makes it very easy to violate the law, and violations are very difficult to catch. In fact, the crime report sections of many newspapers are now completely automated. They pull data directly from the databases of local law enforcement, including mug shots, names, birthdates, and reasons for arrest. Just as in the case of aggregation, increased accessibility creates a potential privacy harm that, though possible in the past, was unlikely to occur.

One other frequent point of confusion about Solove's taxonomy is the difference between "disclosure" and "exposure." Both of these categories of privacy problems involve revealing truthful private information, so it is easy to get them confused. "Exposure" involves the public display of certain highly private aspects of a person's body or emotions. The most common examples involve photographs of people in death, sickness, grief, and so on. For example, a doctor who publishes an x-ray or autopsy photo of a celebrity is committing an act of exposure (in addition to several other types of privacy violations). "Disclosure," on the other hand, focuses on revealing facts, not taboo images. Solove reports on the case of a Japanese author who wrote a book about her extramarital affair with a prominent politician. This information was truthful, but its publication clearly harmed the politician.

Solove's main idea is that rather than endlessly debate what is or is not "privacy," we ought to get on with the business of solving privacy problems. His taxonomy is an attempt to give names to the various types of privacy problems that occur today, so that we can more easily deal with them. It also provides technology makers with a checklist of common privacy problems that they can use when analyzing their products for potential dangers.

### Reflection Questions

1. POSITION One might argue that information collection is never a privacy violation, only information dissemination. Defend or refute this position.

2. APPLICATION Some Americans refuse to fill out census forms on the grounds that it is a privacy violation. Under which of Solove's categories does this fall?

## 3.3.6 Applying Solove's Taxonomy

Solove's taxonomy does not tell us whether a particular action is right or wrong, but it allows us to break a case into pieces so that we can attempt to identify the type of privacy problem it presents. Let's analyze Case 3.2 with this in mind. Professor Hernandez's actions illustrate several kinds of privacy problems. She made a secondary use of Michael's paper—that is, she contributed it to Plagiarism Preventer's database for use in future plagiarism detection. She also committed an act of exclusion by excluding Michael from her decision to submit his paper to Plagiarism Preventer's archive. Professor Hernandez's posting of Michael's grade to Plagiarism Preventer was certainly a breach of confidentiality, but it is less clear whether her posting of the assignment was a breach of confidentiality in and of itself. Many students and professors accept that student work may sometimes be shared with third parties, but most agree that grades should not be.

Professor Bobson's distribution of Michael's paper to the wider Internet community was both a problematic disclosure, and also a breach of the confidentiality that Plagiarism Preventer required when it gave him the file. Note that Dr. Bobson's actions are not really a form of increasing accessibility, because the information (Michael's paper) was not public at the time that Professor Bobson posted it.

The actions of the media, on the other hand, could be viewed as increasing accessibility in a way that harmed Michael.

### Reflection Questions

1.  APPLICATION Consider Plagiarism Preventer's decision to allow Professor Bobson access to the full text of Michael's paper. Which item in Solove's hierarchy is most applicable to this action?

2.  POSITION Keeping in mind Plagiarism Preventer's decision to allow Professor Bobson to download the full text of Michael's paper, did Plagiarism Preventer violate Michael's privacy? Explain your reasoning.

3.  APPLICATION Use Solove's taxonomy to analyze Case 3.1. Which of Solove's sixteen types of privacy breaches apply to the case? Explain your reasoning.

## 3.4  PRIVACY IN PRACTICE AND IN THE LAW

In this section we discuss some practical rules and legal precedents related to privacy and computing in the United States. There are a multitude of laws and precedents, but an exhaustive and shallow catalog of them is not useful. Instead we focus on a few examples that: (1) are so foundational that every citizen should know about them; or (2) provide a current and typical example of how computing is affecting privacy in the law and in practice.

### 3.4.1  Privacy in the U.S. Constitution and Laws

The United States Constitution and Bill of Rights serve as the foundations for most arguments about rights in the United States, both in the courts and in public opinion. For this reason, to verify claims that a "right to privacy" exists in the United States, the Constitution is the first place we should look. You might be surprised to learn, however, that the U.S. Constitution does *not* explicitly describe a broad right to privacy. Instead, various amendments to the constitution define certain narrow areas of privacy. The five privacy-related amendments to the Constitution are listed in Figure 3.2.

First Amendment: Congress shall make no law respecting an establishment of religion, or prohibiting the free exercise thereof; or abridging the freedom of speech, or of the press; or the right of the people peaceably to assemble, and to petition the Government for a redress of grievances.

Third Amendment: No Soldier shall, in time of peace be quartered in any house, without the consent of the Owner, nor in time of war, but in a manner to be prescribed by law.

Fourth Amendment: The right of the people to be secure in their persons, houses, papers, and effects, against unreasonable searches and seizures, shall not be violated, and no Warrants shall issue, but upon probable cause, supported by Oath or affirmation, and particularly describing the place to be searched, and the persons or things to be seized.

Fifth Amendment: ... nor shall [any person] be compelled in any criminal case to be a witness against himself, nor be deprived of life, liberty, or property, without due process of law; ...

Fourteenth Amendment, Section 1: No State shall make or enforce any law which shall abridge the privileges or immunities of citizens of the United States; nor shall any State deprive any person of life, liberty, or property, without due process of law; ...

**F I G U R E 3.2** Privacy-related portions of the U.S. Constitution

The First Amendment guarantees a certain level of "privacy" in the practice of religion, in that the government cannot prevent a person from practicing his or her particular religion. The Third and Fourth Amendments together guarantee a very limited right to privacy in the home. The Third says that soldiers will not be quartered in one's house (which would certainly be an invasion of privacy), and the Fourth guarantees that a person's private papers and effects will not be violated by the government without judicial oversight. The Fifth Amendment can be viewed as providing citizens with privacy of their thoughts and knowledge, at least in cases where exposure would lead to a criminal conviction.

The use of the Fourteenth Amendment to protect privacy is more controversial than the use of the First, Third, Fourth and Fifth Amendments. Though it does not explicitly address privacy, many justices would argue that one of the liberties the Fourteenth Amendment addresses is Warren and Brandeis's "right to be let alone." Consider the 1969 Supreme Court case of *Stanley v. Georgia*. According to court documents, police raided the house of a man suspected of running an illegal gambling operation. They did not find evidence of illegal gambling, but they did find in a desk drawer three pornographic films that were deemed to be "obscene" (and hence illegal). Stanley was convicted of obscenity. Writing for the court in overturning Stanley's conviction, Justice Marshall held that:

> The First Amendment as made applicable to the States by the Fourteenth prohibits making mere private possession of obscene material a crime.

In other words, even if the states wanted to make laws that prohibit the private possession of obscene materials, they cannot. This activity is private and falls outside the jurisdiction of the government.

We have seen that, while the U.S. Constitution does provide citizens some privacy protections against the government, it does not define a general right to privacy. U.S. law, in general, takes a piecemeal approach to privacy. There are many different laws, with each law designed to protect the privacy of one particular kind of data, or one particular medium of communication. For example:

- Contents of first class mail – Title 18, U.S. Code, section 1702
- Contents of a student's academic records – Family Educational Rights and Privacy Act (Title 20, U.S. Code, section 1232g)
- Bank records – Title 12, U.S. Code, section 3403

So while there are many laws dealing with specific privacy issues, there is no law that defines or protects privacy in general.

### Reflection Questions

1. APPLICATION Cellular phone companies can locate you very accurately as long as your phone is turned on and has a signal. This location information is often used by law enforcement to solve crimes. Under the Fourth Amendment, should it be legal for law enforcement to get this information without a warrant? In other words, should cell phone location fall under the category of things ("persons, houses, papers, and effects") protected by the Fourth Amendment? Explain your reasoning.

2. APPLICATION Do you think the court's decision in *Stanley v. Georgia* implies that states cannot prohibit people from watching obscene videos over the Internet? Use an analogy, and explain your reasoning.

3. APPLICATION Which of Solove's sixteen types of privacy breaches (presented in Section 3.3.5) are directly addressed by the consitutional amendments listed in Figure 3.2, and which are not? Explain your reasoning.

### 3.4.2   A Reasonable Expectation of Privacy

The Fourth Amendment makes an important distinction between reasonable and unreasonable searches and seizures. For example, if a man is waving a gun and threatening to shoot someone, it is quite reasonable to seize his gun, even without a warrant. Applied to information privacy, the question often boils down to whether or not the person whose privacy is infringed actually had a reasonable expectation of privacy in that case.

Consider a woman standing in front of the Washington monument, shouting at the top of her lungs. Clearly the words she says are not private, because she is shouting them in public. On the other hand, a teenager using a cell phone in the bathroom of a coffee shop with the door closed might reasonably believe himself to be "in private." In 1967, the Supreme Court indeed upheld this belief in *Katz v. United States*. Without a warrant, the FBI had recorded phone conversations of Mr. Katz, who was using a public telephone booth, and they argued that because the phone booth was in a public place, Katz did not have a reasonable expectation of privacy. However, the Supreme Court disagreed.

New technologies are constantly changing our expectations of privacy and hence affect the protections of the Fourth Amendment. It is legal for an airplane to fly over your house and take pictures, as long as it is at a legal altitude. This did not change with the invention of the high-power zoom lens; it is still legal for an airplane to fly over your house and take pictures, even though cameras and lenses have improved drastically, so that a picture taken from a plane today would reveal far more than a picture taken from a plane fifty years ago. But this means that our expectation of privacy in our backyards has changed, and this in turn changes whether or not a warrant is needed to photograph us in our backyard.

The question of whether or not e-mail is private continues to be contentious. The courts have long held that it is reasonable to expect the contents of physical mail to be private, because they are inside an envelope, while the address and post-mark on the outside of the letter are not. Similarly, the courts have held that telephone conversations are private, and so tapping a call requires a warrant—but the government can record which numbers you call without a warrant.

In 2007, a panel of the United States Court of Appeals for the Sixth Circuit (in their opinion in *United States v. Warshak, et al.*) argued that e-mail was similar to telephone conversations. They argued that even though e-mail messages reside on a third party's server, the third party should not give the messages to law enforcement without a warrant. The court argued that a communication does not become public just because it is *possible* for a third party to access it. The user has a reasonable expectation that his or her Internet Service Provider will not give e-mails to law enforcement without a warrant. In other words, the user has a reasonable expectation of privacy. In the end, however, the court refused to issue this opinion as a final ruling, dismissing the case on other grounds.

District Judge Michael Mosman of Oregon similarly avoided ruling on the central issue in a recent opinion about warrants for e-mail messages stored by third parties. In his opinion, however, he says,

> Much of the reluctance to apply traditional notions of third-party disclosure to the e-mail context seems to stem from a fundamental misunderstanding of the lack of privacy we all have in our e-mails. Some people seem to think that they are as private as letters, phone calls, or journal entries. The blunt fact is, they are not.

In the end, it is still unclear what privacy protections, if any, the Fourth Amendment provides for e-mail. This confusion stems from fundamental disagreements about whether or not a reasonable expectation of privacy exists for e-mail.

## Reflection Questions

1. APPLICATION How does the idea of a reasonable expectation of privacy relate to Case 3.2? Should the FBI be able to get student papers from Plagiarism Preventer without a warrant? Explain your reasoning.

2. CONTEXT If Plagiarism Preventer told students that student papers might be shared with law enforcement, would this remove any reasonable expectation of privacy with regard to papers submitted to Plagiarism Preventer?

3. [CONTEXT] Some experts have argued against the idea of "a reasonable expectation of privacy," claiming that it introduces subjectivity into decisions. The question of whether or not something is private depends on context—that is, on whether or not the person thought there was privacy at the time. Is this dependence on context a strength or weakness when used to interpret the Fourth Amendment? Justify your answer.

## 3.5  MULTICULTURAL PERSPECTIVES

So far in this chapter, we have focused on the Western view of privacy, particularly the legal and philosophical traditions of Britain and the United States. But the definition of what is private and what is public is often affected by culture as well as technology. In *A History of Private Life*, a five-volume treatise written by top French historians of the twentieth century, the editors say:

> Private life is not something given in nature from the beginning of time. It is a historical reality, which different societies have construed in different ways. The boundaries of private life are not laid down once and for all; the division of human activity between public and private spheres is subject to change. Private life makes sense only in relation to public life. (Prost and Vincent)

In this section we provide a few examples of the ways that other cultures conceptualize privacy and how the differences in these views create conflicts between cultures.

### 3.5.1  Libel and International News Reporting

The crime of libel is closely related to distortion as Solove defines it. **Libel** means publishing or broadcasting false statements about another person, usually with the intent of harming the other person's reputation. Almost all legal systems recognize either civil or criminal penalties for libel. For journalists and authors, an understanding of libel laws around the world is particularly important, because it is one of the few restrictions on the press that almost all countries accept.

In most countries a statement cannot be libel if it is true or if it is a matter of opinion. A statement can only be libel if the writer claims it is a fact, but it is actually false. In the United States, for a statement to be libel, it usually must be "(a) a statement of fact; (b) that is false; (c) and defamatory; ... (g) that causes actual injury...." (Glasser 2009, p. 49)

Some countries, however, allow a person to be sued for libel even when the statement is true, based purely on the fact that the statement is intended to be defamatory. In particular, Spanish law may find a person guilty of libel for "the disclosure of facts relating to private life, which affect a person's reputation and good name." (2009, p. 380) This is much closer to Solove's concept of disclosure than distortion. Similarly, in China, "insulting statements may be found actionable even if they do not contain false statement of fact." (2009, p. 83) In one case, for example, a Chinese leaflet-maker was imprisoned for three years for insulting a former premier.

Libel used to be something that only writers and publishers had to worry about, but new technologies like blogs and Twitter are blurring the lines between "journalist" and "citizen." The widespread use of the Internet also makes it easier for people from different countries to interact. On October 28, 2000, *Barron's* magazine online posted an article called "Unholy Gains" that made reference to Joseph Gutnick in a way that he believed to be defamatory. The case was complicated, however, because, while *Barron's* is published in the United States, Mr. Gutnick lives in Australia. Mr. Gutnick attempted to sue Dow Jones (the company that owns *Barron's*) for libel in the Australian courts. Dow Jones asserted that because its Web servers reside in New Jersey, it could be sued under U.S. law, but not Australian law. In rejecting this argument, the High Court of Australia wrote,

> I agree with [Gutnick's] submission that what [Dow Jones] seeks to do, is to impose upon Australian residents … an American legal hegemony in relation to Internet publications. The consequence … would be to confer upon one country, and one notably more benevolent to the commercial and other media than this one, an effective domain over the law of defamation, to the financial advantage of publishers in the United States, and the serious disadvantage of those unfortunate enough to be reputationally damaged outside the United States. (*Dow Jones and Company v. Gutnick*)

This decision set a precedent that left Web-based authors and publishers open to lawsuits from every country and every jurisdiction. The fact that different cultures have different views of what constitutes "libel" can have a chilling effect on Internet writing. The term **chilling effect** is used to refer to a situation in which one feels pressure not to do something, even though it is legal to do so, because of fear of prosecution. In this case American authors may choose to avoid making defamatory but true statements that would be protected under U.S. law because they fear prosecution in other countries. Part of Dow Jones's argument, in its appeal to the High Court of Australia, was that allowing the case to proceed would have a severe chilling effect on free speech on the Internet. The High Court unanimously rejected this argument.

## Reflection Questions

1. RESEARCH Many years have passed since the Gutnick decision. Based on your observations of blogging and Internet news, have the chilling effects and widespread lawsuits predicted by Dow Jones occurred? Explain your answer.

2. POSITION Imagine that a writer from Country A posts an article on a server residing in Country B, about someone who lives in Country C. The article is readable only by people in Country D (readers from other countries trying to access the article receive an error message). If countries A, B, C and D have very different libel laws, which country's laws ought to apply? Why?

### 3.5.2 Case: Drug Tourists

Differences in drug and alcohol regulations from country to country have given rise to **drug tourism**, which is the practice of crossing a national border in order to get access to a drug that is illegal on the other side. One of the most common forms of drug tourism in the United States is for young adults 18-20 years old to cross the border into Canada in order to purchase alcohol.

Jennifer and her friend, Susan, were studying to be elementary school teachers at a small school in the northwestern United States. One weekend they decided to go to Canada to a big party hosted by one of Susan's friends. As it happens, two other students from the same school, Brian and his girlfriend Stephanie, were at the party as well. Stephanie took a picture of all four of them with alcoholic drinks on her cell phone. Brian later posted the photo, along with others, on his blog.

Many teaching colleges have strict rules about law breaking. In the past, students have been expelled from teaching college for illegal, underage drinking. Administrators discovered the picture of Susan, Jennifer, Stephanie, and Brian on Brian's blog, and brought all four up on disciplinary charges. The charges were eventually dropped when it became clear that the party had taken place in Canada, and hence was likely legal.

Susan and Jennifer, however, were upset at Brian and Stephanie for posting the picture without getting Susan and Jennifer's permission. They complained to the college's Student Honor Board that Brian had violated the code of student conduct, which requires all students to respect the privacy of their fellow students. They asked the Board to levy punitive sanctions against Brian and to require him to remove the photo from his blog.

Susan and Jennifer argued that a party is not a public place. Had they been drinking in a public park they would not have expected privacy, but they were in a private residence, at a private party. Hence they feel they had a reasonable expectation of privacy, and Brian should have asked permission before posting the picture.

Brian argued that taking pictures, and posting them online, is a normal activity at a party. By attending the party and posing for the picture they implicitly agreed to be photographed and to have the photograph posted online.

Jennifer and Susan also argued that they expected the picture to be seen by others at the party, but not by the administrators and other students of their college, or by prospective employers. Brian's blog post may create an impression that Susan and Jennifer broke the law, even though they did not. This is what Solove calls distortion.

### Reflection Questions

1. [POSITION] What decision should the Student Honor Board make? Should Brian be forced to take down the picture? Should Brian be punished? Explain your reasoning.

2. [CONTEXT] Should it matter whether Brian's blog is on a server owned by the college or on a separate private server? Explain your reasoning.

3.  CONTEXT Would it matter if the offending picture was a picture only of Susan and Jennifer, and Brian and Stephanie did not appear in it?

4.  CONTEXT Would it change your decision if it was discovered that some other students at the party asked not to be photographed, and Stephanie has respected their wishes?

## 3.6   INTERDISCIPLINARY TOPIC: PANOPTICISM

Michel Foucault is one of the most influential social thinkers of the twentieth century. He studied and wrote about the history of social institutions such as sanitariums, prisons, and clinics. In the essay "Panopticism," (1979) Foucault explores the influence of persistent surveillance on society, comparing modern society to the modern prison.

"Panopticism" takes its name from the Panopticon, a prison design proposed by the English philosopher Jeremy Bentham (1748-1832). Though the Panopticon itself was never built, many modern prisons take significant inspiration from Bentham's proposals. In contrast to medieval prisons, where dozens of prisoners might be crowded into a single dark room, in the Panopticon each prisoner is housed in a separate cell. Unlike the dingy dungeons of the past, the Panopticon is well lit, with each cell including external windows to let in light. An internal window allows the guards in the central guard tower to see each prisoner. According to Bentham's plan, illustrated in Figure 3.3, the guard tower is kept dark, and the windows are covered with venetian blinds to prevent the prisoners from seeing the guards. In this way a very small number of guards can maintain order over a large prison population. Because the prisoners have no way of knowing whether or not they are being watched at a particular time, they must always assume they are being watched. The placement of one prisoner per partition also means that prisoners cannot effectively organize or riot.

Foucault used Bentham's design for the Panopticon as a metaphor for the role of surveillance in modern society. According to Foucault, the Panopticon is not a

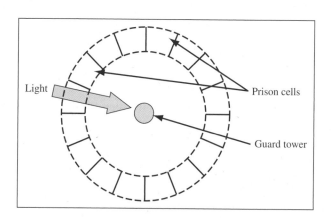

**FIGURE 3.3**
Bentham's Panopticon

method of punishment, but a method of discipline. Each prisoner, assuming that he is being constantly watched, disciplines himself. This use of self-regulation makes the Panopticon much more efficient, in terms of the number of guards needed, than traditional designs.

Foucault observed that many of our society's institutions serve a similar purpose in enforcing discipline in our day-to-day lives. The government uses the public school system to look for evidence of child neglect or abuse, requiring teachers to look for and report any such evidence to police. The fact that all hospitals are required to report instances of specific diseases to the Centers for Disease Control allows the government to detect and track outbreaks. The hierarchical structures of modern corporations, which generally limit the number of low-ranking workers that have daily contact with each other, derive from command structures originally designed for use maintaining discipline in armies. These institutions separate individuals into small groups and then ensure that these individuals are aware that they may be under surveillance. And again, this system is much more efficient than simply punishing wrongdoers; in institutions that follow the panoptic design, people simply refrain from doing wrong because they know they are being watched. They engage in self-discipline.

Bentham's design did not end with surveillance of the prisoners, however. He recommended that the guard tower be open to the public. Anyone could stroll in from outside via a tunnel, and ascend into the guard tower. This way one would not have to worry about prisoner abuse, because the guards would know that they too were (possibly) being watched by ordinary citizens visiting the guard tower. In other words, institutionalized surveillance does not necessarily arise only as a result of a tyrannical government. Instead, surveillance can arise as a means for a society to encourage self-discipline, and thus improve productivity and reliability.

It is important to understand that Foucault (at least in the essay discussed here) was not taking a position for or against panoptic structures. What he wanted to point out is that these structures were invented, that they are a technology that can be used in many places in society. By describing the Panopticon metaphor, he has given us the tools we need to recognize this pattern when we see it in society or in our own work. As with most technologies, whether a panoptic structure is morally good or morally bad depends on how it is used.

As a technology student, you might be involved in creating new systems with panoptic aspects. Foucault wrote about the surveillance society in the early 1970s, before personal computers, before the Internet, before Facebook. Social networking, online retail, and online communication all mean that society today is orders of magnitude more transparent than anything Foucault could have imagined. Nevertheless, many people are unaware that they are under constant surveillance. They don't realize that prospective employers check Facebook and credit records, that employers monitor real-estate listings for early warning that someone is quitting, or that universities routinely monitor student e-mails for keywords like "fake id" or "stoned." Such surveillance is not truly panoptic,

- ■  A central authority has control over some aspect of people's lives.
- ■  People are kept in small groups, separated from each other.
- ■  Everything a person does can be observed by the authorities.
- ■  A person can never be sure whether or not he or she is currently under observation.
- ■  Awareness of the possibility of surveillance causes self-discipline.

**F I G U R E  3.4**  Key ideas of a panoptic structure

however, as long as society is unaware of it. Without awareness of the surveillance, self-discipline does not occur.

Surveillance is a topic of contention in online forums and blogs. On one side are libertarians, who decry most forms of government surveillance and control. On the other are groups who view law and order as one of the highest goods, arguing that surveillance is perfectly acceptable to anyone who has nothing to hide. Foucault's analysis suggests that both groups may be too simplistic in their understandings of the issue.

Figure 3.4 summarizes the key ideas of a panoptic structure.

## Reflection Questions

1.  APPLICATION  In Section 3.3.3 we discussed Justice Richard Posner's view of privacy as concealment. He argued that, before modern times, people had little privacy because an entire family would often live in a single room. Is this situation of constant surveillance by other family members an example of a panoptic structure? Be sure to refer to the "key ideas" of panoptic structures in your argument.

2.  RESEARCH  We list several beneficial aspects of surveillance, such as preventing child abuse and early detection of flu pandemics. What are some other beneficial systems of surveillance in contemporary society?

3.  APPLICATION  Twitter acted as a tool of liberation during the Iranian elections of 2009 and during the Arab Spring of 2011, allowing pro-reform groups to get their messages out to the world. At the same time, governments have started using pictures and GPS data from social media sites (as well as surveillance cameras) to identify protestors and rioters, something that was not possible in the past. Ultimately, is social networking likely to be liberating or oppressive? In what ways?

## 3.7  CASE: CAMERA PHONE PREDATOR ALERT ACT

On January 9, 2009, U.S. Representative Peter King of New York proposed a new law called the Camera Phone Predator Alert Act (see Figure 3.5). Use the Reflection Questions at the end of this section to help you analyze the potential impact of this bill if it were to be enacted into law. You will have a further opportunity to analyze this bill in the Chapter Exercises.

A BILL

To require mobile phones containing digital cameras to make a sound when a photograph is taken.

*Be it enacted by the Senate and House of Representatives of the United States of America in Congress assembled,*

**SECTION 1. SHORT TITLE.**

This Act may be cited as the 'Camera Phone Predator Alert Act.'

**SEC. 2. FINDING.**

Congress finds that children and adolescents have been exploited by photographs taken in dressing rooms and public places with the use of a camera phone.

**SEC. 3. AUDIBLE SOUND STANDARD.**

(a)    Requirement- Beginning 1 year after the date of enactment of this Act, any mobile phone containing a digital camera that is manufactured for sale in the United States shall sound a tone or other sound audible within a reasonable radius of the phone whenever a photograph is taken with the camera in such phone. A mobile phone manufactured after such date shall not be equipped with a means of disabling or silencing such tone or sound.

(b)    Enforcement by Consumer Product Safety Commission- The requirement in subsection (a) shall be treated as a consumer product safety standard promulgated by the Consumer Product Safety Commission under section 7 of the Consumer Product Safety Act (15 U.S.C. 2056). A violation of subsection (a) shall be enforced by the Commission under section 19 of such Act (15 U.S.C. 2068).

**FIGURE 3.5**   The Camera Phone Predator Alert Act in its entirety

### Reflection Questions

1.    POSITION Does it make sense that this bill singles out camera phones, instead of addressing all digital cameras and video-recording devices? Explain your reasoning.

2.    APPLICATION Based on your reading of the bill, would this law (if enacted) make it illegal to own a camera phone that takes pictures silently? Explain your reasoning.

3.    CONTEXT In the past it was not deemed necessary to require cameras to make a sound so that people would know photographs were being taken. What, if anything, has changed to make people want to enact this bill? Explain your reasoning.

## 3.8   CASE: THE TEXAS INFANT DNA DATABASE

For more than thirty years, the government has taken a blood sample, called a blood spot, from every baby born in the United States. The main purpose of this policy is to help identify children with serious congenital disorders, such as hypothyroidism or phenylketonuria, so they can be treated. This test does not require parental consent. In fact, in most states, parents cannot opt out of it.

You might assume that, after the tests are performed, the blood spots would be disposed of, but this is not true in most states. The Texas state health department, for example, was turning over the blood samples to the U.S. military. This fact was discovered after parents started complaining about Texas's policy of keeping the blood spots. In 2010, Emily Ramshaw, of the Texas Tribune, reported,

> When state health officials were sued last year for storing infant blood samples without parental consent, they said it was for medical research into birth defects, childhood cancer and environmental toxins. They never said they were turning over hundreds of dried blood samples to the federal government to help build a vast DNA database—a forensics tool designed to identify missing persons and crack cold cases.

Before the twenty-first century, there was little motivation to keep such samples. However, with the advances in DNA sequencing and the creation of computerized DNA databases for various uses, DNA samples have become a valuable source of information for scientists and law enforcement alike. What rights, if any, should we have to keep our DNA private?

## Reflection Questions

1. POSITION Imagine that you were one of the state health officials making the decision about whether or not to pass on DNA sequences to the U.S. military. Would you support the action? Explain why or why not.

2. CONTEXT What if the group responsible for compiling the database was a for-profit corporation instead of the U.S. military? Would this be better or worse? What if the group making the database was the U.S. Red Cross? Explain your reasoning.

3. CONTEXT Does it matter that the individuals whose DNA was being collected were infants? Would you be more comfortable if DNA was not released to the U.S. military until 18 years after it was collected? Why or why not?

4. POSITION Is this a problem of *computing* ethics, *medical* ethics, or both? Explain your reasoning.

5. POSITION The United Kingdom keeps a national DNA database for use in solving crimes. In 2009, the BBC News Service reported a retired police superintendent saying, "It is now the norm to arrest offenders for everything if there is a power to do so. It is apparently understood by serving police officers that one of the reasons, if not the reason, for the change in practice is so that the DNA of the offender can be obtained: samples can be obtained after arrest but not if there is a report for summons. It matters not, of course, whether the arrest leads to no action, a caution or a charge, because the DNA is kept on the database anyway." Should all people arrested for a crime be required to submit a DNA sample to a national DNA database? Explain your reasoning.

## 3.9 CASE: LOWER MERION SCHOOL DISTRICT

Lower Merion School District (LMSD), in Pennsylvania, has launched a progressive, "Twenty-first Century Learning" initiative. As part of this initiative, the district provides each high school student with a laptop computer. Soon after the initiative was launched, the district found itself embroiled in controversy related to policies designed to protect the computers against loss or theft.

In February 2010, student Blake Robbins sued LMSD, alleging that,

> [T]he school district has the ability to remotely activate the embedded webcam at any time the school district wished to intercept images from that webcam of anyone or anything appearing in front of the camera… (*Robbins v. LMSD*)

The suit further alleges that students became aware of the practice only after Blake was called into a meeting with an assistant principal. The assistant principal allegedly informed Robbins that he had been "engaged in improper behavior in his home" as evidenced by "a photograph from the webcam embedded in [his] laptop." Parents and the media are concerned that student privacy might have been violated, and that in some cases minors might have been photographed unclothed.

At the heart of the problem is a piece of software called LANrev, which has a Theft Track feature intended to help school administrators track down missing laptops. The idea was that, when a computer was reported missing, administrators could remotely turn on the computer's webcam, in the hopes of being able to identify the computer's location based on what could be seen from the webcam. Robbins (and the other parties to his suit) alleged that school officials abused this feature to spy on students, and they kept the feature secret from students.

To further complicate issues, LANrev allegedly has some major security vulnerabilities. According to a report in *Wired* (Zetter 2010), Leviathan Security Group (a computer security consulting company that studied LANrev after Robbins's allegations were reported in the press) discovered that the encryption key used to secure LANrev is a stanza of German poetry and is the same for all computers. This means that, after deciphering this key, a hacker on the same network as a student running LANrev could remotely take complete control of the student's computer.

So far, the legal fees in the case have reached one million U.S. dollars. The school had issued 2,300 laptops to its students.

### Reflection Questions

1.   RESEARCH  At the time of the writing of this chapter (June 2010), the case was ongoing, and not all the facts were known. Search for news stories that have appeared since that time. Write a summary of the new information that has come out since June 2010.

2.  APPLICATION Who are the morally significant parties in this case? List them. Next, list the components of Solove's taxonomy that are most appropriate to the case. Which components apply to which parties?

3.  APPLICATION Use an act utilitarian argument to evaluate whether or not the LMSD should have installed the remote Theft Track software on student laptops. (*Hint*: Compare the costs of the lawsuit to the costs of laptop thefts. Also consider the probability of being sued versus the probability of a laptop being stolen.)

## SUMMARY

- The dictionary definitions of privacy conflict with each other, complicating our attempts to reason about privacy issues.

- Warren and Brandeis argued that there is a right to privacy that is separate from property rights and contractual obligations.

- Justice Richard Posner argues that the right to privacy did not exist in the past and will not exist in the future. He argues it is an illusion created by the current form of our culture.

- Law Professor Daniel Solove argues that attempts to define privacy are doomed to failure. Instead, he proposes a taxonomy of types of privacy problems that can be used in decision making.

- The Bill of Rights contains some basic and very specific privacy protections, but no general right to privacy.

- The Fourteenth Amendment is sometimes (but not always) interpreted as a protection for the right to be let alone.

- The approach to privacy in U.S. law is to focus on particular kinds of data or particular communication media.

- Changes in technology affect our expectations of privacy, which in turn affects our protection from government searches under the U.S. Constitution.

- Differences in the definition of libel from country to country may have a chilling effect on certain kinds of speech.

- Michel Foucault's work on the use of surveillance in modern society is based on a metaphor to a prison called the Panopticon, designed by philosopher Jeremy Bentham.

- Panoptic structures appear in many social institutions, and the Panopticon metaphor helps us understand how and why they work.

## CHAPTER EXERCISES

1. REVIEW State the dictionary definition(s) of "privacy."

2. REVIEW State the definition of "a right."

3. REVIEW State Warren and Brandeis's formulation of the right to privacy.

4. REVIEW Define "private life" and "public life."

5. REVIEW State Posner's definition of "privacy."

6. REVIEW Concisely state Posner's argument that privacy is "greatly over-rated" as a social good.

7. REVIEW Restate the "I have nothing to hide" argument.

8. REVIEW List and define the twenty terms from Solove's taxonomy of privacy problems.

9. REVIEW Restate the five amendments to the U.S. Constitution that protect specific forms of privacy.

10. REVIEW Explain what is meant by the phrase "a reasonable expectation of privacy," and what role it plays in deciding whether or not the government needs a warrant for a search.

11. REVIEW Define libel. Give both the general definition that applies to most countries and the more specific U.S. definition.

12. REVIEW Define "chilling effect."

13. REVIEW Describe the Panopticon of Jeremy Bentham. Draw a picture to illustrate your description.

14. REVIEW Restate the key features of a panoptic structure.

15. APPLICATION Referring to Case 3.1, use one of the ethical theories from Chapter 1 to explain what Professor Bobson ought to do and why.

16. APPLICATION Recall from Chapter 2 that codes of professional ethics usually take the form of rules, principles, or ideals. The National Education Association's Code of Ethics of the Education Profession explicitly requires teachers to safeguard student privacy, stating that the educators "Shall not disclose information about students obtained in the course of professional service unless disclosure serves a compelling professional purpose or is required by law." With this in mind, consider Case 3.2. Did Professor Hernandez violate the code of ethics? In particular, did Hernandez "disclose information" about Michael? If so, did the disclosure "serve a compelling professional purpose"? Explain your answers.

17. CONTEXT Recall from Chapter 2 that codes of professional ethics usually take the form of rules, principles, or ideals. The National Education Association's Code of Ethics of the Education Profession explicitly requires teachers to safeguard student privacy, stating that the educators "Shall not disclose information about students obtained in the course of professional service unless disclosure serves a compelling professional purpose or is required by law."

With this in mind, consider Case 3.2. Did Professor Bobson violate the code of ethics? In particular, does it matter that Michael is not Professor Bobson's student? Is Professor Bobson's duty to safeguard student privacy limited to only his own students, or does it apply to all students everywhere?

18. POSITION Should a college professor connect as "friends" with her students on Facebook? Explain your reasoning. In particular, be sure to describe pros and cons for both positions, and be sure to describe what the teacher-student relationship ought to be like.

19. POSITION In Case 3.7 you read the Camera Phone Predator Alert Act, a law that was proposed to try to prevent child predators from using cell phone cameras. Imagine that you are a technology advisor to Representative King. You need to draft a better bill and convince him that your version is better. Rewrite the bill so that it will be more effective in preventing child exploitation. (You do not have to use the precise format of a bill or law; focus on the main overarching ideas of what should be prohibited and how it should be enforced.) Also write an explanation of how your bill improves on the original.

20. POSITION In Case 3.7 you read the Camera Phone Predator Alert Act, a law that was proposed to try to prevent child predators from using cell phone cameras. Imagine that, as part of your work for a libertarian think tank, you are writing an article for a national news magazine. Your goal is to persuade the public and lawmakers not to enact Representative King's bill into law. Write a detailed rebuttal of Rep. King's proposal by demonstrating that American citizens have a right to possess a silent camera phone.

21. RESEARCH In Case 3.8, you learned that the government was collecting DNA samples to be used (among other things) for identifying criminals. Would a court be likely to rule that this collection of blood spots constitutes an unreasonable warrantless seizure under the Fourth Amendment? You will need to find and present other court cases about other warrantless seizures of DNA as evidence to support your position.

22. RESEARCH In Case 3.9 you read about one school district's use of remote monitoring software. Either critique or defend the following position: Schools should never install remote monitoring software on computers used by minors, because the dangers outweigh the benefits. You may need to research some of the other uses and benefits of remote access software.

## WORKS CITED

*Dow Jones and Company Inc v. Gutnick.* [2002] HCA 56. High Court of Australia. 2002.

Foucault, Michel. "Panopticism." *Discipline and Punish: The Birth of the Prison.* New York: Vintage, 1977. 195-230. Print.

Glasser, Charles J. *International Libel and Privacy Handbook: A Global Reference for Journalists, Publishers, Webmasters, and Lawyers,* 2nd Edition. New York: Bloomberg Press, 2009. Print.

Mosman, Michael. "Opinion and Order in cases regarding search warrants for electronic mail." 08-mc-9131 and 08-mc-9147. District Court of Oregon. 2009. Web. 6 Jul 2011.

"Police making arrests 'just to gather DNA samples'" *BBC,* 24 Nov 2009. Web. 6 July 2011.

Posner, Richard. "Posner on Privacy." *The Becker-Posner Blog,* 8 May 2005. Web. 6 July 2011.

Posner, Richard. "Privacy." *BigThink.com,* 2008. Web. 6 July 2011.

Prost, Antoine et al. *History of Private Life, Volume V: Riddles of Identity in Modern Times.* Cambridge: Belknap Press of Harvard University Press, 1998. Print.

Ramshaw, Emily. "DSHS Turned Over Hundreds of DNA Samples to Feds." *The Texas Tribune,* 22 Feb 2010. Web. 24 July 2011.

Solove, Daniel J. *Understanding Privacy.* Cambridge: Harvard University Press, 2010. Print.

*Stanley v. Georgia.* 394 U.S. 557. U.S. Sup Ct. 1969.

*United States v. Warshak, et al.,* 2010 WL 5071766. United States Court of Appeals for the Sixth Circuit. 2010.

Warren, Samuel V., and Louis D. Brandeis. "The Right to Privacy." *Harvard Law Review* 4.5 (1890): 193-220. Print.

Zetter, Kim. "School Spy Program Used on Students Contains Hacker-Friendly Security Hole." *Wired.com Threat Level,* 20 May 2010. Web. 6 July 2011.

## RELATED READINGS

### Novels

Orwell, George. *1984.* New York: New American Library, 1961. Print. (The culture explored in *1984* is a classic "panoptic" system. Big Brother watches the citizens through telescreens in the home. In real life, almost all computers now come with video cameras built into them, and as video-conferencing becomes more popular it is possible that cameras will be built into televisions as well. Is it possible that one day the authorities *will* watch us through our televisions and computers?)

### Short fiction

Bradbury, Ray. "The Murderer." *The Golden Apples of the Sun.* New York: Harper Perennial, 1997. Print. (Ray Bradbury's story, originally published in 1953, of a man driven to kill all of his personal electronic and communication devices. Much of the dialog is eerily reminiscent of Twitter communication or Facebook status updates.)

### Film and television

*Gattaca.* Dir. Andrew Niccol. Columbia Pictures, 1997. Film. (Like *1984, Gattaca* is a dystopian story. In this story, one's position and opportunities in life are decided by the genetic predisposition towards favorable or unfavorable traits. Are the protagonist's problems mainly due to the lack of genetic privacy in his society?)

"To Surveil with Love." *The Simpsons*. Fox. 2 May 2010. Television. (In response to a nuclear disaster, the city of Springfield installs ubiquitous security cameras, monitored by Ned Flanders. Though the cameras were installed to prevent terrorism, they end up being used primarily to nag and tattle on Springfield's residents.)

## Nonfiction books

Solove, Daniel J. *Understanding Privacy*. Cambridge: Harvard University Press, 2009. Print. (The summary of Solove's work provided in this chapter necessarily oversimplifies his arguments. As you will see by reading his book, his arguments are more thorough and more nuanced than the brief summary provided in this book. He also discusses many real life cases to illustrate his points.)

## Scholarly essays

Foucault, Michel. "Panopticism." *Discipline and Punish: The Birth of the Prison*. New York: Vintage, 1977. 195–230. Print. (This essay is a classic in the analysis of how societies establish discipline and control, and is the foundation for much of what has been written about surveillance in society. Foucault was not really talking about technological surveillance, but many of his ideas have direct analogs in today's culture of the Internet and social networking. The essay is relatively easy for a general audience to read.)

Solove, Daniel J. "I've Got Nothing to Hide and Other Misunderstandings of Privacy." *San Diego Law Review* 44 (2007): 745–772. Print. (For readers who want to understand more of Solove's thinking, but do not have the time to read *Understanding Privacy*, this work may be a good substitute.)

# Chapter 4

# Intellectual and Intangible Property

The U.S. Constitution says that the Congress has the right to "promote the Progress of Science and useful Arts, by securing for limited Times to Authors and Inventors the exclusive Right to their respective Writings and Discoveries" (Article I, Section 8). By including this passage, the writers of the Constitution recognized that creativity and invention are essential to improving the quality of human life, and that people are more likely to engage in such activities if they can make a living doing so.

The products of creativity and invention are typically called "intellectual" property, to distinguish them from tangible property such as a house or a pair of shoes. In this chapter we describe the types of intellectual property that are most affected by computing and the Internet, and we look at new types of intangible property that arise due to computing, but do not seem to be creative in nature. We then give some background on current intellectual property law and the philosophical basis for these laws. We conclude with a number of case studies.

## 4.1 CASE: SONY BMG ANTIPIRACY ROOTKIT

Throughout this book we use the term **piracy** to refer to the intentional illegal copying of copyrighted material. We use "piracy" instead of "theft" to emphasize the fact that there are morally significant differences between copying intangible property and stealing physical objects.

In 2005, in an effort to stop music piracy, Sony BMG started using a copyright protection scheme on its CDs. When the music CD was inserted in a CD player, it worked normally, but when it was inserted in a computer, the user was asked whether to install "Enhanced CD" content, which might contain photographs, music-playing software (similar to iTunes), or other materials.

The installation program also used a rootkit to change the computer's operating system. A **rootkit** is a piece of software that allows an unauthorized user to override security and get administrator access to a computer; it gets its name from the fact that the main administrator account on many computer systems is called the "root" account.

If the user chose "Agree" when playing the CD on a computer, the "Enhanced Content" did three main things:

- It used a rootkit to get administrator access to the computer, even if the person playing the CD did not have administrator privileges.

- It modified the operating system to place limits on how the CD's contents could be copied or used. In particular, it limited the number of times the user could convert the CD to MP3 files and the number of copies of the CD the user could "burn"; it also prevented people from using the CD with nonapproved music-playing programs or devices.

- It used a technology called cloaking to make it hard to tell whether or not the user's computer had the software installed.

Sony BMG was most likely concerned about people converting its CDs into MP3 music files and posting them on the Internet for people to download illegally. Several other companies addressed this problem by making CDs that could not be played in a computer at all. When the CD was inserted in a computer, the computer simply ejected the CD. Other companies did not use any antipiracy technology. Sony BMG knew that many users wanted to use their computers as home stereos and to listen to their music on MP3 players, so the company opted to go with a copy protection scheme that limited casual piracy while allowing users some flexibility.

In a commentary in *Wired*, security expert Bruce Schneier expressed concern that antivirus and antispyware companies originally chose not to detect or remove the rootkit. He noted that the Symantec Corporation, publisher of numerous widely used security programs, explained its lack of action by saying that the "rootkit was designed to hide a legitimate application." Schneier rejected this claim, saying that "the only thing that makes this rootkit legitimate is that a multinational corporation put it on your computer, not a criminal organization."

## Reflection Questions

1. POSITION If you legally purchase a CD, should you have the right to convert the CD to MP3 files and post those files publicly on the Internet? Explain your reasoning.

2. POSITION If you legally purchase a CD, should you have the right to convert the CD to MP3 files and use them on your personal music player? Explain your reasoning.

3. **CONTEXT** Consider Symantec's argument and Schneier's counterargument, presented earlier. Should antivirus companies distinguish between rootkits from major corporations and rootkits from criminals, allowing the former but detecting and removing the latter? Explain your reasoning.

## 4.2 CASE: VIRTUAL INVESTMENT FRAUD

Investment fraud schemes are common in massive multiplayer online games such as *Second Life* or *EVE Online*. These games almost always have some form of virtual currency, and players are often looking for ways to earn a quick (virtual) buck. In 2006, a character named "Cally" in the popular game *EVE Online* started the EVE Intergalactic Bank. Cally would take deposits of the game's currency (the Interstellar Kredit, or ISK) and pay interest on these deposits. He claimed that he was reinvesting the money, but in actuality he was pocketing most of the money. It has been reported (though widely disputed) that when Cally's scheme started to fall apart, he walked away with 790 billion ISK. It is important to understand that there are many Web sites that allow players to exchange ISK for U.S. dollars and vice versa. At the time Cally's bank failed, the 790 billion ISK that he had allegedly stolen was worth about 170,000 U.S. dollars.

Cally bragged about his scam, admitting it openly, but he was not punished. Why not? *EVE Online* is a computer game about piracy and commerce in outer space. Players are encouraged to steal each other's cargo, attack each other, or extort money by threatening to attack. As a commentator writing under the name Ralphedelominius reported in the blog *Ten Ton Hammer*, CCP hf. (the company behind *EVE*) decided that what Cally did was within the rules of the game. In other words, although creating fake investments is wrong in real life, it is perfectly acceptable within the *EVE Online* game.

### Reflection Questions

1. **POSITION** Either defend or refute the following claim: Fraud is fraud regardless of whether or not it occurs in a virtual world; if something stolen can easily be converted into real currency, then it is a real fraud and should be punished.

2. **POSITION** Either defend or refute the following claim: Committing fraud in *EVE Online* is like bluffing in poker. Everyone knows and accepts that bluffing is part of poker, and therefore it is morally permissible. For the same reason, scams and frauds inside *EVE Online* are morally permissible. You agree to those risks when you play the game.

3. **POSITION** Assume that you live in a society (such as the United States) that has a personal income tax. Should ISK earned in *EVE Online* be subject to income tax? Or should only U.S. dollars earned by selling ISKs be subject to income tax? Explain your reasoning.

## 4.3  INTELLECTUAL PROPERTY LAW IN THE UNITED STATES

In a letter he wrote in 1813, Thomas Jefferson pointed out the difficulty of owning one's ideas.

> If nature has made any one thing less susceptible than all others of exclusive property, it is the action of the thinking power called an idea, which an individual may exclusively possess as long as he keeps it to himself; but the moment it is divulged, it forces itself into the possession of everyone, and the receiver cannot dispossess himself of it.

The purpose of intellectual property law is to make sure that people with good ideas can profit from those ideas, even after the idea is known to everyone. As noted in the introduction, the framers of the U.S. Constitution thought this would encourage more people to get involved in creative arts or invention, to the benefit of everyone.

The production and distribution of intellectual property accounts for a significant fraction of the U.S. economy. As a result, intellectual property law is very complicated; we cannot hope to give a full summary of it here. Instead, we will focus on three key types of intellectual property protections that directly affect computing: copyright, patent, and trademark. Over the course of the next few sections, we will define each of these in turn. With each type of intellectual property protection we study, it's helpful to ask the following five key questions.

- What type of thing can be protected? (For example, patents protect inventions, not artworks.)
- What rights are reserved for the creator of the work? (For example, one cannot publish a photograph without the photographer's permission.)
- What rights are reserved for the public? (For example, a book critic has the right to use short quotes from a book in her criticism, and the book's author cannot prevent this.)
- How does one obtain the protection for a work?
- How long does the protection last?

### 4.3.1  Copyright

Copyright is the main mechanism for protecting creative works such as art, music, and writing. More precisely, in the United States, copyright protects "original works of authorship fixed in any tangible medium of expression" in the areas of literature, music, drama, pantomime, graphic art, sculpture, motion pictures, sound recordings, and architecture (Title 17, U.S. Code section 102). Note that copyright cannot cover ideas, facts, or common knowledge. Copyright also does not cover creative works until they appear in a tangible fixed form. The classic example of this is dance choreography; in order to protect their work, dance choreographers often make video recordings of a dance during a rehearsal.

The creator of a copyrighted work does not have to do anything to get a copyright. As soon as one's creation appears in a fixed medium, it is automatically protected by copyright. Under U.S. law, the default length of a copyright is the lifetime of the author plus 70 years after the author's death. (Note that in U.S. copyright law, the term **author** is used for all creators, including choreographers, architects, and so on.)

It is a common misconception to think that copyright gives authors 100 percent control over their work. In fact, U.S. law (Title 17, U.S. Code section 106) recognizes four main rights of the author:

- The right to reproduce the copyrighted work
- The right to prepare derivative works based upon the copyrighted work
- The right to distribute copies of the copyrighted work to the public by sale or other transfer of ownership, or by rental, lease, or lending
- The right to perform or display the copyrighted work publicly (Note: In the U.S. Code, this right is broken into three separate cases depending on the nature of the work. We have combined them for simplicity.)

The author, and only the author, has the right to use the copyrighted work in these ways, although she can sell her copyright to others or authorize others to exercise these rights on her behalf.

Most activities not covered by the four main rights of the author belong to the public. For example, if you legally obtain a DVD, you are allowed to display the work privately in your own home. The author has the right to control public displays of the movie, but private viewings are allowed under the law. There are two main rights reserved for the public that deserve special attention: fair use and the doctrine of first sale. We cover these next.

### Reflection Questions

1. APPLICATION Sports leagues often include a copyright notice in their public broadcasts that claims that one cannot publish accounts or descriptions of their games without getting written consent. Regardless of whether or not you think this claim is actually true, explain which of the four rights of the author might be used to support this claim.

2. CONTEXT Some software companies claim that one cannot publish reviews of their software without getting written consent. Is this claim more likely, or less likely, to be true than the one in the previous question? Explain your reasoning.

**4.3.1.1 Fair Use**     Throughout this book, we repeatedly use copyrighted material. For example, in the last paragraph of Case 4.1, we quoted from a copyrighted work: an article in *Wired* magazine written by Bruce Schneier. We are allowed to use short extracts from his writings without his permission, because U.S. copyright law specifically allows us to make **fair use** of copyrighted works without permission. The U.S. Code states the following:

The fair use of a copyrighted work…for purposes such as criticism, comment, news reporting, teaching (including multiple copies for classroom use), scholarship, or research, is not an infringement of copyright.

In determining whether the use made of a work in any particular case is a fair use the factors to be considered shall include—

(1) the purpose and character of the use, including whether such use is of a commercial nature or is for nonprofit educational purposes;

(2) the nature of the copyrighted work;

(3) the amount and substantiality of the portion used in relation to the copyrighted work as a whole; and

(4) the effect of the use upon the potential market for or value of the copyrighted work.

The fact that a work is unpublished shall not itself bar a finding of fair use if such finding is made upon consideration of all the above factors. (Title 17, U.S. Code section 107)

This law does not give clear rules about which uses are fair and which are not. Instead, it specifies four factors that should be considered when a court or other arbitrator evaluates a particular case.

The first factor, purpose and character of the use, means that a noncommercial use is more likely to be fair than a commercial one, and an educational use is more likely to be fair than other uses. The fourth factor, effect on market or value, means that a use is more likely to be fair if it does not damage the copyright holder's ability to make money from the work.

The second factor, the nature of the work, is not clearly defined in the law, but there are two main standards that are consistently adopted by the courts. The first is that the use of a nonfiction work is more likely to be fair than the use of a fictional work. The second is that the use of a published work is more likely to be fair than the use of an unpublished work.

The third factor, amount and substantiality of the used portion, means that using short extracts of a work is more likely to be a fair use than reproducing large portions. One important point, however, is that sometimes a very small portion of a work may still be substantial, hence not a fair use. A classic example is the "Son of Man" by Rene Magritte. According to the World Intellectual Property Organization (WIPO):

"The Son of Man," a painting from René Magritte, depicts a man whose face is obscured by an apple. If you would only use the face with the apple, you may still require permission. While, in fact, this is only a small part of the total painting, it is seen as a vital or recognizable part of Magritte's painting. (Verbauwhede)

Understanding fair use has become very important because computer technologies make reusing copyrighted material much easier than it used to be. For example, the results of a Google image search include copyrighted images, which many people might think they can use in their documents. Also, bloggers borrow extensively from material copyrighted by the Associated Press. Finally, many journalists copy material from Wikipedia. Before using copyrighted content without permission, one should consider whether or not it is a fair use.

### Reflection Questions

1. **APPLICATION** Imagine that an instructor in a college course on computer ethics wants to provide students with Bruce Schneier's *Wired* article, which was referenced in Case 4.1. Rather than direct students to the Web site where it is posted, she makes copies and hands them out in class. Is this a fair use? Give your reasoning.

2. **APPLICATION** Imagine that an instructor in a college course on computer ethics is using a textbook other than this one but wants to provide this chapter to students as a supplement. The instructor makes a PDF copy of the chapter (not the whole book) and posts it on a public Web site. Is this a fair use? Give your reasoning.

3. **CONTEXT** What if the instructor in Question 2 decides to place the PDF on a password-protected site rather than a public one, so only her students can access the article? Is this more likely to be a fair use than the use in Question 2? Give your reasoning.

4. **APPLICATION** What if the instructor in Question 2 decided she did not want students to have to buy any book? She takes the intellectual property chapter from one book, the privacy chapter from a second book, the chapter on professionalism from a third book, and so on. She takes only about 10 percent from each book and posts all of these extracts on a password-protected site for students to access. Is this a fair use? Give your reasoning.

**4.3.1.2 Doctrine of First Sale**    Although copyright law is designed to protect something intangible (an expression of creativity), until recently, consumers purchased these goods in a tangible form. To purchase the right to listen to a music recording, you would purchase a physical record, tape, or CD. To purchase the right to read a novel, you would purchase a printed copy of the book. This can create a certain amount of confusion in the minds of consumers. It would be natural to think that the same set of rules (about resale and copying) applies to CDs and books as to shovels, but this is not the case.

Consider the textbook you are now reading. If you purchased a new copy of the textbook, then we (the authors) received a percentage of what you paid as our royalty. Now imagine that you sell that book back to the bookstore, then they resell it as a used book. Should we get another royalty?

The **doctrine of first sale** says that we are not entitled to a second royalty. In particular, copyright law (Title 17, U.S. Code section 109) says "the owner of a particular copy…lawfully made under this title…is entitled, without the authority of the copyright owner, to sell or otherwise dispose of the possession of that copy." Once you purchase a copy of a book, that copy is yours to resell, and the copyright owner is not involved as long as no new copy is made. This policy has proved to be workable since it was first created in 1908. But as consumers shift from physical books to e-books, and from CDs to MP3s, first sale may no longer make sense. And the reason for this has to do with modern copyright protection schemes, collectively called digital rights management, which is discussed in the next section.

### Reflection Questions

1. POSITION  The doctrine of first sale has a big effect on college students. Many students prefer to buy a used copy of a textbook, rather than spending more to get a new copy. On the other hand, if the used textbook were only 1% cheaper than the new one, we suspect that most students would probably choose the new one. How big does the price difference have to be for you to prefer the used book? Explain your reasoning.

2. CONTEXT  While the doctrine of first sale seems to have a big effect on textbook sales, it doesn't have much effect on CD sales. Why do you think this is? Explain your reasoning.

**4.3.1.3 Eroding Fair Use and First Sale**   We conclude the section on copyright by briefly discussing how Internet distribution of copyrighted material is changing fair use and the doctrine of first sale. Many consumers now buy their music, novels, and TV shows electronically on the Internet. Instead of receiving a physical product, you receive a computer file that can be displayed or played on a variety of digital devices.

If you have ever used an Apple iPod, Microsoft Zune, Amazon Kindle, or Barnes and Noble Nook, you have probably had to deal with issues related to digital rights management. The term **digital rights management (DRM)** refers to a collection of technologies that work together to ensure that copyrighted content can be only viewed by the person who purchased it. When you purchase content for devices protected by DRM, the content is often locked so that it can only be used on your device. For example, a book purchased for your Amazon Kindle cannot be read on your friend's Kindle, and vice versa.

Consider what happens to your fair use and first sale rights if you use an e-book. With an e-book that is protected by DRM, you may not be able to copy and paste a quote from the book into a word processing file. Even though it is your right to do so, the DRM technology may make it impossible, and you will have to retype the quote manually. These systems also typically make it impossible to exercise your right to resell a book. For example, imagine you gave a copy of an e-book to a friend, then immediately deleted your own copy. Although this seems to meet the spirit of the first sale doctrine, it will not work, because the e-book will work only on your e-reader, not on your friend's reader.

In a DRM system, the copyrighted material is encrypted. This means that it cannot be read, and looks like gibberish, unless you have a special numerical key to unlock it. When you view the DRM-protected material, your device must contact the company that sold you the material and obtain the key. The computer server that gives you the key can tell which device you are using and will give the key only to an authorized device.

No system of encryption is foolproof. Computer security experts and hackers are often able to decrypt the material and produce a version that is usable on any device. To prevent this, the U.S. Congress passed a law in 1998 called the **Digital Millennium Copyright Act (DMCA)**. The law updated many parts of the U.S. Code to deal with modern copyright issues. The part we are interested in here is called the anticircumvention clause, and it reads as follows:

> No person shall circumvent a technological measure that effectively controls access to a work protected under this title. (Title 17, U.S. Code, section 1201)

This law has been criticized on the grounds that it makes fair use, and exercising one's right under the doctrine of first sale, legally impossible. Even though the copyright law explicitly gives the public these rights, it is usually not possible to exercise them without circumventing (sometimes called "breaking") the DRM system.

### Reflection Questions

1.  POSITION Author Cory Doctorow summarizes the anticircumvention clause of the DMCA this way: "It would be illegal for me to break the DRM on a Kindle to access my own novels, were they sold with Kindle DRM." In other words, if Doctorow bought his own novel (to which he holds the copyright) on an Amazon Kindle, it would be protected by the Kindle's DRM system. He could not legally remove the encryption from that e-book (breaking the DRM lock), even though he owns the copyright on the book itself. Does this mean that the DMCA is a bad law? Explain your reasoning.

2.  APPLICATION Apply the anticircumvention clause of the DMCA to Case 4.1. In particular, imagine that the Sony BMG rootkit had been installed on your computer. Is it ethical for you to remove the rootkit without Sony BMG's permission? Explain your reasoning.

**4.3.1.4 Comparing Plagiarism to Copyright Violation**    Many people confuse plagiarism with copyright violation. Richard Posner (whose work was first introduced in Chapter 3), an Appeals Court Judge and University of Chicago law professor, defines **plagiarism** as "copying that the copier claims (whether explicitly or implicitly, and deliberately or carelessly) is original with him and the claim causes the copier's audience to behave otherwise than it would if it knew the truth" (Posner 106). Plagiarism does not necessarily imply copyright infringement. Consider a situation in which a student pays a friend to write an essay. The student turns this essay in as her own work, with the friend's permission. This would be plagiarism, but it would not be a copyright violation. Because the friend gave permission for this distribution of the work, copyright is not violated. Charges of plagiarism are still applicable, however, even though the author of the work gave permission for it to be used, because: 1) the student claimed it was her own work, 2) the claim was false, and 3) this could cause the professor to give a higher grade than she otherwise would have. Plagiarism harms the audience of the plagiarized work as well as the original author; simply getting permission from the original author is not sufficient to avoid charges of plagiarism.

Similarly, copyright infringement does not necessarily imply plagiarism. If we were to include a copy of Art Rogers's photograph, "Puppies," in this book we could be charged with copyright violation unless we obtained Rogers's permission. Simply giving him credit in the picture's caption would not be sufficient, but it would allow us to avoid charges of plagiarism.

## Reflection Questions

1. RESEARCH  The IEEE (Institute of Electrical and Electronics Engineers) is a large professional organization and also a major publisher of scientific journals. If a paper published in an IEEE journal is found to be plagiarized, what are the consequences for the plagiarists? You might want to do an Internet search for "Notice of Violation of IEEE Publication Principles," as well looking at the *www.ieee.org* pages about plagiarism.

2. POSITION  Do you think the consequences you discovered in the previous question are sufficient to deter plagiarists from submitting to IEEE journals? Explain your reasoning.

**4.3.1.5 Sharing versus Selling**    Until the mid-1990s, most copyright piracy involved counterfeiting—that is, the illegal duplication of physical media. Many shops, especially in foreign countries, specialized in producing bootleg CDs, DVDs, and the like. The DMCA was not created to deal with this type of copyright piracy, because trademark and anticounterfeiting laws were already sufficient. The DMCA (along with other laws, such as the No Electronic Theft Act, discussed later in this section) were designed to stop the casual piracy that has become common among ordinary people.

In fact, most people who engage in casual copyright violations would not call their actions "piracy," but sharing. Until the mid-1990s, copyright infringement through sharing (for example, sharing a computer program disk with a friend so he could illegally install the software) had only a small impact on businesses, because each legal purchaser would only share his or her media with a few close friends. With the advent of the Internet, it became possible for one person to share a single legal copy of a work with thousands of other people. Furthermore, the fact that these items were shared, not sold, turned out to be legally relevant.

In 1994 a Massachusetts Institute of Technology student named David LaMacchia was charged with criminal copyright infringement. He allegedly ran a computer bulletin board (similar to a private Web site) that illegally provided copyrighted software (such as Microsoft Excel and SimCity 2000) for download.

The case was thrown out of court. At the time, the law said that copyright infringement was criminal only if the infringer acted "for [the] purpose of commercial advantage or private financial gain" (Title 17, U.S. Code, section 506). Because the alleged crime did not involve private or financial gain, the infringement could not be classified as a criminal offense.

As a result, in 1997 the U.S. Congress passed the **No Electronic Theft Act** (or **NET Act**). This act amended U.S. copyright law so that the definition of the term "financial gain" includes receiving copyrighted works for free (Title 17, U.S. Code, section 101). This means that quid-pro-quo swapping of copyrighted material (I'll give you movie A if you give me movie B) is now clearly illegal. The NET Act also made it a criminal offense to share copyrighted works with a total value of more than $1,000 within any 180-day period. Penalties include up to five years in prison and a fine of up to $250,000, even if the copyright holder cannot show any financial harm from the infringement.

## Reflection Questions

1. APPLICATION Imagine that you routinely swap music albums or movies with friends. Are you likely to accidentally cross the "$1,000 within any 180-day period" threshold? In other words, are people who are acting in a morally permissible way likely to accidentally commit the crime of sharing too much? Explain your reasoning.

2. POSITION In this section we looked at criminal penalties for copyright infringement, which means that the U.S. government is in charge of (and pays for) prosecuting the infringer. In the next section we will learn more about civil penalties, which means that the copyright holder is in charge of (and pays for) suing the infringer. Make the best case you can that copyright infringement must have criminal penalties, because civil penalties are not sufficient.

**4.3.1.6 Peer to Peer Sharing and Searching**   It is easy to understand that it is illegal (and probably morally wrong as well) to post a copyrighted song or movie to an Internet site. But this is not the only type of action that can lead to an infringement claim. As in many areas of the law (and in morality), those actions that enable an illegal (or immoral) act might also deserve blame.

Consider the case of Napster. Napster provided a software program that enabled users of a peer-to-peer file sharing service to search for files to download. In order to understand the case, you need to understand a bit about how peer-to-peer sharing works. In a traditional file-sharing system (such as the one described in the previous section), users upload computer files to a central server so that other users can download them. A user can easily see what files are contained on the server, select whichever ones she wants, and download them. A peer-to-peer system has no central server that stores all the files. Instead, the users' computers contact each other directly. If User A has a file that you want to download, your computer contacts User A's computer directly, and User A uploads the file to you, instead of uploading it to a central server. See Figure 4.1 for a diagram of the differences between the two systems.

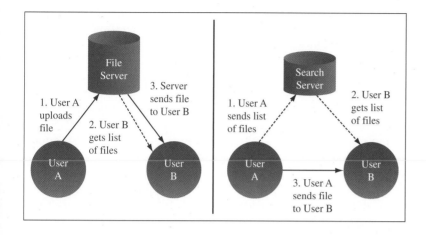

**FIGURE 4.1** Traditional file distribution compared with peer-to-peer distribution

The big problem with peer-to-peer systems is finding out which files are available for download. In computer science, this is known as a "search problem." If there is no central server, then how do we find out which files are available for download? Even if we know a file is available for download, how do we find out which users are offering it? Napster was one of the first companies to provide a service to solve this problem. The Napster program was a peer-to-peer file-sharing program, but it also provided access to a search service that allowed users to find which files were shared by other users. Napster did not download, upload, or store copyrighted files, but the company's software allowed users to swap copyrighted files with each other.

Napster was found to have violated copyright law, even though the company did not directly traffic in copyrighted files. Various courts found that Napster committed contributory infringement and vicarious infringement. We will not give precise legal definitions of these terms, but a rough definition of each is useful. **Contributory infringement** occurs when an infringement committed by another person would not have happened without your help. **Vicarious infringement** involves an infringement that occurs in an area under your supervision, and when you should have been policing and preventing such acts. For example, a business or university that willfully and knowingly ignores the use of its computer network in a software piracy scheme might be found guilty of vicarious infringement.

The courts held that the users of Napster would not have been able to solve the search problem without Napster's software; this led to the charge of contributory infringement. It was also held that Napster could have, and should have, prevented its users from listing copyrighted files on its search service. Napster clearly knew what its users were doing, and the company allowed people to continue because it benefited the company financially; thus, the courts shut down the Napster service.

These kinds of cases continue to arise. The most common peer-to-peer file-sharing protocol used today is known as BitTorrent. The BitTorrent technology is used by software and movie pirates to share files, but it is also used by large software companies. **BitTorrent**, and other peer-to-peer systems, are very helpful for companies that need to deliver one large file to millions of users. In BitTorrent, a large file (such as a video game or DVD movie) is broken into thousands of small pieces. The company uploads the pieces to a few thousand users (a process known as seeding the file), and then those users pass it out to everyone else. Once your computer obtains a piece of the file, it rebroadcasts that piece to other users who are also looking for it. BitTorrent is beneficial for large corporations that need to distribute large software updates to their users. In the traditional model, if a company needed to distribute a 2-GB file to 1000 customers, it would need 2000 GB of Internet capacity. It would send the file to each of the 1000 customers individually. With BitTorrent, it needs to send only a few pieces of the file to each user, then the users can swap pieces with one another, saving the company both time and money.

Of course, this technology also makes it much easier for pirates to distribute files. A pirate would not have been able to afford to distribute files under the old model, because the bandwidth needed is too expensive. Before the advent of peer-to-peer sharing, pirates would sometimes hack into servers owned by other people and hijack them to distribute the files—in itself an illegal act. With technology like BitTorrent, a pirate has only to seed the file and then walk away.

The BitTorrent protocol, however, does not provide a solution to the search problem—that is, the protocol does not provide a way for you to find out what files are available for download. For that, you receive a special key from the person who originally seeded the file. The sites that provide search functionality for BitTorrent are called **index sites**, and the authorities have repeatedly shut them down. An index site provides a service very similar to the service Napster provided; it allows you to find out which files are available for download. (Note that not everyone objects to index sites. In Case 4.7.2 we will see one case of an index site, The Pirate Bay, that may one day be part of the Swedish government.)

The Napster case was very controversial at the time. There was a great deal of concern that the result of the case would open up all search engines to copyright infringement lawsuits. Based on the illustration in Figure 4.1, it is hard to see any major technical difference between important search engines like Google, and the services provided by Napster. In the end, the decision seemed to depend on Napster's intent. Napster's business plan seemed to depend on widespread copyright infringement by its users, and so the various judges involved in the case ruled that Napster not only enabled copyright infringement, but also did so intentionally and willfully. Traditional search engines like Google may sometimes enable copyright infringement, but this is not their primary business.

### Reflection Questions

1. APPLICATION Is it true that what Google does is morally superior to what Napster did? Explain your reasoning, using one of the ethical theories from Chapter 1 to support your answer.

2. APPLICATION Was what Napster did morally permissible? Use one of the ethical theories from Chapter 1 to support your answer.

3.  APPLICATION Should Napster's business have been considered "fair use?" Explain your answer. Be sure to address all four standards from Section 4.3.1.1 for evaluating whether a use is fair or not.

**4.3.1.7 Copyright Duration**   In the introduction to this chapter, you read a quote from the U.S. Constitution, which says that Congress has the right to "promote the Progress of Science and useful Arts, by securing for limited Times to Authors and Inventors the exclusive Right to their respective Writings and Discoveries" (Article I, Section 8). The writers of the Constitution apparently believed that intellectual property protections should expire at some point so that the public could use intellectual properties for free, once the creators had gotten a fair chance to profit from their work.

Debates persist of about how long each type of intellectual property protection should last, but copyright has been particularly controversial. The duration of copyright protection has grown steadily and significantly. Figure 4.2 summarizes these changes. Note that the figure assumes that the author lived sixty years after the work was created, so that we can compare the old versions of the law with the newer ones. Also note that the figure addresses only copyrights held by individuals; different rules apply to copyrights held by corporations. Because the term extensions apply retroactively, some items published in 1923 are still under copyright.

Two changes in copyright law are especially significant. The first is that the copyright duration was increased with each new copyright act. The second change

| Which Law | Maximum copyright term (years) | Details |
|---|---|---|
| Copyright Act of 1790 | 28 | Default duration was 14 years, renewable for another 14 years if author still alive |
| Copyright Act of 1831 | 42 | Default duration was raised to 28 years, renewable for another 14 years if author still alive |
| Copyright Act of 1909 | 56 | Default duration remained at 28 years, but renewable was increased to 28 years if author still alive |
| Copyright Act of 1976 | 110 | Default duration calculated in a new way; the author's lifetime, plus 50 years |
| Copyright Term Extension Act of 1998 | 130 | The author's lifetime, plus 70 years |

**F I G U R E  4.2**   Maximum duration of copyright in U.S. law over time

has to do with how copyright duration is calculated. As expressed in the Copyright Act of 1790, the expiration date of a copyright was originally calculated by taking the date of creation and adding a certain number of years. Beginning in 1976, this changed. The expiration date of a copyright is now calculated by taking the date of the author's death and adding a certain number of years. According to the Copyright Term Extension Act of 1998, the most recent law, a work is copyrighted until 70 years after the author's death.

Let's take a closer look at the issue of copyright duration—also referred to as the **copyright term**. An author might argue that the copyright term should be as long as possible, certainly at least as long as the author's lifetime. Imagine that at age thirty-six you wrote a very popular novel. The novel is assigned as reading in many schools and continues to sell well for more than forty years—well enough to provide you with a comfortable living that whole time. Under the Copyright Act of 1790, you would have lost your copyright after twenty-eight years (at age sixty-four), and you would no longer be entitled to a royalty. You might feel that this is unfair, because the book is still profitable at its current price. If the book enters the public domain, its price would drop to zero (or close to it), even though lots of people are still willing to pay for it. Many authors think that the term of the copyright ought to extend beyond their own lifetimes, so that their works can continue to support their families after they die.

But what are the downsides of long copyright terms? Why should they expire at all? One argument is that it is often difficult to track down the current owner of a copyright many years after the creation of the work. Because copyrights can be sold or traded, it is hard to know whether anyone owns the right once the original author has died. A copyrighted work that is still within its copyright term, but no longer has a copyright owner, is called an **orphaned work**. For example, a museum might have hundreds of photographs from the presidency of Harry S. Truman, but might not know who took them. The museum could not publicly display them with any confidence until at least the year 2073, because the copyright for unpublished anonymous works lasts 120 years after the date the work was created. If the Copyright Act of 1790 was still in effect, the museum could have confidently started using the photographs in their displays in 1981 (twenty-eight years after the end of Truman's presidency).

Another argument against long copyright terms has to do with the social cost, especially in education. Every year millions of students in the United States read Shakespeare's plays. They can be obtained legally, for free, on the Web because they are no longer under copyright. They can also be included in textbooks for free. How much more would education in the United States cost if Shakespeare's heirs were still collecting a royalty on each new copy of his plays? Some authors, and their representatives, have testified before Congress that they believe the copyright term should be infinite. If this were the case, would we even be able to track down the current copyright holder for *Hamlet* to get permission to make new copies?

These are just a few examples of the types of arguments that shape the debate around the length of copyright protection; they are not meant to be exhaustive.

### Reflection Questions

1.  POSITION Should it be legal to print a T-shirt with the Mona Lisa on it, without paying a royalty? Note that we are asking about what should be allowed, not about what the law actually says.

2.  POSITION Should it be legal to print a T-shirt with Disney's Phineas and Ferb on it, without paying a royalty? Again, we are asking about what ought to be, not about the law.

3.  CONTEXT Throughout this section we focused on works that are owned by a particular person, the author. Many copyrighted works, however, are owned by corporations. When a work is created as work for hire, the copyrights end up belonging to the corporation that commissioned the work. Should such works receive more or less protection than works owned by an author? Explain your reasoning.

### 4.3.2    Patent Law

In the previous section, you saw that copyright law protects works of creative authorship that have a fixed and tangible form. However, many types of useful intellectual work do not fall into this category. Consider, for example, the universal serial bus (USB) interface. The invention of USB technology greatly simplified the configuration of computer systems, because peripheral devices can now use the USB system to connect to the computer. In the past, each type of device had its own plug. Keyboards used the AT connector, mice used the PS/2 connector, printers used the parallel port connector, hard drives used the SCSI connector, and so on. Now all of these devices, and more, can connect with the USB connector.

The USB connector, however, is not a work of creative authorship. You will not see it on display in an art museum or listen to it on the radio. It is an **invention**. The value of a creative work is largely aesthetic and is not based purely on its usefulness. An invention, on the other hand, involves the discovery of "any new and useful process, machine, [article of] manufacture, or composition of matter, or any new and useful improvement thereof" (Title 35, U.S. Code, section 101). Intellectual properties of this type—inventions—are protected by patents.

In the United States, a patent is obtained by filing an application with the United States Patent and Trademark Office (USPTO). The USPTO examines the patent to make sure the invention specified is patentable—that is, they make sure it truly is an invention. They also make sure that it meets two criteria:

- **Novelty**—An invention is novel only if it has not previously been invented by someone else.

- **Nonobviousness**—A solution to a problem that is obvious to another specialist in the appropriate area cannot be patented. There is no widely accepted definition of, or test for, obviousness, which is why many court cases to invalidate patents focus on challenging the obviousness of the invention. We will see an example of this in a case study later in the chapter.

Once a patent is issued, it typically lasts twenty years from the date the application was filed.

Obtaining a patent can be expensive. Many different fees are associated with filing a patent in the first place. Additional fees are associated with maintaining an existing patent. Under ordinary circumstances, these fees can easily add up to $10,000 during the lifetime of the patent. However, this expenditure can be a good investment, because once an invention is patented, no one can "make, use, offer to sell, or sell" the invention without the patent holder's permission.

Patents were originally designed to stimulate the advancement of the "technological arts" by allowing inventors of new technologies to profit from them. These days, many of the most significant advancements of the technological arts involve new and improved computer software, not machines. As a result, many companies that produce computer software are attempting to use patents to protect their inventions. This use of patents is highly controversial, but we will put off further discussion of the topic until Section 4.6, where we consider the various intellectual property protections available for software.

### Reflection Questions

1. RESEARCH Create a list of the five most important (in your opinion) computer software inventions of the past 20 years. For each item, very briefly explain why you think it is an "invention" and why it is important.

2. RESEARCH Many pharmaceutical companies are now using patents to protect genetic sequences. Research the issue, and then explain why you think this is, or is not, a good use of patent protection.

### 4.3.3  Trademark

A trademark is a legally registered word, phrase, symbol, or other item that identifies a particular product, service, or corporation. In the world of marketing, the term "trademark" and "brand" are sometimes used synonymously, although "brand" is also used to describe the product's identity as a whole, whereas a trademark is one specific element of that identity. Trademark protection is most often used to protect a word or logo related to a product, so that consumers can be sure that products bearing those logos are authentic. It is also possible to register a trademark that protects other identifying characteristics of a product, including:

- Colors—T-Mobile holds a trademark for the color magenta when used to promote wireless telecommunication products and services; in 2008, it requested that the blog *Engadget Mobile* stop using the color in its logo. (*Engadget Mobile* refused. In fact they, and several other gadget blogs, changed their entire color-scheme to magenta in protest.)

- Sounds—Tivo holds a trademark on the "six pops" sound that Tivo video recorders make when fast-forwarding. Motorola holds a trademark on the "chirp" sound its phones make when using direct-connect technology. (To listen to it, visit the "Trademark Soundex" on the USPTO Web site.)

- Shapes—Coca-Cola holds a trademark on "bottles, jars, or flasks with bulging, protruding or rounded sides" for use in marketing carbonated soft drinks. Apple Inc. holds trademarks on the designs of its iPod music-playing devices.

In order to receive a trademark, you must already be using the mark to represent a product or service, and your mark must not be easily confused with a competing product's trademark. If such is the case, you can register your trademark with the USPTO for a fee of a few hundred U.S. dollars. A trademark lasts ten years but can be renewed indefinitely.

As long as you hold a trademark, no one else can use it in a way that is likely to cause confusion among consumers. No other cell phone company can adopt magenta as its company color (because this would be confusingly similar to T-Mobile's trademark), but the soft-drink Tab is welcome to use magenta (because no one would confuse Tab for a cellular phone company).

One important area of trademark law is called trade dress. The **trade dress** of a product involves the look and feel of the product or its packaging. Several companies have attempted to use trade dress protection to prevent others from copying the look and feel of their Web sites.

### Reflection Questions

1. POSITION Write an argument that either defends or refutes the following position: It should not be legal to trademark a color.

2. RESEARCH The Nintendo Wii has a particularly recognizable design and trade dress. Immediately after its release, a variety of companies started releasing knock-off game systems that looked like the Wii and had a similar price. Research some of these systems on the Internet, and then either defend or refute the following position: Nintendo should have been able to stop these companies from selling game systems that looked similar to the Nintendo Wii.

## 4.3.4 Trade Secrets

Thomas Jefferson's quote, with which we began Section 4.3, reminds us that the only natural way to keep an idea for one's own personal use is to keep it completely secret. With some products, it is actually possible to do this. For example, most Internet search companies keep their search algorithms secret, so that their competitors cannot steal them. Such secrets are called **trade secrets**. Intellectual property laws are not needed to protect trade secrets. If someone breaks into your computer or company to steal the secret, they can be prosecuted for trespassing. Employees can be prevented from leaking secrets through the use of nondisclosure agreements in their employment contracts.

Many ideas, however, cannot be both profitable and secret. If you have invented a better mousetrap, anyone who buys one will be able to look at it and figure out your design. Intellectual property laws are necessary so that inventors can charge money for their inventions even after the public knows about them, and artists can charge money for their work even after it has been publicly displayed. In this section, we have described the three main types of intellectual property protection that apply to computer-related fields: copyright, patent, and trademark. In Section 4.6 we will return to these ideas and attempt to understand how the intellectual property behind a computer program can be protected.

### Reflection Questions

1. POSITION One of the most famous trade secrets is the formula for Coca-Cola. Imagine that someone was able to figure out the formula without stealing it. Should he be allowed to make and sell a drink that tastes exactly like Coca-Cola? Explain your reasoning.

2. APPLICATION Imagine that you work for the Coca-Cola Company, advising them on intellectual property issues. If you were asked to recommend a way to use one of the intellectual property protections discussed in this chapter (copyright, patent, or trademark) to protect the formula of Coca-Cola, which one would you choose? Explain your reasoning.

## 4.4  VIRTUAL GOODS

Intellectual property laws concern the value of ideas. Most societies create intellectual property laws to create incentives for people to work on developing useful new ideas. But intellectual property is not the only type of valuable intangible good. The rise of the Internet, particularly the sale of online games, digital books, and music, has given rise to a whole new class of intangible property: virtual goods.

Vili Lehdonvirta is one of the first scholars to study virtual economies and virtual goods. In his dissertation, "Virtual Consumption," written for his doctorate from the Turku School of Economics, he writes the following:

> Unlike goods, virtual goods do not need to be shipped. Unlike services, virtual assets are not perishable and can be re-sold. And unlike information goods (such as music, software and news), virtual goods are rivalrous: one person's use of a virtual good excludes others from using it. What are being bought and sold on the virtual goods markets are therefore not data, services or objects, but permissions: the exclusive right to use this feature or that corner of an online environment frequented by thousands of people (9).

According to this definition, then, **virtual goods** are items of property that are rivalrous, nontangible, not services, and which rely on some online system for their existence.

It is easier to understand the nature of virtual goods through examples:

- In the online game *World of Warcraft*, players invest hundreds of hours to obtain weapons and armor that exist only in the game.

- The ISK, the currency described in Case Study 4.2, is a virtual currency.

- In the online world *Second Life*, it is possible to purchase or rent virtual land with real money. Many people make a real-life living by purchasing land in *Second Life*, then subletting it to renters. (Figure 4.3 shows a *Second Life* resident on his virtual homestead.)

- In *Habbo Hotel*, an online game that Lehdonvirta discusses in his dissertation, users can purchase items to decorate rooms in a hotel. Although these items have no function other than decoration, some of them sell for hundreds, even thousands, of U.S. dollars.

Taken as a whole, the value of these virtual goods in the world economy is quite high. Just counting **real money transactions (RMTs)**, virtual goods purchased with real money, the world market for virtual goods has been estimated at between $2 billion and $10 billion per year. *Wired* contributor and author Julian Dibbell estimates that this places the gross domestic product of the virtual world

Courtesy of Bo Brinkman

**F I G U R E 4.3** *Second Life* resident in front of his virtual homestead

somewhat higher than Afghanistan's actual GDP. The total value of all virtual goods that exist is likely in the hundreds of billions of U.S. dollars.

### Reflection Questions

1. POSITION Is it reasonable to spend real money on virtual items? Explain your reasoning.

2. POSITION Many Web sites allow game players to trade their virtual currency for real currency. Is there any difference between such virtual currencies and real ones? In particular, is the U.S. dollar more "real" than the ISK used in *EVE Online*? Explain your reasoning.

## 4.5  COMPLICATIONS SURROUNDING INTANGIBLE PROPERTY

The following three case studies demonstrate some issues that computer and Internet technologies are raising in the area of intangible property.

### 4.5.1  Case: *Bragg v. Linden Lab*

Almost all virtual goods depend on some online service. For example, if you play the game *Farmville*, your farm and all the items on it exist on servers belonging to a company called Zynga.

Virtual property can be destroyed in a variety of ways. If you were a regular player of *Farmville* and Zynga went out of business, all your *Farmville* items would cease to exist. Similarly, if you owned virtual currency worth thousands of U.S. dollars, as Cally did in Case 4.2, this money could instantly vanish if CCP hf. (the company that owns *EVE Online*) failed to maintain the game servers properly. Virtual property can also be destroyed by a hacker breaking into a player's account to steal items or even delete the account. A company's servers could be destroyed by a natural disaster, or they could be turned off as a result of bankruptcy. For most virtual goods, there is no way to make a backup copy or transfer it to another system. Only the hosting company is capable of preventing the loss of a virtual good. In a dispute between a consumer and a hosting company, the consumer currently has very little recourse. This case illustrates that point.

Marc Bragg is a lawyer from Pennsylvania who participated in the popular online world called *Second Life*. Mr. Bragg became involved in a dispute with Linden Lab, the company that runs *Second Life*, and apparently as a result of the dispute, Linden Lab terminated Bragg's account. Bragg then sued Linden Lab.

Judge Eduardo C. Robreno, in an opinion on the case, wrote the following:

> This case is about virtual property maintained on a virtual world on the Internet. Plaintiff, March Bragg, Esq., claims an ownership interest in such virtual property. Bragg contends that Defendants, the operators of the virtual world, unlawfully confiscated his virtual property and denied

him access to their virtual world. Ultimately at issue in this case are the novel questions of what rights and obligations grow out of the relationship between the owner and creator of a virtual world and its resident-customers. While the property and the world where it is found are "virtual," the dispute is real (1).

In the same opinion, Justice Robreno summarized the central dispute:

> The dispute ultimately at issue in this case arose on April 30, 2006, when Bragg acquired a parcel of virtual land named "Taessot" for $300. Linden sent Bragg an email advising him that Taessot had been improperly purchased through an "exploit." Linden took Taesot [sic] away. It then froze Bragg's account, effectively confiscating all of the virtual property and currency that he maintained on his account with Second Life (6).

According to Bragg, the virtual goods and virtual currency confiscated by Linden Lab were worth between $4000 and $6000 in real U.S. dollars.

To join a virtual world, you usually have to agree to a set of terms and conditions called the **terms of service**, or **ToS**. One of the clauses of the ToS that Marc Bragg agreed to when he signed up for *Second Life* was as follows:

> [Clause 2.6] Linden Lab has the right at any time for any reason or no reason to suspend or terminate your Account, terminate this Agreement, and/or refuse any and all current or future use of the Service without notice or liability to you. In the event that Linden Lab suspends or terminates your Account or this Agreement, you understand and agree that you shall receive no refund or exchange for any unused time on a subscription, any license or subscription fees, any content or data associated with your Account, or for anything else.

When Marc Bragg first logged into *Second Life*, he was presented with a copy of this document and had to click "I Agree" in order to play the game.

## Reflection Questions

1. ☐APPLICATION☐ Sometimes a contract is invalidated because the courts decide it contains elements that are not morally permissible. Such a contract is called "unconscionable." Is Clause 2.6 of the *Second Life* ToS morally permissible? Explain your reasoning, using one of the ethical theories from Chapter 1 to support your argument.

2. ☐CONTEXT☐ Imagine you rented an apartment and your renter's contract contained wording similar to Clause 2.6 of the *Second Life* ToS—that is, the landlord can evict you at any time for any reason or for no reason. Would this contract be morally permissible? Compare and contrast your thinking with your thinking on the previous question.

3. ☐APPLICATION☐ In another clause of the *Second Life* ToS, users had to agree not to sue Linden Lab and instead submit to binding arbitration

under an arbitrator selected by Linden Lab. Use a rule utilitarian analysis to analyze the following proposed rule: In contracts between individuals and large corporations, the large corporation may require individuals to waive their right to sue when disputes arise.

### 4.5.2   Case: Reusing Images Found on the Internet

Many types of creative works, such as textbooks and magazine ads, use photographic illustrations. Rather than hire a photographer to take a picture for a specific use, it is often sufficient to go to a Web site and purchase a license to use a stock photograph. The license fee is based on the intended use of the image.

However, people looking for images are turning to Internet search engines and to social networking sites like Flickr and deviantART, where they can download photos or artwork without permission. Consider some examples:

- When Capcom rereleased a game called *Okami* for the Nintendo Wii, they wanted to use the same cover art that they used on the original version of the game (made for the PlayStation 2). Rather than finding and reusing the original art, they just downloaded a photograph of the art from the Internet. The site they downloaded the art from, IGN, had placed a watermark containing the IGN logo on the image. The logo was clearly visible on the game box. Apparently no one at Capcom noticed this until people who purchased the game wrote about it on blogs and Internet forums.

- The blog *youthoughtwewouldntnotice* chronicles instances of plagiarism. In one typical case, a 19-year-old American photographer who posted her work on the social networking site deviantART discovered her self-portrait on T-shirts being sold across Eastern Europe.

- Danielle Smith, the author of the blog *extraordinarymommy*, was surprised to find out that life-size pictures of her family were appearing on signs in grocery stores in the Czech Republic. Ms. Smith, who lives in the United States, discovered this through a Facebook friend who lives in the Czech Republic. The store most likely took the image from Danielle's Web site.

Capcom may have been embarrassed by the IGN watermark that appeared on the cover art for *Okami* (because it made them seem sloppy and unprofessional), but it did not violate the image's copyright. The other two cases are pretty clear cases of copyright violation, however, assuming that the alleged facts are accurate.

An interesting related case is the famous "Hope" poster, featuring then presidential candidate Barack Obama, created by artist Shepard Fairey. Many of Fairey's artworks are based on posterized images, which are images that have been reproduced with a very small number of colors. See Figure 4.4 for an example of a posterized image.

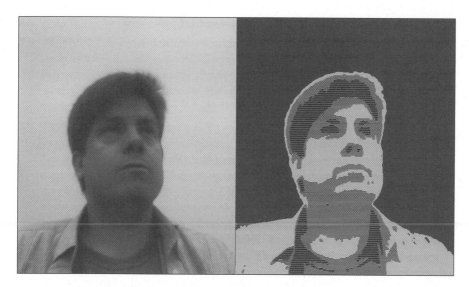

**FIGURE 4.4**  Posterized portrait in the style of Shepard Fairey

Fairey's "Hope" poster is clearly based on a 2006 photograph of President Obama taken by freelance photographer Mannie Garcia, who was temporarily filling in for an Associated Press photographer. Soon, there were three parties involved in a dispute about the interpretation of copyright law with regard to this photograph. Their positions were as follows:

- The Associated Press believed it held the copyright to the photograph and should therefore have been credited by Mr. Fairey and received monetary compensation for the photograph's use.

- Mr. Garcia believed he held the copyright to the photograph. He claimed he never signed anything assigning the copyright to the Associated Press.

- Mr. Fairey believed that his use of the photograph, regardless of who held the copyright, was a fair use and hence not a copyright violation.

Note that, although we would like to print both the original photograph and Mr. Fairey's poster in this book, we have elected not to do so. Because it is not clear who owns the copyright to either image, we do not know whom to contact to purchase the right to reproduce the images. In addition, we are not certain that using the image without permission would be a fair use.

## Reflection Questions

1.  APPLICATION  Consider our decision not to reproduce Mannie Garcia's photograph or Shepard Fairey's poster in this textbook. If we had chosen to reproduce them here, would we have been protected under fair use? Explain your reasoning, including an analysis based on the four factors of fair use discussed in Section 4.3.1.1.

2. **RESEARCH** Was Fairey's use of Garcia's photograph a fair use? In order to answer this question you will probably need to search the Internet for more information. In particular, be sure to look at Fairey's poster, the original photograph by Garcia, and Fairey's statements about whether or not he made a profit from the poster. Give an analysis based on the four factors of fair use discussed in Section 4.3.1.1.

3. **APPLICATION** Recall the term "chilling effect," defined in Chapter 3. Is our decision to not reproduce Fairey's poster and Garcia's photograph an example of a chilling effect? Explain your answer.

### 4.5.3  Case: PlaysForSure

In most DRM systems, the files that you download to your device are locked using cryptography. The key to unlock the file that contains your book, sound file, or game is specific to you, your device, and the file being unlocked. When you use a file for the first time (and, in some systems, every time you access the file), your device must contact a **key server**, which is a computer on the Internet that provides the key to unlock the file to authorized users. This means that even if you give the file to friends, they will not be able to use it because the key server will not give them the key.

PlaysForSure, a digital media standard created by Microsoft, contains many features, one of which is a DRM system meant to prevent unauthorized copying of digital music files. Music purchased from the MSN Music Store is protected by this system. On April 22, 2008, Microsoft informed MSN Music Store customers that it would be turning off the key servers on August 31, 2008. After that date, it would not be possible to reauthorize a music file. This means that while music files would continue to play on the owner's current computer, they would not be usable if the owners 1) upgraded or reinstalled their operating system, or 2) got new computers.

Response from customers and antiDRM advocates was immediate and vocal. Microsoft quickly reversed its decision, announcing that the MSN Music Store key servers would continue to operate at least until the end of 2011.

### Reflection Questions

1. **APPLICATION** Some commentators have suggested that Microsoft should distribute an "unlocker" program that permanently removes the encryption from the affected music files. Explain why this is not a decision that Microsoft can make on its own. Who else would need to give permission for this to happen?

2. **POSITION** When consumers "buy" songs, they are not purchasing the copyright. Instead, they are purchasing a private use license to listen to the song. The MSN Music Store situation demonstrates that most consumers think these licenses should last forever—and that indefinite licenses are impractical. When a consumer licenses a song for private use, how long should that license last, and why? In other words, how long should the company selling the content guarantee it will keep the key servers running? Explain your reasoning.

## 4.5.4 Case: DeCSS

As discussed earlier, the DMCA prohibits circumventing the DRM on a copyrighted work. The law also makes it a crime to traffic in (buy and sell or otherwise distribute) circumvention devices, which are tools that are intended to help in this process.

One of the most interesting cases based on this law involves a program called DeCSS. **DeCSS** is a program that removes the copy protection from DVDs. Normally it is not possible to copy the video from a DVD onto your computer or to view the DVD on a computer without an approved player (one that has been licensed by the **DVD Copy Control Association**, or **DVDCCA**). DeCSS made such copying possible and also allowed people to watch DVDs on open-source operating systems like Linux. DeCSS is a circumvention device, in the sense meant by the DMCA, though it has some uses that most people would consider morally positive.

The controversy about DeCSS comes from the fact that it is extremely simple. The computer source code of DeCSS is very short. As a result, many people posted it on their Web sites or added it to their e-mail signatures. One person, Eric Corley, went to prison for sharing DeCSS through his Web site and encouraging people to use it to violate copyright. Corley was asked to remove the code from his Web site; he did so, but he added links to other sites that had the code. The court decided that this linking, combined with his intent, still constituted "trafficking in circumvention devices."

Many Internet activists felt that Corley's conviction was unfair and that it should not be possible to ban the distribution of programs like DeCSS. Many people came up with innovative ways to spread the DeCSS program without directly placing it on the Web. Some sites sold T-shirts and ties with the code printed on it. Artists embedded it into paintings or used it as the lyrics for a song. Should those people have also gone to prison, or were they protected by the First Amendment right to freedom of speech? If they were protected, why wasn't Corley?

### Reflection Questions

1. RESEARCH The anticircumvention clause of the DMCA also bans trafficking in any technology that can circumvent DRM. Eric Corley was convicted of violating the DMCA because his Web site linked to other Web sites that provided programs capable of removing DRM from DVDs. Read the Wikipedia summary of the court case *Universal City Studios, Inc. v. Reimerdes*. Do you think Corley ought to have been convicted, or should he have been found innocent? Explain your reasoning.

2. CONTEXT What role did Corley's intent have in the outcome of the case? If he had consistently said that DeCSS should be used only to play DVDs on open source operating systems (where no official DVD player was available), do you think he would have been convicted? Provide evidence to support your position.

3. CONTEXT Whether you agree with it or not, write the best argument you can refuting the following claim: While Corley was fairly convicted for trafficking in DeCSS, because his intent was to help people steal,

the people that made DeCSS T-shirts could not have been convicted, because their main intent was to make a political statement about the DMCA, and this is protected speech.

4.   POSITION One of the arguments against Corley's conviction was that the particular form of DRM that DeCSS was designed to counteract was just too simple to count as a true DRM system. Is the ease of circumventing a DRM system relevant in deciding whether or not circumventing the DRM system was morally permissible? Explain your reasoning.

## 4.6  INTELLECTUAL PROPERTY PROTECTION FOR SOFTWARE

As technology advances, older systems of rules and regulations no longer fit perfectly. We say that technological changes "complicate" the intellectual property regime, because although the old regime no longer quite fits, it is unlikely to be completely discarded. The law gets stretched to fit new cases, and it gets modified in the places where it cannot be made to fit, but it will likely survive these latest upheavals in mostly the same shape. In this section, we discuss two major changes in the way people think about and work with intellectual property—changes that are complicating the rules.

In Section 4.3, we saw that the appropriate type of intellectual property protection varies depending on what you want to protect. For example, copyright protection is for creative works in a fixed form, patent protection is for inventions, and trademark protection is for identifying characteristics used in commerce. All three types of protection can be used to protect parts of a computer software product. Let's consider each in turn, starting with copyright and trademark law.

### 4.6.1  Copyright and Trademark Protection for Software

Copyright is used to protect the parts of a computer program that are works of creative authorship. Here are some examples:

- The source code of a computer program (see Figure 4.5) is a creative work of authorship and is copyrighted. Note that certain very short snippets of code may not be copyrighted for the same reason that very short phrases cannot be copyrighted, because they are not sufficiently original or creative. Also note that the code itself is not always enough to tell you whether two programs are, or are not, the same. For example, Figure 4.5 shows source code for the same program written in two different languages, Java and Scheme. (Both programs, when given "5" as input, produce the output "5 4 3 2 1 Blastoff!".) Even though these programs look very different, they could be considered the same program because they use exactly the same logic.

- The look and feel of a game as a whole can be copyrighted. In *Atari v. North American Philips*, Atari alleged that Philips' game *K.C. Munchkin!* infringed on Atari's copyright for *Pac-Man*. The court agreed with Atari, and sales of *K.C. Munchkin!* were halted. This case is interesting because, in many situations, trademark law is used to protect "look and feel," not copyright.

```java
public class Blastoff{
  public static void blastoff(int seconds){
    if(seconds <= 0){
      System.out.print("Blastoff!");
    } else {
      System.out.print(seconds + " ");
      blastoff(seconds-1);
    }}}
```
Java

```scheme
(define (blastoff seconds)
  (if (<= seconds 0)
    (cons "Blastoff!" '())
    (cons (number->string seconds)
          (blastoff (- seconds 1)))))
```
Scheme

**F I G U R E  4.5**   Two examples of computer code for a launch countdown

Trademark, on the other hand, is used to protect the parts of a program that uniquely identify it, and make it distinctive, for the purposes of commerce. For example, Blue Nile, an online jewelry store, sued Ice.com, another online jewelry store, for allegedly copying its look and feel. Although no decision has been reached in the case, Justice Lasnik has left open the possibility that trade dress law (discussed earlier in Section 4.3.3) might protect the look and feel of Blue Nile.

Notice that both copyright and trademark can be used, in some circumstances, to protect the look and feel of a computer program. In the case of Pac-Man, it was determined that the look and feel of Pac-Man was a work of creativity (like a painting), and hence copyright was most appropriate. In the Blue Nile case, it would be a stretch to say that their Web design was a work of creativity, but it is certainly true that the design of the site is a big part of Blue Nile's identity. As a result, it is at least plausible to try to protect that identity using trademark law.

### Reflection Questions

1.   RESEARCH  Look at the computer software and Web sites that you use every day. Give one example each of a piece of software (or a feature of a piece of software) that could be protected by: 1) copyright, and 2) trade dress.

2.   RESEARCH  Do an Internet search to find screenshots of *K.C. Munchkin!* and *Pac-Man*. Do you agree that *K.C. Munchkin!* violated the copyright on *Pac-Man*? Explain your reasoning.

## 4.6.2  Patents for Software

The biggest controversy over intellectual property and software revolves around the use of patents to protect software. It would be reasonable to patent a piece of software if it was a genuine invention, but experts cannot agree which pieces of software are genuine inventions, or even on whether or not a piece of software can even be an invention. Because this question is unsettled, we will not take a position on the issue. Instead, the following sections present some examples of software patents that have fueled the controversy.

**4.6.2.1 The Amazon 1-Click Patent and the Nonobviousness Test**    The traditional model for online shopping requires users to add items to a virtual shopping cart and then pay for the item(s) via a check out process. During checkout, the user enters payment and shipping information. In 1997, Amazon.com began offering a different option, called 1-Click. Amazon's 1-Click option allows a customer to enter payment and shipping information into her account settings, and then change the 1-Click setting to "Yes." After that, the customer can just click the "Buy now with 1-Click" button to purchase an item. The item is then charged to the customer's prespecified payment option and shipped to the prespecified address. On September 28, 1999, the U.S. Patent Office issued Amazon a patent for this invention, "Method and system for placing a purchase order via a communications network." Amazon successfully used the patent to prevent Barnes and Noble from using a 1-Click ordering system. Apple Inc. has subsequently licensed the patent, which means they have paid Amazon for permission to use it, so they can provide 1-Click ordering in their online store and on iTunes.

The patent is controversial for a variety of reasons, but here we focus on one main question: Was this idea sufficiently nonobvious to be considered an invention? An idea usually cannot be patented if it would be obvious to skilled practitioners in that particular field. So if most people designing an online shopping site would hit on the idea of 1-Click shopping, then 1-Click shopping is an obvious idea, hence not patentable.

This leads to the first main criticism of software patents. Many people argue that the U.S. Patent Office is not competent to decide whether the idea behind a piece of software is nonobvious, and that it therefore regularly awards software patents for things that are not truly inventions. This benefits large corporations over small companies or individuals because of the prohibitive cost of a patent application. It also makes developing new and innovative software very difficult, because it is difficult to know, in advance, whether a piece of software violates one of the thousands of existing software patents.

### Reflection Questions

1. [POSITION] How *useful* is the 1-Click purchasing invention? If buying items takes more clicks, how might this affect the amount of items that people buy or the sites they buy from? Explain your reasoning.

2. [CONTEXT] When purchasing items through a Web browser on a computer, 1-Click purchasing is fairly useful; but it may be even more useful on other devices. Consider the Amazon Kindle. Its e-ink display refreshes much more slowly than the LCD displays used by laptops and tablet computers (like the Apple iPad). If you have never used such an e-ink device, either try one that belongs to a friend or go online and watch a video of one being used. How is this scenario different (if at all) from the previous question? In this context, how useful is the 1-Click purchasing invention?

**4.6.2.2 The Patentability of Algorithms**    An **algorithm** is a mathematically precise set of steps for computing something. Some algorithms are faster than others, and so scientists and corporations spend a lot of money and time trying to find the best algorithm for a particular problem. One of the major controversies surrounding software patents has to do with the question of whether or not a patent can be used to protect an algorithm.

It is not possible to patent a basic mathematical fact. For example, consider the method of addition that you learned in elementary school: You add up the columns, one column at a time, from right to left. If the result from any column is more than one digit, you carry the extra digits over to the next column. What would happen if this method of addition were to be patented? That might make it almost impossible to write new software or create new algorithms for other purposes, because you would not be able to add two numbers without the permission of the patent holder. So an algorithm that is a "basic mathematical fact" cannot be patented, because it would seriously harm the public good.

On the other hand, some algorithms seem like genuine inventions. Consider, for example, Google's search algorithm. It was so superior to its competitors that Google quickly became the dominant company in Web searching. Google's main method for estimating the importance of a Web page, the PageRank algorithm, is patented. In a sense, PageRank might be viewed as a basic mathematical fact; the mathematical formulas that define PageRank are relatively simple to write down and can be found on Wikipedia. On the other hand, they were not simple to discover. PageRank was invented by Larry Page; it was not some basic fact that everyone in the world already understood, like the algorithm for addition. And unlike the algorithm for addition, it is unlikely that someone else, working from the same information Larry Page had, would invent the exact same set of formulas for estimating the importance of a Web page.

## Reflection Questions

1. APPLICATION As you learned in math class, a prime number is a number that is divisible only by 1 and itself. Write down the steps you would use to figure out, in your head, whether or not 49 is prime. This is your "primality testing algorithm." Should you be able to patent your primality testing algorithm? Explain your reasoning.

2. RESEARCH Look up the PageRank algorithm on Wikipedia. Do you think (based on your current understanding of patents) the PageRank algorithm should be patentable? Explain your reasoning.

**4.6.2.3 Summary**    The question "Which type of intellectual property protection should apply to software?" contains a trap. By asking the question in this way, it makes it appear that there should be one single correct answer to the question. As we have seen, however, each of the existing types of intellectual property protection has its place in protecting computer programs. At the same time, the technical complexity of computer software has resulted in controversial (and in some cases outright incorrect) decisions by courts and the U.S. Patent Office about how to apply intellectual property law.

### 4.6.3  The Creative Commons

In the preface to his book *Free Culture*, Harvard Law Professor Lawrence Lessig writes the following:

> [W]e come from a tradition of "free culture"—not "free" as in "free beer[,]" but "free" as in "free speech," "free markets," "free trade," "free enterprise," "free will," and "free elections." A free culture supports and protects creators and innovators. It does this directly by granting intellectual property rights. But it does so indirectly by limiting the reach of those rights, to guarantee that follow-on creators and innovators remain as free as possible from the control of the past. A free culture is not a culture without property, just as a free market is not a market in which everything is free. The opposite of a free culture is a "permission culture"—a culture in which creators get to create only with the permission of the powerful, or of creators from the past (xiv).

In many societies there are a great many resources that are not owned by any one person—fish in a public stream, grass on public land, a picnic table in a public park, and so on. These resources, which are held jointly by everyone, are sometimes called **the commons**.

Lessig argues that, historically, most creative work has been in the commons rather than privately owned. This has been crucial to the creative process, because it means that new creators are able to learn from and use the creative works of the past. One example of this is Renaissance art. According to *Gardner's Art Through the Ages*, "The familiar premium that contemporary Western society places on artistic originality is actually a fairly recent phenomenon. Among the concepts Renaissance artists most valued were imitation and emulation (Kleiner, 431)." Computers in general, and the Internet in particular, have changed all this. Mechanical reproduction and Internet distribution of intellectual property has pushed intellectual property owners into a corner, where they feel they must fight tooth and nail to hold on to their livelihoods.

As a result, according to Lessig, current copyright law allows very little material to enter the creative commons. Because the term of a copyright is effectively 100 years or more, today's creative works will not enter the commons (by becoming public domain) for three or four generations. To address this problem, Lessig, along with renowned computer scientist Hal Abelson and others, founded an organization called Creative Commons. Creative Commons is devoted to helping people release their creative work into the creative commons. Current copyright law makes this very difficult. And even if you were able to overcome the copyright hurdles and make your work available for free, there was no easy way to let the world know that your work was available. To overcome these problems, Creative Commons came up with a variety of copyright-compatible licenses and symbols that can be used to indicate that you have licensed your work for reuse by others. Some Creative

Commons licenses allow items to be reused for commercial purposes, while others do not.

Many popular media-sharing Web sites, like Flickr, YouTube, Google's Picasa, blip.tv, and Wikimedia Commons, allow users to set the license terms of their content using the Creative Commons licenses. This makes it easy for other creators to download, reuse, and remix their work without fear of lawsuits. Through these efforts, Creative Commons has been very successful in setting up a new creative commons for photographs; if you need a photograph, you can almost certainly find something you can use, as long as you credit the creator, on Flickr or Picasa. So far, these efforts have not been as successful with respect to video and music. Figure 4.6 shows a search for images available via Flickr that are licensed for commercial use as long as credit is given to the creator.

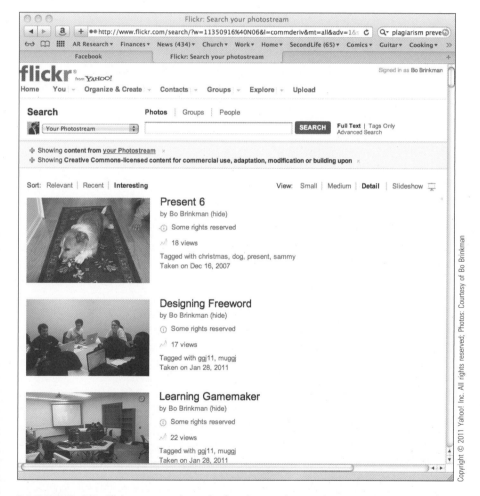

**FIGURE 4.6** Flickr.com search results for pictures that are free to use in a commercial product

Music is a particularly interesting case. In June of 2010, the American Society of Composers, Authors and Publishers (ASCAP) sent a fund-raising letter to its members specifically criticizing the efforts of Creative Commons and allied groups. According to the blog *techdirt*, the letter stated the following:

> Many forces including Creative Commons, Public Knowledge, Electronic Frontier Foundation and technology companies with deep pockets are mobilizing to promote "Copyleft" in order to undermine our "Copyright." They say they are advocates of consumer rights, but the truth is these groups simply do not want to pay for the use of our music. Their mission is to spread the word that our music should be free. (Masnick)

Are ASCAP's criticisms of Creative Commons (CC) and the Electronic Frontier Foundation (EFF) well founded? As Lessig pointed out, the two meanings of "free" in this context create ambiguity and cause misunderstandings. Furthermore, there are groups of pirates who think "music should be free," and they often support groups like CC and the EFF. So, while Creative Commons explicitly says that they support copyright and promote only copyright-based licensing schemes, intellectual property owners sometimes see them as the enemy.

This is the heart of the current controversy around Creative Commons; the debate is portrayed as "pirates" versus "intellectual property owners." Both the pirates and the intellectual property owners tend to think that Creative Commons is on the side of the pirates. Lessig, in *Free Culture*, points out that this is a misunderstanding. It is possible to believe that true piracy is wrong and harmful to creativity and yet also believe that the current copyright regime goes too far and is harmful to creativity.

### Reflection Questions

1. RESEARCH Do you post any of your photographs online? Would you consider allowing others to use them, free of charge? Look at the four conditions used in Creative Commons licenses as described at *http://creativecommons.org/about/licenses/*. Which of these conditions would you require, and why?

2. RESEARCH Look over the types of licenses offered by Creative Commons at *http://creativecommons.org/about/licenses/*. Based on this, do you think the people behind Creative Commons are in favor of abolishing copyright protection? Explain your reasoning.

## 4.7  MULTICULTURAL PERSPECTIVES

Globalization creates special challenges in the realm of intellectual property regulation. The Internet has made it very inexpensive to reproduce music and video and distribute it worldwide. This means that pirates wanted for copyright infringement in the United States can operate in countries with lax law enforcement. And copyright holders, who used to benefit from the difficulty in distributing copyrighted materials, have had to invent new technological schemes to prevent their works from being distributed contrary to their wishes.

## 4.7.1 Region Coding for Video Discs

One of the four main rights that authors have, under copyright, is the right to distribute copies of their work as they see fit. Consider the case of the movie *Juno*. It was released in theaters in the United States and Canada on December 25, 2007, and the DVD version of the movie was released on April 15, 2008. The movie was not released until much later in Japan. There, Juno appeared in theaters on June 14, 2008 and in DVD format on November 7, 2008.

This type of scheduling is very common, because movie studios need time to translate the movie into a new language. This creates a bit of a dilemma, however. What is to stop someone living in Japan from buying the American version of the DVD? For a group of two or more people, it is less expensive to purchase a single DVD and watch it together than to buy multiple tickets at the theater.

In order to prevent DVD sales from cannibalizing theater ticket sales, movie studios may choose to use a technology called **region-coding**. Any company that makes a DVD or Blu-Ray player is obligated to include region-coding technology, which prevents the user from playing videodiscs from other parts of the world. For example, the American DVD of Juno is a Region 1 DVD, which means it can be played only in the United States and Canada. Japan is in Region 2, so even if someone imports the DVD from the United States, it will not play on an ordinary DVD player made for sale in Japan. So a movie studio can, if it chooses, use region-coding to discourage people from importing movies before their official release date.

Critics of region-coding focus on a practice called **price discrimination**, which is the practice of charging different people different prices for the same thing (usually richer people pay more, and poorer people pay less). People in different parts of the world have very different amounts of money, and this influences the amount that one is willing or able to pay for a DVD or Blu-Ray disc. For example, a DVD on Amazon's Chinese site might cost 20 yuan, or about $2.95. The same DVD, in English, costs over $20 on Amazon's U.S. site. Because DVDs cost so little to produce, the movie studio can still make a profit selling them at $2.95 in China, but it would like to charge U.S. consumers more. Region-coding makes this price discrimination based on geography much easier. Without region-coding, someone might be able to buy thousands of cheap DVDs in a foreign country (where they are very inexpensive), then import them into a country where they are more expensive, hence defeating the movie studio's attempt to price discriminate.

### Reflection Questions

1.  POSITION Should region-based price discrimination be prohibited? Explain your reasoning.

2.  APPLICATION Explain why, under U.S. copyright law, region-based price discrimination is legal. In particular, which of the copyrights gives

the copyright holder permission to charge different people different amounts of money?

3.  [APPLICATION] Whether you agree with it or not, use Rawls's principles of justice to write an argument in favor of the following proposition: One ought to charge people in poor countries less than one charges people in rich countries. Then briefly comment on whether or not you agree with this argument, and explain your reasoning.

### 4.7.2  BitTorrent, The Pirate Bay, and the Pirate Party

As explained earlier in this chapter, BitTorrent is a peer-to-peer file-sharing protocol that is used for distributing files over the Internet. BitTorrent has a decentralized design that facilitates transmission of very large files, but searching for available files requires a separate index site.

The most popular index site in the world is The Pirate Bay, which is based in Sweden. It allows users to search for **torrents** (which are the keys used to locate files), and also allows users to find other users with whom to swap file pieces. The Pirate Bay has come under legal attack by copyright holders because it openly traffics in copyrighted material. Although it does not, itself, store or redistribute any copyrighted material, its service makes this process simpler for those who do. As we saw in the discussion of the Napster and DeCSS cases, this facilitation of copyright violation can be illegal. The Pirate Bay has repeatedly been shut down by Swedish authorities, but each time it has simply re-located to a new Internet service provider (ISP), and re-opened.

The movement to reform intellectual property law is particularly strong in Sweden, and many protestors turn out to support The Pirate Bay whenever they have a court appearance. There is also an entire political party in Sweden called the Piratpartiet (Swedish for "Pirate Party"). This party focuses on three main issues: 1) privacy protection, 2) copyright reform, and 3) the reduction or elimination of patents and other private monopolies. The Piratpartiet's statement of principles includes the following: "The copyright will encourage the creation, development and dissemination of culture... We claim that widespread and systematic abuses of today's copyright actively oppose these purposes by limiting both the creation of culture and cultural access." In the 2009 European Parliament election, Piratpartiet captured two of the 736 seats.

Though still small, Piratpartiet's political power has had implications in Hollywood's attempts to get The Pirate Bay Web site shut down. In May 2010, The Pirate Bay's Internet service provider was forced to cut off the site based on an injunction filed in a German court. The Piratpartiet took over these duties, providing The Pirate Bay with Internet service, eventually offering to do even more. Party leader Rick Falkvinge, in an editorial in the Swedish language newspaper *Aftonbladet*, stated:

> [The Swedish Constitution] says that [members of parliament] cannot be sued or prosecuted for anything that is done as part of the political mission... Some of the [Piratpartiet's] prospective MPs are planning to

use this to drive the Pirate Bay from within the parliament, if today's operators accept this. (Falkvinge)

The Pirate Party has spread to 22 nations. It remains to be seen whether the movement can attract enough members to win further political power, but its support of The Pirate Bay (which is one of the 100 most popular sites on the Internet) makes it an important target for intellectual property holders.

### Reflection Questions

1. POSITION Is the Piratpartiet's intention to shield The Pirate Bay from prosecution morally permissible? In other words, is there anything inherently immoral about The Pirate Bay's work? Explain your reasoning.

2. CONTEXT Is it possible that violating copyright might be immoral in one country (i.e., the United States) but moral in another country (i.e., Sweden)? Explain your reasoning.
   a. If you said "yes," is your position an example of cultural relativism? Explain why or why not.
   b. If you said "no," is it morally acceptable for one country to have strong copyright protection while another does not? Explain your reasoning.

## 4.8   INTERDISCIPLINARY TOPICS

The fight over intellectual property has had the greatest impact on industries that are clearly based on distributing creative works, such as the recording, publishing, news media, and video game industries. It reaches much farther than these direct effects, however. In this section we briefly discuss two examples. In one case, intellectual property protection led a mathematician to publish data that he knew (and admitted) was incorrect. In the other case, the remix culture of the Internet (where new creative works are made by combining pieces from existing works) is leading literary critics to question the definition of "writing."

### 4.8.1   Intellectual Property Protection Through Intentional Errors

The word "computer" predates the existence of the modern mechanical computer. Since the birth of modern science and engineering, it has been necessary to compute values of critical functions, such as the sine, cosine, and logarithms. This was once done by hand, and the humans who performed these computations were called "computers." It was possible to purchase manuals that contained, for example, the base-10 logarithm of every number from 1 to 100,000—which were all computed by humans.

Computing and double-checking these numbers was tremendously time consuming and expensive. It is not clear, however, that this valuable intellectual property is covered by any of the protections we have discussed in this chapter.

The creators of these tables were interested in catching plagiarists, but this is very difficult when the information included is purely factual. Everyone who calculates a logarithm to a certain number of places should get the same answer.

One famous compiler of mathematical tables, L.J. Comrie, wrote the following in the introduction to one of his books: "In no case should any error greater than +0.52 units of the last decimal be found. Moreover, it is confidently believed that the cases where the error exceeds +0.51 units of the last decimal could be counted on the fingers of one hand; those that are known to exist form an uncomfortable trap for any would-be plagiarist (vii)." In other words, he was aware of some errors in the book, and suggests (perhaps tongue-in-cheek, perhaps not) that these errors were left in intentionally, so that he could prove any plagiarism.

Plagiarism identification schemes of this type still exist today, in the form of digital watermarking of images. **Digital watermarking** means embedding small errors into a digital image so that someone viewing the image cannot see the errors with the naked eye, but a special computer program can use the errors to identify the source of the image.

### Reflection Questions

1. APPLICATION Assuming that Comrie was serious about using the errors in his book to catch plagiarists, would Immanuel Kant have viewed Comrie's decision to leave known errors in his table of logarithms as moral or immoral? Explain your reasoning.

2. APPLICATION Assuming that Comrie was serious about using the errors in his book to catch plagiarists, would a utilitarian be able to support Comrie's decision? Explain your answer. In particular, be sure to describe the potential negative consequences of his actions, and evaluate whether or not these are significant.

3. POSITION Let us assume that, all else being equal, it is not morally permissible to intentionally release a logarithm table with known errors. Does Comrie's need to catch plagiarists justify his actions, hence rendering them morally permissible? Explain your reasoning.

### 4.8.2  Plagiarism, the Web, and Writing

Helene Hegemann's first novel, written when she was just seventeen, was released to critical acclaim. The book rose to number five on the German-language best-seller list. Shortly afterward, however, bloggers identified several passages that were plagiarized from other books. Hegemann was widely condemned for failing to acknowledge her sources, and it appears that these revelations have severely affected the rating of her book on Amazon.de (Amazon's German site).

But unlike similar instances in the past, the revelation of plagiarism did not cause literary critics to reject Hegemann's book. Even after the allegations were well known, Hegemann was selected as a finalist for the "best novel" prize at the Leipzig Book Fair, an award worth $20,000. Nicholas Kulish of the *New York Times* reports that at least one member of the prize jury continued to support Hegemann.

Kulish also reported on Hegemann's response to the allegations:

Although Ms. Hegemann has apologized for not being more open about her sources, she has also defended herself as the representative of a different generation, one that freely mixes and matches from the whirring flood of information across new and old media, to create something new. "There's no such thing as originality anyway, just authenticity," said Ms. Hegemann in a statement released by her publisher after the scandal broke.

Hegemann seems to be arguing that, in a creative culture based on remixing, it is acceptable to cut-and-paste short passages from someone else and use it without attribution. The argument is that if the new work created by mixing is original and authentic overall, it does not matter if some of the sentences are taken from elsewhere.

### Reflection Questions

1. CONTEXT Which is more acceptable, to "borrow" sentences without attribution when writing a novel for publication, or to do so when writing an assignment for school? Explain your reasoning.

2. APPLICATION Review Posner's definition of plagiarism at the end of Section 4.3.1.4. If Hegemann had given credit, in the preface of her book, to the people whose work she borrowed, would she still be guilty of plagiarism? If she had given credit, would her borrowing be morally permissible? Explain your reasoning.

3. RESEARCH A significant amount of research shows that plagiarism in college is a growing problem. Some claim that this is the result of students growing up in a remix culture that does not understand plagiarism. Others claim it is simple laziness that is exacerbated by the ease of finding and copying information on the Web. Interview five of your classmates and/or teachers to try to determine why people plagiarize. You may wish to read Trip Gabriel's article, "Lines on Plagiarism Blur for Students in the Digital Age" (*www.nytimes.com*) for background.

## 4.9 PHILOSOPHICAL FOUNDATIONS OF INTANGIBLE PROPERTY LAW

In this chapter we have focused on the law much more than we do in the rest of the book. Intellectual property law affects ordinary people every day, and so we think it is important to understand the differences between copyrights and patents, and to understand one's legal rights (or lack thereof) with respect to one's virtual property.

In this section, however, we want to ask bigger questions. Which ethical theories support the legal protection of intellectual or virtual property? Should there be any intellectual property at all, or should all intellectual property immediately enter the public domain? Does the owner of a virtual good have any rights to that good, or does the owner of the virtual world have complete control? We will look at intellectual property using a consequentialist argument and virtual property using a deontological one.

### 4.9.1 Intellectual Property: The Consequentialist Argument

As we note in the introduction to this chapter, the U.S. Constitution says that the Congress has the right to "promote the Progress of Science and useful Arts, by securing for limited Times to Authors and Inventors the exclusive Right to their respective Writings and Discoveries" (Article I, Section 8). This is an inherently consequentialist argument. It seems to imply that one would not normally, all things being equal, give authors and creators a monopoly on their ideas. But it also recognizes that we, as a society, need authors and inventors. And so to encourage more people to create and invent, the founders decided to allow limited time monopolies on ideas. The argument is not based on the rights of the authors, or on notions of justice or caring, but just on the idea that such monopolies will increase the overall happiness of our nation.

The problem with the consequentialist argument is that there are an increasing number of examples that seem to contradict it. Consider the Linux operating system, and other open source software products. Anyone can use Linux for free, and anyone can download and modify the source code for Linux to make new products. Linux is now used on more than 10% of server computers worldwide. Thousands and thousands of other high quality open source products are also freely available, for anyone to use and modify. The authors of these open source products willingly give up most of their intellectual property rights. In most cases, they simply demand: 1) to be given credit, and 2) that if you reuse their code in your own code, you make your code available to be reused in the same way. The main motivation for the authors of open source products appears to be altruism, not compensation based on intellectual property laws.

Another example that contradicts the consequentialist argument is Wikipedia. Thousands of editors, from all walks of life, have contributed articles or edits to Wikipedia. Contributors to Wikipedia don't get paid for their work. One might expect academics' contributions to Wikipedia to count for promotions or raises, but this is usually not the case because of Wikipedia's editorial structure (for more on this, see Chapter 6).

Until recently, it was assumed that intellectual property laws were necessary to ensure progress in technology, the arts, and scholarship. Because we have concrete examples of extremely valuable projects, like Linux and Wikipedia, that have been created for free, we need to re-examine this assumption. People on both sides of the argument would like to find evidence that either supports or refutes the claim that limited time monopolies on ideas are, ultimately, beneficial to society. Furthermore, even among those who believe intellectual property laws are necessary, there is a significant debate about how long the "limited time" of the monopoly should last. Again, it seems that more evidence is needed.

Unfortunately, it is hard to imagine any kind of empirical evidence (evidence that comes from experiment or direct observation) that everyone involved would accept. Because we wish to evaluate the effects of intellectual property laws on a society as a whole, it seems impossible to take an experimental approach. We are unlikely to just eliminate all intellectual property laws so that we can see what happens.

Some economists have tried to use virtual worlds (like *Second Life*) to explore this question further. Some virtual worlds make it very easy to copy another person's creative works, while others make it very hard. In the case of *Second Life*, early versions of the *Second Life* client program had some bugs that made it possible to duplicate another person's creations. Some of the top content creators of the world (people who made virtual clothes, virtual houses, and so on, to sell to other residents) closed up shop when this became widely known. They threatened to stay away (wrecking the in-game economy) if Linden Lab did not fix the problem. This could be seen as evidence supporting the idea that intellectual property laws are necessary, because it shows that some authors and inventors will refuse to work if such laws don't exist.

The consequentialist argument forms the basis of most arguments in favor of intellectual property, and appears to be the basis for the U.S. Constitution's language about inventions and useful arts. But, as an argument, it suffers from the fact that not everyone agrees that such laws are necessary to promote progress. Indeed, we saw (in Section 4.6.2) that Lawrence Lessig, among others, thinks that progress would be accelerated if the creative commons were larger and if intellectual property laws were less strict.

## Reflection Questions

1. POSITION Give one example of a product that you use every day that you think would not have been created if there were no intellectual property laws. Explain your reasoning.

2. POSITION Supporters of the consequentialist argument would point out that open source software creators also benefit from copyright law; open source software licenses use copyright to require re-users to give credit to the original author. Because there is currently no U.S. law against plagiarism, copyright law is the usual way to sue to prevent plagiarism. Would you support creating a law that makes plagiarism illegal, with penalties similar to the penalties of copyright theft? Explain your reasoning.

## 4.9.2   Intangible Property: The Deontological Argument

Recall that deontological theorists (such as Kant) focus on the rights and duties of individuals, instead of the consequences of actions. It might seem natural, given the problems with the consequentialist argument in the previous section, to turn instead to a deontological argument in support of intellectual property. However, when viewed through the deontological lens, the rationale behind intellectual property law loses focus. In fact, deontological theories inevitably lead us to question the very foundations of the idea of property. Does a "right to property" exist at all? As we saw with the "right to privacy" in Chapter 3, the question of whether or not a natural right to property exists is not completely settled. Thus, before we can begin to think about a "right to intellectual property" we should look at the reasoning behind the more general case.

One of the most enduring explanations of personal property comes from political philosopher John Locke (1632-1704) and his *Second Treatise of Government*. Locke's ideas, introduced in Chapter 5 of his *Second Treatise of Government*, are controversial and are mostly outside the scope of our current inquiry. The main ideas are useful, though. Locke says that the natural resources of the earth are held in common by all people, but that each person has a natural right to his or her self. In particular, each person has a total right to benefit from the labor of his or her own body. Furthermore, he says, a natural resource becomes ours if: 1) there is plenty for everyone else, and 2) we transform it into something new through our own labor. Locke's example of this is the picking of wild fruit. If there is a wild orchard that no one is tending, and you pick some fruit to eat, it becomes yours.

Now, in real life, this is just the start of a complicated theory. Locke has quite a bit of work to do to incorporate scarcity, rivalrousness, and money into his theory. But he claims that when the raw materials to make something are themselves plentiful, then a person has every right to take them and make things. And whatever is produced is, by rights, the property of the person that produced it.

This is exactly the case with some types of virtual property. Again, we take *Second Life* as our example. In *Second Life*, residents can build very sophisticated objects, such as vehicles that speed up travel, a swimming pool with a working water slide, a garden that accurately simulates the life cycles of real plants, and so on. These complex goods are created from primitive objects (known colloquially as **prims**) that look like simple shapes such as cubes, spheres, cones, and tubes. They can be colored, resized, repositioned, and hooked together. A person with the necessary know-how can add complex and automated behaviors through computer programming. The raw materials (the cubes and spheres) are infinitely abundant, and you can get as many as you want at the touch of a button. Making them into something that other people will want to buy just requires labor and skill.

Locke's argument indicates that when you create virtual property, through your own labor, you have an exclusive right to it. No one else should be able to take it from you, or claim ownership of it, so that they have it but you do not. Locke's argument is that once you mix your labor with a common, to make something new, it becomes uniquely yours, and it cannot be rightfully taken away from you. In the current setting this argument has two problems.

The first problem is that this does not seem to tell us anything about intellectual property. Because intellectual property is not rivalrous, you may copy my intellectual property without directly breaking my right to property. Locke's argument is based on the rivalrousness of physical goods. Certainly one could try to extend Locke's ideas to intellectual property by arguing about being deprived of income from the copies, but his basic argument does not directly apply.

The other problem has to do with applying his theory of property to virtual property. It doesn't account for the fact that the virtual goods live on a server computer maintained by a third party. If you create virtual property in *Second Life* (for example), the corporation Linden Lab must pay a bit of money every day to see that your property continues to exist. They pay for the electricity to run the server, they own the server itself, they pay for staff to keep the server in good repair. If Linden Lab decides to turn off *Second Life* one day, have they violated the virtual property rights of the people that have made things there? Locke's theory does not seem to address this consideration.

## Reflection Questions

1. POSITION Imagine that you play an online game and obtain a valuable virtual object that you don't want. You sell it through an online auction for $10,000 (actual U.S. dollars), but after handing the item over to the purchaser, he puts a stop order on the payment, effectively stealing the item. Should the police treat this theft the same as the theft of a real $10,000 item, such as a car? Explain your reasoning.

2. RESEARCH Search the Internet for stories about crimes similar to the one described in the previous question. What is the usual outcome of such cases? What should it have been?

## SUMMARY

- The United States Constitution instructs Congress to make laws to protect intellectual property in order to promote progress in science, technology, and the arts.

- Creative works are protected by copyright. The following four main rights are reserved for the author: reproduction, derivative works, distribution, and performance.

- In many cases, members of the public are allowed to use copyrighted works without permission or royalty. Such use of a work is often referred to as fair use.

- Digital rights management technologies help protect copyrighted works, but also interfere with fair uses.

- Criminal penalties for copyright infringement are relatively new and were created by the No Electronic Theft Act (NET Act).

- The Napster case showed that contributory and vicarious infringement charges can sometimes be leveled against Internet search providers.

- Patents protect new and useful inventions.

- Trademarks protect the identifying characteristics of a product.

- Virtual goods make up a significant and growing piece of the U.S. economy, but they are creating new technological and legal challenges.

- Software is protected by all three of the major categories of intellectual property protection. Patents can protect the algorithm a program uses, copyright can protect the original source code, and trademark can protect the look and feel.

- The Creative Commons License is intended to allow authors to share their copyrighted works for re-use and/or redistribution by others.

- There are both consequentialist and deontological arguments in favor of intangible property laws, but there is not yet a strong consensus on what form such laws should take.

## CHAPTER EXERCISES

1. REVIEW Quote the clause of the United States Constitution that allows the protection of intellectual property.

2. REVIEW Explain the main functions of a rootkit.

3. REVIEW Answer the "five key questions" from Section 4.3 for each of the following types of intellectual property protection: 1) copyright, 2) trademark, and 3) patent.

4. REVIEW List and briefly explain the four main rights granted to the author by copyright.

5. REVIEW Explain the fair use exception to copyright, including the four factors used to determine whether or not a use is fair.

6. REVIEW Explain the doctrine of first sale.

7. REVIEW Describe the purpose of digital rights management (DRM).

8. REVIEW Summarize the main purpose of the anticircumvention clause of the Digital Millennium Copyright Act (DMCA) and describe its impact on fair use.

9. REVIEW Define plagiarism. If your definition is different from Posner's, explain why you think yours is superior to his.

10. REVIEW With respect to copyright, what is an orphaned work?

11. REVIEW In your own words, explain the difference between a work of creative authorship and an invention.

12. REVIEW Define "novel" in the context of a patent.

13. REVIEW Define trade dress.

14. REVIEW What is a trade secret? Explain why intellectual property laws are not needed to protect trade secrets.

15. REVIEW Define virtual goods (in particular, list and explain Lehdonvirta's four criteria for whether or not something is a virtual good).

16. REVIEW Define "real money transaction (RMT)."

17. <u>REVIEW</u> Explain what terms of service (ToS) are and why they are important.

18. <u>REVIEW</u> Explain what a key server is in the context of digital rights management.

19. <u>REVIEW</u> Define "algorithm."

20. <u>REVIEW</u> Define "commons," as the term is used when talking about public property.

21. <u>REVIEW</u> Define "region coding," and explain its main purpose.

22. <u>REVIEW</u> Define "price discrimination."

23. <u>REVIEW</u> Define "digital watermarking" and briefly explain how it works.

24. <u>REVIEW</u> Briefly describe Locke's theory of the right to property.

25. <u>RESEARCH</u> Research the concept of "hyperinflation." The case of Germany in the 1920s is particularly interesting, as is Zimbabwe during 2007–2009. Based on what you find, either critique or defend the following claim: "National currencies are inherently safer than virtual currencies."

26. <u>RESEARCH</u> Many, and perhaps most, Americans have violated copyright law at some point. Most people, when challenged, have some justification or explanation for why they did it. Usually (though not always) they claim that what they did was morally acceptable. In discussion with your classmates, friends, and family, produce a list of the top reasons that people give for violating copyright law.

27. <u>POSITION</u> Either defend or refute the following multistep argument in favor of illegally copying software:

    a. I cannot afford to buy this expensive software.
    b. Therefore, if I copy the software illegally, the copyright holder is not losing any money.
    c. Therefore, the copyright holder is not hurt by my copying.
    d. Therefore, my copying is morally permissible.

28. <u>CONTEXT</u> Consider the argument about copying software illegally from the previous question. Part (a) of the argument seems to imply that how much money one has might impact whether or not it is moral to copy software illegally; it might be morally permissible for a poor person to do it, but not a rich person. Is this true? Explain your reasoning.

29. <u>RESEARCH</u> Many video game retailers make a great deal of money by taking advantage of the doctrine of first sale. They purchase and re-sell used games. Recently, some video game makers have tried to stop this practice by charging people who bought the used game an additional fee for online play, a fee that they do not charge to the first purchaser. Does this practice violate the doctrine of first sale? Is this policy fair? Explain your reasoning.

## WORKS CITED

Bragg v. Linden Research, Inc., 487 F. Supp. 2d 593 (U.S. District Court, E.D. of Pennsylvania. 2007.).

Comrie, Leslie John. *Chambers's Six-figure Mathematical Tables*. n.p.: W. & R. Chambers, 1963. Print.

Dibbell, Julian. "Recalculating the Global Virtual GDP, Yet Again." *Terra Nova* 26 June 2007. Web. 2 Aug. 2010.

Doctorow, Cory. "Brazil's copyright law forbids using DRM to block fair use." *Boing Boing* 10 July 2010. Web. 2 Aug. 2010.

Falkvinge, Rick. "Vi Ska Driva Pirate Bay Från Riksdagshuset." Trans. Google Translate. *Aftonbladet* 2 July 2010. Web. 17 July 2011.

Gabriel, Trip. "Lines on Plagiarism Blur for Students in the Digital Age." *NYTimes.com* 1 Aug. 2010. Web. 2 Aug. 2010.

Jefferson, Thomas. Thomas Jefferson to Isaac McPherson, 13 Aug. 1813. In *The Writings of Thomas Jefferson*. Washington: Riker, Thorne, & Co., 1855. Print.

Kleiner, Fred S. *Gardner's Art Through the Ages: The Western Perspective, Volume I*. 13th ed. Boston: Wadsworth Publishing, 2009. Print.

Kulish, Nicholas. "Author, 17, Says It's 'Mixing,' Not Plagiarism." *NYTimes.com*. 11 Feb. 2010. Web. 2 Aug. 2010.

Lehdonvirta, Vili. "Virtual Consumption." Diss. Turku School of Economics, 2009. Web. <http://info.tse.fi/julkaisut/vk/Ae11_2009.pdf>.

Lessig, Lawrence. *Free Culture: The Nature and Future of Creativity*. New York: Penguin, 2005. Print.

Linden Lab. "Terms of Service Archive/Through 29 April 2010 – Second Life Wiki." Web. 2 Aug. 2010. <http://wiki.secondlife.com/wiki/Linden_Lab_Official:Terms_of_Service_Archive/Through_29_April_2010>.

Locke, John. *Second Treatise of Government*. Indianapolis: Hackett Publishing Company, 1980. Project Gutenberg. Web. 24 July 2011. <http://www.gutenberg.org/ebooks/7370>.

Masnick, Mike. "ASCAP Claiming That Creative Commons Must Be Stopped; Apparently They Don't Actually Believe In Artist Freedom." *Techdirt* 25 June 2010. Web. 2 Aug. 2010.

Piratpartiet. "Principprogram Version 3.4." Trans. Google Translate. 25 Apr. 2010. Web. 17 July 2011. <http://www.piratpartiet.se/principer>.

Posner, Richard A. *The Little Book of Plagiarism*. New York: Pantheon, 2007. Print.

Ralphedelominius. "CCP Speaks Out on the EIB Scam." *Ten Ton Hammer* 26 Sept. 2007. Web. 2 Aug. 2010.

Schneier, Bruce. "Real Story of the Rogue Rootkit." *Wired.com* 17 Nov. 2005. Web. 2 Aug. 2010.

Smith, Danielle. "Stolen Picture." *Extraordinary Mommy* 28 May 2009. Web. 2 Aug. 2010.

Verbauwhede, Lien. "Legal Pitfalls in Taking or Using Photographs of Copyright Material, Trademarks and People." Web. 2 Aug. 2010. <http://www.wipo.int/sme/en/documents/ip_photography.htm>.

## RELATED READINGS

### Nonfiction Books

Dibbell, Julian. *Play Money: Or, How I Quit My Day Job and Made Millions Trading Virtual Loot*. New York: Basic Books, 2007. Print. (Dibbell, a well-known author for *Wired* who focuses on social aspects of computing, chronicles a year spent trying to earn a living by playing online games. The book includes interesting interviews and stories from people who make a real living "farming" gold and trading in virtual goods.)

Lessig, Lawrence. *Free Culture: The Nature and Future of Creativity*. New York: Penguin Press, 2005. Print. (Due in part to his role in founding the Creative Commons, Harvard Law Professor and *Wired* columnist Lawrence Lessig is one of the most widely cited and read authors studying modern copyright issues. Any one of the three books listed here is a good starting place for an in-depth study of the controversy over modern copyright law and why it matters to ordinary people. *Free Culture* is creative commons licensed for free download (and also for free reuse and remixing for noncommercial purposes) through various sites, including *www.bookpub.org* and *www.free-culture.cc*.)

---. *Remix: Making Art and Commerce Thrive in the Hybrid Economy*. New York: Penguin Press, 2008. Print.

---. *The Future of Ideas: The Fate of the Commons in a Connected World*. New York: Vintage, 2002. Print.

### Essays and Articles

Benjamin, Walter. "The Work of Art in the Age of Mechanical Reproduction." *Illuminations*. New York: Schocken, 1969. 217-252. Print. (A German scholar and cultural critic who was also a Marxist and an outspoken critic of fascism, Benjamin died while trying to escape Nazi Germany in 1940. In "The Work of Art," he explores the role of technology in changing the meaning and significance of art. This essay is widely read in many areas of the humanities, but we are particularly interested in his contribution to the debate about whether or not movies are "art." One of Benjamin's key ideas is that the ease with which film (and photographs) can be reproduced fundamentally changed the meaning of the word "art," to the point that the question "Is film art?" was misleading.)

### Film and TV

*Pirates of Silicon Valley*. Dir. Burke, Martyn. Turner Home Entertainment, 1999. Film. (This made-for-TV biopic starring Noah Wyle and Anthony Michael Hall chronicles the formative years of both Apple and Microsoft from 1984 through 1997. Of particular interest are the exchanges between Steve Jobs and Bill Gates on the "look and feel" lawsuit surrounding the Windows operating system.)

# Chapter 5

# Trust, Safety, and Reliability

Suppose you want to know the sum of one thousand numbers. Then suppose you give the list of numbers on paper to three different people. To perform the calculations, one person uses pencil and paper, one uses a calculator, and the third uses a spreadsheet program on a computer. No two answers are alike, and they differ from one another by significant amounts. Suppose further that you are on a tight deadline and do not have time to have everyone recalculate the sum. Which result would you be most likely to trust?

Now suppose you need a Russian poem translated into English. You ask a friend, who is a Russian major, for a translation. You also use a computer program to translate the poem. Finally, you Google the poem's title and find a translation on the Internet. The Internet source provides no indication of who did the translation; it just gives the poem in Russian and in English. The three translations are very different from one another. Which would you be more inclined to trust as a good translation?

Chances are, you were more inclined to trust the computer in the first case than in the second. We tend to trust computers to do large numbers of calculations accurately, but we are inclined to distrust them in other areas. In some cases, we are wrong to trust computers and at other times we are wrong not to trust them.

In this chapter we explore various ways in which people trust computers to perform important tasks. We also examine how and why computers sometimes fail to justify that trust, and we consider the consequences of such failures. Finally, we discuss possible ways to minimize the likelihood of computer failures.

## 5.1   CAUSES OF COMPUTER FAILURE

When a computer fails to do what we think it should, it's usually possible to identify a human who made an error which led to the computer's failure. Of course, physical damage to a machine or some sort of external interference such as an electrical storm can be factors, but in the vast majority of cases, computer failures are caused by a person associated with building the computer, developing the software, or inputting data. Before we look more closely at the various ways that humans can cause computers to fail, we will briefly survey the ways in which computers let us down.

Here are a few of the most important ways a computer might fail to meet expectations:

- **Hardware errors** – The hardware might malfunction, causing erroneous results.

- **Software errors** – Sometimes called bugs, software errors are mistakes in either the programming or the design of the software. The origins of the term "bug" supposedly go back to a moth that was found in 1947 in the circuitry of an early computer known as the Mark II. The Mark II was the second in a series of four computers financed by the U. S. Navy and built at Harvard University under the direction of physicist Howard Aiken (1900-1973). The project was financed by the U. S. Navy and IBM. The Mark II bug, which truly was a bug, was actually the cause of a hardware problem, and although the term "bug" is still used to refer to small problems or "glitches" in hardware, today it most often refers to software errors. The story of the moth is one that was often told by an early pioneer in computing, Grace Hopper (1906-1992), who as a young naval lieutenant (junior grade), was instrumental in implementing the programming language COBOL on the Mark I. She ultimately became the first female admiral in the U. S. Navy. She was largely responsible for popularizing the term "debugging" as the process of finding and removing errors from software. In reality, the term "bug" had been used often by engineers much earlier—it was even used by Thomas Edison. The great computer scientist Edsgar Dijkstra (1930-2002) asserted that computer scientists should never use the term "bug," but should always say "mistake" in order to emphasize that it is a human who was at fault. Despite Dijkstra's objections, however, the term has become part of the standard language of software developers and is also the term we will use.

- **The computer solves the wrong problem** – Every program is written by one or more programmers in order to satisfy a want or need of some human being, usually one or more users or clients. Usually, the programmers are not the clients. When the programmers do not correctly understand the wishes of the clients, the program, even if it was programmed correctly to do exactly what the programmers intended, does not actually do what the client wants and expects.

■ **Misuse** – Misuse of a computer system involves attempting to use a computer for the wrong purpose or using one incorrectly for the right purpose. One common example is to supply a program with incorrect input. When a program is given erroneous input data, the results will generally also be incorrect. The old cliché, "garbage in, garbage out," is valid.

■ **Communication failure** – Software often interacts with humans. Sometimes the person who is prompted for some action misunderstands what is being asked. For example, as actually happened once, people refueling an aircraft using a computer monitoring system for determining the amount of fuel needed, did not realize the program was reporting the amount of fuel in liters rather than gallons. The result was that an airliner actually ran out of fuel over Lake Superior. Fortunately, the plane was able to land safely and no one was injured. The program worked properly, in a sense, but the result was still a near disaster.

■ **Malice** – In recent years, malicious computer software has been growing more prevalent. In some cases it is simply a form of vandalism. In the popular imagination, a teenage hacker is often to blame. But malicious software is often the product of a full-blown vendetta, for-profit crime, terrorism, or warfare.

### Reflection Questions

1. APPLICATION Suppose your word processor marks a sentence in your text as a fragment, but you know the sentence is correct. What type of error is that most likely to be? If you see several possibilities, list each. Explain your reasoning.

2. APPLICATION Suppose your ATM gives you less cash than was charged to your account. What type of error is that most likely to be? If you see several possibilities, list each. Explain your reasoning.

3. POSITION Think about a situation where you have had some sort of interaction with a computer where you misunderstood what was being asked of you, and you got an undesired result because you misunderstood what the computer asked. Explain what the creators of that software should have presented to you so that you responded properly. Examples might include automatic checkout lines at the grocery store, online class registration systems, software installation programs, or an ATM.

## 5.2  CASE: ARIANE 5 FLIGHT 501

The Ariane 5 Flight 501 was an unmanned test flight sponsored by the European Space Agency as part of the development of its Ariane 5 system. The flight, which consisted of a cluster of four rockets, came to an end when the rockets self-destructed due to a computer error. The error arose from a particular kind of arithmetic error that could have been prevented if the program developers had not decided to gain efficiency by gambling that such an error would not occur. The bug did not cause a loss of life, but it did result in a loss of $3.5 million and was included on *Wired* magazine's 2005 list of the ten worst bugs in history.

Numbers can be stored in a computer in a variety of ways. One type of numeric value, a **floating point** number, is similar to scientific notation, used in the natural sciences. For example, using scientific notation, one might represent the number 250,000,000 as $2.5 \times 10^8$. Floating point numbers are useful in programming because they allow the program to handle a larger range of magnitudes than would otherwise be possible. In fact, many of the calculations done today in scientific applications would be impossible without the use of floating point numbers. The downside to floating point numbers is a loss of precision. For example, representing exactly the number $1.23 \times 10^{45}$ would require 46 digits. To be precise, the representation $1.23 \times 10^{45}$ consists of a number of significant digits (in this case the digits 1, 2, and 3) and a scale factor or magnitude (in this case, 45). The number of significant digits determines the precision, while the number of digits in the scale factor determines the range of magnitudes.

We could, for example, choose to represent a floating point number by exactly five digits. We could choose to have the last two of those five digits represent the magnitude, and the first three the digits of precision. In that case, we would have three significant digits followed by two digits of magnitude. We could also assume a decimal point after the first digit. We could, therefore, represent a very large range of numbers using just five decimal digits. In our discussion, we will prefix floating point numbers with an 'F' to avoid confusing them with integers. For example, the floating point number F12345 would represent $1.23 \times 10^{45}$, with the decimal point and the power of ten assumed. Similarly, the floating point number F62131 would represent $6.21 \times 10^{31}$ and F72003 would represent $7.20 \times 10^{03}$. The problem with using such a notation is that we lose precision; many numbers will have the same representation because we have only three significant digits. For example, if we were using our five-digit scheme as just described, all of the integers, 123451, 123452, 123453, 123454, 123455, and numerous others, would be represented as the floating point number F12305, which represents $1.23 \times 10^5$. Also, if we are limited in the number of digits we allow in an integer, some floating point numbers cannot be represented as integers. Suppose for example, a computer had a limit of five decimal digits for any integer. Then the floating point number F12311, which represents $1.23 \times 10^{11}$, could not be represented in that computer as an integer because the integer it represents would require twelve digits, seven more than the maximum allowed. If we programmed such a computer to convert F12311 to an integer, an error would occur when we tried to put twelve digits in a memory cell that had room for only five. That kind of error is called an "arithmetic overflow." In a computer, of course, numbers are not represented with decimal digits, but with binary digits (bits). The same principles apply to binary digits as to decimal digits, but all digits are either one or zero. In the computer system used in the Ariane 5, floating point numbers were represented as sixty-four bits and integers were represented as either sixteen bits or thirty-two bits. Another complication that we have omitted is that computers must allow for negative numbers and for negative magnitudes to represent small fractions. That simplification will not affect the discussion of any of the cases we consider.

The first fifty seconds of the Ariane 5 flight were controlled by a software system that had been reused from the earlier Ariane 4 system. Unfortunately, the Ariane 5 accelerated much faster than the Ariane 4, forcing the old software to deal with values that became larger much faster than in the old system. At one point, a 64-bit floating point number, which was converted to a 16-bit integer, proved too large to fit into 16 bits. This caused an arithmetic overflow error, as explained above. This error ultimately caused the destruction of the rockets. The whole problem could have been avoided. The software did not contain error-handling code that would have been able to deal with an arithmetic overflow of the type generated during the Ariane 5 flight. This error-handling code was left out to make the software run more efficiently.

The program monitored seven key values stored as variables. Seven of those variables were at risk of overflowing, but only four were protected by error-handling code. In an investigation after the fact, a memorandum turned up indicating that there was a plan to add code later that would have protected the other three variables. However, the memorandum did not explain why these variables were ultimately not protected. All we know is that the error was not detected and no corrective action was taken.

A further irony was that, at the time the software failed, the specific program that failed was not actually doing anything useful. The code containing the unprotected variable was there to stabilize the rockets during the countdown period. That code had no real function after liftoff, but continued to run for an additional forty seconds after liftoff in case something happened during the countdown to delay the flight. The additional forty seconds was to give the ground equipment time to resume control of the rockets. The error occurred well after liftoff, just four seconds before the software would have stopped executing. The result was a 3.5 million dollar accident.

## Reflection Questions

1. POSITION Suppose you were able to identify the particular person or persons who made the decision to omit the code necessary to handle the arithmetic overflow error. Would you hold the person or persons responsible for the accident? Why or why not?

2. POSITION Suppose you were able to identify the particular programmers who omitted the code necessary to handle the arithmetic overflow error. Suppose further that these programmers reported to their superiors that omitting the code could cause the flight to fail, and that their superiors ordered them to release the software anyway, along with a memorandum indicating that further code should be added later to correct the potential problem. Should the programmers who warned their superiors be held responsible for the accident? Why or why not?

Should the superiors who gave the orders be held responsible for the accident? Why or why not?

3. POSITION Suppose lives had been lost due to the Ariane 5 disaster. Should anyone be considered guilty of criminal negligence? Explain your reasons. Base your argument on what you think the law should be, not what the law actually is.

4. APPLICATION Does reusing software seem like a good idea to you? What are the advantages and disadvantages of reusing software? (Note: This is not a research question. You should formulate your answer according to your current knowledge of software development.)

5. RESEARCH Software reuse is a common goal in software engineering. Research the term "software reuse" and explain the advantages and disadvantages of software reuse in current software development.

## 5.3 CASE: PENTIUM FLOATING POINT DIVIDE

In October, 1994, Professor Thomas Nicely, a professor of mathematics at Lynchburg College in Virginia, notified Intel Corporation about an apparent flaw in the Intel P5 Pentium chip. The flaw had to do with floating point division. According to Professor Nicely, the division of one floating point number by another floating point number sometimes produced invalid results. These invalid results only occurred under certain circumstances and were unlikely to be noticed by most users.

While this problem might not seem significant, it proved to be a serious issue, affecting most of the numerical calculations performed by PCs at that time. Even though the erroneous values were significant only for those calculations requiring high precision and were quite rare (approximately once in every nine billion floating point divide operations), the total number of such operations that were done every day by PCs was enormous, so that the number of faulty values was also very large.

According to Nicely, people at Intel indicated they had been aware of the problem for several months, but had not announced it to the general public. The following month, a report on CNN turned the bug into real news. Intel argued that the bug was not very important and affected very few users. The company offered to replace chips only for those users who could demonstrate a need for high precision. Public outrage ensued, with critics arguing that Intel had an obligation to deliver a product that behaved as it was supposed to. They also argued that users should not be required to predict their future needs for precision, and instead should be able to count on their computers to provide the precision defined by current computational standards as defined be standards agencies. Soon, probably because of the public outcry, Intel reversed its position and agreed to replace all of the flawed chips.

The cost to Intel for the floating point divide bug has been estimated at approximately one-half billion dollars. The loss of trust by the public is difficult to measure in dollars, but there can be no doubt that Intel's image was tarnished by the bug and by the company's initial reluctance to disclose the problem and replace the faulty chips.

### Reflection Questions

1. **POSITION** When employees of Intel first discovered the bug, did they have an ethical responsibility to make the problem public? Why or why not?

2. **APPLICATION** Did Intel have a moral obligation to replace the defective chips, even for those users who had no need for high precision? Why or why not?

3. **POSITION** Suppose a bank was relying on computers that had the Intel Pentium 5 chip to perform extensive computations relating to investments. Suppose further, that the error in the chip caused the bank to lose a significant amount of money. Is Intel morally obligated to compensate the bank for its loss? Note that we are not asking about legal liability here, only the moral liability, if any. Give arguments to support your answer.

4. **RESEARCH** The floating point divide error in the Pentium chip was not really a software error issue, because it was a problem with a chip. As it happens, we do not consider it a hardware error either because it involves a bug in a kind of program, known as firmware, that is burned into silicon. Research the term "firmware" and explain how it is used in modern computers.

5. **CONTEXT** The floating point divide error caused a small error in certain calculations. We have seen, however, that floating point numbers can represent a large range of magnitudes—in exchange for a loss in precision. Hence one could argue that all floating point calculations potentially involve small errors and so Intel should not have had to replace any chips. Is that argument valid? Explain.

6. **APPLICATION** Both the Ariane 5 flight failure and the Pentium floating point chip error involved floating point numbers, but the ethical issues in these two cases are quite different. Identify the ethical issues for each case.

## 5.4  CASE: WHY SOFTWARE FAILS

Developing software is a complicated task. Even when done diligently by competent people with good intentions, failure is a possibility. This section discusses some causes of software failure. As we shall see, a programming bug isn't the only possible cause of software failure. The following case, although inspired by real events, is fictional.

Some years ago, before the time of the Internet, over six thousand chemists from all over the world registered to attend a particular professional conference. Some were to come alone, while others were to be accompanied by their families. The conference organizers planned to have receptionists provide each chemist with a packet of registration materials (such as room assignment, convention schedule, etc.), which were to be stored in large cardboard boxes. The boxes, and the envelopes within the boxes, were to be arranged alphabetically by the last name of the registered chemist. Naturally, in order for this plan to work, it had to be possible to identify each chemist's last name on the registration form. Unfortunately, the form included only a single blank labeled "Name." That made it difficult to identify each chemist's last name because of the variety of ways people had chosen to write their names in the blank. Some example entries were:

Mr. Thomas Dobbs Jr.
Dr. Mary K. Stone
Smith, Verlynda L.
Wayne Thomas MD
Peters Susan MD

The organizers transcribed all the names from the forms into a text file, hired a programming student, and asked her to write a program that would identify the last name of each registrant.

Writing such a program is tricky. An inexperienced programmer might write a program that mistakenly identifies titles (e.g., Mr., Ms., Jr.) as last names. Even a very clever programmer would find it harder to write a program that could account for the many forms of human error apparent in the registration forms. For example, when writing "Peters Susan MD" on her form, Dr. Peters probably left out a comma. She probably really meant to write "Peters, Susan MD." But there is no way to tell whether "Wayne Thomas MD" is actually Dr. Wayne Thomas, or whether Dr. Thomas Wayne chose to write his last name first, and like Dr. Peters, mistakenly omitted the comma.

The conference organizers in this example made some significant errors, beginning with the design of the registration form. They also gave the programmer the wrong problem to solve. The real problem was to unite each registrant with his or her registration packet. The problem presented to the programmer was actually just a means to the end of solving the real problem, but it wasn't an end in itself. As we have already seen, there was no way to determine with certainty the last name in the entry "WAYNE THOMAS MD" without information beyond what the entry supplied.

As you can see then, even if the programmer was exceptionally clever, she was unlikely to solve the problem satisfactorily. For each incorrectly identified last name, there was a person whose registration packet could not be found and who was consequently inconvenienced. Had the registration form designer, the programmer, the organizers, and the receptionists worked together, virtually all such problems could be avoided.

To get started, a programmer needs a logical plan that defines the steps necessary to determine the solution to the problem the program is supposed to solve. The specific sequence of steps constitutes an algorithm which, as explained in Chapter 4 (Section 4.6.2), is a mathematically precise description of a procedure. The program, when it is finished, is a kind of translation of the algorithm into a programming language. A software error could arise because of a faulty algorithm (a certainty in this case, since there is no infallible algorithm for the problem) or because of a faulty representation of the algorithm in the chosen programming language.

Suppose the programmer in our example decided to focus on the position of initials, the location of any common titles, and the presence or absence of commas. First the name entry is checked for a comma. If one is present, the first word is assumed to be the last name. If no comma is present, then any common titles are deleted. Then, if the last item is an initial, the first word is assumed to be the last name. Otherwise it is the last word. The term "common title" is defined as "Mr.," " Ms.," "Mrs.," "Miss," "Dr.," "M.D.," "Prof.," "Ph.D.," "Jr.," or "Sr."

The plan has some significant flaws. The idea of a list of common titles is a good one, but more than ten will surely be necessary. Foreign titles have been entirely overlooked. The plan fails to anticipate an entry of the form "John, Sally, and Ellen Brown" as well as the possibility of a name such as "Dr. Miss," which will be eliminated altogether when common titles are deleted. The plan also assumes a consistent use of periods used by the person filling in the blank. It is almost certain that there would be a significant number of cases where that would not be true. The resulting algorithm would therefore, even if implemented correctly, produce erroneous results.

The programmer in question did a good job with her assignment, such as it was. She ran tests on a sample of the applications, and out of the one hundred applications arbitrarily chosen for testing purposes, only one was assigned the wrong last name. The program, in a sense, worked perfectly. That is, it correctly implemented the algorithm she had developed to try to solve the given problem. She believed that an algorithm that would find the correct name in all cases was impossible. Since the one she created, when tested, worked in ninety-nine out of one hundred cases she decided that her program was sufficient.

Unfortunately, the story did not have an entirely happy ending. Most registrants were given the right packet as expected, but there were 296 people whose packets were misfiled and that led to delays. After the conference was over, further investigation revealed at least some of the reasons for the unexpectedly high number of misplaced packets:

1. Even if everything had worked as the testing suggested it should, there would have been sixty people whose name would have been identified incorrectly. Only one out of a hundred is, after all, sixty out of six thousand. That level of error would, by itself, cause a lot of inconvenience to those 60 conference attendees.

2. The arbitrary selection of applications for testing had not been representative. The programmer had started testing early in order to be

completely finished in plenty of time for the conference. Not all of the applications had arrived when the test applications were selected. The early arrivals had been almost entirely from the United States and had last names that were relatively easy to identify. Consequently, the actual results were worse than the one in one hundred failure rate suggested by the test cases.

3. The forms selected for testing had been prepared by the programmer herself and were completely free of typing errors. However, the complete set of last names, transcribed into a text file, did contain typing errors. Those typing errors prevented the program from working correctly.

4. The program actually had a minor programming bug in the implementation that caused the wrong name to be selected under very special circumstances. Those circumstances never arose in the test applications. The implementation bug accounted for only 10 of the 296 misidentified names.

Once the conference organizers realized there was going to be a problem with determining the last name of each registrant, they were correct in choosing to use a computer to mitigate the problem. Computers are tireless and can be of great service in tedious work like carefully examining six thousand names. But, as mentioned earlier, the organizers did not give the programmer the correct problem. Had they done so, the result might have been much better.

There were a number of things the programmer might have done to solve the real problem instead of solving some kind of text puzzle as she was asked to do. For example, once the program had eliminated titles, initials, abbreviations, and other similar words that were clearly not names, the number of remaining words would be small. Her program could then choose one of the words to be the name associated with the packet and then create a cross-reference table for other words in the list, indicating for each the name under which the packet is filed. How the program chose the word under which to file the packet would not matter much. It would not even matter much if the word chosen was not really a name. The correct last name would be one of the words in the list of remaining words and would be in the cross-reference table. The registration worker could then consult the cross-reference table whenever a packet failed to be under a person's last name. Because the number of possibilities for the packet's location would be small, there would be little delay in providing the person with his or her packet. The programmer's final program using a cross-reference table would have been quite different. Her goal would have been to reduce the size of the cross-reference table so that it was manageable, but correctly identifying the correct last name would be, at most, of secondary importance. Her program, if implemented correctly, would have been a poor solution to the puzzle she was actually given, but would probably have been a good solution to the real problem.

## Reflection Questions

1. APPLICATION The consequences of the faulty program in this case were not especially costly in terms of money, and no humans were injured or killed. The bad consequences involved some people (296 registrants,

some with their families) to be inconvenienced. Is that sufficient for either the conference organizers or the programmer to have any moral responsibility? Explain your reasoning, making sure to specify the moral theory you are using.

2. APPLICATION The consequences of the faulty program in this case were not especially costly in terms of money, and no humans were injured or killed. The bad consequences involved some people (296 registrants, some with their families) to be inconvenienced. Is that sufficient for either the conference organizers or the programmer to have any ethical responsibility? Explain your reasoning, making sure to specify the relevant group whose ethics you are considering.

3. APPLICATION Assuming the conference organizers had a limited budget, was their decision to hire a student to do the programming for their problem a moral one? Explain.

4. APPLICATION Assuming the conference organizers had a limited budget, was their decision to hire a student to do the programming an ethical one? Explain.

5. CONTEXT Was the programming student's decision to use the program morally permissible, given that one error out of one hundred tested occurred?

6. CONTEXT Suppose the programmer had been a professional programmer. In that case, would the decision to use the program have been ethical, given that one error out of the one hundred tested occurred?

## 5.5  BUGS AND PUBLIC SAFETY

In the previous sections, two of the three cases we considered involved very costly errors, but in neither of those cases were lives lost. However, in some situations, a computer failure can lead directly to death. In this section we discuss a series of tragic accidents that were caused by computer bugs. We will discuss the reasons for those failures and examine the current software engineering processes relevant to producing reliable computing systems, especially when public safety is at stake.

### 5.5.1  Safety-Critical Software

**Safety–critical software** is software that may affect someone's safety if it fails to work properly. This category usually includes software that could potentially harm the environment, as that would presumably indirectly harm humans. A few obvious examples of such systems are air traffic control software, software that controls processes within a nuclear power plant, software associated with braking systems of automobiles, or patient monitoring software in an intensive care unit. The standards of creating, testing, and maintaining safety-critical software are much stricter than other software, for obvious reasons.

Clearly, it is important that safety-critical software be as reliable as possible because its failure could potentially have dire consequences. Throughout the computing disciplines, most people agree that there is no way to be absolutely certain that a nontrivial computing system will function correctly. However, many disagree about how best to maximize software reliability. In many cases, it's also not clear how reliable a complex computing system will actually be even after it has achieved the maximum reliability possible.

The most obvious approach to making sure a program has no bugs is to test it. Testing, while obvious, is not the complete answer. The ideal way to test a program would be to test every possible execution and make sure that no matter what the input, the program will work correctly. Unfortunately, that approach is not feasible because of the large number of tests that would be required. The number of different possible instruction sequences executed by even a moderately sized program is enormous, making it impossible to test all possible sequences.

It's actually possible to roughly calculate the number of executions required to exhaustively test a program. To make this calculation, you need to understand the concept of decision points. A **decision point** is a place in computer code where the next instruction executed depends on input data. A program could have thousands of decision points, but even one hundred decision points could result in over $10^{30}$ different executions of instruction sequences. If a computer required one picosecond to execute each sequence (a speed that is actually much faster than current computers' capabilities), the time required to execute all those sequences would exceed ten billion years.

To make matters worse, many safety critical programs are **control programs**, which are programs that control some sort of machinery. Testing control programs is much more problematic than testing ordinary programs which, as we just saw, is already a formidable task. In the past, some prominent computer scientists have argued that the complexity of computer software is simply too great to be used in safety-critical systems and software should never be trusted when human lives are at stake. If society took that approach, many aspects of our lives would be very different; there are many different ways in which we rely on software to control devices and systems we consider vital.

Control programs are particularly difficult to test because they are commonly multiprocess programs with real-time constraints. The term **real time** simply means that the program must do something within a specific amount of time. For example, a program that initiates evasive action in a military plane upon detection of an approaching missile obviously must be capable of responding before the missile actually arrives. Hence, not only must the program execute correctly, it most do so within precisely defined real-time constraints. To respond late, even if the response would have been the correct one, would be a failure. The term **multiprocess** is used to refer to programs that execute at the same time as one or more other programs. Multiprocess programs must coordinate with each other so that they do not get in each other's way. For example, the software controlling acceleration when a car is on cruise control must coordinate with the braking system so that it does not attempt to accelerate when the driver is applying the brakes. If those programs do not coordinate properly, they could prevent a car from stopping in time to prevent an accident.

Software engineering has made many advances that have improved our ability to produce reliable programs. Despite the hopelessness of exhaustive testing, software has continued to grow more complex and play a larger part in our society. So far, the dire predictions of regular catastrophes from software failures have not materialized because software engineering methods for improving software reliability have kept pace with the growing complexity of software systems. To be sure, there have been failures. We have already seen some, and we will examine others shortly. Despite such failures, today many trillions of computer instructions are executed every day correctly performing some safety-critical function.

These advances stem from the following four improvements in the industry:

- Better education and training of software engineers, programmers, and analysts
- More sophisticated testing procedures
- Better maintenance
- Refocusing the software development process on the prevention of bugs rather than the detection and correction of bugs

Studies continue to show that the single most important component of reliable software is the quality of the people who create it. The quality of software developers depends on natural aptitude as well as their education, experience, and training. The former cannot be altered, but the latter has improved considerably in the last three decades. The proper education of software developers involves, of course, technical subjects in computer science and software engineering, but should also address the societal and social impact of computing. Educating software developers on the communicative, psychological, and ethical aspects of both the users of software and the developers themselves has led to attitudinal changes in software developers. That, in turn, led to a greater emphasis on the social impact of software, including reliability and safety.

Our ability to test more thoroughly has also improved. Despite the intractability of exhaustive testing, testing is still one of the most important ways in which we attempt to ensure software reliability. Testing procedures have developed so that it is often possible to automatically run many tests without human intervention. Even though exhaustive testing remains impractical, it is possible to devise tests, sometimes with automated tools, so that the most likely execution sequences are tested. Also, it is possible to test all of the program's instructions, even though not all sequences of instructions can be tested. Of course, the automated tools themselves could be faulty and introduce new problems. Testing is useful and important, but it can never be foolproof.

Some tests cannot be reasonably conducted because of the nature of the application. Software that initiates the self-destruct sequence of a rocket that has gone off course, for example, cannot be directly tested without actually having a rocket go off course. That is one place where creating a simulation of the system can be beneficial. The idea is straightforward: create a virtual rocket, much like might be done in a game, and launch that rocket under a number of environmental conditions, which are also simulated. Simulations can be used many times under a multitude of conditions. Particularly for control systems, simulations are extremely valuable. Of course, there are additional problems with using simulations. The simulation of computer systems, like the simulation of natural systems, may not accurately represent the system being simulated. Moreover, the simulation itself is commonly a complex program subject to errors. Hence, even if the simulation indicates that the system works perfectly, it could be that both the simulation and the software being tested are faulty. As with program testing, simulation testing, even after many hours of simulation, will not exhaust all of the possible ways the program could execute. Hence, there is still the possibility that something could go wrong. Simulations do, however, have a good track record, and software systems that have been extensively tested in simulations have been generally successful. For very critical systems, simulations often continue as long as the software is in use in the hope of finding a problem in the simulation before it occurs in the real system.

Maintenance of programs is another area where real progress has been made. Sometimes programs need to be updated because of new developments in the application environment. Sometimes, despite developers' best efforts, software fails. When it fails, it is important that the cause be identified and a remedy found. High-quality software requires a high-quality maintenance system for reporting, documenting, and correcting problems when they happen. Once a problem has been detected and a correction implemented, the testing needs to be done again. Sometimes, fixing one error creates a new one elsewhere in the system. It is therefore important that previous tests be repeated to be sure that no new problems have arisen.

Finally, real progress has been made in the way the people and tasks are organized to produce reliable software. We will explore that further in the following section.

## Reflection Questions

1. RESEARCH Make a list of three instances where, in your opinion, your safety could be affected by a faulty computer program. In each case, explain how you could potentially be harmed and whether you believe there is a real danger. Interview four to seven of your friends and determine whether their views are the same as yours.

2. POSITION Make a list of three instances where the same safety-critical task could be done by a computer or by a human. In each case, specify which one you trust more to protect your safety and explain why you think so.

3. POSITION Make the strongest argument you can that the world would be a safer place if computers completely replaced air traffic controllers.

## 5.5.2  The Software Development Process

Advances in software engineering are largely related to improvements in the software development process. It is common to think of software as being developed in a process that is similar to the way the program was developed in the chemical conference case described in Section 5.4. In such a process, a client hires a single programmer who then writes and tests the program according to that client's wishes. In reality, however, developing any commercial software system, and particularly safety-critical software systems, involves multiple tasks, which are usually performed by many different people. Frequently, specialists concentrate exclusively on one particular task, leaving other tasks to other specialists.

The major tasks of software development are as follows:

- Requirements—Literally what is required of the software. For large projects, specialists called "requirements engineers" interview clients to determine exactly what the system needs to do to best serve the clients. Had our student worker in Case 5.4 investigated the requirements of the system instead of simply accepting the assignment as given, the resulting program probably would have been much better. Requirements are commonly written in English (or other natural human language), specialized diagrams, and sometimes in formal mathematical notation.

- Specification and Design—Once the requirements of a system are established, designers develop the particular set of component program modules, or subprograms of the software system. Specifications are developed that describe what each module must do. Specifications, like requirements, are commonly expressed in natural human language sentences, diagrams, and formal mathematical notation.

- Implementation—Programmers then use the design to create code in an appropriate programming language. The program is considered a correct program when it matches the specification. When the specification is expressed in a formal mathematical notation, the correctness of the program may be established by an actual mathematical proof that demonstrates that the program matches the specification.

Testing typically occurs regularly as portions of the implementation are completed and proceeds throughout the lifetime of the software as discussed above. The philosophy of the modern development process is to prevent errors rather than discover them after they have occurred. That is the motivation behind the formal mathematical notations in requirements and specifications. Formal mathematical notation potentially allows a mathematical proof that the program matches its specifications. When a program works correctly in a test case, there could still be a bug. It is a maxim of programming that you cannot prove a program is correct by testing it. You can only prove it is incorrect. Formal proofs can in a sense prove that a program is correct, but such proofs are usually very difficult to achieve, and as we shall see shortly, also very expensive.

Note also that the word "correct" in this context means that the program matches a specification. A correctness proof for a program does not prove that the specification itself is correct. The specifications are based on requirements, which are derived largely through human communication. That is one of the reasons human communication is considered so important for reliable software.

One of the ways in which the overall software process has improved is to concentrate on human communication. In a typical software project, some people will work on more than one task, but some will work on only one. It is important then that the people working on one task communicate clearly with the people who will be working on a later task. In fact, communication is frequently cited as the most important aspect of software development.

Human communication is the basis of "Brooks's Law," which states, "Adding people to a late project makes it later." (1995) The reasoning is straightforward: adding people adds many new lines of communication and because the process requires reliable communication, the additional lines increase the chances of miscommunication or missed communication, leading to delays and a lack of reliability. Empirical evidence in recent years suggests that Brooks's Law is valid.

Advances in software engineering have been significant, but not nearly so dramatic as in computer hardware. Most advances in the techniques or tools for software involve a gain of five to thirty-five percent in productivity or reliability. That differs significantly from computer hardware. In fact, many of the gains in software techniques exist entirely because faster computers with more memory allow methods that previously were unthinkable. The two programming languages used most commonly fifty years ago, FORTRAN and COBOL, have much in common with the modern programming languages such as Java or C++. That's not to say that the differences between the old and new languages are insignificant, but they are not as great as the differences in the hardware of today compared to the hardware of fifty years ago. In the early 1960s, the biggest, most powerful commercially available computer in existence had 32K words of memory (32K is 32 times 1024). Today, many smart phones have over one million times that amount of memory.

## Reflection Questions

1. POSITION Many executives of software producing companies, as well as some famous computer scientists, have asserted that the most important skill needed by a software developer is an ability to communicate. Defend or refute that assertion.

2. APPLICATION Would more extensive testing of the software have been likely to prevent the Ariane 5 flight failure? Explain your reasoning.

3. POSITION Creators of pharmaceuticals must test their products before they can put their drugs on the market. They, like software developers, face daunting testing problems because of the enormous complexity of the human body. As with computer software, sometimes their tests fail to reveal a problem. Nevertheless, pharmaceuticals continue to play an important role in modern society. Which are more difficult to test, software systems or drugs? Explain your reasoning.

4. POSITION In the United States, pharmaceutical companies must submit test results to the Food and Drug Administration before a drug can enter the market. Would a similar approach be suitable for safety-critical software? Explain your reasoning.

5. APPLICATION We have mentioned some of the roles that are associated with a software development project. When safety-critical software is involved, which, if any, of those roles should be filled by professionals? Explain your reasoning.

### 5.5.3   Case: Therac-25

Probably the most well-known accidents to date caused by computer bugs are those accidents involving the Therac-25. The Therac-25, which we first introduced in Chapter 2, was a machine designed for cancer treatments, known as a medical linear accelerator. It was one of a series of such machines marketed by Atomic Energy of Canada Limited (AECL). The "25" designation referred to its power, which was substantially greater than its predecessors, the Therac-6 and the Therac-20. Unlike earlier versions in the series, the Therac-25 relied much more heavily on the machine's software for control and hence for safety. That reliance on software proved to have tragic consequences; there were six serious accidents involving the Therac-25. All six accidents seriously harmed patients, and three patients actually died directly because of the Therac-25.

The Therac-25 case has been described and analyzed in many places, most extensively by Nancy Leveson in her book, *Safeware: System Safety and Computers*. Although the Therac-25 case is not a recent one, it clearly illustrates some significant issues and merits close study.

### Reflection Questions

1. POSITION Suppose you had a choice of being x-rayed by an x-ray machine for which the x-ray dosage was set by computer software with input from an x-ray technician, or by a machine that had a set of dials and switches that were set by an x-ray technician. Which would you choose? Explain your reasoning.

2. POSITION Suppose you were going to be x-rayed by a machine where the x-ray dosage was set by computer software with input from an x-ray technician. If the dosage turned out to be wrong, where do you think the greater likelihood of error is: from incorrect input from the technician, or from the computer software? Explain your reasoning.

3. APPLICATION Suppose a new graduate in, say, economics, who had completed several courses in programming with good grades, was offered a job programming for a company that made x-ray machines. Suppose also that the first project for that person was to write a program

that controlled the dosage for a new x-ray machine. The new programmer would have sole responsibility for developing and testing the program.

a.  Would it be morally permissible for the new graduate to take that job? Explain.

b.  Would it be morally permissible for the company to offer the new graduate that job? Explain.

**5.5.3.1  Summary of the Accidents**    The first Therac-25 accident, a radiation overdose, occurred at the Kennestone Oncology Center in Marietta, Georgia in 1985. A middle-aged woman undergoing radiation therapy for breast cancer suffered a terrible burn in her shoulder. Although she reported severe pain (and her reaction was consistent with intense pain) and she reported a "blue flash" that she had been able to see though closed eyes, the attending physicians were simply unable to believe that the machine had burned her. The machine had worked many times before, and in their minds, simply could not have done that. One physician suggested that she had a mild radiation burn and recommended some salve to put on her skin problem. It was not a mild radiation burn, but a very serious radiation burn that had, in fact, effectively burned a hole through her shoulder. Radiation burns do not show up right away. In fact, it can take days or weeks for the true extent of the damage to become apparent. Hence it was some time before it became clear that the woman had been very seriously burned. By that time she had consulted a lawyer and had filed a lawsuit. She died in an automobile accident before her lawsuit was finished.

Less than two months after the first accident, another accident occurred involving the Therac-25. A woman was being treated for carcinoma of the cervix. She received a severe radiation burn to her hip. She died not very long thereafter, but her death was shown by the autopsy to have been caused by her cancer, not radiation. However, the autopsy also revealed that had she lived, she would have needed to have her hip replaced due to damage caused by the radiation burn (Leveson and Turner 23).

The following December, yet another radiation overdose occurred—this time in Yakima, Washington. Again, although the burn was severe, it was not fatal. In fact, the patient was still alive ten years later. The next three accidents, however, were all fatal overdoses. Two occurred in Tyler, Texas and another in Yakima, Washington. Ultimately, it was discovered that two separate software bugs caused these tragic radiation overdoses. As we shall see, however, programming errors only partially explained the problem.

Both inside and outside of AECL, people had such trust in the Therac-25 machine and its software that they discounted their own powers of observation. For example, in the first case, the medical staff at Kennestone were unable to accept the idea that the patient had suffered more than a minor radiation burn. Nevertheless one of Kennestone's medical physicists did call AECL to inquire if it were possible for the Therac-25 to operate in a way that would cause a radiation overdose, but AECL assured him that it was not, in fact, possible. The details of the accident were not reported to AECL or to the FDA, because the physicians in charge didn't even agree that an accident had occurred. Today, we still do not know the exact nature of the failure that burned the Therac-25's first victim.

### Reflection Questions

1. POSITION Make the strongest argument you can in support of the following position: The Therac-25 machine killed three people and injured three others. Although that is tragic, it is much less tragic than most passenger plane crashes, most passenger train wrecks, most ship sinkings, and even many automobile accidents, all of which usually involve more than three people. Hence, despite three human deaths, it is not really important enough to merit much study.

2. POSITION Make the strongest argument you can for the following position: Companies that produce safety-critical software are subject to expensive lawsuits if their software fails and harms someone. That threat is sufficient to motivate such companies to produce the best product possible.

3. POSITION Do you think the doctor who dismissed the first victim's radiation burn as minor behaved ethically? Explain your reasoning.

4. POSITION Do you think the physicist, who called AECL for confirmation that the Therac-25 could not have delivered a radiation overdose, behaved ethically? Explain your reasoning.

**5.5.3.2  Accountability and Moral Responsibility**  Professor Douglas Birsch of Shippensburg University is a well-known applied ethicist and author who analyzed the moral responsibilities of some key people in the Therac-25 case. He argues that, if we make reasonable assumptions about what the key people at AECL knew, or should have known, both the programmer who designed the software and the company's quality assurance officer bear significant moral responsibility for the accidents. (A quality assurance officer is the person responsible for the policies, personnel, and budget required to monitor and enforce a company's quality standards.) However, without more information about the accidents, Birsch explained, it is not possible to assess the exact degree of moral responsibility. Note that he doesn't argue that the programmer and the quality assurance officer bear legal responsibility; that is a matter for the courts.

Birsch identifies three criteria that must be met for a person to bear moral responsibility: "(1) The person's actions must have caused the harm, or been a significant causal factor. (2) The person must have intended or willed the harm, or it must be a result of his or her negligence, carelessness or recklessness. (3) The person must be able to have known, or must know the consequences of the action, or must have deliberately remained ignorant of them." (241)

For the sake of simplicity, let's focus solely on the moral responsibility of the programmer. Birsch argues that the Therac-25 programmer meets the criteria for moral responsibility. A paraphrase of his argument is as follows:

1. The programmer, as the person who wrote the software, made or at least allowed the software errors that directly caused the radiation overdoses.

2. The programmer, as the software expert, knew (or at least, ought to have known) that such a complex program could have bugs that were unlikely to be detected by testing. He should have notified management of that fact.

3. The programmer knew the machine was potentially lethal and understood the possible consequences of a software failure.

The problem with this analysis is that it does not adequately consider the context of the time. By today's standards, we need to consider several additional points:

1. The program was entirely developed by one person, working alone. Today this would be considered extremely poor programming practice.

2. The software contained elementary errors, indicating that the programmer lacked formal training. Today, software used to control such potentially dangerous equipment would not be developed by amateurs. In 1985, however, a great deal of the software in existence—probably most of it—had been developed by people without formal training in computer science or software engineering. Computer science is a very young discipline and software engineering even younger. Standards of software engineering had not yet become accepted practice in 1985. Indeed, the very term "software engineering" was not yet widely accepted as a meaningful term.

3. The programmer worked in an **assembly language**—a very low level language that is very similar to machine language. Using assembly language was a decision that was dependent upon the time the software was developed. At that time, there really weren't any other good options, because, although some high-level languages did exist for the computer being used, they did not allow the programmer direct access to the machine's components so that the computer could directly control the linear accelerator. And even if they had been available, the real-time constraints of the Therac machines required such a high degree of efficiency, only an assembly language program was feasible.

4. The Therac-20 software was reused almost intact in the Therac-25 because it appeared to be error free. The Therac-20 software had a good record for reliability, but part of that reputation was unearned. Later, it was learned that the software in the Therac-20 had sometimes failed, but because the hardware safeguards had done their work properly, no accidents occurred. No one even realized a software failure occurred. However, in the Therac-25, the hardware safeguard features were omitted, leaving the software entirely responsible for all safety issues. Safety was delegated entirely to the software because of its perfect record for safety. Because the "perfect" record of that

software was an illusion, accidents were inevitable. In 1985, the entire discipline of computing was still quite new and its practitioners did not have a firm grasp on the complexity of software systems. Today, when developing safety-critical systems, software engineers would consider it foolish to remove hardware safeguards and rely entirely on software for safety.

Although we do not know much about the programmer who programmed the Therac-25, we do know that he was not working by today's standards, because they did not yet exist. We think it is likely that the programmer was quite confident that his software was correct. Today, few programmers would have such confidence; we know a great deal more about the pitfalls of producing the kind of software used in the Therac-25. It is therefore likely that, while the programmer might bear some moral responsibility, his transgression was more likely to be hubris than negligence. It is plausible that he simply had no way of knowing what he did know and did not know about the system he was developing.

### Reflection Questions

1. APPLICATION Did anyone involved in the Therac-25 accidents behave in an immoral way? Explain your reasoning.

2. APPLICATION Did anyone involved in the Therac-25 accidents behave in an unethical way? Explain your reasoning.

3. POSITION What, if anything, should have happened to the programmer who programmed the Therac-25? Explain your reasoning.

4. RESEARCH Read Birsch's arguments concerning the moral responsibility of AECL's quality assurance officer. Make the best argument you can that Birsch's analysis is correct.

5. RESEARCH Our discussion of the Therac-25 case did not touch on the error messages issued by the machine and the way the operators dealt with them. Consult accounts of the Therac-25 case and explain how communication problems associated with the error messages contributed to the problem.

6. POSITION Suppose you are the supreme ruler of the world and you wish to dispense justice in the Therac-25 case. You are not concerned with legal issues, because your powers are absolute. Who, if anyone, involved with any of the Therac-25 accidents would you punish and with what punishment? Explain your reasoning.

### 5.5.4 Lessons Learned

The Therac-25 case is just one example among many of the dangers of an over-reliance on computers. (Look back to Chapter 2 and the recall of 300,000 Prius hybrids by Toyota for another good example.) The Therac-25 case is also an example, and to some extent a cause, of how methods, abilities, and attitudes of the people involved in software development have changed. Finally the Therac-25 case is an example of how people, despite considerable evidence to the contrary, are willing to trust a computer despite serious risks.

The way the software for the Therac-25 was developed was fairly typical of that time. Programmers often wrote important code in assembly language and often preferred it to languages that were safer. Efficiency of the program, in terms of how rapidly it executed and how much memory it used, was of paramount importance and programmers believed that their ingenuity was more than adequate to deal with the complexities of programming and debugging. It was also common, as in the Therac-25 case, for a lone programmer to complete an entire system and to be the only person to understand the program fully. It was also common for that one person to ultimately discover that he or she really did not in fact understand the program. That meant no one, in reality, understood the program. Such was the situation with the Therac-25 software.

The Therac-25 disaster, along with other famous computer system failures, have led to major changes in the way we produce software, particularly safety-critical software. The potential for future disasters has not, however, been eliminated. The hazards of computer failures are real, and as computer systems continue to grow, the complexity of those systems also continues to grow.

The way various people reacted when the first accidents occurred was also fairly typical of that time. The belief that the Therac-25 was controlled by a computer, and so simply could not do the things it seemed to be doing, was so strong that even when it should have been clear that the machine was malfunctioning, people in charge denied that anything was wrong. That attitude has diminished in many respects, but certainly is not gone. We rely on computers more and more each year, and each year additional questions arise as to whether computers can really be trusted.

The Therac-25 accidents are important for programmers and developers to study because they revealed a misplaced confidence by software developers in their ability to produce reliable software. The accidents, and their subsequent investigations, revealed that the explosion in software development occurring at that time was creating thousands of applications that could potentially harm people and it was not obvious that we were capable of containing the risks. Although many software failures contributed to the grave concern over risks to the public due to faulty software, the Therac-25 accidents were the first to actually take human lives. That provided a strong incentive for the entire computer industry to change direction. The famous computer scientist, C. A. R. Hoare, who argued fiercely for a more disciplined approach to software development, had in 1980 pointed out in his Turing Award lecture, "There are two ways of constructing a software design. One way is to make it so simple that there are obviously no deficiencies. And the other way is to make it so complicated that there are no obvious deficiencies." The Therac-25 software was the epitome of the second way, and it revealed the potential dire consequences of that way. The software in the Therac-25, although seemingly fully tested by actual use and fully reliable, was in reality a time bomb. No one knew for sure how many other such unpleasant surprises awaited the public from software with no obvious deficiencies.

### Reflection Questions

1. APPLICATION The way in which the Therac-25 software was developed probably contributed to the errors. Describe how the Therac-25 software development process differed from current software engineering practices for safety-critical software. For each difference, explain why you do or do not think that contributed to the accidents.

2. RESEARCH Consult the literature on the Therac-25 case to identify the kinds of bugs in the Therac-25 software and the effects they produced. Discuss how the AECL should have responded to those bugs.

3. APPLICATION Using Douglas Birsch's criteria for moral responsibility, evaluate the moral responsibility of the team that created the faulty software that caused the Ariane 5 Flight 501 accident.

4. APPLICATION What software do you encounter in your life that could be hazardous to you if it were to malfunction? List at least three kinds of software and the hazards associated with each.

5. POSITION Should safety-critical software be regulated? If so, why? What sort of regulation do you suggest, and who should do it? If it should not be regulated, why not?

## 5.6  CASE: A&P'S CASH REGISTER SCANDAL

In 1974, a scandal occurred in New York City at the A&P Supermarket at 220 East 46th Street. Inspectors from the New York City Department of Consumer Affairs alleged that the cash registers in the markets systematically overcharged customers when the number of items purchased and the total bill for the purchases was larger than a specified amount.

The scam depended on the fact that people trusted computers (in this case, computers in the form of programmed cash registers) to add correctly and that therefore the added amount would not be noticed. Very few people would actually add the numbers to see if the total bill was correct. Ultimately, the manager and two part-time checkers were fired. The allegations were that the manager had programmed the registers so that if the amount of a purchase was greater than a certain amount, the total would be increased by an additional percentage. The reasons for the checkers being fired were not specified. The manager, at least in his public statements, insisted he knew nothing of such a scheme, and that he had no awareness of the registers overcharging anyone.

Stuart Baur (1974), writing for *New York Magazine*, suggested that the store manager might have been innocent, and that only the checkers deserved the blame. Baur had observed checkers at a different market surreptitiously preventing the register from closing a small transaction after a customer had paid. The checker then retained the transaction amount as a subtotal which was then added to the total of the next person in line. The additional charge, however, would not appear on the second person's receipt; only the items the person had actually bought appeared on the receipt. Unless the customer actually mentally added up all the items on the receipt, she wouldn't notice that the total was actually higher than it should have been. Without noticing the error, the second customer would pay the inflated total, allowing the checker to pocket the money paid by the first customer. Because the second person's payment would go into the register, everything balanced at the end of the day. By zeroing in on pairs of customers in which the first had a small order and the next had both a large order and some sort of distraction, such as a cranky child, the checker could proceed with the deception unnoticed.

In the A&P case, we don't know whether the manager was guilty, or if checkers were using a scam like the one observed by Baur. No public disclosure was given concerning the final dispensation of the case. Note, however, that the overcharges, no matter who perpetrated the scam, were possible only because customers trusted that the addition performed by a computer was correct. In both cases, if the customer had checked the items on the receipt against the actual purchase, everything would have matched. To detect the overcharge, the overcharged customer would have to add up all the charges and compare it to the total on the receipt. Except for the occasional calculating prodigy, most people would find that too difficult to accomplish in a busy checkout line at a grocery store. And besides, most people assume that the computer in a cash register adds numbers correctly.

## Reflection Questions

1. APPLICATION The A&P scam was possible only because people trusted a computer to do arithmetic correctly. It worked only because people accepted the computer's addition without actually checking it. What occasions can you think of where you accept a computer's arithmetic without checking it? (List several.) Should you?

2. RESEARCH Because computers are so good at adding, one way in which people think computers could be used is to count votes in an election. Do some research and make a list of the pros and cons of using computers for this purpose. Do you think it is that a good idea? Why or why not?

3. CONTEXT Suppose you had a long grocery bill and for some reason you decide to add up the prices of the individual items by hand. Suppose further that your answer is considerably more than the total on the bill you paid. You add them again, adding the individual prices in a different order from your last addition. Suppose you got the same answer as before. Would you assume that you had added incorrectly, or would you assume that the computer had added incorrectly? How, if at all, does your evaluation of the computer's reliability compare to the doctors at Kennestone who assumed the Therac-25 could not have given the patient a radiation overdose?

## 5.7 MALWARE

**Malware** is short for "malicious software." It can take many forms. The most prevalent types are:

- **Worm**—A program that makes copies of itself and propagates those copies through a network to infect other computers.

- **Virus**—Malware that is similar to a worm, but which resides in another program. That program must execute in order for the virus to propagate itself. The term "virus" is sometimes used as a general term for malware, but that is not the way it is used by computer professionals.

- **Spyware**—A computer program that is secretly installed for the purpose of collecting information about the computer's user or users.

- **Trojan horse**—A piece of software that masquerades as an innocent, and perhaps useful, program, but that is actually designed for a malicious purpose.

- **Rootkit**—A program that embeds itself into a computer's operating system and acquires special privileges that would normally be available to the operating system. For example, when you first log on to your system, it is the operating system that asks you for your password. It similarly decides whether the password you provide is the correct one. A rootkit, once installed, could potentially override the authority of the operating system, gaining access to your password and all of your files. You may recall that we first saw an example of the use of a rootkit in Section 4.1, where Sony BMG used it to monitor the use of music files.

The people who write and deploy malware are commonly called **hackers** and the activity of doing it is called **hacking**. The term "hacker" today generally has a negative connotation. However, especially among older practitioners, "hackers" and "hacking" have dual meanings. Originally, it was a common term for discovering some way to work around a problem. Good hackers were therefore simply people who were good at problem solving via programming. The older meaning seems to be fading fast and most people today use the term to describe someone who uses computer knowledge for unethical purposes.

The ethical implications of malware are generally straightforward. That we call it "malware," indicating malice, has direct moral and ethical implications. There are, however, complications, and in some contexts the issue is far from clear. Often, the people who are creating and deploying malware do not consider themselves to be malicious, and sometimes the particular context of their actions allows for strong arguments on their behalf. It is clearly immoral in most contexts for a person to vandalize another person's property, to steal from another person by illegally using that person's credit card, to trick people into hurting themselves, or to spy on a person. However, ethical debates concerning particular uses of malware do arise. We explore these next.

### 5.7.1 Ethical Hacking

Some people have legitimate jobs in which they are paid to break into systems by the people who own the systems. These people are sometimes called "white hat hackers;" their goal is to seek out vulnerabilities so they can be removed before a malicious intruder discovers them and launches an attack. The team of people involved in this activity are sometimes called a "tiger team" or a "red team." This activity raises some ethical and legal issues:

- Hiring a team of hackers is always a risk, because it's possible that, despite the team's supposedly legitimate intentions, some or all members of the team may actually have illegitimate goals. If the hired hackers get caught doing something that appears unethical, they can claim that they were merely "doing their jobs." Particularly problematic are cases where the ethical hacker is, in fact, a person who was previously convicted of illegal hacking, who has been hired because of his or her ability to gain unauthorized entry into private systems.

- Sometimes even legitimate hacking necessarily violates the law. For example, in one case, a bank employee who had transferred away from his tiger team decided to check that the security measures instituted by his group were still sound. They appeared to be inadequate. He broke into the system and immediately notified the tiger team of the vulnerability. However, new security measures had identified him as an intruder, and because he no longer had legal authority to crack the system, he had broken the law. He was arrested and spent some time in jail before eventually being released. Although there are generally exceptions for hacking with permission of the system owners, networks today cross state boundaries and even national boundaries, making the legal issues murky at best.

- The education and training of ethical hackers is controversial. The proponents of teaching ethical hacking argue that learning the techniques of hacking better equips a person for preventing hacking. Opponents argue that teaching hacking skills is in effect teaching someone how to be a criminal. They also argue that teaching people to hack does not make them good at preventing hacking, any more than teaching people to bat makes them better pitchers.

The methods employed by white hat hackers are the same as those employed by other hackers. Their methods sometimes rely on technical expertise, sometimes on exploitation of human weaknesses, sometimes on trickery similar to that employed by con artists, and sometimes on direct physical force.

The rootkit that we encountered in Chapter 4 was a good example of using technical knowledge to gain access to the inner workings of a computer system. Such vulnerabilities are common in complex software, and hackers are constantly trying to find them. Frequently, when a potential vulnerability is discovered, the person who discovers it does not actually exploit the vulnerability but instead makes the information public. There are even Web sites devoted to providing such information so that would-be hackers can attempt to devise a way to exploit known vulnerabilities. Similarly, when companies discover vulnerabilities in their computer systems, they naturally want to keep that information secret until they can remove the vulnerabilities. Each day that goes by after the vulnerability is discovered increases the probability that it will be exploited. Most often, when hackers attack, they exploit vulnerabilities that have been previously discovered. An attack that exploits a previously unidentified vulnerability is known as a **day zero attack** or a **zero day attack**. Zero day attacks are commonly the most dangerous and unexpected.

One of the most common ways of exploiting human weaknesses is a **phishing scam** which attempts to fool or frighten a person into revealing key information. For example, one such scam that is very common occurs on college campuses each fall shortly after the arrival of new students. The scam is an e-mail that claims to be from the school's IT department indicating that something is wrong with the student's e-mail account. Usually some sort of jargon cites some sort of error code, regulation, or security hazard. The student is instructed to click a Web link, which opens a Web page that requests the e-mail address and password. Students who comply, of course, give the hacker access to their account. More sophisticated schemes mimic the Web site of a bank or some other well-known business. For example, an e-mail might suggest a problem with an account and provide a link to the phony site. When the victim logs into the bogus site, the password and user identification are stored for future use by the criminal. The victim is then asked to verify some minor matter and given a message that everything has been properly reconciled. Frequently the victim will leave the site without ever realizing that he or she has just been scammed.

Sometimes a hack is simply human trickery. For example, a respectable-looking person might show up at the reception area of a corporation with a flash drive that he claims to have found in the parking lot. In such a case, a receptionist might think nothing of inserting the flash drive in her computer to review the file list, so she could figure out to whom the flash drive belongs. If the perpetrator loaded the flash drive with temptingly named files (such as "Upcoming Layoffs" or "Salary Comparisons") it's very likely that receptionist might be unable to resist the urge to open at least one. If the file she opens contains a virus, the company's computing environment might become infected.

Physical attacks may involve breaking and entering or may be associated with some sort of listening device or camera. For example, in one case, a cable to a server was accessed in an elevator shaft and the electronic traffic was recorded, resulting in many stolen passwords. In an even more straightforward case, intruders used a crowbar to pry open office doors and steal the computers and all the information they contained.

### Reflection Questions

1.   POSITION   Suppose you discovered your local bank used a former safe cracker and bank robber to try to break into the building so that they could monitor and maintain the bank's physical security. Would you consider that a positive or negative aspect of doing business with that bank? Why or why not?

2.  APPLICATION Another group of hackers, who consider themselves ethical, write worms or viruses that perform some kind of beneficial task. For example, such a hacker may write a worm that will seek out a particular vulnerability in an operating system, fix the problem, and then destroy itself. Are these hackers really acting in an ethical manner? Explain.

3.  POSITION Suppose your university was considering offering a course on ethical hacking. Under what circumstances, if any, would you consider that appropriate for your university?

4.  POSITION Hackers sometimes take over systems that are not properly maintained and that therefore lack security safeguards. Unknown to the system's owner, the hacker's software takes up residence on the system. Such infiltrated systems are called zombies. Zombies are useful to hackers who are distributing malware because it makes it hard to trace the malware back to the hackers. Suppose your machine became a zombie and a hacker used your machine as a launch site for malware. What is your moral responsibility for the harm caused by that malware?

5.  APPLICATION Suppose you discover a vulnerability in an operating system. Although you notified the vendor, they have not, so far as you can tell, done anything about it. In order to call attention to the issue, you post the vulnerability on the Internet so that the information becomes public to the people who tend to exploit such vulnerabilities. Is your action moral? Is your action ethical? Explain.

6.  APPLICATION Suppose you have posted a vulnerability on the Internet. A teenage hacker writes an exploit that uses that vulnerability to destroy files on a system with that vulnerability. Unfortunately, the virus created by the teenager destroys some key files in a manufacturing control system which causes thousands of dollars' worth of damage to the manufacturing facility. Do you have any moral responsibility for that damage? Explain.

## 5.7.2   Case: Stuxnet Worm

The Stuxnet worm has been in the news a lot recently, but you might not be familiar with the worm's name, as it is often not included in the news stories on the subject. Stuxnet is a computer worm that has significantly set back the Iranian nuclear development program. It is an extremely sophisticated piece of software, and in fact, is so sophisticated that many experts believe that it could have been developed only by a nation state. A common speculation is that the CIA and the Israeli government jointly developed the worm. Its sophistication is manifest in various ways:

- The worm attacked three different operating systems, including Windows.

- There were four (an unprecedented number) instances of a zero day attack for Windows systems.

- In addition to the above exploits, the worm also exploited other previously identified, vulnerabilities, and included a Windows rootkit.

- It was a very large worm, consisting of over 500,000 bytes of programming.

- The worm was very specific in its target. Although it would propagate indiscriminately, through removable memory devices such as USB Flash drives, it would unleash its attack only on Siemens Supervisory Control And Data Acquisition (SCADA) systems, which were used in the centrifuges in Iran's nuclear program. The attack included a **man-in-the-middle** capability that ensured that, after the worm caused the centrifuges to malfunction, it replaced the signals drawing attention to the problem with signals that all was well, so that the centrifuges were not shut down until they were destroyed. Although detailed information is not available, it appears that approximately one thousand centrifuges were destroyed by the worm. Moreover, so many systems were infected that it is not clear that the problem is over for the Iranians.

- The worm was released in several variants to explicitly attack five different sites in Iran.

At the time of this writing, the Stuxnet worm is clearly the most sophisticated worm to date. The kinds of sophistication involve expertise in computer software, but also expertise in industrial processes, not to mention detailed knowledge of Iran's nuclear program. The computers infected in Iran were not connected to the Internet, so it's clear that various clever methods had to be employed to infect them with the virus. It seems that a large team of experts would be necessary to have created such a sophisticated piece of software. Hence, the assertion that this is an instance of "cyber warfare" seems warranted.

### Reflection Questions

1. CONTEXT It is likely that the people who wrote the Stuxnet worm consider themselves ethical hackers. Are they? Why or why not?

2. CONTEXT Suppose the Stuxnet worm, instead of just destroying centrifuges, had caused some other sort of damage that had taken human lives. Would that affect whether the people who created and deployed the worm were ethical hackers? Explain.

3. CONTEXT Suppose that, despite all appearances, the author of the Stuxnet worm was actually someone working independently living in the United States. Would that person be an ethical hacker? Explain.

4. CONTEXT Suppose that, despite all appearances, the author of the Stuxnet worm was actually a person working independently living in Iran. Would that person be an ethical hacker?

5. APPLICATION Suppose the Stuxnet worm, although it appeared to be explicitly targeted to Iran, caused major damage in other countries. Would the creators of the worm bear moral responsibility for that damage? Explain.

## 5.8  PUBLIC TRUST

Some computing systems potentially have a wide spread impact across our entire society. Here we will consider three examples. Our first example illustrates some of the problems and expenses associated with implementing safety-critical software. Our second topic, concerning election technology, examines software that, while not safety-critical, is of great societal importance. Finally we explore how computers can actually entice us into overuse.

### 5.8.1  Nuclear Shutdown System

The Darlington Nuclear Generating Station near Toronto was the first Canadian nuclear station to use computers to run the emergency shutdown systems for its reactors. Two independent shutdown systems were planned, each with its own program, to monitor various parameters of the plant's operation and to shut down the four selected reactors if safety required it. Shutting down a reactor would require software, rather than a human, to control the switches and devices. Each of the two programs required around ten thousand lines of code, which by current standards is not particularly large. Moreover, the programs were relatively simple compared to many other control programs.

The programming itself went smoothly. However, after the programming was finished, Ontario Hydro, the company that owned the plant, faced an uphill battle convincing the Atomic Energy Control Board (AECB), Canada's federal regulatory agency for nuclear power plants, that the programs were reliable. The process required more time that the original programming effort and was very costly.

The AECB first ruled that the programs were so complex that determining their correctness by simply examining the code was impossible. The board then consulted David L. Parnas, a leading software engineer, to evaluate the programs. Parnas was well known as a software expert and for his outspoken criticism of other software projects, including the Strategic Defense Initiative, perhaps better known as the Star Wars Project, which was a United States defense system for intercepting intercontinental ballistic missiles.

In Parnas's initial evaluation, he indicated that he could not possibly assert definitively whether the programs were correct. He suggested a major effort at documenting the requirements and specifications of the programs so that the program code could be compared to those specifications. This turned out to be an outstanding example of the problem faced by experts, in this case nuclear engineers, attempting to communicate unambiguously with each other and with officials in a regulatory agency.

Although Parnas could not reveal specific aspects of the programs' specification, he was later able to make up a fictitious example that he said was analogous to the problems in the specification: "Shut off the pumps if the water level remains above one hundred meters for more than four seconds." Although most of us would probably think the meaning of this sentence is clear, Parnas pointed out that it becomes difficult to interpret in a situation in which the water level varies during a four second span. Parnas thought up three different interpretations that depended on how one calculated the average water level. He discovered, however, that the programmers had not used any of his three interpretations when creating the programs. Instead, they had implemented a system that would be consistent with an entirely different interpretation, as follows: "Shut off the pumps if the minimum water level over the past four seconds was above one hundred meters." That interpretation would be very different in practice if the water was moving in large waves, as might happen, for example, in an earthquake.

Parnas's critique convinced the AECB to require a complete software review, including new documentation for the requirements and formal specifications. (Recall from Section 5.5 that by formal specification, we mean precise mathematical models of the specification of the requirements in addition to the English statements that were provided as part of the standard specification.) Parnas also insisted that the system undergo random testing, with input data selected according to statistical models for the kind of data the programs were designed to process. He argued for random data instead of made-up data because, he said, when people make up data they are likely to overlook the same issues that the programmers overlooked when writing the program. Hence, input that would cause a problem might not really be tested. As a general rule, random sampling avoids the psychological blind spots to which humans are prone. After numerous additional analyses of the programs and after additional testing, some minor errors were found and corrected, but neither Parnas nor the AECB were convinced of the programs' reliability. Ultimately, the AECB required a thorough formal mathematical verification of the programs. That kind of verification is extremely difficult and can also be very tedious for the people involved in the process. Hundreds of ambiguities, omissions, and errors were ultimately found, virtually all of them harmless. The formal verification process took an extra year.

Ultimately, the power plant was licensed and began operation. It is not clear that the additional efforts prevented a future failure, but it is clear that, at this point, the AECB had legitimate reason to trust that the programs were reliable. However, the story was not really over. Although the AECB was confident that the programs, in their current state, were reliable, the organization was concerned about the potential effect of future changes to the programs. Thus, the AECB ruled that the programs should be redesigned so that future changes would be easier to check for bugs or weaknesses. Before the redesign could begin, however, the AECB needed to develop standards for specifying safety-critical programs so that the redesigned programs would meet standards for safety and also for modification.

### Reflection Questions

1. **POSITION** The programmers who wrote the shutdown programs were nuclear engineers rather than software engineers. They therefore knew much more about nuclear power plants than do typical software engineers. David Parnas was a software engineer who was not particularly knowledgeable about nuclear engineering. Yet the AECB generally followed David Parnas's advice about the reliability of the

software rather than the advice the nuclear engineers. Was that the right decision? Explain your reasoning.

2. POSITION The shutdown programs were written by nuclear engineers who knew how to program. Hence, they were experts in the domain of the application for which the program was intended. In general, is it better to have experts on a particular technology write safety-critical programs or to have software engineers write them? Explain your reasoning.

3. APPLICATION Writing detailed specifications of anything in English can be very difficult. As an exercise in understanding the difficulty of exact specification of something you know well, try to write a complete specification that differentiates a can from a box. Once you have your specification, switch specifications with another student and try to test his or her specification by thinking of all the possible examples of cans and boxes and determining whether the specification successfully differentiates the two concepts.

4. APPLICATION The shutdown programs were programs that could affect many lives if they failed to perform their tasks properly. No doubt, that was one reason the AECB insisted upon expensive and time-consuming measures to maximize their reliability. Make the best argument you can that the AECB was correct in its decision to require a rigorous mathematical verification of the programs.

5. APPLICATION The shutdown programs were programs that could affect many lives if they failed to perform their tasks properly. No doubt, that was one reason the AECB insisted upon expensive and time consuming measures to maximize their reliability. Some, however, argue that the decision of the AECB was overkill and simply made the software much more expensive—which in turn, would ultimately make nuclear power more expensive. Make the best argument you can that these critics are correct.

## 5.8.2 Elections and Voting Technology

Counting votes is something you would expect computers to be very good at. Especially since the election of 2000, it also seems as though the United States has a need for better technology for vote counting. Counting votes obviously is not a safety-critical task, but equally as obvious, it is one of enormous importance. If computers are going to perform such an important task, the reliability of the software that does that task has reliability constraints similar to safety-critical systems. Unlike most safety-critical systems, there is a clear danger of the system being attacked by people who either wish to disrupt the election or to determine the winner. In this section, we will discuss the election of 2000, where technology failed in more than one way. We will then present a case of where a voting machine was hacked by some white-hat hackers for the purpose of exposing the machine's vulnerabilities and the dangers it posed to the integrity of any election using it.

**5.8.2.1  Case: The 2000 Presidential Election**   The presidential election of 2000 was an extremely close one between then-Vice President Al Gore and George W. Bush. Ultimately, because of the way presidents are elected in the United States, the winner of the election came down to whoever would be the winner of the popular vote in the state of Florida. When we cast our votes in a presidential election, we do not actually vote for any of the presidential candidates, but rather vote for an elector who pledges to vote for a particular candidate. Those electors ultimately cast their votes, called electoral votes, in the real election that occurs well after what we think of as Election Day. Each state has as many electors as it has representatives in Congress–two for its two senators and one for each member of the House of Representatives. All the states except Maine and Nebraska appoint their electors for the winner of the popular vote in the state. Hence, the winner of the popular vote in Florida would win all twenty-five of Florida's electoral votes, and that would decide the winner. The vote in Florida was so close that it was difficult to tell, even days afterwards, who had won. On election night, television news anchors declared Gore the winner, then Bush, then declared the election too close to call. At one point, Al Gore actually called George W. Bush to concede, but then retracted his concession. The political pundits were in no better position to determine the results than was the news media. Ultimately, the U.S. Supreme Court became involved. One of its decisions effectively decided the election with certainty and on December 13, 2000, over a month after election night, Al Gore conceded to George W. Bush in a televised speech. George W. Bush had won the election in Florida, and hence the nation, by 537 votes. Technology played a significant role in both the reporting of the results by the news media and in some of the problems with counting the vote. We shall look at each of these issues.

The news media uses statistical models and exit polls to predict the result of an election. We are all familiar with the map where the states are all colored gray until a winner is declared and then it usually becomes red or blue depending on the party of the winning candidate. Frequently, winners are declared when only a small portion of the actual vote has been counted; until the election of 2000, the media was almost always right when they declared a winner. In the 2000 election, however, a number of factors caused the projections of the news stations to be inaccurate. Every major news network made bad projections on that night until eventually all networks called the election as undecided. Although there were a number of factors contributing to the confusion and incorrect reporting, here we will focus only on the technological issues. In particular, we consider the problems with the punch card technology used in Florida and its apparent failure to correctly record all of the votes cast.

On election night in Florida in the 2000 election, the discrepancy between exit polls and the actual reported count was particularly large. One reason was that many ballots were declared invalid. In Florida, voters used a small pin to punch a hole in a card in the right place to indicate their preferred candidate. The hole is a little square piece of the card, called a chad, that is attached at its four corners. When a voter pushes a voting pin into the indicated place for his or her candidate, the chad is detached, allowing a laser to later scan the card and record the vote. If the voter does not punch the card firmly, the chad may not detach fully and the card reader cannot record a vote for that ballot.

When election night ended in what was essentially a tie, a manual recount was started. There were many problems with the recount, in part because Florida law did not specify an objective criterion for declaring a ballot valid, but rather indicated that hand recounts should count ballots whenever it was possible discern "the voter's intent." There was no clear consensus as to what constituted a reasonable way to do that. For example, if a chad was detached at three of the four corners, it seems reasonable that the voter had intended to punch out that chad. If, on the other hand, a chad still had all four corners attached but there was an indentation in the chad, should that indicate a voter's intention to punch that chad? Eventually, the contention over what ballots would be recounted and how they should be counted resulted in a legal battle that involved a number of court cases, some in the Florida Supreme Court and some in the United States Supreme Court. The final decision that settled the matter was issued on December 12, when the court ruled that the manual recounts ordered by the Florida Supreme Court violated the equal protection clause of the United States Constitution because the standard was too vague and would lead to inconsistent counts in different districts. The following day, Al Gore conceded the election.

## Reflection Questions

1. POSITION Had the Florida ballot been recorded and counted electronically, there could not be any problems with partially-detached chads. There could, of course, be problems with the electronic recording and counting. Would recording and counting the vote electronically be superior to the punched card ballot? Explain your reasoning.

2. APPLICATION Had the Florida ballot been recorded with indelible ink on a paper ballot, there could not be any problems with partially-detached chads. Would recording votes on paper ballots, and then counting those ballots by hand, therefore be superior to the punched card ballot? Explain your reasoning.

3. POSITION Should news reporters be ethically required to wait until a candidate has been officially declared a winner before declaring a winner in the news media? Explain your reasoning.

**5.8.2.2 Case: Hacking The Diebold Voting Machine** One way Congress reacted to the 2000 Election was by passing the Help America Vote Act of 2002. That act, among other things, provided funding for states to modernize their voting systems and eliminate punch card and lever systems. One of the more obvious approaches was to consider some form of electronic voting system, and computers were naturally considered one of the better possibilities. There were obvious risks with using computers, particularly in view of the strong motivation of people to subvert the systems. For example, any person or group who wanted to disrupt the democratic process might use hacking in an attempt to prevent the machines from recording votes or to destroy the record of votes already cast. A person or group might attempt to hack the machine to record votes incorrectly to favor a particular candidate. Hence any computerized voting system would necessarily have to have very robust security measures as well as rigorous audit procedures so as to guarantee a correct vote count. Not only must the systems be secure, the voting public needs to believe they are secure in order to have confidence in the process. Those are formidable challenges.

As an example of just how difficult the problem is, consider one of the leading computerized voting machines, the Diebold AccuVote-TS and its successor, the Diebold AccuVote-TSx. Those machines were used in real elections, and by September of 2006 were the most widely used electronic voting machine in the United States. A number of computer scientists had expressed alarm at the rapid proliferation of computerized voting machines, claiming that they were not sufficiently secure. Their concerns were convincingly confirmed by a research group at Princeton University. The Princeton group's research showed that someone who was alone with the machine for only two or three minutes could install malware on the machines. The following is a paraphrase of their main findings:

1.  The installed malware, installed on a single machine, can steal votes without leaving any evidence of the hack. Audit trails would indicate that the tally was entirely correct.

2.  Anyone who had physical access to the machine could install the malware in two or three minutes. With a little practice, it could actually be done in less than one minute.

3.  While installing the malware, it is equally easy to install a virus on the memory card of the machine. That allows the malware to be transmitted to other machines when the memory cards are used to update the machines and so the malware is likely to infect all of the machines in the voting precinct.

4.  In order to prevent the kind of hack used by the Princeton group, Diebold would need to make changes in the hardware and new election procedures would have to be adopted. (Feldman, Halderman, and Felten 2006)

In addition to their paper, the Princeton group produced a video that illustrated how quickly the malware could be installed. The video is available at *http://citp.princeton.edu/voting*.

The hack used by the Princeton research group required physically breaking into the voting machine. They reported, and their video clearly demonstrated, that breaking into the machine was very easy and could be done very quickly. Once the machine had been opened, they simply installed the malware. Any printing or querying of the vote tally, or any portion of the vote tally, was performed by the machine's software. Hence, corrupting the software corrupted the tally. And further, any audit of the voting records would likewise not show any irregularities. In principle, one could contact all of the voters and ask how they voted, but that method is 1) not practical, and 2) would violate the voter's right to cast a secret ballot.

The video, once posted on the Web, became quite famous and surely influenced Diebold and other makers of voting machines to immediately address the issues raised. Perhaps even more importantly, it made a large portion of the general public very aware of the risks associated with voting machines with inadequate means of maintaining a secure and accurate audit track.

Despite the negative findings of the Princeton group's research, the researchers believed that a secure voting system could be devised. Such a secure system would have to integrate appropriate hardware security measures, paper audit trails, and a variety of other safeguards.

### Reflection Questions

1. POSITION View the video that demonstrates the hack created by the Princeton group. Was their action of placing that video on the Internet a morally permissible action? Explain your reasoning.

2. APPLICATION The hack shown in the Princeton video required physical access to the machine after it had been deployed. From what you know of the software development process, are there other people who, if malicious, might be in a position to tamper with voting results from those machines? Explain your reasoning.

3. RESEARCH Determine and describe the voting technology used in your state.

## 5.8.3   The Opponents of Microsoft PowerPoint

In Switzerland, the Anti-PowerPoint Political Party (APPP) is attempting to get a referendum on the ballot to ban PowerPoint and possibly other presentation software. As of this writing, the APPP is circulating petitions, and if it can get 100,000 signatures, the issue will be voted on in a national referendum. The APPP claims that PowerPoint costs Swiss citizens about two and one half billion dollars each year in wasted time, arguing that 85% of the people who attend PowerPoint presentations are bored and get nothing out of them.

Matthias Poehm, the leader of the APPP, expresses an interesting moral position, "I don't want to be right, I only want the best result." The best result, according to his argument, is to ban PowerPoint and to use other presentation methods, such as flip charts, which he says are more engaging and less wasteful of the audience's time.

Matthias Poehm is not the only opponent of PowerPoint presentations. Edward Tufte, noted statistician, artist, graphic designer, and computer scientist, believes that the cultural effect of PowerPoint presentations weaken both verbal and spatial reasoning. Unlike Matthias Poehm, Edward Tufte does not argue that PowerPoint should be banned. Tufte's position is that it should be avoided as a means of delivering important information, especially quantitative information. His position is that presentation software, because of the way it presents information hierarchically, strongly encourages people to use only that one architecture of knowledge. That is, information is presented in categories, which are then each divided into subcategories, and so on. All of this is due to the fact that it is extremely easy, in PowerPoint, to compress information into bullet points which are divided further into more bullet points.

Tufte argues that the "slideware" view of presenting information reduces our ability to really understand the material presented. He also argues that the way of thinking fostered by PowerPoint presentations contributed significantly to the destruction of the Space Shuttle Columbia. In his essay on the topic, he focuses on one slide in particular, which he asserts presented a catastrophic misrepresentation of the truth. The slide described a piece of debris that damaged Columbia's heat shield. According to Tufte, the slide obscured the grave danger that such damage posed to Columbia. His analysis was taken seriously by the Columbia Accident Investigation Board, whose extensive report includes Tufte's analysis. The board's report also included a highly critical comment concerning the way important critical information was communicated at NASA:

> As information gets passed up an organization hierarchy, from people who do analysis to midlevel managers to high-level leadership, key explanations and supporting information is filtered out. In this context, it is easy to understand how a senior manager might read this PowerPoint slide and not realize that it addresses a life-threatening situation.
>
> At many points during its investigation, the Board was surprised to receive similar presentation slides from NASA officials in place of technical reports. The Board views the endemic use of PowerPoint briefing slides instead of technical papers as an illustration of the problematic methods of technical communication at NASA. (191)

Obviously, PowerPoint and similar presentation software cannot be blamed for all bad presentations. Nor is it reasonable to assert that the blame for a misleading presentation rests more with the presentation software than with the author and presenter. Presentation software, like so many other technologies that provide a convenience, allow, perhaps even tempt, humans to rely on it more that they should. Many technologies throughout the years have both improved our lives and tempted us to misuse them. Automobiles do not prevent us from walking, but without them we certainly would walk more. Wikipedia does not require people to ignore primary sources any more than any previous encyclopedia, but more people would consult primary sources if Wikipedia didn't exist. Cell phones do not require people to text while driving, but without them no one would text while driving. The PowerPoint issue is an exemplar of a great many of the ways in which we come to rely on computers. People easily become dependent on technology, from presentation software and word processors to spell checkers and e-mail programs. We shall address this issue again in the next chapter as we explore the various ways in which computers alter our behavior.

## Reflection Questions

1. POSITION The Anti-PowerPoint Political Party claims that 85% of people get nothing out of PowerPoint presentations. Describe your own experiences as to whether PowerPoint has been a positive or negative influence on the quality of presentations you've attended.

2. POSITION Suppose The Anti-PowerPoint Political Party's claims were correct concerning the two and a half billion dollars lost each year due to PowerPoint. If you were a Swiss citizen, would that convince you to vote to ban PowerPoint? Explain your reasoning.

3. POSITION Suppose your school were to ask students to vote on a school policy to ban the use of PowerPoint or similar presentation software in the classroom. Would you vote for it? Explain your reasoning.

4. POSITION Is Matthias Poehm's position, "I don't want to be right, I just want the best result," morally permissible? Explain.

5. RESEARCH Consult *The Columbia Accident Board Report*, volume 1, section 7.5, and evaluate Tufte's claims, as presented there, on the influence of PowerPoint in the Space Shuttle Columbia's crash. Make the strongest argument you can that Tufte is correct.

6. RESEARCH Consult *The Columbia Accident Board Report*, volume 1, section 7.5, and evaluate Tufte's claims, as presented there, on the influence of PowerPoint in the Space Shuttle Columbia's crash. Make the strongest argument you can that Tufte is not correct.

## SUMMARY

- We often trust computers over humans, sometimes with justification and sometimes not.

- Computer failures are sometimes expensive and sometimes threaten human safety.

- The most common categories of computer system failures are hardware errors, software errors or bugs, solving the wrong problem, misuse, communication failures, and malice.

- The Ariane 5 Flight 501 disaster cost 3.5 million dollars due to a failed rocket launch. The cause was an arithmetic overflow caused by converting a 64-bit floating number to an integer.

- The Pentium floating point divide error cost an estimated one-half billion dollars and a great deal of public trust. Although the error in the calculation was small, it was large enough to be significant in some important applications.

- Safety-critical software is software that can jeopardize human safety if it fails. Often safety-critical software is control software with real-time constraints that make it more complicated.

- Software engineering has improved software reliability in a number of ways: better education and training of programmers and software engineers, better tools for creating software, better testing methods, and better ways of specifying and verifying systems.

- The modern software development process for any substantial computer system (especially safety-critical systems) includes people who define the system's requirements, develop the specifications necessary to meet those requirements, create the overall system design, implement the design, test the implementation, and develop maintenance processes. All aspects of the development are documented extensively.

- A number of advances in the software development process have improved program reliability. Much of the progress has been made in preventing bugs rather than finding and correcting them.

- The most important single factor in developing quality software is the quality of the people who do the development.

- The most important single issue in the software development process is communication.

- The Therac-25 was a medical linear accelerator that malfunctioned and ultimately killed three people and seriously injured three others. The machine relied entirely on software to protect against radiation overdoses. The software was developed in the 1980s by one person using a low-level programming language that increased the likelihood of mistakes. This was not unusual for the 1980s.

- Malware is a term for malicious software. Malware comes in a variety of forms, including worms, viruses, Trojan horses, spyware, and rootkits. Malware is commonly written by programmers called hackers—usually a negative term today.

- The Stuxnet worm is a highly sophisticated worm that was probably responsible for substantial damage to Iran's nuclear development program. The worm was explicitly targeted to systems used in Iran's nuclear program. It is widely believed that the worm was created by some national governmental intelligence agency, probably in the United States or Israel.

- The shutdown programs written for the Darlington Nuclear Generating Station are programs designed to shut down nuclear reactors if safety demands it. The programs were originally written by nuclear engineers. With the help of David Parnas, a prominent software engineer, the programs were formally and mathematically verified to maximize the certainty of their reliability. Although the process was successful, it was very costly and time consuming.

- The presidential election in 2000 hinged on the vote in Florida, which was too close to call at the end because the number of ballots in dispute exceeded the difference in votes between the two candidates. Every major network covering the election at some point made erroneous predictions about who had won. Some of the problems with the disputed ballots stemmed from the technology used. In particular, many of the voting cards were not punched properly, making them hard for the machines to accurately read. The Florida Supreme Court ordered a recount, but the United States Supreme Court ultimately overruled the Florida court, citing the vagueness of the Florida law that required a manual recount.

- The most popular computer voting machines in 2006 were made by Diebold. A research group from in Princeton University demonstrated that those machines could be hacked. The Princeton group illustrated that the machine could be hacked in less than a minute; that malware capable of stealing votes without detection could be loaded; and that the malware could infect other machines.

- A political party in Switzerland is attempting to ban PowerPoint, claiming that PowerPoint results in a costly waste of time. Edware Tufte, a well-known statistician and graphic designer, argues that PowerPoint contributed to the crash of the Space Shuttle Columbia. These arguments against PowerPoint do not suggest that PowerPoint by itself is harmful, but that it entices humans to potentially do harm and therefore should be avoided, according to Tufte, or illegal, according to the Swiss party.

## CHAPTER EXERCISES

1. REVIEW Both the Ariane 5 Flight and the Pentium floating point divide cases involved problems with floating point numbers. These seem to be problematic, so why do computers use such numbers?

2. REVIEW What was Intel's justification for initially replacing the chips only for those users who could show a need for high-precision computing?

3. REVIEW According to Intel's critics, why was Intel obligated to replace all defective chips?

4. REVIEW Name the three criteria that Birsch uses to determine moral responsibility for an action.

5. REVIEW What standards for safety-critical software development, as practiced today, appear to have been violated by the programmer of the Therac-25 case?

6. RESEARCH Of the ten worst software bugs discussed in the *Wired* article on history's worst programming bugs, this chapter explored only three: the Ariane 5, the Pentium floating point divide bug, and the Therac-25 accidents. Choose another important bug from this list and identify the mistakes that led to the failure.

7. RESEARCH Since the *Wired* article on history's worst programming bugs appeared in 2005, other candidates for the history's worst bugs have come

to light. Do some research and compile your own list of candidates for an updated top-twenty list.

8. REVIEW What modern standards of software development were violated by the Therac-25 software development process?

9. REVIEW The A&P scam was possible only because people trusted a computer to do arithmetic correctly. In that case, faith in the computer's arithmetic was, as far we know the facts of the case, justified; it was people's greed that caused the scam, not computer error. In some of the cases presented in this chapter, however, computers were the cause of error. Give some examples of situation in which faith in a computer's arithmetic abilities was not justified.

10. APPLICATION Chances are, your instructor uses a spreadsheet to calculate the final grade for your course. How might you or your instructor verify that the arithmetic done by the spreadsheet is really correct?

11. RESEARCH Prior to the Stuxnet worm, the most famous worm was, without question, the Morris worm. Robert Morris was a student at Cornell University who unleashed a worm that quickly swept across the country and changed the nation's attitude towards worms. Do some research on the Morris worm and discuss the impact of the event.

12. RESEARCH We often think calculators are infallible at arithmetic. As with computers, however, this is not necessarily true. Search for information on the fallibility of calculators and present a list of examples in which calculators were shown to give incorrect results. One place you could start would be the chapter of Ivar Peterson's book (Peterson 1995) on the Pentium floating point divide error.

13. RESEARCH Consult Leveson and Turner's paper on the Therac-25 case and write an analysis, similar to Birsch's analysis, on the moral responsibility of two people involved in the case who were outside of AECL.

14. RESEARCH One area that we have not examined in this chapter is the simulation of natural systems via computer models. Such simulations require a combination of a mathematical or some other formal model of a system and a computer implementation of that model. Such simulations are used to predict the weather, climate change, the effects of automobile crashes on passengers, and the outcomes of many other complex processes. Select an example of a computer simulation and try to explain why you do or do not trust the simulation. For simulations you do not trust, is it the model, the computer implementation, or both you do not trust? Some possible examples are: (a) prediction of a hurricane track, (b) the existence of global climate change, (c) the trajectory of a spacecraft, (d) the grammatical correctness of an English sentence, (e) economic growth of the United States for the next 12 months, or (f) life expectancy of a newborn infant.

15. POSITION If you were the CEO of a software company that produced safety-critical software, what policies would you insist on to prevent the kind of problems illustrated in the Therac-25 case?

16. POSITION Are white-hat hackers moral? Are they ethical? Why or why not?

17. RESEARCH A great deal of software is written for various medical devices, such as life support systems, diagnostic systems, databases of medical information, and diagnostic devices such as MRI, CAT scan machines, and x-rays. Should such software be subjected to additional regulation, similar to the way drugs are regulated? Why or why not?

18. RESEARCH The most famous Trojan horse to date involved a CIA ploy to lure the Soviet Union into stealing some intentionally faulty software. The Soviets did in fact steal the software, which was associated with control of natural gas pipelines. When they used it, the program reportedly caused a pipeline explosion in the Soviet Union that was supposedly the largest nonnuclear explosion in history. According to the story, this explosion occurred in the Siberian wilderness, where such an explosion might conceivably have gone unnoticed. Public knowledge of the Trojan horse came from former Air Force Secretary Thomas Reed, who served under President Ronald Reagan. Some have said that Reed was simply playing an April Fool's joke on Congress. Some members of the former Soviet Union claim that no such explosion ever occurred. Research the literature on the Soviet pipeline explosion and explain what allegedly happened.

19. CONTEXT Recall the following question from Chapter 2: *Suppose you are the chief information officer (CIO) for a large hospital and you are considering bids from two different companies. One of the companies is a startup consisting of only five people, all of whom are recent graduates of a well-known engineering college. They have had few previous contracts, but they have done well on the jobs they have done so far. The other company is a well-established major firm. As CIO, you are aware that The Software Engineering Institute, a federally-funded research and development center that evaluates companies' software development processes (referred to as capability maturity models), has assessed the major firm at the highest level. The software system you are accepting bids for is used to schedule room occupancy. This can be quite complex in a hospital. Room assignments can be made simultaneously from various places within the hospital, and many factors have to be considered. Although patients are clearly affected by how well the software functions, there is no evident direct risk to patients in the event of a software failure. Suppose the bid from the small startup company is for $100,000, with a delivery date of six months, and the bid from the major firm is $300,000, with a delivery date of 18 months.* In Chapter 2, you were asked how you would choose which firm to hire and to justify your choice. This time, you should again choose a firm, but your justification should include a discussion of the following:

    a. Even though the question explicitly states there is no direct risk to patients in the event of software failure, should the software be considered as safety-critical software? Explain.

    b. Suppose you chose the cheaper company, and due to major failure of the room scheduling software, a very chaotic situation developed that caused much confusion and inconvenience to the hospital staff and to the patients. No actual physical harm was suffered by any patient, but in some cases patients experienced frustration and discomfort. Do you bear any moral responsibility for the inconvenience, frustration, and discomfort suffered by the people in the hospital? Explain your reasoning.

20. REVIEW What is a zero day attack?

21. REVIEW Why is it so extraordinary that the Stuxnet worm generated four zero day attacks?

22. REVIEW What is a white hat hacker?

23. REVIEW Why were the shutdown programs at the Darlington nuclear power plant considered safety-critical software?

24. REVIEW Why did the AECB call in David Parnas as a consultant for creating shutdown programs for the Darlington nuclear power plant?

25. REVIEW Why did the AECB require the shutdown programs at the Darlington nuclear power plant to be mathematically verified?

26. REVIEW What were the major reasons for the incorrect predictions by the news media in the 2000 elections?

27. POSITION Make the strongest argument you can that America should use computerized voting machines in its elections.

28. REVIEW How did the Princeton group hack the Diebold voting machines?

29. REVIEW Why does the Swiss APPP want to ban PowerPoint?

30. REVIEW Why does Edward Tufte want people to avoid using PowerPoint?

31. REVIEW What evidence does Edward Tufte give to show that PowerPoint contributed to the crash of the Space Shuttle Columbia?

32. REVIEW What does the Columbia Accident Investigation Board think about Tufte's arguments?

33. POSITION Do you think PowerPoint should be banned? Why or why not?

## WORKS CITED

Baur, Stuart, "The Long-Playing Widespread Check-out Counter Rip-off," *New York Magazine*, September 2, 1974. Web. July 10, 2011. <http://books.google.com/books?id=jOkCAAAAMBAJ&q=Stuart+Baur+Supermarket#v=snippet&q=Stuart%20Baur%20Supermarket&f=false>.

Birsch, Douglas, "Moral Responsibility for Harm Caused by Computer System Failures," *Ethics and Information Technology*, Vol. 6, 2004: 233-245. Print.

Feldman, Ariel J., J. Alex Halderman, and Edward W. Felten, "Security Analysis of the Diebold AccuVote-TS Voting Machine," Center for Information Technology Policy. September 13, 2006. Web. August 22, 2011. <http://citp.princeton.edu/pub/ts06full.pdf>.

Garfinkel, Simson, "History's Worst Software Bugs," *Wired,* Nov. 8, 2005. Web. May 10, 2011. <http://wired.com/news/technology/bugs/0,2924,69355,00.html?tw=wn_tophead_1>.

Hoare, C. A. R., "1980 Turing Award Lecture," *Communications of the ACM,* Vol. 24, No. 2, February 1981: 75-83. Print.

Leveson, Nancy, *Safeware: System Safety and Computers*, Boston: Addison-Wesley, 1995. Print.

Leveson, Nancy and Clark S. Turner, "An Investigation of the Therac-25 Accidents," *IEEE Computer,* Vol. 26, No. 7, July 1993: 18-41. Print.

National Aeronautics and Space Administration, *Columbia Accident Investigation Board Report*, Volume 1. Washington: National Aeronautics and Space Administration and the Government Printing Office, 2003. Web. August 7, 2011. <http://www.nasa.gov/columbia/home/CAIB_Vol1.htm,>.

Tufte, Edward, "PowerPoint Does Rocket Science: Assessing the Quality and Credibility of Technical Reports," Sept. 6, 2005. Web. August 20, 2011. <http://www.edwardtufte.com/bboard/q-and-a-fetch-msg?msg_id=0001yB>.

## RELATED READINGS

### Essays and Articles

Brooks, Fred, "No Silver Bullet: Essence and Accidents of Software Engineering." *IEEE Computer* Vol. 20, No. 4, April 1987: 10–19. Print. (This is one of the most famous papers in software engineering. The phrase "no silver bullet" refers to the fact that there is no definitive way to kill what Brooks refers to as the "werewolf of software complexity." More specifically, Brooks argues that no "order of magnitude" improvement is possible in software.)

Nissenbaum, Helen, "Computing and Accountability," *Communications of the ACM,* Vol. 37, No. 1, January 1994: 73-80. Print. (Nissenbaum examines the reasons that computing appears to be reducing the degree to which individuals are held accountable for their actions. This is a very thoughtful article and is not very technical; one of the main examples is an excellent analysis of the Therac-25.)

Safire, William, "The Farewell Dossier," *New York Times*, Feb. 2, 2004. Web. May 10, 2011. <http://www.nytimes.com/2004/02/02/opinion/the-farewell-dossier.html>. (This article is the primary source of the story concerning the Soviet pipeline explosion.)

### Nonfiction Books

Brooks, Fred, *Mythical Man-month: Essays on Software Engineering*, Boston: Addison-Wesley Professional, 1995. Print. (Brooks's book is one of the classic works of software engineering and can be read by people with limited knowledge of computing. In this book he states what came to be known as "Brooks's Law." Though he did most of his work in the 1970s, Brooks is still one of the most quoted software engineers in the discipline.)

Erickson, Jon, *Hacking: The Art of Exploitation*, San Francisco: No Starch Press, 2008. Print. (This tutorial in hacking is best suited for people who are reasonably comfortable with programming and programming literature. It is not too advanced for undergraduate computer science majors, but would be difficult for people with no programming background. It starts at the beginning, but advances rapidly beyond the material covered by most introductory programming courses.)

Gillman, Howard, *The Votes that Counted: How the Court Decided the 2000 Presidential Election*. Chicago: The University of Chicago Press, 2001. Print. (Gillman's work is a thorough report on all aspects of the 2000 election. Since it was written shortly after the election, later issues such as the Help America Vote Act and the 2004 election are not covered.)

Harper, Allen, Shon Harris, Jonathan Ness, Chris Eagle, Gideon Lenkey, and Terron Williams, *Gray Hat Hacking: The Ethical Hacker's Handbook*, Third Edition. New York: McGraw-Hill, 2011. Print. (This handbook, although written for security professionals, has something for everyone interested in hacking. The first five chapters are suitable for people with little programming background and are very informative on a number of issues, including the authors' views on the ethical and social factors of hacking. Later chapters go into detail on some very technical topics.)

Herrnson, Paul S., Richard G. Niemi, Michael J. Hanmer, and Benjamin B. Bederson, *Voting Technology: The Not-So-Simple Act of Casting a Ballot*. Washington, D.C.: Brookings Institution, 2008. Print. (This book is an excellent overview of voting technology. It covers the many different kinds of technology, issues with user satisfaction, reliability, and voter confidence.)

Lee, Leonard, *The Day the Phones Stopped: How People Get Hurt When Computers Go Wrong*, New York: Donald Fine Inc., 1992. Print. (Leonard Lee is a journalist and a very good writer. This book is easy to read, and although a bit dramatic in spots, is highly interesting and informative. It is written for a nontechnical audience.)

Leveson, Nancy, *Safeware: System Safety and Computers*, Boston: Addison-Wesley Professional, 1995. Print. (Leveson is at times rather technical, but her account of the Therac-25 accidents, which updates and elaborates Leveson and Turner's earlier paper on the subject, is probably the most complete account of the accidents to date.)

Peterson, Ivars, *Fatal Defect: Chasing Killer Computer Bugs*, New York: Vintage Books, 1995. Print. (Peterson writes in depth about eight major computer bugs. The book is very readable and was the major source for the details of the Darlington shutdown programs. The book contains much more detail and background than was covered in the chapter.)

# Chapter 6

# How Computing is Changing
# Who We Are

Having read the first five chapters of the book, you are most likely comfortable with the idea that computing in general, and the Internet in particular, have radically changed our social institutions. We have seen how advances in computer technology have eroded the twentieth-century conception of privacy and changed the way we think of property. We have also seen the tremendous harm that software can inflict, with evidence that safety issues in software are taken less seriously than safety issues in physical products.

Chapters 3 through 5 really focus on changes in society. Though issues of privacy, property, and safety can at times affect us each personally, the questions raised by these issues are mainly questions about what society ought to do as a whole. In this chapter we turn our focus inward, to consider how computing is changing each of us individually. Computing is transforming our sense of personal identity, affecting the meaning and significance of our interpersonal relationships. Internet services like Google and Wikipedia are changing the way we construct knowledge. This has tremendous implications for who we are as individuals—whether these changes are beneficial or detrimental is a subject of heated debate.

## 6.1 CASE: KRATOS AND POSEIDON'S PRINCESS

In the very successful *God of War* series of videogames, the player controls a Spartan warrior named Kratos on a mission of revenge against the Greek gods.

Kratos displays many of the symptoms of dissocial personality disorder, which, according to the World Health Organization, is characterized by:

> … disregard for social obligations, and callous unconcern for the feelings of others….. There is a low tolerance to frustration and a low threshold for discharge of aggression, including violence; there is a tendency to blame others… (ICD-10, 204)

Jamal is the father of two boys, one 17 and one 14. He enjoys playing video games with his sons, but he usually plays through the games himself, first, to make sure that they are suitable for his kids to play. Jamal is generally not concerned with cartoonish violence in games, or even the semirealistic violence in games where there are clear good guys and bad guys, or in situations that are clearly self-defense or otherwise morally justified by the story.

*God of War III* is another story, however. While playing through *God of War III*, Jamal was particularly disturbed by a sequence involving a computer character named Poseidon's Princess. At this point in the game Kratos is blocked by a metal gate. The gate can be opened by turning a heavy crank, but as soon as Kratos lets go of the crank, the door closes again.

The solution to this puzzle is to "rescue" the Princess from a room where she is trapped, and then push her into the crank mechanism. As Kratos walks towards the door, the Princess begs for mercy, but Kratos ignores her. As Kratos continues towards the door, the player hears the Princess begin to scream, and then the gruesome sounds of the princess being crushed by the mechanism.

Jamal finds himself disturbed by this scene, and spends some time looking for alternate solutions to the puzzle, but there are none. The player cannot complete the game without pushing Poseidon's Princess into the crank.

## Reflection Questions

1. APPLICATION Based on this description of Kratos's behavior, do you agree that Kratos (if he were real) should be diagnosed with dissocial personality disorder? Explain your reasoning.

2. POSITION Jamal felt disturbed by the Poseidon's Princess scene. Does that mean that he is more moral than someone who was not disturbed by the scene? Would you consider him to be more moral than someone who actually enjoyed the scene?

3. APPLICATION In Section 1.4.4, we discussed Aristotle's idea that we become virtuous by mimicking and repeating virtuous acts. Explain why Aristotle might argue that Jamal should not let his sons play this game.

4. CONTEXT In Section 1.4.6 we presented Kant's "principle of the end in itself." If the player does, as the game requires, sacrifice the Princess, is the player violating Kant's principle? In particular, does it matter that the Princess is not a real person, but simply a computer construct?

5.  POSITION Do you believe that playing this type of video game, where the player is forced to mimic immoral actions, can cause a person to become less moral? Explain your reasoning. You may wish to do some online research to provide evidence for your position.

## 6.2  CASE: VIRTUAL TWO-TIMING

Mitch and Meghan have been close friends since junior high. They attend the same college, but they rarely see each other because they are pursuing different majors. Last year, Meghan started dating Erik, who is in many of Mitch's classes. Mitch discovered that he and Erik share an interest in massively multiplayer online games and they've recently started teaming up in one game.

Erik is part of an online guild, a group of players with whom he regularly meets to work on challenging parts of the game. A month or two after Mitch joined the guild, he started to notice that Erik spent the majority of his time in the game teaming up with a female guild member named Raquel. Mitch did not think much of it until Valentines Day. On Valentines Day the game has a special event that allows players to wear a sash that says "—'s Sweetheart." Erik's character was wearing a sash that said "Raquel's Sweetheart" and Raquel was wearing one that read "Erik's Sweetheart."

Mitch started to worry about his friend Meghan. Was Erik cheating on her with Raquel? Mitch confronted Erik about this, but Erik's position was that he was not doing anything wrong. His reasoning was that:

- They were playing a role-playing game. Raquel and Erik were only pretending to be boyfriend/girlfriend. Even though they were emotionally very close, and spent a lot of time together online, the boyfriend/girlfriend relationship was just part of the game.

- Raquel and Erik have never physically met, so they cannot really be considered boyfriend/girlfriend anyway.

- Because Meghan does not care about or understand online games, it is best not to tell her about Raquel; she will misinterpret the relationship.

### Reflection Questions

1.  POSITION Was Mitch right to approach Erik, and question him about his relationships? If possible, use one of the moral theories from Chapter 1 to support your position.

2.  POSITION Is it possible to cheat on a boyfriend/girlfriend with someone you have never met face to face? Name some behavior that does not occur face to face that would be evidence that a person was being unfaithful to his/her significant other.

3.  CONTEXT Does it matter that the role-playing game that Erik and Raquel are playing is online? Would your assessment of the situation

be different if Erik, Mitch, and Raquel were all part of a gaming group that met face to face to play Dungeons and Dragons, and Erik and Raquel's characters were dating within the game? Explain your reasoning.

## 6.3   THE INTERNET AND THE SELF

You probably have an intuitive idea of what we mean when we say "my self," but in the rest of this chapter it is important for us to distinguish between the terms **self** and **self-concept**. The Blackwell Dictionary of Sociology (by writer and activist Allan Johnson) defines these terms:

> From a classical sociological perspective, the self is a relatively stable set of perceptions of who we are in relation to ourselves, to OTHERS, and to SOCIAL SYSTEMS. The self is organized around a self-concept, the ideas and feelings that we have about ourselves. (277)

Over the past twenty years in the United States, parents and educators have worked tirelessly to instill children with a positive self-concept. Many maladies, including eating disorders and depression, can be aggravated by a negative self-concept. On the other hand, an undeservedly positive self-concept might lead to complacency, narcissism, or irresponsible behavior.

Our self-concept greatly shapes our behavior and affects our interactions with others. In this section we will examine some ways that Internet technologies, especially social networking and virtual worlds, are reshaping our concepts of our selves.

### 6.3.1   Case: A Health Warning for Fashion Photos

We start with a simple case study revolving around the use of digital image manipulation in the fashion and advertising industries. The portrayal of women in popular culture and advertising can have tremendously negative effects on self-concept. The prevalence of exceedingly skinny models can lead healthy people to mistakenly believe themselves to be overweight. Women's rights groups, such as the National Organization of Women (NOW), and psychologists are particularly concerned because such misperceptions can trigger eating disorders and lead people to seek risky elective cosmetic surgery.

In October 2009, a series of advertisements for Ralph Lauren's "Blue Label" line of clothing brought new scrutiny to the use of digital image manipulation in fashion photographs. A picture of model Filippa Hamilton was modified to make her appear even skinnier than she is in real life, so skinny that bloggers took notice and started circulating (and mocking) the image. Most assumed that posting the image would be a fair use, under copyright law, because they were posting it for the purposes of news reporting and commentary.

Journalist and novelist Cory Doctorow reported that Ralph Lauren attempted to block this criticism by filing a Digital Millennium Copyright Act (DMCA) infringement notice with the Internet Service Providers of those who posted the image, including his site, BoingBoing.net. (Recall that we discussed some of the effects of the DMCA on fair use in Chapter 4.) A DMCA infringement notice requires the Internet Service Provider to remove the offending item, in order to shield itself from prosecution for copyright infringement. In this case, Boing Boing's Internet Service Provider felt that the use was a fair one, and so they simply passed the notice on to Boing Boing, and otherwise ignored it. The image and the story about the DMCA notice are still available for viewing on Boing Boing.

There is a growing movement, particularly among English and French health agencies, to regulate the use of digital image manipulation to modify images that are meant to be realistic. Sophie Hardach, a reporter for Reuters, reported that the French government is considering requiring "health warning" disclaimers on heavily modified photographs. Hardach states that,

> Under the proposed law, all enhanced photos would be accompanied by a line saying: "Photograph retouched to modify the physical appearance of a person."

This is similar to the way cigarette advertising is regulated in the United States. Every cigarette ad printed in the United States now includes the following: "Warning: The Surgeon General has determined that cigarette smoking is dangerous to your health."

The approach in Britain is slightly different. In the summer of 2011, the British Advertising Standards Authority banned two cosmetics ads because it ruled that the manipulation of the images made them misleading. This ruling did not specifically address the question of how these images affect self-concept, but the lawmaker who filed the complaints about the ads, Member of Parliament Jo Swinson, was clearly motivated by this concern. In discussing the case with reporters for the *Daily Mail*, she cited her concern about how "these idealized images are distorting our ideas of beauty." (Poulter)

## Reflection Questions

1. POSITION Do you agree with the proposed French law? Should the United States enact a similar law? Explain your reasoning.

2. CONTEXT It has always been possible to modify photographs. Before digital image manipulation, it was common to airbrush photographs to remove wrinkles or spots. (An airbrush is a spray-painting device that gives the artist a very high degree of control.) Why do you think people are more concerned about digital image manipulation than they are about airbrushing?

3. CONTEXT Fashion photographers are not the only ones using digital image manipulation. *Newsweek* used it on the cover of its March 7, 2005 issue to make Martha Stewart look thin. *Paris Match*, a celebrity tabloid, removed the love handles of French President Nicolas Sarkozy in the

August 9, 2007 issue. Of these three uses of digital image manipulation (the Ralph Lauren ad and the two mentioned here), which is the most ethically troubling, and why? Which is the least ethically troubling, and why?

### 6.3.2   Multiple Online Personas

The case of health warnings for digitally manipulated images demonstrates a very specific threat to self concept. In this section we consider a much broader challenge to our self-definition, the increasing use of aliases and multiple online personas.

Author and editor Chris Gonsalves writes about technology for business audiences. He introduces the idea of online personas by discussing several different online personas with whom an advertiser or business person might want to interact:

- Bill on Facebook.com and Fark.com—A professional in his 40s who should be approached in a professional way.

- TrakBurner115 on CarSpace.com—A potential car buyer who focuses on a car's performance specifications when deciding whether or not to buy one.

- NecroticOne1 on MySpace.com—A music fan who likes heavy metal music, as well as clothing and jewelry that promote his favorite bands; he is inclined to buy things that make him feel unique and noticeable.

He concludes:

[These online personas] all have traits and desires unique to their online personalities. They all communicate in ways specific to their virtual environments, ways businesses need to understand to reach all of them. The difficulty? They're all the same person.

Gonsalves and others have argued that it is counter-productive to think of people as having "true selves" or "true personas" that explain all of their actions, all of their likes and dislikes. Adam Sarner, an analyst for the technology consulting company Gartner Group, says that businesses should "Sell to the persona, not the person. A persona will show you how it wants to be treated." (Pettey)

In other words, how a person acts and what he or she likes is shaped by context. For example, how you act at the office will be different from how you act on a business trip, at the doctor's office, or at a baseball game. Though Gonsalves and Sarner clearly recognize that this segmentation of the self into multiple personas predates the Internet, they believe that Internet technologies are causing the typical person to adopt a much greater number and variety of personas. In the 1980s and 1990s, it was common to talk about the "work/life balance," which implied that most people had two main personas, an "at work" persona and an "at home" persona. Today it is not uncommon for people to have up to a dozen distinct personas. Some people have multiple Facebook accounts, multiple Twitter accounts, and multiple Amazon.com accounts to help them manage these personas and keep them separate.

This has moral and ethical implications. Though in Chapter 1 we argued that morality ought to be based on reason, we also know that the choices people end up making often depend on context. Consider two professional basketball players who are close friends, but play for different teams. It happens fairly often that a disagreement over a call or a foul can lead to physical violence between the players. Yet this physical violence between the players would be unlikely in the extreme if they had a disagreement during a picnic with their families. Each player has a "during the game" persona and an "after the game" persona, and the moral decisions they make seem inconsistent.

In other words, having multiple personas allows a person to maintain two (or more) mutually incompatible value systems. A safety inspector for the Occupational Safety and Health Administration can also be a demolition derby driver. The manager of a nonprofit that provides food aid to the poor can also be a pirate in an online game, profiting by stealing from other players.

Many people believe that this division of the self into separate personas is harmful. They argue that, in order to be a good and happy person, we must eliminate the incompatibilities between our different selves. TV host Dr. Phil McGraw calls this ideal of having only one persona, not multiple personas, the "authentic self." (Other sources sometimes call it the "integrated self.") One might argue that a person who maintains multiple personas risks becoming a hypocrite—that is, someone who claims to follow a particular moral code but then acts contrary to that code.

## Reflection Questions

1. APPLICATION Make a list of your personas, along with a brief description of the context in which each persona becomes active. It might be helpful to give each persona a descriptive name (for example, "The Rule Enforcer" or "The Social Butterfly"), so that you can refer to them later.

2. APPLICATION Do your personas share a common set of values, or are there conflicts between them?

3. POSITION Do you think that having multiple personas with conflicting systems of values is inherently immoral? Explain your reasoning.

4. APPLICATION How many of your personas depend on the Internet for their existence? In other words, if there were no cell phones, Facebook, Twitter, text messaging, and so on, which personas would still be applicable? Explain your reasoning.

5. APPLICATION Reflect back on our discussions of professional ethics in Chapter 2. Explain why it might be *necessary* for a person to have multiple personas with conflicting systems of values in order to do certain jobs. Give at least one example of such a profession, and explain your thinking.

### 6.3.3  Griefer Madness: Sociopathic Behavior on the Internet

One area where online personas are often used as cover is in online bullying and harassment. Several recent cyberbullying cases have drawn attention to the ways that social networks and video games can be used to emotionally abuse others and cause real harm. In this section we will explore the question of whether the Internet, in particular, is encouraging people to develop sociopathic tendencies, such as cyberbullying and related behaviors. In other words, is cyberbullying just normal bullying in a new form, or is Internet technology causing bullying to expand? When we use the word **sociopath** we mean someone who suffers from the dissocial personality disorder described in Case 6.1.

In a 2008 article in *Wired* magazine, Julian Dibbell described a type of online sociopath called a **griefer**.

> Broadly speaking, a griefer is an online version of the spoilsport — someone who takes pleasure in shattering the world of play itself. Not that griefers don't like online games. It's just that what they most enjoy about those games is making other players not enjoy them.... Their work is complete when the victims log off in a huff. Griefing, as a term, dates to the late 1990s, ... [b]ut even before it had a name, grieferlike behavior was familiar in prehistoric text-based virtual worlds like LambdaMOO, where joyriding invaders visited "virtual rape" and similar offenses on the local populace.

Individual griefers have existed for many years, but Dibbell argues that the Internet has led to something new:

> [T]he rise of organized griefing, grounded in online message-board communities and thick with in-jokes, code words, taboos, and an increasingly articulate sense of purpose. No longer just an isolated pathology, griefing has developed a full-fledged culture.

Griefers are one example of a new type of creature who lives on the Internet and finds its entertainment in hassling others. Another example is a **troll**, a user who posts in a public forum or chat room, with the goal of either subverting the conversation or otherwise provoking an emotional response. A third type is the **cyberbully**, or **cyberstalker**, who uses the Internet to harass a particular target, often using fake identities or public Web sites to enable the harassment. Unlike with trolls and griefers, who often seem to select random or ideologically-motivated targets, cyberbullies tend to target people they know from everyday life.

What makes cybersociopathy (that is, sociopathic behavior specific to the Internet) particularly troubling is that the Internet seems to be making these behaviors easier. The Internet allows trolls and griefers to find like-minded people. Banding together gives them a shared sense of purpose, and they receive positive feedback and attention for their exploits. The Internet makes it much easier for cyberstalkers to invade another's privacy and to mask their own identities. The following examples of griefer, troll, and cyberbully behavior may be helpful in understanding the issue:

- Cyberbullying—A Long Island woman was charged with aggravated harassment after she posted an ad offering sexual services on Craigslist, giving the name and phone number of one of her daughter's rivals. The girl targeted was nine years old. This resulted in more than twenty harassing phone calls to the girl's home. In another case, a woman from Santa Ana reported that her ex-boyfriend and sister-in-law were sending her threatening text messages, and had them arrested. It turned out, however, that she had impersonated her sister-in-law to purchase the phone, and was using it to send harassing messages to herself, in an attempt to frame her ex-boyfriend and sister-in-law.

- Griefing—In EVE Online, an online role-playing game, the most powerful spaceship is called a Titan. Making a Titan costs the equivalent of about $10,000 US dollars, so there are very few of them in existence. The GoonFleet, a team of self-described griefers, organized an attack that focused on finding and destroying the first Titan. Describing the attack to Dibbell, GoonFleet's leader said, "The ability to inflict that huge amount of actual, real-life damage on someone is amazingly satisfying.... The way that you win in EVE is you basically make life so miserable for someone else that they actually quit the game and don't come back." Although griefing seems less worrisome than cyberharassment, developers of online games and services take it very seriously. Griefers tend to drive away current customers and ruin a new customer's first impression of a service. Linden Lab (creators of the Second Life virtual world) often deploys friendly greeters to parts of the world intended for new players, much like Walmart places friendly greeters at the entrances to their stores.

- Trolling—There are many sites on the Internet where users can post questions, which are then answered by other users on the site. It is fairly common for trolls to respond to these questions with bad advice. For example, a user might ask how to save a file in a particular photo-editing program. A troll might tell them to "press Ctrl+Alt+Delete" (which reboots the computer) or "press Alt+F4" (which closes the current window, possibly losing unsaved work).

The central question of cybersociopathy is, "Are these behaviors really wrong?" Many griefers can give articulate explanations for why they do what they do, along with justifications for why it is (in their view) morally permissible. Others might argue, however, that cybersociopathy should be diagnosed as a mental illness. In diagnosing mental illness, the *DSM-IV* (*Diagnostic and Statistical Manual of Mental Disorders, or DSM-IV*) is one of the most commonly used references in the United States. In Case 6.1 we introduced one type of sociopathy, dissocial personality disorder. A more detailed diagnostic guide is provided by the *DSM-IV*, which calls the condition **antisocial personality disorder**.

**Pervasive pattern of disregard for and violation of the rights of others ... as indicated by three (or more) of the following:**

1. Failure to conform to social norms with respect to lawful behaviors as indicated by repeatedly performing acts that are grounds for arrest

2. Deceitfulness, as indicated by repeated lying, use of aliases, or conning others for personal profit or pleasure

3. Impulsivity or failure to plan ahead

4. Irritability and aggressiveness, as indicated by repeated physical fights or assaults

5. Reckless disregard for safety of self or others

6. Consistent irresponsibility, as indicated by repeated failure to sustain consistent work behavior or honor financial obligations

7. Lack of remorse, as indicated by being indifferent to or rationalizing having hurt, mistreated, or stolen from another

**F I G U R E 6.1** Description of antisocial personality disorder as it appears in the *DSM-IV* (classification 301.7)

Figure 6.1 provides the description of antisocial personality disorder as it appears in the *DSM-IV* (classification 301.7).

It is interesting that these criteria, particularly 4 and 5, do not take into account mental or social harms, instead focusing on physical harms. This is particularly interesting in light of recent research into the mental effects of bullying.

In a September 2010 press release, the National Institutes of Health (NIH) announced new findings about the links between bullying and depression in children from grades 6 through 10. The study looked at physical bullies and their victims. Some people may be surprised that physical bullies are substantially more likely to be depressed than the victims of physical bullying. However, cyberbullying shows the exact opposite effect. The victims of cyberbullying are significantly more likely to be depressed than cyberbullies. In other words, there is some evidence that, from a mental health perspective, cyberbullying is significantly different from traditional bullying. The authors of the study speculate that "...unlike traditional bullying which usually involves a face-to-face confrontation, cybervictims may not see or identify their harasser; as such, cybervictims may be more likely to feel isolated, dehumanized or helpless at the time of the attack."

Because computers are changing the way we interact with others, they are also changing the ways we perceive ourselves and our perception of what is "normal." This process, the way that an aspect of society becomes "normal," is called **normalization**. The prevalence of online griefing and harassment is causing some people to start to view these behaviors as normal. This, in turn, makes it more difficult to stop such behaviors, because not everyone agrees about whether or not they ought to be stopped. This principle of normalization applies to the other topics of this chapter as well.

## Reflection Questions

1. POSITION Consider the activities and statements of griefers presented here. Do you think that they are "sociopathic" in the general sense? Explain your reasoning.

2. APPLICATION Based on the described activities and statements of griefers presented here, which of the seven *DSM-IV* criteria do griefers definitely violate, definitely *not* violate, or probably violate? For each one, explain your reasoning in a sentence or two.

3. POSITION In the diagnostic criteria for antisocial personality disorder, criteria 4 and 5 seem to focus on physical acts of violence. Should they be broadened to include nonphysical harms? Explain your reasoning.

4. APPLICATION Is griefing in online games morally wrong? Use one of the ethical theories from Chapter 1 to explain your answer.

5. POSITION Do you think the existence of Internet forums, social networks, and multiplayer online games is causing people to develop sociopathic tendencies, when they might not have otherwise? Give evidence and explain your reasoning.

## 6.3.4 Virtual and Online Addictions

In the previous section we discussed two definitions of an antisocial personality disorder, a mental disorder that seems to be encouraged by the Internet. In that case, the mental disorders we studied are widely recognized, and the controversy revolves around whether or not griefers, trolls, and cyberbullies meet the diagnostic criteria for those disorders. In this section we look at a more controversial topic, behavioral addiction. By **behavioral addiction** we mean addiction to certain online behaviors like gambling, video games, internet surfing, sex, extreme sports, and so on.

Is it really possible to be "addicted" to video games, surfing the web, or online gambling? This concept is controversial because up until very recently psychologists did not officially recognize any addictions other than addictions to substances, like alcohol or drugs. New scientific results, however, are casting some doubt on this interpretation. Researchers have found that problem gamblers, in particular, experience symptoms similar to alcoholism or nicotine addiction. Furthermore, the same types of treatments work for all three conditions. For these reasons, in the new edition of the *DSM*, "problem gambling" is likely to be moved to the "addiction" category from the "impulse control" category. (Recall from the previous section that the *DSM* is the manual that American psychologists use to diagnose and categorize mental disorders.)

Figure 6.2 provides a proposed revision to the *DSM* (for the upcoming *DSM-5* edition) that lists criteria for gambling disorder.

**Persistent and recurrent maladaptive gambling behavior as indicated by five (or more) of the following:**

1.  Is preoccupied with gambling (e.g., preoccupied with reliving past gambling experiences, handicapping or planning the next venture, or thinking of ways to get money with which to gamble)

2.  Needs to gamble with increasing amounts of money in order to achieve the desired excitement

3.  Has repeated unsuccessful efforts to control, cut back, or stop gambling

4.  Is restless or irritable when attempting to cut down or stop gambling

5.  Gambles as a way of escaping from problems or of relieving a dysphoric Mood (e.g., feelings of helplessness, guilt, anxiety, depression)

6.  After losing money gambling, often returns another day to get even ("chasing" one's losses)

7.  Lies to family members, therapist, or others to conceal the extent of involvement with gambling

8.  Has jeopardized or lost a significant relationship, job, or educational or career opportunity because of gambling

9.  Relies on others to provide money to relieve a desperate financial situation caused by gambling

**F I G U R E  6.2**  Proposed *DSM-5* criteria for gambling disorder

The proposed criteria for sex addiction, and the existing criteria for drug addiction, are very similar to the criteria listed in Figure 6.2, with the word "gambling" removed and replaced with "sex" or "substance use," respectively. Currently, the American Psychological Association (APA) is not proposing to add "Internet addiction" or "video game addiction" to the *DSM*. This is because there is not yet enough scientific evidence to show that these negative behaviors result from psychological processes similar to the other addictions. Many psychologists and lay people have already been using these terms, however, because the outward behaviors do seem similar to other addictions.

Is it really true that video gaming can become an addiction? We do not know the answer to this question, but by applying the proposed *DSM-5* diagnostic criteria for gambling (in a form modified for video games) we can see whether or not it is at least plausible that video gaming addiction is real. We will focus on addiction to MMOGs (massively multiplayer online games), because it fits the addiction model particularly well. Figure 6.3 provides possible diagnostic criteria for a multiplayer online game disorder, which we have based on the proposed *DSM-5* criteria for gambling disorder.

Behavioral addictions to Internet-enabled behaviors are a particular area of concern for a number of reasons. First, unlike substance use or real-life gambling, Internet activities do not require face-to-face interaction. A drug user

**Persistent and recurrent maladaptive game-playing behavior as indicated by five (or more) of the following:**

1. Is preoccupied with game playing when not playing (e.g., preoccupied with reliving past game playing experiences, planning the next venture, or thinking of ways to get game currency)

2. Needs to tackle increasingly difficult "boss" monsters in order to achieve the desired excitement

3. Has repeated unsuccessful efforts to control, cut back, or stop playing games

4. Is restless or irritable when attempting to cut down or stop playing games

5. Plays games as a way of escaping from problems or of relieving a dysphoric mood (e.g., feelings of helplessness, guilt, anxiety, depression)

6. After losing money, items, or "experience points" during one gaming session, often returns another day to get even ("chasing" one's losses)

7. Lies to family members, therapist, or others to conceal the extent of involvement with game playing

8. Has jeopardized or lost a significant relationship, job, or educational or career opportunity because of game playing

9. Relies on others to provide money to relieve a desperate financial situation caused by game playing

**F I G U R E  6.3**  Possible diagnostic criteria for a multiplayer online game disorder

must meet someone in person to purchase drugs, and a traditional gambler must be with someone to gamble. This means that their behaviors are often observable in public spaces. If you lie to your family about your (traditional) gambling addiction, there is a chance that you will bump into a family friend at the casino and get caught in the lie. With online gambling and other online behaviors, there is a feeling of being in a private place. Even though we know that the government (and hackers) may be able to observe what we are doing on the Internet, most people assume that no one is watching when they go online. This eliminates one of the major deterrents for engaging in addictive or destructive behavior: the fear of getting caught.

The second major concern is convenience—the Internet makes it easy to engage in an addictive behavior any time and from any place. With traditional gambling, you have to go to a casino or other gambling place. This requires making plans, driving, being absent from work or home, and so on. With online gambling, people can gamble at home or at work, fitting it into any free time they have in their schedules. Internet gambling and pornography use are particularly problematic in this way. There is substantial evidence that many workers spend hours each day, while at work, gambling, looking at pornography, or playing online games. Here is just some evidence of this phenomenon:

- A 2007 survey commissioned by game publisher PopCap Games showed that 24% of white-collar workers play video games while at work, and this rises to 35% for top executives. Of those who do play games at work, most players play only during lunch or other official breaks. Some (14%) admitted to playing games during meetings or conference calls, and 84% averaged between 15 and 60 minutes of gameplay per day while at work (PopCap Games).

- Jonathan Karl, reporting for ABC News, said that government investigators had found evidence that many of the Securities and Exchange Commission's top managers spent a significant amount of time each day visiting pornographic Web sites, including one senior attorney who had filled his entire government-owned computer with pornography.

So, although substance abuse, problem gambling, and sex addiction have all existed for thousands of years, the Internet is increasing our opportunities to engage in these types of behaviors. Computers also give rise to new types of behavioral addictions, like online gaming addiction, which did not exist in the past.

## Reflection Questions

1. RESEARCH The nine criteria we suggested for our proposed "multiplayer online game disorder" make sense only if the behaviors actually occur in real life. Search the Internet for recent media reports about "gaming addiction" (there are many of these). Use these stories to provide evidence of whether or not there are actually people who meet the nine criteria. You may also find it helpful to interview friends who are game players to find evidence.

2. POSITION Write the best argument you can that there is no such thing as video game addiction.

3. CONTEXT Look at your argument for the previous question. Would the argument apply equally well to showing that there is no such thing as gambling addiction? If so, explain whether or not you believe in gambling addiction, and why. If not, explain the key differences between gaming addiction and gambling addiction that cause your argument to not apply to gambling.

4. APPLICATION Psychologists treat compulsive behaviors differently from addictive behaviors. Some people seem to be addicted to checking their Facebook or Twitter updates. Do you think this is an addictive behavior or a compulsive one? Explain your reasoning. One way to answer this question without doing further research is to see whether or not the nine diagnostic criteria for gambling disorder make sense when adapted to this new problem. If not, it is probably not an addictive behavior.

## 6.4   INTERDISCIPLINARY TOPICS: SOCIAL NETWORK ANALYSIS

Today we use the phrase **social network** to describe Internet sites like Facebook and LinkedIn. Long before the invention of the Internet, however, sociologists developed a branch of applied mathematics called **social network analysis** to help them understand and explore social organization. In the past, long before the Web existed, the term "social network" was already being used to describe the structure formed by human relationships. A social network, in this original sense, means a visual representation of the people and organizations in society, and the various types of **one-to-one** relationships between them. Social network analysis, then, uses a branch of mathematics called **graph theory** to analyze these social networks.

Before we can illustrate this approach, we need to briefly introduce ideas of graphs and graph theory. In mathematics, a **graph** is a construct in which individual entities are represented as **nodes**, with related nodes connected by an **edge**. Graphs are very useful for representing relationships in a social network. For example, Figure 6.4 shows a graph of the one-to-one relationships between five friends. Each node (illustrated by a circle) represents a person. Each edge (illustrated by a line) represents the fact that the two people know each other. Graphs of this type, which show the relationships between people, are the basis for modern social networks; the word **network** is sometimes used as a synonym for "graph."

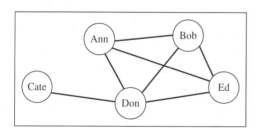

**FIGURE 6.4**  Graph of the one-to-one relationships between five friends

Sociologists have discovered that it is possible to describe and test hypotheses about social and economic phenomena using graphs like the one shown in Figure 6.4. One example of such a phenomenon is the well-known "six degrees of separation" hypothesis. In a social network graph, your friends are one step away from you; the friends of your friends are at most two steps away from you, and so on. The **six degrees of separation** hypothesis says that, in the social network graph of the whole world, everyone in the world is at most six steps away from you.

A mathematician would describe the six degrees of separation hypothesis in terms of **paths** in a graph. A path in a graph is a sequence of edges that leads from one node to another. A **shortest path** (between two particular nodes) is the path that uses the least number of edges. For example, in Figure 6.4, you can trace a path from Bob to Cate, which goes from Bob, to Ann, to Don, to Cate.

We say that this path has **length** three, because it uses three edges. The shortest path, however, has length two; it just goes from Bob to Don and then directly to Cate. Using this terminology, the "six degrees of separation" hypothesis states that the length of the shortest path between any two people in the world is less than or equal to six.

Social psychology professor Stanley Milgram, then at Harvard University, tested the six degrees of separation hypothesis through an imaginative experiment. He sent letters to randomly-selected people in Wichita and Omaha and asked them to forward the letter to a particular acquaintance of his in Boston. The catch was that, if they did not know the Boston addressee personally, they could not send it directly to him. Instead, they were asked to forward it to someone they *did* know personally, who they felt was more likely to know the target. Though most of the letters never arrived at their destination (because recipients refused to participate), those that did make it arrived in an average of 6.5 steps. He published his results in 1967 in the inaugural issue of the magazine *Psychology Today*. Though the experiment has some design flaws, it (along with the "Kevin Bacon" game from the mid 1990s and the concept of the Erdős number in mathematics) has helped keep the six degrees of separation hypothesis alive in our cultural imagination.

Today's social networks are an attempt to directly represent and leverage the social connections between people and institutions. As you probably have already seen on Facebook, you can click a "Like" button to show that you like a particular post, photo, product, or other item. Everything you "like" becomes a node in Facebook's social network, and each time you click "Like," a new edge is created in the network. **Social network analysis**, a field originally pioneered by sociologists and economists, now allows marketers and scholars alike to use Facebook's massive social network to study our society. Scientists are trying to use social network analysis to predict human social behaviors, such as the outcome of elections, which Internet videos will "go viral," or how quickly a pandemic flu will spread.

Network analysis techniques developed for Internet applications can also be repurposed to tell us things about society. For example, consider Google's PageRank algorithm. The job of PageRank is to identify which Web pages are the most important. PageRank treats the Web as a big graph in which each Web page is a node. Within this graph, two nodes are linked by an edge if there is a hyperlink from one to the other. Using this graph structure, PageRank can determine which pages are the most important. By applying algorithms similar to PageRank to social networks, sociologists can estimate the prestige or importance of individual persons.

## Reflection Questions

1. APPLICATION Several government agencies (the Defense Advanced Research Projects Agency, DARPA, in particular) have explored using social network analysis to identify potential terrorists. They would like companies like Facebook and Twitter to provide them with the social

network of all users (even those not under suspicion of any crime or criminal intent), because this is necessary for network analysis algorithms to work. Should social networking companies comply with these requests voluntarily, or should they hold out until they receive a court order? Explain your reasoning. In particular, be sure to describe and analyze the privacy implications of releasing the network structure to the police, even if identities are not released.

2. CONTEXT Marketers and business people also want to use social network analysis, but in this case they want to use it to help them more efficiently target their advertising dollars towards potential customers. They would like companies like Facebook and Twitter to sell access to the social network of all users, so network analysis algorithms can be used to help in this process. Make the strongest argument you can that to sell access to the social network to marketers is better, morally, than giving access to law enforcement without a warrant. Then make the strongest argument you can for the opposite position.

## 6.5 HOW THE INTERNET CHANGES *HOW* WE KNOW

When you look at a piece of information on the Internet, how do you decide whether or not it is trustworthy? While much of the information on the Internet is both true and useful, examples of false or misleading information also abound. Of course, false and misleading information also abound outside the Internet. Determining what's true and what's not has always been an issue.

The branch of philosophy that studies this problem is called epistemology. **Epistemology**, roughly speaking, studies the nature of knowledge and how we know what we know. In this book we stress the role of reason as the primary way of constructing knowledge, but reason alone is clearly not sufficient. We also need to use our senses to acquire data, and we need language to transmit knowledge to and from other people.

Knowledge can be acquired either directly or indirectly. By "directly" acquired, we mean knowledge that you build for yourself by observing phenomena with your senses or by working it out using math and reason. In this section we are particularly concerned with knowledge that is acquired indirectly—knowledge that is given to us by others through language. We receive most of what we know in this way. Someone teaches it to us, and we accept it even though we cannot directly verify the information through our senses or through reason. For example, most people (though not all) trust the consensus of the scientific community. The reason for this trust is because we believe that members of the scientific community are motivated primarily by the search for truth and that they work together to check the validity of scientific papers before they are published.

Since the start of the Enlightenment (in the eighteenth century), society has depended on individual experts to apply reason to construct knowledge. When the experts are in consensus, the rest of us tend to accept their claims.

The Internet, however, is challenging this model. As we will see, some Internet technologies lend themselves to bias (instead of reason), with a decreased role for experts in defining and codifying knowledge. Some view these changes as disastrous, but others view them as leveling the playing field between ordinary people and intellectual elites. We start by looking at the growing role of intentional bias in Internet searching and advertising.

### 6.5.1   Birds of a Feather, and the "Like" button

It is probably not a surprise that you have many things in common with your friends. We usually choose as friends people who like the same books or movies we do, and who have similar political views, similar educational backgrounds, and so on. In the social sciences, this tendency for people to have close friendships primarily with people similar to themselves is called **homophily**. (*Philia*, the Greek word for the dispassionate love between friends, is the root word.)

Homophily comes about in several ways. The first, and most obvious, is that you are more likely to become friends with someone who agrees with you and has similar life experiences. Homophily also comes about because often your friends exert influence over you, and vice versa; you become more like each other over time. If your friend likes a particular music group, you are likely to listen to them and come to like them as well. Facebook uses homophily to increase the effectiveness of online advertising.

The Facebook "Like" button is at the heart of this. Any company can partner with Facebook and place Facebook's Like button on its Web pages. Whenever a Facebook user clicks the Like button on a Web page, Facebook learns something about that user's attitudes and preferences. As it begins to compile information about what a particular user likes, and about what that user's friends like, Facebook can start to make guesses about what products are likely to interest the user. For example, if many of your friends have liked a particular band, and you have not, then that band might pay Facebook to target you with ads. An understanding of homophily tells the marketers at Facebook that you are probably predisposed to enjoy a particular kind of music; targeting you with an ad for a band that your friends like is much more likely to pay off than showing the same ad to a random person.

Facebook calls this service, which makes it possible to present you with ads and content specifically suited to you, "instant personalization." Many companies use Facebook's instant personalization system on their Web sites to tailor content to the user. (The first time a Facebook user visits a site that uses instant personalization she will be given the option to either enable or disable it.) Some examples of instant personalization are:

- Microsoft's search engine Bing.com—This site searches not only the Web, but also the users' Facebook friends to find items the friends like that also match the search query.

- Movie review website RottenTomatoes.com—This site provides movie ratings and recommendations based on your Facebook friends.

- Music site Pandora.com—This site makes it easy to listen to music that is "Liked" by your friends on Facebook.

- Location-based search and review site Yelp.com—When you use Yelp to search for a restaurant, you receive links to reviews written by your Facebook friends for nearby restaurants.

All four of these companies are in the search business, helping the user find Web pages, movies, music, and food. For all of these companies, the goal is to take advantage of homophily, by using your network of friends to improve the usefulness of your search results. The better the search results, the more likely you are to keep using their services. This in turn gives those search companies more opportunities to target you with ads.

It is important to understand why using homophily to personalize search results can increase the usefulness of those results. Consider, as an example, the problem of searching for a movie to watch this weekend. Every movie Web site usually has ratings from movie critics, but is that really the most useful information? If you happen to really enjoy cheesy science-fiction movies, then you are likely to often disagree with the critics about which movies are the best. But if you are a science fiction fan, then your friends will probably "like" many science fiction movies on Facebook. By providing you with a list of the movies most "liked" by your friends, the movie search Web site is giving you information that is even more useful than the published reviews of movie critics.

This leads to an important question: What if search engines start reordering search results based on what your friends like? How would that affect society? For example, imagine that you are searching for information about the effect of government-run health-care systems on health outcomes. Should your political views or the political views of your friends change the outcome of the search?

As this chapter was being written, a new search engine called blekko.com was launched that allows users to filter their search results to focus on a particular point of view. For example, a search for "health care/liberal" returns Web pages about health care that would be of most interest to those who are politically liberal, while "health care/conservative" would return more politically conservative results. On the one hand, the ability to filter search results by political philosophy could be positive, because it allows users to quickly find what they are looking for. On the other hand, it also makes it easier to avoid seeing anything that conflicts with one's own beliefs.

## Reflection Questions

1.  POSITION When searching for information about political issues on the Internet, would you prefer that the pages be sorted by quality *only*, or would you like your beliefs taken into account (so that high-quality pages that agree with you are shown closer to the top than high-quality pages that disagree with you)? Explain your reasons.

2.    [POSITION] Assume that, no matter what, the Internet will always include advertisements. Would you prefer to see advertisements that are randomly selected, or would you prefer to see advertisements for things that your friends like? Explain your reasoning.

### 6.5.2   Why Some Experts Fear *Wikipedia*

Now let's explore the role of experts in the creation of knowledge by focusing on a question college students frequently ask their professors: "Is it okay to cite *Wikipedia* as a source of evidence?" (As you probably know, *Wikipedia* is the popular online encyclopedia that can be edited by anyone.) Most, but not all, college professors answer "No," but not always for the same reason. There are two very different arguments to support the position that students should not cite *Wikipedia* as an authoritative source.

The first argument focuses on the fact that *Wikipedia* is a **tertiary source**, that is, a survey or summary of other work that does not include full evidence, sources, or technical details. Usually (but not for every piece of information in an article), a tertiary source points you towards other sources. By definition, it does not stand on its own as an authoritative source. By contrast, a **secondary source** discusses information presented elsewhere. For example, if you were writing a biography of Benjamin Franklin, an authoritative history of the Revolutionary War would be just one of the secondary sources you would consult. A **primary source** is a source that is as close as possible to the topic being studied. For example, Benjamin Franklin's letters would serve as primary sources for a biographer. According to this line of argument, citing *Wikipedia* is just as ill-advised as citing a print encyclopedia, a textbook, or other tertiary sources. This argument is a bit simplistic in its assumption that *Wikipedia*, as well as textbooks and encyclopedias, are tertiary sources. In some cases, an article in an encyclopedia or textbook might be considered a secondary source because it is authoritative, or presents sufficient evidence that it can stand on its own. *Wikipedia* is not an exception to this in that some of its articles can be considered secondary sources.

The second argument focuses on the fact that *Wikipedia* can be edited by anyone. Thus, according to this line of argument, its contents are not authoritative. For the purposes of this chapter, we are more interested in this second argument, because the concern about the lack of editorial control is the biggest sticking point for many professors and experts. According to a study reported by Jim Giles in the journal *Nature, Wikipedia* is comparable in accuracy to the *Encyclopedia Britannica*, at least for natural science articles. *Nature* evaluated articles on forty-two different science topics, and only eight serious errors were found, four in *Wikipedia* and four in the *Encyclopedia Britannica*. On the other hand, examples of errors in *Wikipedia* abound (as we will see shortly), and stories about these errors are sometimes reported in the news. This understandably makes scholars nervous. In order to understand why *Wikipedia*'s editorial model is so successful and so controversial, we first need to understand the differences between *Wikipedia*'s model and the traditional model for publishing an encyclopedia.

If you are compiling an encyclopedia, whether in print or online, you have at least three major problems:

- What topics do you want to cover and what topics do you want to exclude?
- Once you have selected a topic, how do you find an author to contribute an article on that topic?
- Once you receive a contributed article on a particular topic, how do you ensure that the article is accurate, fair, and well written?

In the traditional model of encyclopedia publishing, most of the decision-makers involved have expertise in the subject area. Each editor and contributor usually has a Ph.D. or some other advanced degree in a field directly related to the topic under consideration. For example, consider the process of creating articles about the American Revolution. The supervising editor for this topic (who likely has a Ph.D. in some area of American history) would develop an outline of the required articles. For each article, she would then find an expert to write the first draft. In this case, this expert would probably be a world-recognized authority on the topic. The draft is then fact-checked and evaluated for fairness by more editors, who are also likely to have advanced degrees in the same area as the topic of the article.

Contrast this with *Wikipedia*'s model. In *Wikipedia*, any registered user can create and write a new article. In other words, *Wikipedia*'s editorial model is a crowdsourcing model. **Crowdsourcing**, in this context, means taking tasks that would normally be performed by experts (such as writing and editing articles), and allowing the public to do them. *Wikipedia*'s editors and contributors are volunteers, whereas the editorial staff of a traditional encyclopedia is paid. With *Wikipedia,* this translates into a drastic reduction in both the cost of writing articles and the time between the writing of an article and its appearance on *Wikipedia.*

It is not necessary to have a Ph.D. to contribute an article to *Wikipedia;* no one checks the credentials of contributors to see if they are experts. Nor is there a supervising editor who decides which topics to include or exclude, nor a team of content editors who check the articles' accuracy. As a result, duplicate articles—that is, two different articles on the same topic—are common in Wikipedia. Another result of the lack of editorial control is that *Wikipedia* tends to focus on items of popular interest, instead of items of scholarly interest. For instance, the *Wikipedia* article about John Locke, the philosopher, whom we discussed in Chapter 1, is currently 3,576 words. The article about John Locke, the character from the TV show *Lost*, is 4,396 words.

In *Wikipedia* anyone can be an author, anyone can be a supervising editor, and anyone can be a content editor. *Wikipedia* does, however, empower certain users (called "admins") to lock, or protect, articles if it appears that vandalism is taking place or to encourage warring editors to come to consensus.

These characteristics mean that *Wikipedia* is much larger than traditional encyclopedias. It also means that errors easily arise in *Wikipedia.* Conversely,

> - In March 2009, a student added a fake quote to the *Wikipedia* page of composer Maurice Jarre a few hours after Jarre's death. The fabricated quote subsequently appeared in newspaper obituaries for Jarre, including in Britain's "The Guardian" newspaper.
>
> - At various times, *Wikipedia* has prematurely announced the deaths of public figures, including Senator Edward Kennedy and teen pop star Miley Cyrus.
>
> - At the time of this writing, there is a minor edit war in the article on "NP Completeness," a key topic in the theory of computer science. One editor is attempting to add a quote from *Nature News*. Though the quote could be considered informative, it is technically incorrect, and so it has been repeatedly removed by other editors. So far it has been added, and then removed again, at least three times.

**F I G U R E  6.5**  Some instructive examples of errors in *Wikipedia*

errors in *Wikipedia* are also easier to correct than in a traditional encyclopedia. Figure 6.5 gives some examples of notable errors in *Wikipedia*.

### Reflection Questions

1. POSITION In evaluating the quality of information you use in your academic work, how important is it to you that the author is an expert in the topic? For example, would you be more likely to trust a *Wikipedia* article on U.S. history if the author is a history professor, instead of an average person? Why or why not?

2. POSITION Imagine a scenario in which a traditional encyclopedia (like *Encyclopedia Britannica*) were able to retain its current editorial model (using expert authors and editors), but make the encyclopedia available online for free. Would you be more likely to use *Wikipedia*, or would you switch to the expert-created online encyclopedia whenever possible? Explain your reasons.

3. APPLICATION If you notice a significant error in *Wikipedia*, do you have a *moral* duty to correct it? Justify your position, using one of the theories from Chapter 1.

4. APPLICATION If a scholar or expert notices a significant error in *Wikipedia* in his area of expertise, does he have a *professional* duty to correct it? Justify your position using what you learned in Chapter 2.

### 6.5.3  Is Cyberdating Really Dating?

We conclude this exploration of how the Internet changes how we know by discussing the link between self-concept (the topic of section 6.3) and epistemology (the topic of section 6.5). In Section 6.3.2 we contrasted the idea of one's "authentic self" with the idea that each person is a combination of multiple context-dependent selves, or personas, all of which are equally valid. There is still considerable debate about whether one approach is better than the other. Some say we ought to strive to be our authentic selves, and that anything else is dishonest. Others claim that all human interactions are context-dependent performances, and there is no such thing as an authentic self.

This debate takes on real significance when we consider the problem of finding a partner or mate. According to a survey of 7,000 people commissioned by Match.com, 17% of U.S. couples that married in the past 3 years met through an online dating site. A growing number of people have significant online relationships, sometimes lasting months or years, before they ever meet face to face.

Traditionally, people in the United States have found potential partners through work, school, or family acquaintances. After being introduced, they usually spend time together, to try to get to know one another, and to try out the possibility of forming a long-term relationship. One might reasonably claim that the purpose of dating is to get to know the "authentic self" of the other person, so that you can decide whether or not you want a long-term relationship.

Consider the following scenario: Ryan and Kayla are two high school sophomores who live 500 miles apart. They met through a mutual friend on Facebook. Over time they communicated more and more through Facebook's chat feature, then started texting each other, and eventually started video-chatting several times per week over the Internet. They eventually updated their status on Facebook to indicate that they were "in a relationship." Ryan and Kayla even went so far as to introduce their parents over video chat. Finally, Kayla convinced her parents to visit a family member who lives near Ryan so that she and Ryan could meet in person.

Is it really possible or reasonable to fall in love with someone you have never met in person? Some would argue that any feelings of intimacy or affection that you feel for a person are illusory if you have not met the person face to face. One way to analyze this question is to consider the medium of interaction, and whether or not it is useful in discovering the authentic self of the other person. Consider the following ways of interacting with a potential partner:

- Sharing a meal in a restaurant or going to a movie together
- Volunteering together on a service project
- Going on vacation together
- Text chat via text message or private Internet chat
- Voice conversation via phone or Internet
- Video chat via the Internet
- Text or voice chat in a public forum, such as a public chat room or virtual world
- Play an online game together (such as World of Warcraft or EVE Online), which includes either voice or text chat

Now think about how likely these methods of interaction are to shed the most light on these key questions about a potential mate:

- Is the person generous?
- Is the person trustworthy?
- Do you enjoy talking with the other person?

- Do you enjoy working together with him or her on shared problems?
- Does the person listen when you talk and value your point of view?

Meeting a person face to face is not a guarantee that you will not be fooled or tricked by the other person. Each year stories appear in the news about people with two families, each of whom is unknown to the other. In a recent case a woman discovered her husband had a second family when she browsed his Facebook account; he had photographs of his wedding to his secret second wife posted on his account.

### Reflection Questions

1. POSITION Here's a quotation from the preceding section: "The purpose of dating is to get to know the 'authentic self' of the other person, so that you can decide whether or not you want a long-term relationship." Do you agree with this claim? If not, give your alternative explanation of the purpose of dating.

2. POSITION Which of the ways of interacting with other people, listed above, gives the best information about whether or not the person would be a good long-term partner? Explain your reasoning. If you think there are important methods of interaction, or important questions you would want to discover about a potential mate, that we have forgotten, list them and address them in your answer.

3. RESEARCH Do an Internet search for "dating never met face to face," and make a short list of the most interesting opinions you see about whether it is possible to date or love someone that you have not met personally. Pick three of these, and explain why you agree (or disagree) with the reasoning.

4. POSITION Is it possible or reasonable for people to fall in love if they have never met face to face? Explain your reasoning.

5. POSITION Is it possible or reasonable for people to be in a long-term committed relationship if they have never met face to face? Explain your reasoning.

6. RESEARCH Many people seem to have a negative opinion of meeting people, dating, or falling in love online. Why do you think this is? Be sure to present evidence, as well as an explanation of your position.

## 6.6  DIVERSE PERSPECTIVES: RACE IN VIDEO GAMES

Designers of video games are currently struggling to incorporate racial diversity in their games. Most big-budget video games feature white protagonists, though video game studios recognize that they ought to portray a wider spectrum of human experience. Attempting to do so, however, comes with a wide variety of pitfalls.

One classic example is Carl "CJ" Johnson, the African American protagonist of *Grand Theft Auto: San Andreas*. Like many of the most successful big-budget video games, *Grand Theft Auto: San Andreas* is highly scripted. The player solves puzzles and completes missions, and after most missions is rewarded with a **cut scene**, a short movie that advances the plot. The game follows CJ, a gang member, as he attempts to resurrect his defunct gang, take over various criminal businesses, and get revenge on crooked cops and treasonous former friends.

In an article in the *New York Times Magazine*, Michel Marriott criticizes *Grand Theft Auto* for its portrayal of African-Americans like CJ:

> The sense of place, peril and pigmentation evident in previews of the game, *Grand Theft Auto: San Andreas*, underscores what some critics consider a disturbing trend: popular video games that play on racial stereotypes, including images of black youths committing and reveling in violent street crime.

The article quotes Joe Morgan, a Manhattan telecommunications executive, who describes these games as "nothing more than pixilated minstrel shows."

Mr. Morgan knows his history. A minstrel show was a type of comic performance, popular in the 1840s and 1850s, in which white actors appeared in blackface; that is, made to look black by darkening the skin, often with burnt cork. In his history of African-American comedy, *On The Real Side*, Mel Watkins says,

> By the 1840s, a systematized form of blackface stage entertainment— minstrelsy—would emerge as the rage of American popular culture, the first concerted appropriation and commercial exploitation of a black expressive form. African American humor (along with elements of song and dance) was lifted from its original context, transformed and parodied, then spotlighted for the entertainment and amusement of nonblack audiences. (82)

Minstrel shows portrayed black Americans as foolish, ignorant, lazy, and criminal. The shows were immensely popular, with at least one minstrel show being performed for President Tyler at the White House in 1844. In the words of Watkins, minstrelsy was "methodically demeaning" and "lastingly damaging" to African Americans because they created, spread, and reinforced many negative stereotypes and caricatures of African Americans. Critics of games like *Grand Theft Auto: San Andreas* accuse it of being a modern form of minstrel show. Whereas the original minstrel shows created parodies of slaves and the poor, *Grand Theft Auto* makes a parody of gang life. Some people argue that, when you play *Grand Theft Auto: San Andreas*, you are like a performer in a minstrel show, acting out a parody of hip-hop culture and street violence.

In this book, we use the phrase **digital minstrelsy** to refer to types of role play that meet the following criteria:

- A person who is a member of an advantaged group in real life plays the role of a person from a disadvantaged group
- The role play purposefully demeans members of the disadvantaged group
- The experience is primarily played out on a computer or gaming console

Note that some authors use "digital minstrelsy" as a synonym for "digital role-playing" or "digital dress-up," but we reject those definitions because they don't convey the demeaning nature of the original minstrel shows. According to our definition, digital minstrelsy is inherently bad because it is demeaning to a disadvantaged group. Game developers who are unaware of the history of minstrel shows are likely to inadvertently cause offense and damage their own reputations by perpetuating the demeaning imagery of minstrel shows.

### Reflection Questions

1. RESEARCH Find plot summaries of *Grand Theft Auto: San Andreas* online. Is the portrayal of the main character, CJ, demeaning? Is *Grand Theft Auto: San Andreas* an example of digital minstrelsy? Explain your reasoning.

2. POSITION Our definition of "digital minstrelsy" specifically focuses on disadvantaged groups. Based on this definition, a game that makes fun of the rich would be less problematic than one that makes fun of the poor. Do you agree that games that make fun of disadvantaged groups are ethically worse than ones that make fun of advantaged groups? Explain your reasoning.

## 6.7   INTERDISCIPLINARY TOPIC: UNDERSTANDING MEDIA

One of the most powerfully disruptive consequences of computing and the Internet has been the growth of many new forms of media. The Web, Twitter, Facebook, e-mail, Google, e-books, word processing, computer spreadsheets, podcasts, video games, and apps are all examples of media that did not exist (for all practical purposes) thirty years ago. Most of these new media were not invented by media scholars, or people who worked in traditional media like newspapers, publishing, or television. They were invented by computer scientists and computer hobbyists. For those who create successful new media, the financial rewards are often enormous.

To understand the many ways these new media are changing our society, and to predict the ways they are likely to change society in the future, it's helpful to turn to the work of one of the most influential media scholars of the twentieth century, Marshall McLuhan. McLuhan was a professor at the University of Toronto when, in 1964, he published his most famous book, *Understanding Media: The Extensions of Man.* The book was an unexpected hit, making McLuhan a bit of a celebrity. (He even had a cameo in Woody Allen's classic movie *Annie Hall.*) In *Understanding Media*, and in the closely related *The Medium is the Massage*, McLuhan foresaw many of the societal changes that are now taking place.

Let's consider some of McLuhan's key ideas, starting with his definition of "media." As the subtitle of McLuhan's first book suggests, he considers **media** to be extensions of humanity. In other words, each media extends some natural human process. In *The Medium is the Massage,* he says, "the book is an extension of the eye ... electric circuitry [is] an extension of the central nervous system" (34-37, 40). In fact, he also says "the wheel is an extension of the foot" and "clothing, an extension of the skin." (31-32, 38-39)

McLuhan often used the word "technology" interchangeably with "media." Most people, when they say "media," are thinking only about methods of communicating information. However, McLuhan's definition reminds us that new technologies "work us over completely," even those that seem unrelated to communication. (2005, 26)

For example, consider the wheel. Without the wheel, we could never have developed the mass-produced novel, because there would have been no efficient way to transport heavy paper books from the place they were made to the readers. Even though we don't normally view it as a "method of communication," the wheel in fact totally remade the way that we interact with others.

A second major claim of McLuhan's work is that "societies have always been shaped more by the nature of the media by which men communicate than by the content of the communication." (2005, 8) One of McLuhan's catchphrases is that "the medium is the message." He completely rejects the position that technologies are not inherently good or bad, that it is only what one does with a technology that makes it good or bad. McLuhan says,

> Suppose we were to say, "Apple pie is in itself neither good nor bad; it is the way it is used that determines its values." Or, "The smallpox virus is in itself neither good nor bad; it is the way it is used that determines its value." Again, "Firearms are in themselves neither good nor bad; it is the way they are used that determines their value." (1994, 11)

He argues that the medium itself really does shape us, and society, and ethics. In McLuhan's view, media are not neutral. Understanding the medium itself, he argues, is more important than understanding its contents.

To understand McLuhan's argument, think about language itself, which is a medium that has a profound effect on the way we think. Some ideas are easier to communicate in one language than in another, and this in turn makes it more likely for those ideas to catch on with people who speak the appropriate language. One example, from Stanford psychology professor Lera Boroditzky, is that many aboriginal groups in Australia have no words for "right," "left," "forward," and "back." Instead, they use cardinal directions, so one might say "There's an ant on your southeast leg." She explains that research shows that speakers of such languages "are much better than English speakers at staying oriented and keeping track of where they are, even in unfamiliar landscapes or inside unfamiliar buildings."

According to McLuhan, this type of phenomenon occurs with all media—that is, the medium shapes what is possible or reasonable to say. The more time that we spend in a particular medium (novels or e-mail or Twitter for example), the more this shapes how we think.

McLuhan takes his critique of media even further, arguing that the effects of media are particularly insidious because the media themselves quickly become invisible to us. We focus on the contents, instead of the medium itself. The medium then becomes part of the environment, similar to the way the illumination from an electric light becomes part of the environment of a room. You might not be inclined to see an electric light as a type of medium because it has no message at all. Most people do not view it as a method for communication. But McLuhan sees this comparison as more than just an analogy:

> Whether the light is being used for brain surgery or night baseball is a matter of indifference. It could be argued that these activities are in some way the "content" of the electric light. This fact merely underlines the point that "the medium is the message" because it is the medium that shapes and controls the scale and form of human association and action. The content or uses of such media are as diverse as they are ineffectual in shaping the form of human association. (1994, 9)

Thus, according to McLuhan, the electric light is a medium that allows us to extend our actions and associations into new times and places. In general, McLuhan felt that people who studied the media mostly studied the wrong thing. *Understanding Media* was his attempt to redirect attention away from the contents, to the medium itself.

We cannot hope to cover all of McLuhan's ideas in this chapter, but the ideas just presented are a good start. To summarize:

- Media—any new technologies—are extensions of humanity.
- The medium is the message; the contents are always less important than the medium itself.
- Media are often overlooked because people are focused on the contents, not the medium.

McLuhan introduced four questions, called the **tetrad**, designed to help us analyze a new medium and foresee its effects. (The term "tetrad" means "set of four.") The four questions in the tetrad are as follows:

- What does the artifact enhance or intensify or make possible or accelerate? This can be asked concerning a wastebasket, a painting, a steamroller, or a zipper, as well as about a proposition in Euclid or a law of physics. It can be asked about any word or phrase in any language.
- If some aspect of a situation is enlarged or enhanced, simultaneously the old condition or unenhanced situation is displaced thereby. What is pushed aside or obsolesced by the new 'organ'?
- What recurrence or retrieval of earlier actions and services is brought into play simultaneously by the new form? What older, previously obsolesced ground is brought back and inheres in the new form?
- When pushed to the limits of its potential (another complementary action), the new form will tend to reverse what had been its original characteristics. What is the reversal potential of the new form? (1988, 98-99)

| Enhances<br>Speed of doing laundry | Reverses into<br>Process: continuous laundry |
|---|---|
| Retrieves<br>Antiseptic house | Obsolesces<br>Scrub board and tub |

**F I G U R E  6.6**  Marshall McLuhan's tetrad for "Washing Machine" (1988, 190-191)

We illustrate the use of this by presenting and explaining one of McLuhan's tetrads, the one for "washing machine." McLuhan's tetrad is presented in Figure 6.6. Note that we have omitted his explanations, presenting only the tetrad itself. In presenting a tetrad, McLuhan placed the questions of the tetrad in a two-by-two grid formation, laid out as shown in the figure. In each space he wrote some notes about the effects of a new technology, based on the questions of the tetrad.

The washing machine tetrad shown in Figure 6.6 is based on a very influential book, *More Work for Mother*, by Ruth Schwartz Cowan, a sociology professor at University of Pennsylvania who studies the sociology of science and technology. McLuhan has simply put her arguments into his tetrad form. In her book, Cowan argues that the effect of the introduction of the washing machine (in the 1920s) eventually led to an increase of work for homemakers, not less. She describes how the electric washing machine made washing much easier and faster, by replacing the physically demanding scrubbing board and washtub. These are the first two elements of the tetrad; the washing machine enhances the speed and ease of washing laundry and makes hand scrubbing obsolete.

Cowan argues that this led to a change in behavior and expectations. By the 1920s, when the electric washer was introduced, most households no longer had household servants, and people had come to accept the fact that clothes, sheets, and rugs would not be perfectly clean. The introduction of the washing machine restored the expectation that clothes and sheets would immaculately clean. This is the third element of the tetrad—the expectation of perfect cleanliness in the house was brought back from history and brought down from the upper classes to the lower and middle classes.

This, in turn, led to an increased amount of laundry to wash. Cowan points out that, in the 1920s, the cuffs and collars of men's shirts were detachable. Normally only cuffs and collars would be washed; the shirt would be worn several times between washes. After the introduction of washing machine, it became customary to wash the whole shirt after each wearing. Similarly, in the 1920s it was common to wash only one bed sheet at a time, not both. The bottom sheet got washed, the top sheet was moved down to the bottom, and the freshly cleaned sheet placed on the top. After the introduction of the washer, it became customary to wash both sheets each time the bed is changed. As a result, the washing machine actually increased the amount of work involved in laundry, not decreased it. Instead of paying servants or cleaning services to clean the clothes, it is now all done in the home. The technology has reversed itself (this is the fourth element of the tetrad). The washing machine, which originally decreased the work involved in laundry, has now actually increased the amount of work involved in laundry.

Cowan's book gives many more examples of ways that household technologies have reversed themselves, leading to, as Cowan says, "more work for mother," not less. McLuhan's book contains many more examples of tetrad-based analyses of various technologies.

### Reflection Questions

1. POSITION You may recall that, in Section 3.6, we made the argument that panoptic structures in society are not inherently good or bad, and that their goodness or badness is a function of how they are used. Both Foucault and McLuhan would agree that the panoptic design is a medium, and Foucault in fact called it a "political technology." According to McLuhan, however, such a blanket statement is not valid, because: 1) you have to look carefully at the medium to decide how it will affect society; and 2) the "way it is used" is the least important part of the analysis. Which position do you find more persuasive? Explain your reasoning.

2. APPLICATION Apply McLuhan's tetrad to Twitter, the social network that allows people to communicate in short 140-character-or-less messages. Structure your answer similar to the four-part grid in Figure 6.6.

3. RESEARCH Analysis using the tetrad is very context-dependent. Because the tetrad asks how the medium changes society, it requires a good knowledge of what life was like before the new medium. Try applying the tetrad to e-mail. Then, after you have produced your own answers to the four questions, interview friends or family members who, because of their age, experienced e-mail differently from you. If you are thirty-five years old or younger, interview people in their 50s or 60s—that is, interview people for whom e-mail was a radically new technology. If you are over thirty-five, interview people in their late teens or early 20s—that is, interview people who have used e-mail nearly all their lives. How do the answers of the people you interviewed differ from your own answers?

## 6.8  OUR CYBERNETIC FUTURE

In this chapter we have looked at the subtle ways that computer technology is changing who we are. Citing Marshall McLuhan, we argued that these subtle changes are the most important changes, because we mostly ignore them as we go about our everyday lives. In this final section we focus on something that is more directly changing the nature of human beings, cybernetic technology, which involves grafting computer (or machine) parts onto living organisms.

The definition of cybernetics is not universally agreed upon. According to one definition, **cybernetics** is the study of self-regulating or self-controlling systems. One example of such a self-regulating system is a human's internal heat regulation system. When we overheat, we perspire, so that we will be cooled by the evaporation of sweat. When we are too cold, we shiver. The rapid contractions of our muscles, in shivering, burns energy, and gives off heat, which warms us back up.

Engineers who study cybernetics often use examples from nature to try to solve similar problems in machines. For example, like a human, your computer has an internal heat regulation system that consists primarily of a variable-speed fan that blows air across the computer CPU. This heat regulation system is a lot less efficient than the human version, because it uses air-cooling rather than liquid cooling. However, some of the most expensive custom-built computers have efficient liquid cooling systems, which mimic the human circulatory system.

The word "cybernetic" is also used to refer to a biological organism that has computer or machine components. Some people use the word **cyborg**, short for **cybernetic organism** to distinguish between the scientific study of cybernetics and such hybrid organisms.

These two definitions of "cybernetic" seem, at first, totally unrelated. Norbert Weiner, in his National Book Award-winning *God and Golem Inc.,* hints at the connection. Weiner is often credited with coining the term "cybernetic," perhaps based on the Greek word *kybernetes*, which means "steersman." He was not thinking about cyborgs; he was thinking about the role of human beings in a society where machines and computers do most of the work. According to Weiner:

> The future offers very little hope for those who expect that our new mechanical slaves will offer us a world in which we may rest from thinking. Help us they may, but at the cost of supreme demands upon our honesty and our intelligence. (1965, 69)

The common usage of "cybernetic" to refer to organism-machine hybrids reflects this understanding that the machines give us new powers, but the organism remains in control, the one thinking, the one steering. In Weiner's view we are all already cyborgs because of our dependence on and use of technology in every part of our lives.

We are on the cusp of a new age, when cybernetic augmentations will start to be available. By **cybernetic augmentation** we mean a computerized prosthesis that gives the user abilities that normal human beings do not have. The first experiments to augment vision by implanting a chip in the retina and to allow a direct interface between the brain and computer, have already been carried out. In the next two sections we explore some examples of ethical or social challenges posed by cybernetic organisms.

### Reflection Questions

1.    APPLICATION Based on your reading of Section 6.7, do you think that Marshall McLuhan would agree with the claim that "machines give us new powers, but the organism remains in control?" Explain your reasoning.

2.    POSITION It could be claimed that most humans, today, are cyborgs. For example, many people use smartphones to take notes and keep a schedule. It could be argued that this is extending and taking the place of human memory, so the person that acts this way is a cybernetic organism. Write an argument either defending or refuting this position.

## 6.8.1   Case: Robotic Legs in the Olympics

For the most part, cyborgs, as portrayed by science fiction writers, do not yet exist. The technology for interfacing between biological and computerized systems is still very rudimentary. Instead, we will look at a case about noncomputerized prosthetics to get a sense of the types of precedents that are being set in the area of human modification and augmentation.

Oscar Pistorius is an elite sprinter for South Africa. His specialties are the 400-meter sprint and the 4x400-meter relay; he has a good chance of qualifying for the 2012 Olympics in London. At the time of this writing he needs only one more 400-meter race with a time under 45.25 seconds to qualify. His case is particularly interesting and controversial because he was born without working legs. A double-amputee, he runs on carbon-fiber prosthetic legs.

Pistorius holds the Paralympic records for the 100-meter, 200-meter, and 400-meter sprints. He has also fought for years to be allowed to run in able-bodied (ordinary) athletic events. He was originally banned from competition, because it was feared that his prosthetic legs might give him an advantage of some kind. Pistorius' legs are not "bionic" or "cybernetic." They are simply springy pieces of carbon fiber that are shaped to provide good performance when running.

The International Association of Athletic Federations (IAAF, the group that governs track and field competitions) eventually concluded that his prosthetic legs did not give him an unfair advantage. In the summer of 2011 he competed in the IAAF World Championships, where he qualified for the semifinals of the 400-meter sprint and where he helped his team win second place in the 4x400-meter relay.

In making the decision about whether or not to let Pistorius compete, the IAAF considered the following questions:

- Is an athlete using prostheses more or less likely to get injured than one who does not use prostheses?

- Does the springy material of the prosthetic legs provide a mechanical advantage over ordinary legs?

- Do the prosthetic legs weigh less than ordinary legs? If so, does this provide an advantage in the events Pistorius will enter?

Physiology and kinesiology experts have concluded, so far, that there is no scientific evidence that Pistorius's prosthetics provide any advantage. Therefore, Pistorius has been cleared to compete in normal events sanctioned by the IAAF. It is possible that, if evidence to the contrary is found in the future, his permission to compete may be revoked.

Part of the argument supporting Pistorius's competition in IAAF sanctioned events is that the legs themselves don't provide any sort of artificial power boost. In an opinion article at *CNN.com*, Dr. Fred Vox, of the New England Rehabilitation Hospital and Tufts University School of Medicine, claims that athletes with powered bionic limbs might one day be allowed to participate in able-bodied sporting events. In this case, however, it may be necessary to limit the power and speed of the motors in the bionic leg, to prevent athletes using them from getting an advantage over nonaugmented runners.

There is an inherent ethical problem posed by Vox's idea: How do we decide on the fair level of performance from a bionic leg? Bionic legs designed to perform like the legs of an average person would amount to a disadvantage in a race full of elite runners. On the other hand, legs designed to perform like the legs of the world's best runners would probably offer an advantage.

### Reflection Questions

1. POSITION Either defend or critique the following proposed solution to the problem of designing bionic legs for sport: Any bionic legs used in a competition should be set to perform at the median level of performance exhibited by able-bodied athletes in the previous year's competition.

2. POSITION Given that some people have better genes than others for particular sports, is it true that sports competitions are inherently unfair? Explain your reasoning, paying careful attention to explaining what "fairness" means in sports competitions.

### 6.8.2   Case: Elective Amputation

The availability of high-quality artificial organs, including legs, arms, hands, eyes, and so on, creates a new ethical problem for doctors: whether to take part in elective amputations. An **elective** surgery, such as **elective amputation,** is not medically necessary, but is desired by the patient. This is already an issue with current prosthetics, and it will only get more pronounced as the technology behind body-to-computer interfaces improves.

Many surgeons refuse to participate in surgeries unless there is some clear positive health outcome for the patient. If a limb is damaged to the point that it either places the life of the patient at risk, or inflicts so much pain that it will significantly reduce the patient's quality of life, the surgeon is probably ethically justified in participating in the amputation. But what if there is no immediate medical reason for the amputation? To explore the range of choices doctors might face, let's consider three scenarios.

The first scenario, described by Dan O'Connor, a faculty member at the Johns Hopkins Berman Institute of Bioethics, was a real case that involved a patient with a nonfunctional hand. The patient lost the use of his hand in a motorcycle accident, but the hand was otherwise normal. It was not likely to be infected and was not giving the patient much pain. The hand did have sensation, so the patient was not likely to get an injury without knowing it (something that happens often to patients with serious nerve damage). The patient had requested that a surgeon remove his hand. He wished to get a bionic hand, but there was no way to use it without getting his original hand amputated. Should the surgeon agree to perform the procedure?

The second scenario (which is made up, but based on real cases) involves a very rare and controversial condition: body integrity identity disorder (BIID). The main symptom of this condition is the desire to have a healthy and functioning limb amputated. Most patients with this condition are not irrational about other issues, but strongly feel that their current bodies do not match their images of themselves. Some patients have described their feelings as being similar to the feelings that motivate a person to have gender reassignment surgery or to get piercings or tattoos that others never see. Overwhelmed by the desire to alter their bodies, some people who suffer from BIID will often seek the help of a surgeon. Some, if they fail to find a competent surgeon, will take matters into their own hands, often with disastrous results. Should a surgeon participate in such an operation?

Scenario three looks to the future, and is somewhere in between the other two scenarios. In this scenario a patient with a perfectly healthy and functioning limb asks a doctor to remove it so that he can use a bionic prosthesis. Should a surgeon be willing to participate in such an operation?

## Reflection Questions

1.   RESEARCH What are the standards of medical ethics that apply to cases of elective amputation? Look up the various oaths or codes of ethics that apply where you live.

2.   APPLICATION Apply the oaths or codes you found in the previous question to the three scenarios presented here. In each case, say whether or not you think the surgeon is ethically permitted to participate in the amputation, and support your answer by quoting appropriate parts of the code or oath that you are using.

3.   POSITION Is elective cosmetic surgery (for example, rhinoplasty—a nose job) more ethically acceptable than the scenarios presented here? Explain your reasoning.

4.   APPLICATION Imagine that prosthetic eyes and hands advance to the point that they are vastly superior to human eyes and hands. Imagine further that it is shown that surgeons with bionic eyes

and hands are twice as fast and are ninety percent less likely to make mistakes than human surgeons without prosthetics or bionics. Would all surgeons be morally required to get bionic hands and eyes? Explain your reasoning, using one of the ethical theories from Chapter 1, or the concept of professionalism from Chapter 2.

## SUMMARY

- Computer technology influences an individual's self-concept. Furthermore, digital image manipulation may be changing our very concept of beauty.

- Social networking sites have the potential to change an individual's self-concept from a single true self to multiple explicit personas.

- New forms of Internet-based sociopathy are on the rise. These forms include griefing, cyberbullying, cyberstalking, and trolling. Traditional measures for diagnosing antisocial behavior disorders don't apply to the online world.

- The preceding topics (self-concept and Internet-based sociopathy) are tied together by the concept of normalization, which is the process by which something becomes normal and accepted in society.

- Computers and the Internet appear to be intensifying behavioral addictions. Until recently behavioral addictions were not considered to be real addictions, but scientists are beginning to find evidence that they function like substance addictions.

- A graph or network is a mathematical construct that can be used to represent relationships between people or things. Social network analysis is a branch of sociology that uses math and graphs to try to predict the outcome of social phenomena, such as the spread of disease.

- Online social networks can encourage social homophily, a state of affairs in which we only interact with others who are like ourselves.

- *Wikipedia* threatens the traditional model for creating and codifying knowledge. This is because anyone can contribute to *Wikipedia*, even if they do not have formal training or recognized expertise.

- Digital minstrelsy demonstrates one way that computer technologies can negatively affect self-concept. It is important for video game makers to be aware of the history of minstrel shows if they wish to avoid re-creating them.

- Marshall McLuhan's definition of media equates "media" with "technologies." His set of four questions, called a tetrad, is a useful tool for analyzing or predicting the effects of a new media.

- Cybernetic augmentations, while still relatively rare, are starting to become commercially viable. Society will need to decide when it is, and is not, ethical to use such augmentations.

## CHAPTER EXERCISES

1. REVIEW Define self and self-concept, as used in this chapter.

2. REVIEW Define persona, and contrast with the concept of a person.

3. REVIEW Define griefer, troll, cyberbully, and cyberstalker.

4. REVIEW Define "normalization" as it is used in the context of changing social attitudes.

5. REVIEW List at least three of the diagnostic criteria for gambling disorder. You should select the three that you think are most important, or most indicative of an addiction to gambling.

6. REVIEW Explain the concept of a network, or graph, as it is used in math and computer science. In particular, describe or define each of these terms: node, edge, path and shortest path. It may help you to draw a picture to illustrate your definitions.

7. REVIEW Compare and contrast the current definition of "social network" with the traditional definition from social science.

8. REVIEW State the six degrees of separation hypothesis.

9. REVIEW Define "epistemology" and "reason" as used in this chapter.

10. REVIEW Define "social homophily."

11. REVIEW Define "crowdsourcing" in the context of *Wikipedia*.

12. REVIEW Describe what a minstrel show was, and define "digital minstrelsy."

13. REVIEW Restate McLuhan's definition of "media" and explain what is meant by "the medium is the message" and "the media are invisible."

14. REVIEW List the four questions of McLuhan's tetrad.

15. REVIEW Restate both definitions of "cybernetic."

16. RESEARCH What is an "edit war" in the context of *Wikipedia*?

17. APPLICATION Consider the *ACM/IEEE Software Engineering Code of Ethics and Professional Practice*, as described in Chapter 2. Would someone who adheres to that code be able to work as a software developer on games like *Grand Theft Auto* and *God of War III*? Explain your reasoning.

18. POSITION The word "schadenfreude" is a German word that means taking joy in the misfortune or pain of others. Schadenfreude appears to be one of the main motivations for griefers. Is it ever morally good to feel schadenfreude? In particular, is it okay to feel joy when a bad person experiences misfortune? Why or why not?

19. APPLICATION Have you ever unfriended or unfollowed someone in a social network because you disagreed with something he or she said? (If not, try to find a friend or colleague who has done so, and discuss their reasons with them.) Why did you (or your friend) break the social network connection with another person? Explain how this relates to social homophily.

20. APPLICATION Select a technology or medium that you find particularly interesting, and apply McLuhan's tetrad to analyze its effects. Note that the more invisible the medium is, the more interesting your results are likely to be.

21. POSITION Would you ever willingly have a normal working body part (such as an eye or limb) removed, so that you could have a prosthesis instead? Explain your reasoning. If your answer is "yes," be sure to explain what capabilities the prosthesis would have to have to be worth making this decision.

## WORKS CITED

American Psychiatric Association. *Diagnostic and Statistical Manual of Mental Disorders DSM-IV*. 4th ed. American Psychiatric Association, 1994. Print.

---, "R 31 Gambling Disorder." www.dsm5.org. American Psychiatric Association. Web. 21 Aug 2011. <http://www.dsm5.org/proposedrevision/Pages/proposedrevision.aspx?rid=210>.

Boroditsky, Lera. "How Does Our Language Shape The Way We Think?" *Edge.org*. nd. Web. 6 Sept. 2011.

Cowan, Ruth Schwartz. *More Work for Mother: The Ironies of Household Technology from the Open Hearth to the Microwave*. New York: Basic Books, 1983. Print.

Dibbell, Julian. "Mutilated Furries, Flying Phalluses: Put the Blame on Griefers, the Sociopaths of the Virtual World." *Wired.com*, 18 Jan. 2008. Web. 13 Sept. 2011.

Doctorow, Cory. "The Criticism That Ralph Lauren Doesn't Want You to See!" *Boing Boing* 6 Oct 2009. Web. 4 Aug 2011.

Giles, Jim. "Internet encyclopaedias go head to head." *Nature*, 438.7070 (2005): 900-901. Web. 6 Sept. 2011.

Gonsalves, Chris. "Multiple Online Personas: The Choice of a New Generation." *Baseline* 8 Feb. 2008. Web. 18 Aug. 2011.

Green, Joshua. "Digital Blackface: The Repackaging of the Black Masculine Image." MA thesis Miami University, 2006. *OhioLink Electronic Theses and Dissertations*. Web. 3 Nov. 2010.

Hardach, Sophie. "France mulls health warning for fashion photos." *Reuters* 21 Sep. 2009. Web. 18 Aug. 2011. <http://in.reuters.com/article/idINIndia-42600920090921>.

Johnson, Allan G. *The Blackwell Dictionary of Sociology: A User's Guide to Sociological Language*. Oxford, UK: Blackwell Publishers, 2000. EBSCOhost.com, 13 Sept. 2011.

Karl, Jonathan. "SEC and Pornography: Employees Spent Hours Surfing Porn Sites." *ABC News* 22 Apr 2010. Web. 21 Aug 2011.

Match.com. "Match.com and Chadwick Martin Bailey 2009 - 2010 Studies: Recent Trends: Online Dating." nd. Web. 3 Nov. 2010. < http://cp.match.com/cppp/media/CMB_Study.pdf>.

Marriott, Michel. "The Color of Mayhem." *New York Times* 12 Aug. 2004. Web. 19 Aug. 2011.

McLuhan, Marshall, and Eric McLuhan. *Laws of Media: The New Science.* Toronto: University of Toronto Press, 1988. Print.

McLuhan, Marshall, and Lewis H. Lapham. *Understanding Media: The Extensions of Man.* Cambridge, MA: The MIT Press, 1994. Print.

McLuhan, Marshall, and Quentin Fiore. *The Medium is the Massage.* 1967. Berkeley, CA: Gingko Press, 2005. Print.

Milgram, Stanley. "The Small-World Problem." *Psychology Today* 1.1 (1967) : 61-67. Print.

National Institutes of Health. "Depression High Among Youth Victims of School Cyber Bullying, NIH Researchers Report." 21 Sept 2010. Web. 10 Aug 2011. <http://www.nichd.nih.gov/news/releases/092110-cyber-bullying.cfm>.

O'Connor, Dan. "The Elective/Necessary Myth." *Berman Institute Bioethics Bulletin* 19 May 2011. Web. 28 Aug 2011.

Pettey, Christy. "Gartner Says 'Generation Virtual' Will Have a Profound Influence on Culture, Society and Business." 13 Nov. 2007. Web. 18 Aug. 2011. <http://www.gartner.com/it/page.jsp?id=545108>.

PopCap Games. "Survey: Tens of Millions of 'White Collar' Workers Play 'Casual' Video Games - One in Four Play at Work, and Senior Execs Play Even More." 4 Sept 2007. Web. 21 Aug 2011.

Poulter, Sean. "Julia Roberts and Christy Turlington L'Oreal Adverts Banned over Airbrushing." *Mail Online* 27 July 2011. Web. 4 Aug 2011.

Vox, Ford. "Why Oscar Pistorius Deserves to Run." *CNN.com* 28 Aug 2011. Web. 28 Aug 2011.

Wiener, Norbert. *God and Golem, Inc.; a Comment on Certain Points Where Cybernetics Impinges on Religion.* Cambridge, MA: MIT Press, 1964. Print.

Williams, Dmitri et al. "The Virtual Census: Representations of Gender, Race and Age in Video Games." *New Media & Society* 11.5 (2009) : 815-834. Web. 19 Aug 2011.

World Health Organization. *The ICD-10 Classification of Mental and Behavioural Disorders: Clinical Descriptions and Diagnostic Guidelines.* 1st ed. Geneva: World Health Organization, 1992. Print.

## RELATED READINGS

### Essays and Articles

Dibbell, Julian. "A Rape in Cyberspace." *My Tiny Life: Crime and Passion in a Virtual World.* 1st ed. New York: Holt Paperbacks, 1999. 11-32. Print. (Julian Dibbell's Web site describes the essay this way: "[T]his curious little tale of crime and punishment online has become an all-purpose cybercultural parable, cited by authors, professors, and others looking for a quick way to explain how virtual life is and isn't different from real life." The classic essay raises issues about what should and should not be allowed in cyberspace, and whether or not real world laws should be applied to virtual worlds. The piece originally appeared in the *Village Voice* in 1993.)

McLuhan, Marshall, and Lewis H. Lapham. "The Gadget Lover." *Understanding Media: The Extensions of Man*. Cambridge: The MIT Press, 1994. 41–47. Print. (In this essay, McLuhan contradicts the idea that in a cybernetic organism, the organism remains in control. He claims that, on the contrary, sometimes the technology is in control, forcing humans to change. At one point he claims that humanity's relationship to technology is like the relationship of bees to flowers; the main value of bees is that they help flowering plants to reproduce and evolve.)

## Film and TV

Ephron, Nora. *You've Got Mail*. Warner Bros. 1998. Film. (Tom Hanks and Meg Ryan star as people who meet and fall in love, online. In real life he is the owner of a chain of stores that is trying to buy out and close down her small independent bookstore. Neither one knows the other's true identity, which allows their romance to blossom online in spite of their conflicts in real life. This movie is an example of the growing importance of our relationships with people that we have never met face to face.)

Sloan, Robin, and Matt Thompson. "EPIC 2014." Web. 11 Nov. 2010. <http://robinsloan.com/epic/>. (This short video imagines a future in which social media has replaced traditional journalism, and social homophily is greatly reinforced by personalized search engines and new Web sites.)

Spence, Rob. *Deus Ex: The Eyeborg Documentary*. 2011. Web. 28 Aug. 2011. (Rob Spence is a cyborg filmmaker who shoots video using a prosthetic eye with a built-in camera. This film is a long-form commercial for a science fiction video game in which the main characters are cyborgs. Spence, who calls himself "Eyeborg," travels the world, learning about the current state of cyborg technology from people who have real cybernetic eyes, legs, and hands.)

Weir, Peter. *The Truman Show*. Paramount Pictures. 1998. Film. (This movie contrasts nicely with *You've Got Mail*. Truman, played by Jim Carrey, is an insurance salesman who is the unwitting star of a reality show on television. His entire life, starting from his birth, has been televised, and all the people he knows, from his boss to his wife, are actors. Is Truman's relationship with his wife more real than the online relationship of Hanks's and Ryan's characters?)

# Chapter 7

# Democracy, Freedom of Speech, and Freedom of the Press

At some time about 50,000 years ago, human beings developed the ability to speak, and at least in Mesopotamia, had learned to write by 4,000 B.C.E. (Inglehart, 1). We do not know when the first person got into trouble for saying or writing the wrong thing, but certainly there is a long history of rulers wanting to control what people said and wrote. For example, Solon, lawmaker and ruler of ancient Athens, outlawed speaking evil about the living and the dead in 594 B.C.E. Long before the invention of the printing press in 1450 A.D., there were books, libraries, and book burnings. The printing press, however, like other technologies that would follow, complicated matters. The amount of printed material available increased dramatically and ideas spread with much greater rapidity. The increase was not universally welcomed. For example, the Venetian scholar, scientist, and church reformer, Brother Paolo Sarpi (1552-1623) "There is no need of books, the world hath too many already, especially since printing was invented; and it is better to forbid a thousand books without cause, than permit one which deserves prohibition." (Inglehart, 40) More recent inventions, such as the telegraph, the telephone, radio, and television, brought new complexities to the issues surrounding communication. Recently, the Internet, hailed by many to be the most significant new development since the printing press, has been added to the list of technologies that can greatly increase our freedom of expression or can potentially constrain it.

In this chapter we will look at freedom of expression, particularly as a constitutional right of citizens of the United States. We will examine the history of that freedom and how new technologies, particularly the Internet, have affected our freedom of expression. We also look at how the Internet, as a global entity, affects our relationships with others, both within and outside our borders.

## 7.1 UNDERSTANDING THE FIRST AMENDMENT

The First Amendment of the United States Constitution is well known to most Americans. It is brief and direct:

> Congress shall make no law respecting an establishment of religion, or prohibiting the free exercise thereof; or abridging the freedom of speech, or of the press; or of the right of the people peaceably to assemble, and to petition the government for a redress of grievances.

The apparent simplicity of the amendment is misleading. For one thing, the word "speech" in the amendment was interpreted by both the courts and the public as meaning more than vocalization by a human—even before the age of computers and the Internet. As pointed out by Marjorie Heins, in her acclaimed work on intellectual freedom, *Not in Front of the Children*, "For purposes of the First Amendment, and the values of intellectual freedom that it embodies, freedom of speech necessarily includes the right to read, view, hear, and think about the expression of others." (13) Similarly, "reading" does not apply only to text, but to drawings, paintings, photographs, and electronic representations of visual images.

Another thing to keep in mind is that the text of the amendment speaks only of the ability of Congress to amend our freedom of speech. It does not address the capability of the President, the courts, state governments, local governments, or private enterprises to abridge our right of free speech. James Madison, when addressing the Congress to present the Bill of Rights, originally proposed two amendments: 1) "The people shall not be deprived or abridged of their right to speak, to write, or to publish their sentiments; and the freedom of the press, as one of the great bulwarks of liberty, shall be inviolable." 2) "No State shall violate the equal rights of conscience, or the freedom of the press, or the trial by jury in criminal cases." The final version passed by the Congress did not include any constraints on the states. It wasn't until 1868, with the passage of the Fourteenth Amendment, that the Constitution extended the prohibition to state governments. The Fourteenth Amendment, while still brief, is not nearly as brief the First Amendment. It consists of five sections, but only the first concerns us here:

> **Section 1.** All persons born or naturalized in the United States, and subject to the jurisdiction thereof, are citizens of the United States and of the State wherein they reside. No State shall make or enforce any law which shall abridge the privileges or immunities of citizens of the United States; nor shall any State deprive any person of life, liberty, or property, without due process of law; nor deny to any person within its jurisdiction the equal protection of the laws.

The key point of the Fourteenth Amendment, as it applies to our discussion here, is the clause, "No State shall make or enforce any law which shall abridge the privileges or immunities of citizens of the United States...." That portion was ultimately interpreted to mean that the prohibitions against Congress specified in the First Amendment also apply to the individual states.

Generally (but not universally), the First and Fourteenth Amendments together are interpreted as preventing the government at any level—whether federal, state, or local—from abridging our freedom of speech. This interpretation was definitively established in 1925 by the case *Gitlow v. New York*. Mr. Benjamin Gitlow was a socialist who was arrested and convicted in New York under the New York Anarchy Law of 1902 for distributing communist literature. The United States Supreme Court ruled that the Fourteenth Amendment dictated that state laws were subject to the same restrictions as the federal laws according the Constitution. The court ruled the New York statute violated Mr. Gitlow's Constitutional rights.

Finally, you should note that the seemingly absolute declaration of free speech in the First Amendment is not nearly so protective of our freedom of speech as you might think. The explicit parameters of our freedom of speech are not specified in the amendment, nor anywhere else in the Constitution. It is clear, however, that the First Amendment was never intended to ensure absolute freedom; our speech is constrained in many ways. The fact that the founding fathers explicitly rejected constraining the states is sufficient to rule out an interpretation of absolute freedom of speech for all citizens. Furthermore, laws passed shortly after the Bill of Rights became law, such as the Sedition Act of 1798, discussed later in this chapter, strongly suggest that certain constraints on speech could and often were imposed on the American public.

Prior to *Gitlow v. New York*, states could and did restrict both speech and the press. In fact, in 1814, Thomas Jefferson, the principle architect of the Declaration of Independence and strong proponent of individual freedom, was indirectly involved in a case of censorship. Two years earlier, a Frenchman, M. de Becourt, had written Jefferson concerning a book that Becourt was writing on astronomy and geology. Mr. Jefferson wished to purchase a copy of the finished work and notified his usual bookseller, N. G. Dufief Monticello, of his interest. When the book was completed, Monticello, as a courtesy to Mr. Jefferson, paid Mr. Becourt two dollars for the purchase of the book. That favor caused Mr. Monticello some significant legal problems. Mr. Becourt's book contained some assertions about the origins of the earth that were offensive to some religions and it was illegal to sell it in Virginia. Mr. Monticello appealed to Jefferson for assistance. It is not evident that Mr. Jefferson intervened in any concrete way in the Monitcello case, but he did respond in a two page hand written, often quoted, letter that reads, in part:

> I am really mortified to be told that, in the *United States of America*, a fact like this can become a subject of inquiry, and of criminal inquiry too, as an offence against religion; that a question about the sale of a book can be carried before the civil magistrate. Is this then our freedom of religion? and are we to have a censor whose imprimatur shall say what books may be sold, and what we may buy? And who is thus to dogmatize religious opinions for our citizens? Whose foot is to be the measure to which ours are all to be cut or stretched? Is a priest to be our inquisitor, or shall a layman, simple as ourselves, set up his reason as the rule for what we are to read, and what we must believe? It is an insult to

our citizens to question whether they are rational beings or not, and blasphemy against religion to suppose it cannot stand the test of truth and reason. If M. de Becourt's book be false in its facts, disprove them; if false in its reasoning, refute it. But, for God's sake, let us freely hear both sides, if we choose. [Original emphasis] (Lipscomb and Bergh, 127)

Thomas Jefferson did ultimately get his book, but not through his bookseller. It was sent to him directly by Mr. Becourt. Apparently, Mr. Monticello was able to extricate himself from his legal difficulties without Mr. Jefferson's intervention.

Today, of course, no state could impose the kind of restriction on free speech such as that encountered by Mr. Monticello. Nevertheless, there are many ways in which our speech is limited. For example, it is illegal to advertise tobacco on television; a citizen may be executed for revealing military secrets; and many prohibitions exist concerning images considered by law to be obscene. Exactly what speech is banned and why has been a point of contention ever since the Bill of Rights was adopted. One interpretation is that the amendment applies only to **prior restraint** of speech or of the press. That is, the government may not prevent you from making a statement or publishing a story, but it may prosecute you afterwards as a consequence of having done so.

Proponents of this view often appeal to the writings of Sir William Blackstone. His work, *Blackstone's Commentaries*, was one of the most important legal documents in the early days of our nation. Blackstone held that freedom of speech or of the press required only the right to speak or publish, not to be immune to the consequences of speaking or publishing. He argued that the government was at liberty to create laws that would punish people for certain kinds of speech or publications. Under that interpretation, Congress could not pass a law preventing you from publishing a newspaper story that calls the President a liar, but they could pass a law that would allow you to be imprisoned if you did. In fact, Congress did exactly that less than a decade after the Bill of Rights was passed. The Sedition Act of 1798 made it a crime to write or publish any "false, scandalous and malicious writing or writings" against the government of the United States, either house of Congress, or the president.

The reason the vice president was not protected by the act is an interesting story. The act was passed by a Congress made up of a majority of Federalists who were supporters of President John Adams. They intended the act to prevent Vice President Thomas Jefferson, a Republican, from criticizing Federalist President Adams, his political rival, prior to the upcoming election. The act was used to prosecute several individuals, including Congressman Matthew Lyon of Vermont. Congressman Lyon was found guilty, and was sentenced to four months in prison and fined one thousand dollars. The act was never challenged in court and, in fact, the principle of judicial review would not even be established until five years later. The bill simply expired since its passage included an expiration date of 1801, just before the next inauguration. It was, however, rejected by the electorate. Jefferson made that act a major part of his campaign and charged the Federalist with attempting to return the country to the tyranny of King George III and soundly defeated Adams in the election of 1800. He immediately pardoned those people who had been convicted under the statute.

Freedom of speech has always been a problematic issue in the United States. Today, technology in the form of the Internet, social networks, virtual worlds, and interactive games has complicated this issue even more, as we shall see.

### Reflection Questions

1.  POSITION Suppose someone authored a book giving detailed instructions on how to cheaply make bombs suitable for terrorists. Should the government have the right to prevent that book from being published? Explain your reasoning. Be sure to discuss both the moral issues as well as the legal issues as you currently understand them.

2.  POSITION Suppose someone authored a book giving detailed instructions on how to cheaply make bombs suitable for terrorists. Should the government have the right to punish the author and/or the publisher if the book is published? Explain your reasoning. Be sure to discuss both the moral issues as well as the legal issues as you currently understand them.

3.  POSITION Suppose someone creates a Web site giving detailed instructions on how to cheaply make bombs suitable for terrorists. Would that be different from publishing the same information in a book? Explain your reasoning.

4.  POSITION Suppose a major communication company opposed the policies advocated by a particular political action group. The communication company, which controlled a large portion of the phone communication in the United States, simply blocked the calls to and from that action group. Does the First Amendment prohibit the communication company from censoring the political action organization? Should such censorship be allowed by law? Explain your reasoning.

## 7.2  CASE: *NEW YORK TIMES V. SULLIVAN*

One of the landmark cases of free speech in the United States was the *New York Times v. Sullivan* case. In March 1960, the state of Alabama was prosecuting Martin Luther King Jr. for tax evasion and perjury in a state court. Two organizations, The Committee to Defend Martin Luther King and the Struggle for Freedom in the South, purchased a full-page advertisement in the *New York Times* seeking donations for the defense of Dr. King. The advertisement included an endorsement from many famous people, including celebrities like Jackie Robinson, Marlon Brando, and Nat King Cole, as well as prominent political figures such as Eleanor Roosevelt and John L. Lewis. Additionally, there were endorsements from four well-known African American preachers: Ralph Abernathy, S.S. Seay Sr., Joseph Lowry, and Fred Shulttlesworth.

The advertisement alleged that southern officials were violating the Constitution by arresting Dr. King (as well as protestors) without proper cause and by prosecuting Dr. King for trumped up charges. Although no southern official was identified by name or by explicit office, one official, Mr. L. B. Sullivan, who was a commissioner for the city of Montgomery, sued the *New York Times* for libel. His argument was that he, as a southern official, had been unjustly defamed by the advertisement.

In fact, the advertisement contained some false statements. There were several errors of relatively minor imprecision or inaccuracy. For example, the advertisement mentioned that Dr. King had been arrested seven times, whereas the correct figure was four. Similarly, the advertisement claimed that the police had "ringed the campus." Actually, although there was a substantial police presence on and near the campus, police did not actually ring it. There were also two statements of greater consequence that were not true. The advertisement claimed that students had been arrested for singing "My Country 'Tis of Thee," an allegation that proved to be untrue. The ad also claimed that the dining hall had been padlocked in order to "starve the students into submission." That too was untrue.

The prominent African American preachers, whose names had appeared on the advertisement, were also sued. Each of the four denied knowledge of the advertisement prior to its appearance—implying that their names had been used without their permission.

The Alabama courts ruled in favor of Sullivan and awarded one half million dollars to him. It is likely that if the ruling had been upheld by the United States Supreme Court, the *New York Times* would have gone out of business. Other Alabama officials were also planning to sue and it is likely that the total judgments against the *New York Times* would have been more than enough to drive the paper into bankruptcy. The Supreme Court, however, overruled the judgment of the Alabama Supreme Court and decided in favor of the *New York Times*. In addition, the decision effectively prevented the State of Alabama from retrying the case.

All nine justices of the court favored overturning the Alabama court from the beginning, but they favored it on the narrow legal grounds that the libel had not been proven beyond reasonable doubt. Had the United State Supreme Court overturned the Alabama Supreme Court on that basis, without deciding the constitutionality of the case, Alabama could have retried the case, and with additional evidence, won the judgment. Supreme Court Justice William Brennen wrote eight different drafts of the decision in an effort to arrive at a decision about the constitutionality of the case that would be acceptable to the entire court. Judge Brennan's final opinion went far beyond the original narrow legal grounds initially favored by the court and effectively prevented Alabama from retrying the case. In addition to ruling that the case of libel against the *New York Times* had not been proven, the court also rejected Alabama's assertions concerning the inapplicability of the First and Fourteenth Amendments.

Let's examine Alabama's two major assertions. First, the state argued that the Fourteenth Amendment did not apply because it was directed at state action and not at the action of private parties. The court ruled decisively against that point, as follows:

> That proposition has no application to this case. Although this is a civil lawsuit between private parties, the Alabama courts have applied a state rule of law which petitioners claim to impose invalid restrictions on

their constitutional freedoms of speech and press. It matters not that that law has been applied in a civil action and that it is common law only, though supplemented by statute. (Legal Information Institute, Brennan)

Second, Alabama argued that the First Amendment did not apply because the *New York Times* published the allegedly libelous statements as a paid advertisement. Again, the court clearly rejected that interpretation:

> That the *Times* was paid for publishing the advertisement is as immaterial in this connection as is the fact that newspapers and books are sold. …Any other conclusion would discourage newspapers from carrying "editorial advertisements" of this type, and so might shut off an important outlet for the promulgation of information and ideas by persons who do not themselves have access to publishing facilities -- who wish to exercise their freedom of speech even though they are not members of the press.… The effect would be to shackle the First Amendment in its attempt to secure "the widest possible dissemination of information from diverse and antagonistic sources."… To avoid placing such a handicap upon the freedoms of expression, we hold that, if the allegedly libelous statements would otherwise be constitutionally protected from the present judgment, they do not forfeit that protection because they were published in the form of a paid advertisement. [citations omitted] (Legal Information Institute, Brennan)

Justice Brennan's decision also preempted the Alabama court by ruling that actual malice could not be proven from the evidence. Had actual malice been shown by the evidence, presumably Mr. Sullivan could have won his libel suits. That was not the opinion of the entire court. Despite Justice Brennan's eight drafts, in the end the court issued two concurring opinions, each by two judges. A concurring opinion is written when judges agree with the ruling but not necessarily the reasoning. Both Justice Hugo Black and Justice Arthur Goldberg argued that, even with malice, the protections of the First and Fourteenth Amendments should provide protection of criticism of public officials from libel suits. Justice Black argued that malice is difficult to define and even more difficult to prove. However, the threat of multiple expensive lawsuits alleging malice would have a strong chilling effect on the press's criticism of public officials. He concluded his argument as follows:

> We would, I think, more faithfully interpret the First Amendment by holding that, at the very least, it leaves the people and the press free to criticize officials and discuss public affairs with impunity. This Nation of ours elects many of its important officials; so do the States, the municipalities, the counties, and even many precincts. These officials are responsible to the people for the way they perform their duties. While our Court has held that some kinds of speech and writings, such as "obscenity,"… and "fighting words,"… are not expression within the protection of the First Amendment, freedom to discuss public affairs and public officials is unquestionably, as the Court today holds, the kind of

speech the First Amendment was primarily designed to keep within the area of free discussion. To punish the exercise of this right to discuss public affairs or to penalize it through libel judgments is to abridge or shut off discussion of the very kind most needed. This Nation, I suspect, can live in peace without libel suits based on public discussions of public affairs and public officials. But I doubt that a country can live in freedom where its people can be made to suffer physically or financially for criticizing their government, its actions, or its officials. [citations omitted] (Legal Information Institute, Black)

The *New York Times v. Sullivan* case is one of the most important cases concerning freedom of the press in United States history. It also illustrates another important point concerning the two interpretations of the word "press." One interpretation is to view the "freedom of the press" as equivalent to the "freedom to print." That is, if you have an idea, a point of view, or some information that you wish to make available to the public, you have the right to print that and distribute it. Another interpretation considers the press to be a collection of organizations, most of them for profit, that function to inform the public. The *Sullivan* case, had Sullivan won, might well have made the second interpretation a thing of the past.

## Reflection Questions

1. POSITION Justices Black and Goldberg both argued that criticism of public officials by the press should be protected, even if there is malice. Are they correct? Explain your reasoning.

2. APPLICATION Suppose one presidential candidate makes untrue malicious statements about his opponent in an advertisement in the *New York Times*. Should it be possible, under the *New York Times v. Sullivan* decision, for the wronged candidate to sue the *New York Times* for that? Explain.

3. CONTEXT Suppose a Web site in France makes untrue malicious statements about a United States Senator. Suppose further, that the Web site's creator is a citizen of the United States who is living temporarily in France. Should the Senator be able to sue that person for libel? Explain your reasoning. Note that you are not expected to know the case law for this situation. You are expected to argue for what you think the law ought to be.

4. APPLICATION Suppose a newspaper editorial makes malicious comments about a Senator's daughter. Would the decision in *New York Times v. Sullivan* pertain to such a lawsuit? Explain your reasoning.

## 7.3 CASE: WIKILEAKS

The most famous case involving free speech recently is, without question, the WikiLeaks case. WikiLeaks was created in 2006 by Julian Assange, an Australian journalist, programmer, and Internet activist who considers himself as an ethical hacker. The purpose of WikiLeaks, according to Assange, is to foster more open and transparent governments by revealing things that governments would prefer to hide. According to Stephen Moss, writing in the *Guardian* in July of 2010, the WikiLeaks Web site is dedicated to being an "uncensorable system for untraceable mass document leaking."

Over the years, the site has posted many documents from various governments and corporations. The recent controversies arose in November of 2010, when the site posted the first of many diplomatic communications that were considered classified by the United States government. The *New York Times*, as well as four major newspapers in Europe, began publishing the documents shortly after they were published on the WikiLeaks site. In April of 2011, a similar controversy arose when WikiLeaks, along with a number of news organizations, published documents concerning the interrogation of prisoners at the Guantanamo Bay prison. A soldier in the United States Army, Bradley Manning, was accused of leaking the material, which included documents marked *Confidential* and also some classified as *Secret*. None of the documents were classified as *Top Secret*. The exact number of documents is in dispute, but there is no doubt that it was in the hundreds of thousands.

Secretary of State Hillary Clinton said of the leaks, "This disclosure is not just an attack on America's foreign policy interests, it is an attack on the international community: the alliances and partnerships, the conversations and negotiations that safeguard global security and advance economic prosperity.... It puts people's lives in danger, threatens our national security and undermines our efforts to work with other countries to solve shared problems." (Jackson) Obviously, the repercussions of the published documents were not confined within United States borders and involved multiple countries. The WikiLeaks site was not, of course, located at one physical site, but was hosted at various locations. The United States government had neither the capability nor the authority to eradicate the site, although the Internet sites were subjected to a number of cyberattacks. The *New York Times*, though in the United States, had no action taken against them. Since the information had already appeared, it would be difficult to make a case for revealing secrets.

## Reflection Questions

1. POSITION Suppose Secretary of State Clinton is correct and the leaks put people's lives in danger. Would it be proper to prosecute the *New York Times* for publishing the documents? Explain your reasoning. For this question, you are not being asked to research the case law beyond what is covered in the chapter. Rather, answer the question based on what you think the law *ought* to be, given the cases you have seen.

2. APPLICATION What, if anything, does this case have in common with the court case *New York Times v. Sullivan*?

3. APPLICATION Suppose Assange and was arrested in the United States and brought to trial for publishing the leaked United States documents. Also, suppose that ultimately his case was considered by the United

States Supreme Court. Based on the cases we have discussed, how do you think the Supreme Court would rule? Explain your reasoning.

4. RESEARCH Assange's reputation as an ethical hacker is based on a set of rules for ethical hacking he published. Research his history and write an argument explaining why you do or do not consider him to be an ethical hacker.

## 7.4  CASE: DeCSS

As you learned in Chapter 4, Case 4.5.4, DeCSS is a very simple program that removes copy protection from a DVD. It was widely circulated throughout the world. American courts have ruled that it violates the Digital Millennium Copyright Act (DMCA).

DeCSS was created by three people, only one of whom is known to the public: Jon Lech Johansen, a Norwegian programmer. In 2000, Mr. Johansen was tried and convicted by a Norwegian court for a violation of Norway's criminal code (similar to the DMCA). Eventually, in 2003, an Appeals Court in Norway ruled that his case merited a new trial; however, prosecutors refused to retry the case, so he avoided any punishment.

In the United States, two key cases related to the DeCSS program served as a test of the boundaries of free speech and copyright law. In the first, *Universal City Studios, Inc. v. Reimerdes*, several major movie studios sued Shawn Reimerdes, two other people, and the magazine that posted the DeCSS code on its Web site (*2600: The Hacker's Quarterly*). The defendants, who argued that the DMCA itself was unconstitutional, lost the case and also the appeal. *2600: The Hacker's Quarterly* magazine was barred from posting or linking to the DeCSS code on the Internet. The defendants chose not to appeal to the United States Supreme Court.

In the second case, *DVD Copy Control Assoc. v. McLaughlin*, the DVD Copy Control Association filed suit against seventy-two individuals, one of whom was Andrew McLaughlin, for making DeCSS available online. The plaintiffs argued that the DeCSS code is a trade secret and thus anyone who posts it online has necessarily illegally appropriated the secret. This case, like the previous one, never reached the United States Supreme Court; unlike the previous one, the ultimate ruling, on appeal, was for the defendants. The California State Appeals Court ruled that the code, at the time the defendants had posted it, was already widely disseminated and was pure speech and not subject to prior restraint as a trade secret. In addition, the California Supreme Court ruled that a defendant, Matt Pavlovich, who did not live or work in California, could not be made to stand trial there.

### Reflection Questions

1. POSITION Make the strongest argument you can in favor of the following assertion: Copyright law violates our First and Fourteenth Amendment rights and should be struck down by the Supreme Court.

2. [POSITION] Can information that has already been posted on the Internet be a trade secret? Why or why not?

3. [CONTEXT] Are there differences among supplying an electronic copy of a program to someone, printing the program code in a book, and printing the program on a tee shirt? Explain your reasoning.

4. [APPLICATION] Suppose a computer science professor explained the fundamentals of copy protection for media, including DVDs, in her course. Suppose, further, that one of her assignments was to write a program to remove the copy protection from DVDs. She did not cover DeCSS, only the various ways and means that could be used for copy protection. She was a good teacher and all of her students successfully completed the assignment. Was the professor guilty of illegally appropriating trade secrets? Explain your reasoning.

5. [APPLICATION] Were any of the students in the course described in Question 4 guilty of illegally appropriating trade secrets? Explain your reasoning.

6. [APPLICATION] Were the actions of the students in the course described in Question 4 moral? Explain. What about the professor? Explain.

## 7.5  FOUNDATIONS OF FREE SPEECH

It is reasonable to ask why our speech should be free at all. The principle of free speech, as defined in the United States is best defended by the writings of John Stuart Mill in his essay *On Liberty*. As you read in Chapter 1, John Stuart Mill (1806-1873) was the leading proponent of utilitarianism. Mill argued that the only reason that a government could impose control over an individual is for self protection. He wrote: "… the only purpose for which power can be rightfully exercised over any member of a civilized community, against his will, is to prevent harm to others." (11) His specific justification for permitting and even encouraging expression of any opinion, however distasteful it might be, has two parts.

First, he reminds us that an opinion we find distasteful just might be correct. Even things that seem outlandish sometimes turn out to be true. Second, he argues that, even if an opinion is obviously false, stifling it would be an evil thing. He supports this assertion with a kind of utilitarian argument for maximizing truth, arguing that the public best serves its own interest by championing the truth. Suppression of false arguments weakens the arguments for the truth, thus increasing the likelihood of the public being fooled by false arguments in the future.

Mill was very forceful in his insistence that minority opinions should not be suppressed. He argued that even if only one person holds an opinion and even if that one opinion is abhorrent to the majority, the majority has no more right to suppress the opinion than the one has to suppress the majority. Mill's point is that when a minority opinion is suppressed, both the minority and the majority are harmed: "If the opinion is right, they [the majority] are deprived of the opportunity of exchanging truth for error; if wrong, they lose, what is almost as great a benefit, the clearer perception and livelier impression of truth, produced by its collision with error." (19)

Laws governing free speech in the United States today are generally consistent with Mill's view. However, the issue of free speech is not settled. It remains unclear as to what constitutes "harm" to the degree sufficient to justify suppressing speech. In one way or another, every society has restricted the speech of its citizens. There are numerous reasons why a society may reasonably want some speech to be suppressed, even if there is a general agreement on the importance of free speech. Some categories of speech that people have wanted to control or suppress in the United States over the years include:

- **Dangerous speech**—Sometimes the public's safety is more important than the need to protect free speech. The standard example is yelling "fire!" in a crowded theater—such speech is obviously not protected. Other examples of unprotected speech include such things as posting incorrect speed limits on a highway or certifying contaminated water as pure.

- **Treasonous speech**—Revealing military secrets or scientific secrets concerning weaponry have always been illegal and, in some cases, a capital offense. The rationale is straightforward; the existence of the nation is put at risk by such speech. Particularly, in times of war, speech deemed detrimental to the nation's safety is prohibited. Violating such prohibitions can lead to severe punishment, including death.

- **Seditious speech**—Criticisms of the government, particularly if not true, have often been the grounds for prosecution. In the introduction of this chapter, we discussed an early instance of a sedition law wherein people were prosecuted for criticizing government officials or policies. In times of war, free speech is typically curtailed. During World War I, the Espionage Act of 1917 was particularly broad in its notion of what constituted "harm" to the nation. Over 2,000 people were prosecuted for "disloyal, seditious, or incendiary speech." One of those people, Reverend Clarence H. Waldron, was sentenced to fifteen years in prison for distributing a pamphlet with the words, "If Christians [are] forbidden to fight to preserve the Person of their Lord and Master, they may not fight to preserve themselves, or any city they should happen to dwell in." Those words were deemed to cause insubordination and to obstruct the recruiting service. (Stone, 172) It is difficult to imagine today's courts upholding such a conviction.

- **Hate speech**—In the United States, it is not generally against the law to make derogatory remarks about a particular race, religion, or culture. If you wish to assert that the world would be a better place if all Lower Slobbovians (a fictitious group) were dead, you would obviously be making a bigoted and mean-spirited statement about the people from the country of Lower Slobbovia, but it would not necessarily be making an illegal statement, even if Lower Slobbovia were a real country. There are specific occasions, however, in which such a statement is not permitted. In most cases, the consequences for such statements are civil matters rather than criminal. A teacher, for example, making such a statement about a real nationality, would surely be subject to discipline and perhaps dismissal. If, however, it could be shown that such a statement directly contributed to violence against a Lower Slobbovian, it would be illegal and subject to criminal prosecution. In some countries, laws against hate speech are much stricter than in the United States and, even without direct consequences, are against the law. As we shall see later in the chapter, the Internet can make the enforcement of laws in various countries a problem for Americans.

- **Speech harmful to children**—Certain ideas and images are considered to be hazardous to the development of children. This has been one of the most common concerns relating to free speech and censorship, especially in recent years. Note that prohibition of speech harmful to children is not the basic argument against child pornography. Child pornography is generally not viewed by children but is considered bad for other reasons. We shall discuss this further in Section 7.5.2.

- **Violent Speech**—Some people believe that watching graphic violence makes people more violent, particularly when the viewers are young. There has been much controversy over this issue, and in the past, there have been efforts to regulate movies, TV shows, comic books, and music that present violent images or language, especially to children. The controversy has extended to the Internet and to interactive computer games.

- **Disgusting and psychologically painful speech**—Some images or speech, such as text or images relating to excrement, regurgitation, distortions or piercings of the body parts, are simply unpleasant for a large number of people and have therefore been banned. Sometimes speech can exceed the boundaries of simple disgust and cause direct psychological pain—in some cases severe psychological pain. A recent example of this is the demonstrations in Topeka, Kansas by members of the Westboro Baptist Church at the funerals of military casualties. The members of this church believe that the casualties of the Iraq and Afghanistan wars, along with casualties of mining accidents, Hurricane Katrina, and other disasters, are God's punishment for tolerance towards gay people. As a consequence of that belief, they hold demonstrations protesting the honoring of such casualties at funerals. They also protested at the funeral of twelve miners killed in the mining accident at the Sago Mine in West Virginia. Dozens of laws have been passed in an attempt to limit this type of speech in the United States, but their constitutionality is in question, particularly after a recent Supreme Court Decision declaring the demonstrations constitutional. The various state and local laws have not been directly struck down, but law experts suspect that they would not survive a court challenge.

- **Pornographic speech**—Pornography is big business on the Internet. In fact, as we shall see, it is the biggest business on the Internet. It is of great concern to parents and is the reason that many libraries and schools have filters to prevent pornographic sites from being accessed.

- **Blasphemous speech**—In recent years, material that is considered blasphemous has been especially problematic. There has been great controversy over such material and it is of great prominence because of the violence that sometimes results.

These are all categories of speech that people—in some cases many people—wish to suppress. However, the First Amendment was explicitly intended to protect a speaker from such people. We can think of other categories of speech that are not necessarily protected by the First Amendment. Yelling "fire!" in a crowded theater when there is in fact no danger is a classic example of unprotected speech. This leads to an important question: How do we distinguish between speech that should be protected and speech that should not be protected? There's no simple answer to this question.

The closest we have to a litmus test is from Supreme Court Justice Oliver Wendell Holmes. Interestingly, his most eloquent defense of the ultimate good of the free trade of ideas came in a dissenting opinion, in which he seemed to reverse his view and contradict an opinion that he himself had written just months earlier. The evolution of Holmes's views took place in the context of a sequence of cases involving the Sedition Act of 1918. The Sedition Act of 1918 was actually a set of amendments to the earlier Espionage Act of 1917. That act, which today would probably be considered shockingly harsh, forbad any person from printing or saying any statements that were disloyal, profane, scurrilous, abusive, scornful, or contemptuous about the government of the United States, the Constitution of the United States, a uniform of a person in the United States military, or the flag of the United States. It also forbad displaying a flag of a foreign enemy or to say or do anything that would encourage or support a foreign enemy. It seems very unlikely that such an act would be considered constitutional today.

The first act to be brought to the Supreme Court concerning freedom of speech and the Sedition Act of 1918 was *Schenck v. United States* in 1919. Charles Schenck was the secretary of the American Socialist Party, which held that the military draft was unconstitutional. The group circulated a pamphlet claiming that conscription was a "monstrous wrong" and urged its readers to assert their rights by protesting conscription, lobbying congress, and joining the Socialist Party. The defendants were convicted of violating the Sedition Act of 1918 on the grounds that the pamphlet would discourage men from serving their country. The Supreme Court upheld the conviction with Justice Holmes writing the opinion for a unanimous court:

> …But the character of every act depends upon the circumstances in which it is done. The most stringent protection of free speech would not protect a man in falsely shouting fire in a theater, causing a panic….

> The question in every case is whether the words used are used in such circumstances and are of such a nature as to create a clear and present danger that they will bring about the substantive evils that Congress has a right to prevent. It is a question of proximity and degree. When a

nation is at war many things that might be said in time of peace are such a hindrance to its effort that their utterance will not be endured so long as men fight and no Court could regard them as protected by any constitutional right.... (Stone, 193)

Holmes argued that although the context of war does not alter the principle of free speech, it does alter the government's power to restrict it. Holmes's words in that case have often been quoted both as arguments for protecting speech and for suppression. The first part specifies the "clear and present danger" concept, explaining that the danger must be both clear and imminent. The second part emphasizes that the context of war necessarily alters the state's right to control speech.

Almost immediately following the *Schenck* decision, the court upheld two similar convictions unanimously. In both, Justice Holmes wrote the opinion of the court. Then, later that same year, in the fall of 1919, the court turned to *Abrams v. United States,* a case that appeared to be very similar to the three previous cases. This time, however, although the court upheld the convictions, Justice Holmes and Justice Louis Brandeis dissented.

The defendants in the case were a group of young Russian-Jewish emigrants who were socialists and anarchists. They had written two pamphlets which they secretly circulated to protest an expedition of American troops to Russia. The defendants believed that the expedition was intended to crush the Russian Revolution and they called for a general strike, particularly among defense workers. They were arrested and convicted under the Sedition Act of 1918. Holmes's dissenting opinion is still considered one of the most compelling defenses of free speech, even though he issued it in a losing cause:

> But when men have realized that time has upset many fighting faiths, they may come to believe even more than they believe the very foundations of their own conduct that the ultimate good desired is better reached by free trade in ideas – that the best of truth is the power of the thought to get itself accepted in the competition of the market, and that truth is the only ground upon which their wishes safely can be carried out. That at any rate is the theory of our Constitution. It is an experiment, as all life is an experiment. Every year if not every day we have to wager our salvation upon some prophecy based upon imperfect knowledge. While that experiment is part of our system I think that we should be eternally vigilant against attempts to check the expression of opinions that we loathe and believe to be fraught with death, unless they so imminently threaten immediate interference with the lawful and pressing purposes of the law that an immediate check is required to save the country.

With those words, Holmes gave a much stronger version of the clear and present danger doctrine than he first expressed in *Schenck v. United States.* Interestingly, it was nevertheless the *Schenck* case that became the critical precedent, even though the outcome seemed to have been a case where context of war carried more weight than the "clear and present" aspects of the danger.

## Reflection Questions

1. [POSITION] Suppose the citizens of a small town are arguing over an informational Web site that offers information on birth control. One group argues that the site should be blocked on computers in the public library because they do not want their children to see it, even on someone else's screen. The other group argues that the site is a public service that the public library should provide for its patrons. Give three arguments for each group that a well-intended, reasonable person might make.

2. [APPLICATION] Using Mill's or Holmes's view of free speech (or both), justify defending the right of the group that protests at funerals (the Westboro Baptist Church in Topeka, Kansas). Note that you are not being asked to defend the demonstrations, but rather the demonstrators' right to demonstrate.

3. [CONTEXT] Suppose you are a member of the United States Supreme Court and you must decide whether the following list of sedition convictions should stand. For each case, suppose a federal law was recently passed that specifically forbad the action described. Also suppose that, in each case, the defendant actually did what he or she was accused of doing. Using the opinions of Justice Holmes as precedent, explain why each conviction is or is not constitutional:
   a. The time was shortly after the September 11, 2001 attacks. The defendant went to funerals and memorial services of the victims of the attacks and proclaimed with a bull horn that the dead deserved their fate.
   b. The time was 2003, one week before the second U.S. invasion of Iraq. The defendant leaked original documents from various intelligence agencies about the investigations into the existence of weapons of mass destruction in Iraq.
   c. The time was 2005, shortly before the establishment of a new Iraqi government. The defendant, on a nationally-televised show, burned a copy of the Koran.

# 7.6  CASE: INTERACTIVE COURSE FOR TERRORIST TRAINING

The following case, though inspired by real events, is fictional. A team of iconoclastic gamers, all former military people with considerable skills in artificial intelligence and virtual reality programming, designed a game that teaches would-be terrorists tactical and strategic techniques of urban warfare. A group of concerned citizens want to have the game banned because they claim that the game promotes violence in minors. The team's designers argue that the game is protected by free speech. They point to the lack of any conclusive studies establishing a link between violent video games and the behavior of video game players. They argue, further, that just because the nature of the game bothers certain citizens, the government does not have a right to ban it and thus destroy the business of the company that created it.

The citizens' group argues as follows: The techniques used in this game are simulations of pedagogical methods that have been successfully used for teaching a variety of subjects. Because we accept that it is possible, using the educational methods involved, to teach children conceptual material that is more complex than a mere collection of facts, it stands to reason that this game is also teaching them. In this case, what is being taught is how to kill the maximum number of civilians. The game is further teaching them, by implication, that such violence is an acceptable way to promote a cause. Such an education constitutes a clear danger to our society. It is against community standards to teach children to be terrorists. Hence the game should be banned.

### Reflection Questions

1. APPLICATION Describe appropriate criteria for deciding whether it is appropriate to ban the interactive course on terrorist training.

2. APPLICATION If you were the judge in this case, what would you decide? Explain. You are not expected to be aware of the history of the case law pertaining to all aspects of this case. Base your judgment on the cases we have already covered and on your perception of what the law ought to be.

3. POSITION Make the strongest case you can for the following statement: Video games should be regulated and children younger than eighteen should not be allowed to purchase games that are deemed too violent by a state review board.

## 7.7  PROTECTION OF CHILDREN

James LaRue, prominent librarian and author, relates in his introduction to *The New Inquisition* his first encounter with a library—actually a bookmobile. He describes a bright blue line painted around the whole inside of the bus that had a simple meaning: all the books shelved below the line were available for children to borrow, whereas everything above the line was for adults only. He recalls thinking of the simple logic of the bright blue line. Adults are taller and so they get the high shelves. The idea that children should not have access to all of the literature, art, and other forms of expressions that are available to adults is hardly a new one. One notable person of times past who expressed such a thought was Plato in *The Republic:*

> A young person cannot judge what is allegorical and what is literal;
> anything that he receives into his mind at that age is likely to become
> indelible and unalterable; and therefore it is most important that the
> tales which the young first hear should be models of virtuous thoughts.

Of course, Plato, like many others after him, was concerned generally about the ability of the average person (not just children) to discern false arguments and misrepresentations of truth. In Plato's view, however, young people were particularly susceptible to the problem. Certainly, every culture wishes to protect its young, but there is widespread disagreement about from what exactly children need to be protected. In modern cultures, the four most significant general areas are political ideas, pornography, violence, and religious ideas that run counter to the norm. In all four areas, new technology has complicated things.

In 1957, the L. Frank Baum's series of books about the Land of Oz were banned from Detroit public libraries because they supposedly had no value for children. Specifically, the books were faulted for preaching negativism and dragging young minds down to a cowardly level. Although there may have been religious aspects to the opposition of the Oz books, the official reasons for the ban did not include any of the four main issues listed earlier. Editorials at the time claimed that the real reason was that some people on the board that banned the books had religious objections to books that included positive images of witchcraft. Oz did, for example, have good witches, which some religions consider to be an oxymoron unsuitable for presentation to children. The editorials suggested that people with religious objections focused on psychological objections rather than religious ones for fear of the First Amendment controversy that their religious objections would generate.

Separating children's material from adult material was much easier before the explosion of electronic media—when books, movies, records, and performances were physically located in libraries, bookstores, theaters, record stores, and concert halls. Obviously, it's not possible to install a bright blue line across the Internet. Different countries and different parts of our own country have varying standards as to what constitutes suitable material for children. They differ even on what constitutes a child. Local standards are relatively easy to establish and enforce for physical buildings holding physical books, but the Internet makes that much more difficult. The world of laptops, tablet computers, and smart phones makes it even harder to block material for any particular subset of society without blocking it for all. All across the country, public libraries are wrestling with the issue of how to filter content for juveniles without censoring legitimate reading material for adults.

## 7.7.1 Case : Objections to Santa Claus

The following case, though inspired by real events, is fictional. In a small town, a group of people calling themselves The Truth Tellers were offended by the commercialization of Christmas, particularly the popular depiction of Santa Claus. They decided to attack the problem using a three-pronged approach. First they employed the services of a spammer in another country to send out e-mail messages explaining their point of view. Secondly, they established a Web site with videos, cartoons, and texts that could be downloaded for free. Finally, they published a children's e-book that they made available for free. The group was careful not to include any overtly religious message in any of their literature. Although their plan was not, in fact, very effective, it did raise the ire of a number of parents who successfully convinced local libraries to block the Web site in both the public library and the school libraries and to not provide access to the e-book.

### Reflection Questions

1. POSITION Suppose The Truth Tellers filed suit against the town demanding that their Web site and their e-book be allowed in school libraries. Should they win? Explain. As usual, you are not being asked to make a legal case on the basis of the entire body of current case law. Instead, base your answer on what you believe the law ought to be and any applicable cases that we have studied.

2. APPLICATION Give the strongest argument you can as to why the Truth Tellers message should be blocked from children.

3. APPLICATION Give the strongest argument you can as to why the Truth Tellers message should not be blocked from children.

4. POSITION Suppose a person who opposed the promotion of Santa Claus at Christmas took a direct approach and went to shopping malls and city streets telling children that Santa Claus is dead. The city, in order to stop that behavior, passed an ordinance forbidding anyone from accosting a child with any statement inconsistent with community standards. The term "community standards" was not defined by the law. Suppose further that the person was arrested and convicted of violating that ordinance and eventually the case reached the United States Supreme Court where you are the judge. Using the cases we have examined, explain why the ordinance is or is not constitutional.

### 7.7.2   Case: Texas School Board Bans Wrong Author

In 2010, the Texas School Board banned the classic children's book, *Brown Bear, Brown Bear, What Do You See?*. The book had been selected as part of the standard third grade curriculum. The school board mistakenly believed that the author, Bill Martin Jr., had written another book, *Ethical Marxism*. However, the book *Ethical Marxism* was written by Bill Martin, a professor at DePaul University in Chicago. Bill Martin Jr. who wrote a number of well-known children's books, died four years prior to the publication of *Ethical Marxism*.

### Reflection Questions

1. POSITION Suppose the Texas School Board had been correct and Bill Martin Jr. had written Ethical Marxism. Would that have been grounds for banning *Brown Bear, Brown Bear, What Do You See?* Explain your reasoning.

2. POSITION Suppose a school board somewhere banned a textbook which it had previously adopted, because it was written by a person

who was discovered to be a criminal. Suppose the author then sued the school board. If you were the judge, how would you decide the case? Explain.

3. POSITION Suppose a school board somewhere banned a textbook which it had previously adopted, because it was written by a person who was an atheist. Suppose the author then sued the school board. If you were the judge, how would you decide the case? Explain.

4. POSITION Suppose a school board banned a book because it included Darwin's theory of evolution, which was considered offensive to members of the board. Should the school board be allowed to do that? Explain your reasoning.

5. POSITION Make the strongest argument you can for the following statement: A school board has responsibility for protecting the children attending the schools within its jurisdiction and consequently must apply standards for textbooks consistent with the standards of the community within that jurisdiction.


## 7.8  STATE MANDATED CENSORSHIP

The Internet is hailed as an open communication medium, where free speech is paramount. That, however, is not uniformly the case. Across the globe, the use of state-mandated filters to control information access is quite common. To a large extent, such filtering has been effective. However, recent events in the so-called "Arab Spring" of 2010 and 2011 have shown that the ability of some states to control information through various electronic media is not absolute. Perhaps one of the most striking examples is Tunisia, where the Internet was strongly controlled by the government. Nevertheless, a "people's revolution" overthrew the government with substantial assistance from electronic communication, including the Internet. Even so, there remain many countries where the Internet and all other forms of communication are tightly controlled. Some countries are especially successful at controlling electronic communication. The usual example is China, where political dissent on the Internet, or anywhere else, is not tolerated.

In 2003, a consortium of scholars from the University of Toronto, Harvard University, Cambridge University, and Oxford University formed the OpenNet Initiative (ONI) as an effort to measure and report on Internet filtering and the control of access to various types of information. By **filtering** we mean the interception and removal of messages to prevent them from reaching their destination. The messages are thus filtered out of the network traffic. Although a site cannot actually be filtered, it can be effectively disabled if all messages to or from the site are filtered. The research of ONI, which covered forty countries and in some cases involved considerable risk to the researchers and informants, measured various types of filtering as defined by the kinds of messages being filtered. ONI divided examples of filtering into four categories:

1. Politics and power: Messages that included comments and criticisms of people or policies of government or opposition to the government.

2. Social norms and morals: Messages that addressed ethical issues, religious issues, and issues of manners and customs.

3. Security concerns: Messages that discussed crime and enemies of the state.

4. Network tools: Software that facilitated the sharing of information such as translation software, anonymizers, blogging services, search engines, and so on. Note that, unlike the other three categories, this type of filtering did not block messages because of what they said. Instead, it prevented messages to or from sites that offered the use of certain kinds of software tools. (Deibert et al)

It is interesting to note that, although protection of intellectual property plays an important role in network regulations, ONI's 2008 report on the forty countries investigated indicated that protection of intellectual property was not a major motivating factor for governments that filtered electronic communication. ONI's findings indicate that many countries engage in Internet filtering, and some do so extensively. Some countries focus on filtering political material, others focus on social material, and one country, Tunisia, used a heavy hand with both. China, Iran, Myanmar, Syria, Tunisia, and Vietnam were the biggest offenders when it came to filtering political material, with Bahrain, Ethiopia, Libya, Saudi Arabia, and Uzbekistan also doing a substantial amount. Iran, Oman, Saudi Arabia, Sudan, Tunisia, The United Arab Emirates, and Yemen were found to do the most social filtering.

Some filtering is mandated by law in the United States, but only in relation to social issues such as pornography, particularly child pornography, rather than for political information. We shall return to this issue later in the chapter.

### 7.8.1 Political Censorship

In the United States today, political censorship is prohibited. Certainly criticism of our government is quite common and individuals are not subject to any form of punitive action for such criticisms. Instead, political censorship is likely to be more of the indirect kind. In our global society, where corporations do business in multiple countries, events and laws in another country can indirectly affect Americans. For example, in May of 2000, a French court ruled that Yahoo! Inc., as well as Yahoo! France was in violation of French law because one of its Web sites allowed auctions of Nazi memorabilia. Nazi memorabilia is considered to be anti-Semitic in France and cannot be legally sold. It is hence a matter of law. The French court held that Yahoo! must prevent French citizens from purchasing such merchandise from its site. Yahoo! argued that is not technologically feasible to filter out all purchases from France, but the company lost the case in French court.

Yahoo! was thus in a situation that is familiar to international corporations; it had violated laws in one country but not in another. In order to avoid the penalties for noncompliance, Yahoo! stopped selling the offensive material to everybody, including Americans. In America, Nazi material, though offensive to many, is protected by the First and Fourteenth Amendments. In France, it is not only unprotected, it is explicitly forbidden. Although the United States government cannot ban Nazi material, Yahoo! can and did, at least for a significant portion of the public.

The Yahoo! case may be viewed as an economic decision rather than a political one—indeed it is almost certain that the company's decision was determined by economic factors. However, it is clear that a particular political principle, which is different in France than in the United States, was applied to Americans. As this case demonstrates, political censorship for Americans is seldom applied by our own government, but sometimes is indirectly applied by other governments.

Yahoo! was also involved in another case that involved a requirement to conform to the laws in another country—this time in China. The People's Republic of China is well known for its tight control of the Internet. Numerous sites are banned and users can be tracked there much more easily than in the United States. Political speech is not protected in China and can be a crime.

In 2004 a Chinese journalist, Shi Tao, used his Yahoo! e-mail account to forward a memo to a pro-democracy group, revealing the Chinese government's intention to avoid reporting on the fifteenth anniversary of the Tiananmen Square protests. When the Chinese authorities discovered the leak, they demanded that Yahoo! reveal the identity of the person who sent out the e-mail. Yahoo! complied and the journalist was arrested and sentenced to ten years in prison. A Yahoo! spokesperson defended the decision to comply, saying that as Yahoo! was doing business in China, it was necessarily required to obey Chinese law.

## Reflection Questions

1.   APPLICATION There is no question that Yahoo! was within its legal rights to choose to take the items that were illegal in France off the market for everybody, even though the items were legal in the United States. It is also clear that if many companies systematically make the same kind of decision, the American people will have more constraints upon what they can read, buy, and write than they would otherwise. Is this a potential problem in your judgment? Explain.

2.   POSITION Yahoo! argued that because they were doing business in China, they were obligated to obey Chinese law. Do you accept that argument? Explain your reasoning.

3.   APPLICATION Suppose Google, Yahoo!, and Microsoft, the maker of Bing, were all doing business in China and the Chinese government required them to intentionally exclude any sites on China's banned list from appearing in the search results of any query anywhere in the world. Further suppose that all three agreed in order to continue doing business in China. Would that, according to what you know of the laws, infringe upon your First Amendment rights? Explain your reasoning.

## 7.8.2 Censorship Relating to Social Norms and Morality

Pornography has been banned in many cultures. However, the exact definition of "pornography" varies, sometimes including graphic violence and sometimes sacrilegious material. Legally, definitions within the United States vary between jurisdictions and also vary with the times. Defining pornography is, and has been, a thorny problem.

An interesting United States Supreme Court case from 1964 illustrates the issues involved. Nico Jacobellis, a theater manager in Cleveland Heights, Ohio, was convicted and fined for showing a French film, *The Lovers*. In the original state decision, *Jacobellis v. Ohio*, the film was deemed obscene by the state courts in Ohio. However, after reviewing the case, the United States Supreme Court ruled in a seven-to-three decision that the movie was not obscene. Although they agreed on the ruling, the justices on the side of the majority could not agree as to why it was not obscene. Justice Potter Stewart, concurring with the majority, refrained from attempting to define pornography. In a famous concurring opinion he said:

> It is possible to read the Court's opinion in *Roth v. United States* and *Alberts v. California* … in a variety of ways. In saying this, I imply no criticism of the Court, which, in those cases, was faced with the task of trying to define what may be indefinable. I have reached the conclusion, which I think is confirmed at least by negative implication in the Court's decisions since *Roth* and *Alberts,* that, under the First and Fourteenth Amendments, criminal laws in this area are constitutionally limited to hard-core pornography. I shall not today attempt further to define the kinds of material I understand to be embraced within that shorthand description, and perhaps I could never succeed in intelligibly doing so. But I know it when I see it, and the motion picture involved in this case is not that. [Citations omitted]

After viewing the film, Justice Stewart said he did not see pornography. Justice Stewart's attitude is unsatisfying to some people because it does not specify precise criteria for deciding what material is pornographic; it merely states "I know it when I see it." Still, we cannot dismiss this attitude out of hand.

As explained in Chapter 1, in the discussion of common morality, you can recognize that a concept exists regardless of whether you can articulate a precise definition for it. Educated English speakers know that, "Woe is I!" is a grammatically correct English sentence. We also know it is wrong. Similarly, like Justice Stewart, the vast majority of us believe that we can recognize obscenity when we see it. Unfortunately, that approach is of little help for those works for which there is no clear consensus. If the number of people who see pornography are about the same as the people who do not, then law will be determined by which group the majority of judges on the court deciding the case belong. The law potentially varies over time according to what the judges entering and leaving the court see. When decisions are entirely subjective, we have no basis for ensuring consistency or predictability. The "I know it when I see it" method must necessarily then be a poor one for a jurist if one of the court's goals is to provide a stable and dependable method for determining lawful content.

Here, for working purposes, we will use the test definition that was given by the court in 1973 in *Miller v. California,* known as the **Miller test**. The Miller test consists of three criteria for obscene materials:

1. The average adult person, applying community standards, would find that the work, taken as a whole, appeals to the prurient interest of the viewer.

2. The work depicts or describes, in a patently offensive way, sexual conduct specifically defined by the applicable state law.

3. The work, taken as a whole, lacks serious literary, artistic, political, or scientific value. This test is called the **SLAPS** test.

The Miller test has been criticized by many as being difficult to apply. The first two criteria seem to be somewhat contradictory since the work must "appeal," but do so in an "offensive way." The SLAPS test leaves a lot of room for disagreement with regard to serious redeeming social value.

The difficulty in defining pornography is only part of the problem of regulating pornography in modern life. Another problem is the lack of agreement over why it should be banned in the first place. As mentioned earlier, one common argument for banning pornography is its supposed effect on children. Another argument for banning pornography is the argument that pornography will negatively influence the behavior of the viewer. The counter argument holds that pornography can function as a kind of pressure release that reduces the likelihood of lascivious behavior on the part of the viewer. Research has so far not provided a definitive answer to this debate. This argument has particular significance to people concerned with regulating child pornography on the Internet.

Child pornography is universally condemned due to its clear abuse of children. In the virtual world, however, it is possible to create virtual photographs that appear to be photographs of real children, but which were created without any real children involved at all. Recently, new Web sites have begun making such images available to pedophiles. The images do not involve any real children, and since the correct view of such images on the impact of the viewer has not been definitively established, the justification for prohibiting them is not self-evident. For example, if future research were to show that viewing such images increased the likelihood of a pedophile acting on his (pedophiles are overwhelmingly male) tendencies, then its prohibition would be clearly justified. If, however, future research indicates that such images actually reduce the likelihood of a pedophile acting on his tendencies, then you could make a utilitarian argument that such sites are actually beneficial to society. Of course, the public may have other reasons for banning such sites, despite the potential social benefit.

Other arguments for banning pornography have their foundation in religion. People of varying religious persuasions believe that certain kinds of sexual activities are prohibited by God and hence necessarily bad. When the population of a particular community has an overwhelming majority of people who think alike on that point, a clear community standard can result. That often makes the identification of obscene material relatively straightforward. For example, in many communities, the simple fact that a pornographic image seems to show a child makes it contrary to the community standard, even if no actual child is involved. In America, the existence of such community standards can be legally problematic if the majority's standards infringe upon the legitimate rights of a minority. For example, suppose that a particular community standard holds that a woman wearing shorts in public is obscene. That standard could not be legally applied to women in the community who chose to wear shorts because that standard would infringe upon a woman's legitimate right to wear shorts. Community standards can vary, but cannot deviate from others so much that the standard violates a de facto national standard for legitimacy.

Other arguments for banning pornography are based on the fact that some images strike the overwhelming majority of people as disgusting. That seems to be the point of the second criteria of the Miller test. A famous example is the controversy over an exhibition of photographs by Robert Mapplethorpe in 1990 that included a group of sadomasochistic photographs. The director of the museum was tried in Cincinnati, Ohio for pandering obscenity and ultimately acquitted. The term **pandering obscenity** is a legal term used in various jurisdictions. In Ohio, where the Mapplethorpe trial occurred, it is a felony, with a maximum first-offense sentence of one year in prison.

The case aroused considerable outrage at the time, some of it not entirely due to Mapplethorpe's photographs. In the public's mind, Mapplethorpe's work was linked to the work of another artist, Andres Serrano, who shortly before, in 1987, had angered many with a photograph of a crucifix submerged in what he claimed was his own urine. Serrano's work never led to a legal battle, but it enraged a number of prominent political and religious figures, including Senator Jesse Helms from North Carolina. Senator Helms, as well as other members of Congress, were particularly angry because both Serrano and Mapplethorpe had received funding from the National Endowment for the Arts (NEA).

Senator Helms felt that taxpayer money was being used to sponsor blasphemous obscenity in the name of art. Along with other members of Congress, he considered the Mapplethorpe exhibition to be an important test case. He used it to focus attention on the NEA, which he wanted to abolish.

It is certainly not hard to see why Serrano's work was offensive to many, but it is hard to understand how Serrano's work could have passed the Miller test for obscenity. Serrano's work did not appeal to prurient interests of the viewer and although it was patently offensive to many, it failed the second criterion as well. The second point of the Miller test explicitly specifies sexual conduct as the offending material. Serrano's work did not depict any sex act. Thus, the work fails on at least two of the three points of the Miller test. In fact, it is not clear that it meets any of the points of the Miller test. One could argue that it had no artistic value, and certainly Senator Helms would concur with that view, but since the work had won an award for artistic merit, it could be argued that it failed the third criterion of the Miller test as well.

Mapplethorpe's photographs, however, were a different story. They involved explicit images of homosexual activities and were going to be shown in Cincinnati, where the exhibition was likely to be contrary to community standards. Many of the activities depicted in the Mapplethorpe photographs had not even been legal in Ohio prior to 1974, less than two decades prior to the exhibition. Long before the exhibition was scheduled to open, both sides in the legal dispute were preparing for the showdown in Cincinnati. In the end, both sides claimed victory. The director of the Museum was acquitted of pandering obscenity and those who objected to Mapplethorpe's work got indictments, a trial, and a very public forum to express their objections. The trial, even though it ultimately led to acquittal, had a lasting effect on the art world.

### Reflection Questions

1.  POSITION  Suppose that, using Justice Stewart's criterion "I know it when I see it," you decide that the Serrano photograph of the crucifix in urine was pornographic. (The word, "see", in this context is used metaphorically. You are not being asked to actually view the image. You are to assume that you have viewed the work and that you "see" pornography.) What, if anything, should happen to the artist for creating such a work? What, if anything, should happen to the person who exhibited the work?

2.  POSITION  Suppose the Mapplethorpe photographs included activities that were illegal in Ohio at the time of the exhibition. Should that have determined the verdict in the case? Explain your reasoning. Again, you are not being asked to view or to judge the images. You are simply to assume that they depict illegal activities.

3.  POSITION  Many knowledgeable people considered Serrano and Mapplethorpe to be good artists. These same people claimed that their work had artistic merit. Does this mean that their work cannot be considered pornographic? Explain your reasoning.

4.  APPLICATION  Suppose Mapplethorpe's exhibition were on the Internet rather than at an art museum. How, if at all, would that affect the issue of whether it was pornographic? Explain your reasoning.

### 7.8.3  Case: A Pornographic Artist

In this fictitious case, Rufus Rand is a painter who produces pornographic oil paintings. The paintings are intentionally in bad taste and involve child pornography as well as various other forms of pornography. He does not sell the paintings, but puts on shows where he charges a substantial attendance fee to view the exhibition. He does not allow anyone under the age of twenty-one into the exhibition and is very scrupulous about checking for identification. In one of the cities where he was holding an exhibition, local authorities arrested Mr. Rand for pandering obscenity. The local district attorney was quoted as saying, "I know obscenity when I see it, and in Mr. Rand's paintings, I see it."

### Reflection Questions

1. POSITION Suppose art critics generally agree that Mr. Rand's paintings have no artistic merit. Should Mr. Rand be convicted of pandering obscenity? Explain.

2. POSITION Suppose art critics generally agree that Mr. Rand's paintings have considerable artistic merit. Should Mr. Rand be convicted of pandering obscenity? Explain.

3. POSITION Suppose Mr. Rand changed his rules and allowed anyone to purchase a ticket, regardless of age. Would that change either of your previous answers? Explain.

4. POSITION Suppose a person viewed Mr. Rand's exhibit and shortly thereafter committed a violent sex crime. Should Mr. Rand be held legally responsible? Explain. Note, you are not being asked to give an opinion on Mr. Rand's actual legal responsibility, but rather what you think it ought to be regardless of current law.

5. POSITION Suppose Mr. Rand's exhibits were on the Internet rather than on physical canvases. What effect, if any, would that have on any of your previous answers?

## 7.9  PRIVATE CENSORSHIP AND THE FIRST AMENDMENT

One of the great social concerns of both free speech and a free press is that the "marketplace of ideas" is not necessarily a free market. Without appropriate **communication conduits**—that is the media, such as the Internet, newspapers, and television, through which communication travels—neither is possible. The rise of radio and television networks, along with the consolidation of newspapers and publishing houses, have, at various points in the twentieth century, placed the major conduits of communication into very few hands. This raises a vital question: If a private corporation gains sufficient power to effectively act like a government in censoring our speech, should the government intervene to protect the speech rights of the general public?

Two different interpretations of the First Amendment can help us answer this question. The first, known as the **negative interpretation**, holds that the First Amendment prevents the government from acting in matters related to speech and press. The second, known as the **affirmative interpretation**, holds that the government must sometimes act to ensure free speech or a free press. In the middle years of the twentieth century, the Federal Communications Commission and the United States Supreme Court regularly made decisions based on the affirmative interpretation of the First Amendment. However, beginning in 1980, that conception of the First Amendment became less prevalent. As we will see, the distinction is not merely an academic one, especially in regard to the Internet.

Dawn Nunziato, Professor of Law at George Washington University and author of the acclaimed book *Virtual Freedom*, identified five doctrines that have affected laws governing communication conduits in the United States. The first, the **public forum doctrine**, requires that "the state facilitate and not discriminate against speech by requiring public property be available for 'uninhibited, robust, and wide-open' discussion and debate on matters of public and societal importance." (42) This doctrine stems from a 1939 case, *Hague v. Committee for Industrial Organization*, in which the high court ruled that Frank Hague, mayor of Jersey City, New Jersey, could not constitutionally prevent labor unions from meeting in public places or distributing literature. Mayor Hague, who considered labor unions to be communist organizations, attempted to do just that through a city ordinance. However, the court struck down the ordinance as being contrary to the freedom of assembly and of speech. In its decision, the court declared that "the state may not restrict speech within publicly owned places that are quintessentially well-suited for public discussion and debate within democracies." (Nunziato, 43)

The second doctrine identified by Nunziato, the **state action doctrine**, says that the state is obligated to facilitate free speech within state-owned facilities that are natural for such expression. The state action doctrine also imposes similar obligations on powerful private actors. In the 1946 case, *Marsh v. Alabama*, the United States Supreme Court rejected the argument that powerful private entities, because they are private, are immune to the constraints of the First Amendment. The town of Chickasaw in southern Alabama was a company town that was entirely owned by the Gulf Shipbuilding Corporation. A woman, Grace Marsh, was distributing religious literature within the town without a permit and was told she would not be given a permit. She continued to distribute the material and was arrested and convicting for trespassing. In a five-to-three verdict, the United States Supreme Court found that the town had violated her First and Fourteenth Amendment rights, despite the fact that the town was privately owned. The court looked at the town in terms of its functional role as a municipality rather than its formal role as private property.

The third doctrine identified by Nunziato is the **fairness doctrine**. Adopted by the Federal Communications Commission (FCC) in 1949, it required broadcast licensees to function as fiduciaries for the public interest. A **fiduciary** in this context means a company that functions as a trusted agent of the public for a valuable resource, in this case, information. The fairness doctrine also granted the public limited rights of access to the broadcast facilities, under certain conditions, on matters of public importance. The rationale was that the broadcast licensees were the recipients of a limited public resource and thus owed the public something for the privilege of that license. The doctrine was challenged in *Red Line Broadcasting v. Federal Communications Commission* in 1964. The story of the case is as follows: A man named Fred Cook wrote a book critical of then-presidential candidate Barry Goldwater. A radio evangelist named Reverend Billy James Hargis suggested on Pennsylvania station WGCB that Mr. Cook had communist affiliations. Mr. Cook demanded, under the fairness doctrine, that the station offer him a chance to answer the charge. When the FCC backed Mr. Cook's position, the broadcasters claimed that the doctrine infringed upon their right of free speech. The United States Supreme Court upheld the FCC ruling and the fairness doctrine, arguing that because the rights of the listening pubic were essential to a functional democratic system, the public deserved a fair and balanced treatment of important public issues.

The fourth doctrine identified by Nunziato, the **must-carry obligation**, was encoded into law by the Cable Television Consumer Protection and Competition Act of 1992 and enforced by the FCC. It required cable systems operators to carry, free of charge, the signals of local commercial and noncommercial educational public broadcast television stations located on the same cable channels as their broadcast channels. In *Turner Broadcasting System v. Federal Communications Commission* of 1994, Turner Broadcasting challenged the FCC's enforcement of the statute, claiming that it violated its First Amendment rights to make editorial decisions on what to broadcast. The FCC argued that imperfections in the market necessitated affirmative government action to achieve fairness, just as the fairness doctrine (which by this point was well-established in the law) made affirmative government action necessary in broadcast television and radio. The United States Supreme Court rejected that argument, saying economic disadvantages of one technology over another are not, by themselves, sufficient grounds for government intervention. Nevertheless, the court upheld key provisions of the statute, reasoning that Congress "has an independent interest in preserving a multiplicity of broadcasters."

The fifth and final doctrine identified by Nunziato, the **common carriage doctrine**, obligates private speech conduits, even if privately owned, to facilitate the expression of others. The common carriage doctrine has been applied to transportation as well as communication, but here we are concerned only with the communication issues.

The common carriage doctrine has a long history going back to English common law and has been applied to postal services, telegraph companies, phone companies, and cable providers. Common carriers are prohibited from making decisions on what communication to carry or whose communication to carry. Common carriers are not allowed to discriminate on the basis of content, providing that the content is legal.

When the Internet was first created, access to the Internet was made possible largely through common carriers, such as phone companies. As broadband Internet services became more prevalent, the FCC tended to move away from viewing Internet providers as common carriers. In 2005, in the *Brand-X v. Federal Communications Commission* decision (discussed in detail in the next section), the Supreme Court upheld the FCC's right to remove those obligations from broadband Internet providers.

### Reflection Questions

1. [POSITION] Should broadband Internet providers be considered common carriers? Why?

2. [APPLICATION] Suppose e-mail were given the same protections as regular mail. Would that have any effect on your view of whether broadband Internet providers should be common carriers? Explain your reasoning.

### 7.9.1    Case: *Brand X v. Federal Communications Commission*

The Telecommunications Act of 1994 involved a complex set of regulations and definitions pertaining to telecommunications services. One problem raised by the act was how to regulate cable providers of Internet access. According to the new law, if they were regulated as common carriers, they would be prohibited from discriminating against any type of legal content transmitted through their networks. They would also be required to allow interconnection by nonaffiliated Internet service providers free of charge. That is, even if a particular company holds a monopoly within a given area, it would be required to allow other companies to connect to its network, effectively sharing its physical facilities. The company in question would also have the right to connect to the networks of other companies in other areas. The rationale is that the public gains the benefit of the combined shared facilities of all companies. If, however, they were regulated only as "information service providers," they would not have to conform to the common carrier regulations.

After studying the issue, the FCC ruled that cable broadband service does not entail a separate telecommunications service, and therefore, cable broadband service providers should not be considered common carriers. The decision was challenged by nonaffiliated Internet service providers in the *Brand X v. Federal Communications Commission*. The arguments in the case were largely technical ones involving the way in which data is transmitted by the networks. The case ultimately reached the Supreme Court, which ruled that the FCC's decision was reasonable and that the FCC was authorized to enforce it.

Because only a few corporations control the bulk of the Internet in the United States, the *Brand X* case could greatly influence the character of the Internet. Several incidents suggest that neutrality has already been violated.

**Net neutrality** is a principle, championed by free speech advocates on the Web, that says neither Internet service providers nor governments should impose any restrictions on a user's access to networks that participate in the Internet because of the legal content of the information transferred, computing platform, point of origin, or point of destination. Proponents of net neutrality argue that it is fundamental to maintaining truly open communication on the Internet. However, because the Internet is controlled by relatively few private corporations, systematic censorship is a real possibility.

In the past, most of the incidents involved pragmatic issues of traffic volume. For example, in August 2008, the FCC ruled that Comcast had violated federal network neutrality rules when it practiced bandwidth throttling (reducing the amount of data that can be transferred) to prevent usage of a particular network service called BitTorrent. As you learned in Chapter 4, BitTorrent is a file-sharing service optimized for moving very large files. According to Dawn Nunziato, Comcast was also involved in a political form of filtering. The Web-based organization AfterDowningStreet, which opposed the war in Iraq, sent e-mails to its supporters regarding an effort to lobby Congress to impeach President Bush. Comcast filtered all e-mail containing the text *AfterDowningStreet*, ensuring that they did not reach their intended recipients. Comcast claimed it had been using another company, BrightMail, to filter mail from AfterDowningStreet because of alleged complaints concerning e-mail from that organization. However, the complaints were never produced. BrightMail apparently imposed the same restrictions on the customers of its other clients, which included AOL and Cox Cable. (Nunziato, 6) In a similar incident, AT&T censored lyrics from a Pearl Jam performance that were critical of President George Bush. AT&T said the censorship was the result of a mistake.

There have also been incidents in which communication appears to have been censored for economic reasons. One such incident occurred when the Internet provider Madison River Communications blocked access to Vonage a competitor. In that case, Vonage used the Internet to transmit voice communication via Voice Over Internet Protocol (VoIP). VoIP communications can easily be blocked because such traffic is sent via a specific Internet port. Madison River Communications simply blocked all traffic over that port.

An Internet provider's terms of service agreement, a document that most of us readily accept, but seldom read, sometimes contains provisions that concede some of our rights. For example, Verizon and AT&T include clauses that authorize them to terminate the accounts of subscribers who criticize them or their business partners. (Nuziato, 10)

Search engines also have a great impact on the information we access. If the major search engines, Google, Yahoo!, and Bing, all ignored or greatly reduced the priority of a particular Web site, we, the public, would be much less likely to access that site. Google argues that because its ordering of sites that match a particular search are determined by an algorithm, neutrality is inherently assured.

As of the time of this writing, the issues just mentioned have not been addressed by any court decisions involving free speech. Advocates of net neutrality argue that the Internet is more central to communication than any previous medium. To suggest that free speech is a right available to all, without insisting on free speech on the Internet is folly. Those who oppose any additional regulation of the Internet argue that the competition among the players will necessarily avoid any one-sided bias on the net. Additional regulation will necessarily stifle innovation and reduce the value of the Internet.

## Reflection Questions

1. POSITION Do you agree with Google's argument that its search ordering is necessarily neutral? Explain.

2. POSITION Suppose a particular Web site is the cause for an extreme amount of traffic and one or more Internet providers block all traffic to and from that site in an effort to avoid delays for the rest of their customers. Is that a legitimate curtailing of Internet traffic? Explain.

3. RESEARCH Using a variety of search engines, try searching for Web pages containing articles critical of Google, Microsoft, and Yahoo!. Analyze your results to see if any of the search engines appear to be biased.

4. POSITION Suppose your Internet provider provided automatic spam filtering. Would you consider that to be good thing? Explain. In your discussion, explain whether that would violate your freedom of speech. Would it violate the freedom of speech of the spammer?

5. POSITION Suppose your Internet provider provided automatic filtering of pornography. Would you consider that to be good thing? Explain. In your discussion, explain whether that would violate your freedom of speech. Would it violate the freedom of speech of the creator of the pornography?

6. POSITION Suppose a bill has been proposed that Internet providers, because of their position with regard to communication, should be prohibited from contributing money to a political organization or party. Give the strongest argument you can that might be made by a well-intended person who favored passage of the bill. Give the strongest argument you can that might be made by a well-intended person who favored defeat of the bill.

## 7.9.2   Case: Censoring "The Cartoons that Shook the World"

The Danish newspaper *Jyllands-Posten* published a set of cartoons that sparked violent political rallies in the Middle East in February 2006. The demonstrations were due to what the demonstrators perceived as insults from the Western countries to Islam. A great deal of property damage occurred and people were killed. The exact number of deaths is a matter of some dispute, but estimates range into hundreds. There was much controversy at the time and many misleading statements.

The offensive pictures were twelve caricatures published under the title "The Face of Muhammad." The newspaper invited forty-two illustrators to participate in an experiment to draw an image of Muhammad as they perceived him. The alleged reason for the experiment was that an author of a children's book that included material on Muhammad had been unable to get an illustrator. The magazine was experimenting to see if illustrators were afraid to do such a drawing. Indeed, there was reason to believe that illustrators might be fearful.

Some years earlier, in 1988, Salmon Rushdie published a book, *The Satanic Verses*, which the Ayatollah Khomeini considered to be blasphemous. Khomeini delivered a fatwa in 1989 calling for the death of Rushdie along with all the editors and publishers aware of its contents. The threat was not an idle one. There were a number of attacks around the world on various people connected with the book, and one, the Japanese translator, was killed. Several bookstores that carried the book were firebombed, and a hotel hosting a conference attended by a different translator was burned, resulting in thirty-seven deaths. It was not surprising that only fifteen illustrators responded to the Danish newspaper's challenge. Twelve drawings were ultimately used.

Jytte Klausen, a professor at Brandeis University, investigated the issue at length. She had "loyalties on both sides of the issue," and according to the preface of her book on the subject, wanted to unravel the complexities of the sequence of events in an even-handed way. Her book, *The Cartoons that Shook the World*, was accepted for publication by Yale University Press. The press made the decision to publish the book, but not to publish the cartoons themselves. It also chose to delete all other representations of Muhammad that appeared in the book. Yale did not respond to a direct threat, but rather assumed an implied threat after consulting a number of authorities on the subject. These authorities advised against publishing the work, not because of threats to Yale University Press, but because of the potential for violence in the Middle East. Hence, Yale University Press published a book in 2009 about cartoons that did not actually appear in the book. The reader was required to grasp the nature of the drawings from Professor Klausen's description.

Yale University Press was highly criticized for caving in to bullying. The drawings would not have provided any new material because they were and are readily available on the Internet. Also, shortly after the news broke of Yale University Press's decision, a new book, authored by Gary Hull, in 2009, the same year as Klausen's book, published the cartoons plus all of the other images of Muhammad that would have appeared in Klausen's book. Hull's criticism of Yale University Press is scathing:

> In 1773, at the age of 18, Nathan Hale graduated with first-class honors from Yale College. Three years later, he was hanged by the British for defending America's nascent freedoms, including free speech and freedom of the press. At his hanging, he spoke the immortal words: "I regret that I have but one life to give for my country."
>
> In 2009, some 235 years later, his alma mater preemptively surrendered to modern tyrants, the Islamofascists, thus earning the ignominious motto: "We regret that we have but one life to surrender to our masters." Without even putting up the mildest fight, Yale abandoned the "life of the mind" to the barbarism of the mindless. (Hull 5)

Not every criticism of Yale's decision was as fiercely stated as Hull's, but the overwhelming opinion in academic circles was that Yale had made the wrong decision. However, the matter was unquestionably a highly sensitive one with risks of further violence. At the time of this writing, however, there is no evidence that Gary Hull or anyone else associated with his book has experienced any retribution for publishing the images.

## Reflection Questions

1. POSITION  Was Yale University Press's decision to expunge the images of Muhammad from Jytte Klausen's book morally permissible? Explain.

2. POSITION  Did Yale University Press's decision to expunge the images of Muhammad from Jytte Klausen's book violate, in any way, anyone's First Amendment rights? Explain.

3. POSITION  Did the illustrators who chose to create the drawings act morally when they made the caricatures of Muhammed? Explain.

4.  POSITION Did the people who demonstrated violently behave in a morally permissible way? If so, would Christian demonstrators have been justified in similar demonstrations because of Serrano's work? Explain. If not, what should the demonstrators have done instead? Explain.

## SUMMARY

- Freedom of speech and freedom of the press are guaranteed by the First and Fourteenth Amendments of the United States. The First Amendment prohibits Congress from abridging freedom of speech or freedom of press (among other rights), and the Fourteenth Amendment prohibits states from abridging individuals' fundamental rights as guaranteed by the Constitution.

- A landmark case that preserved the freedom of the press was *New York Times v. Sullivan*, decided in 1964.

  - The *New York Times* had printed a paid advertisement seeking funds for the legal defense of Dr. Martin Luther King, who was being prosecuted in Alabama. The ad accused Southern officials of violating the constitution and a number of them, including L. B. Sullivan, filed suit against the *New York Times*.

  - The Supreme Court ruled in favor of the *New York Times* despite some inaccuracies in the ad. Speaking for the majority, Justice William Brennan, rejected Alabama's arguments that neither the First nor the Fourteenth Amendments applied in the case.

  - The *Sullivan v. New York Times* case is often cited as saving America's free press as we currently know it.

- In 2010, the WikiLeaks site published many United States government documents that were classified as either *Confidential* or *Secret*. The United States was unable to prevent the documents' publication, and so far, have been unable to prosecute the site's creator. A soldier, Bradley Manning, was accused of leaking the material.

- DeCSS, a program that removes copyright protection from DVDs, raises a freedom of speech issue. Two cases were of particular significance in the United States. One resulted in *2600: The Hacker's Quarterly Magazine* being barred from including the program on its Web site or linking to another site that had the program. In the second case, the defendants charged with illegally appropriating trade secrets were acquitted by the California State Court of Appeals on the grounds that the program had already been too widely disseminated to be a trade secret.

- The American concept of free speech was espoused by John Stuart Mill, the philosopher who so strongly promoted utilitarianism. Mill argued that even seemingly outlandish ideas may upon closer inspection turn out to be valid. Even if an argument is fallacious, it is better to hear it and refute the bad argument than to suppress it.

- Although the language in the First Amendment is consistent with an absolute freedom of speech, it has not been interpreted as such. Various kinds of speech are considered by some to be objectionable leading to attempts to control or prohibit them. Among them are:

  - Dangerous speech, such as yelling "fire!" in a crowded theater

  - Treasonous speech, such as revealing military secrets

  - Seditious speech, such as promoting the cause of a foreign enemy

  - Hate speech, such as calling for the death of a particular race or religious group; although hate speech is generally protected under the First and Fourteenth amendments, it sometimes directly contributes to violence and forfeits that protection

  - Speech that is unsuitable for children, such as explicit sex or graphic violence

  - Violent speech such as violent video games

  - Speech that causes disgust or psychological pain, such as demonstrations criticizing the dead at funerals

  - Obscene speech, such as pornography

  - Blasphemous speech, such as lewd drawings of major religious icons

- The most common standard for declaring speech beyond the protection of the First and Fourteenth Amendments comes from Justice Oliver Wendell Holmes. That is the "clear and present danger" standard, which holds that there must clearly exist an explicit danger and that danger must be imminent. Justice Holmes also argued that the degree of protection awarded to speech was context dependent. In times of war, the state can and should exercise less tolerance.

- The most prevalent reason for censorship is protection of children. It is widely believed that some speech, images, and literature are in some way harmful to children and so controls are needed to prevent children from being exposed to such harmful things.

- Restrictions on freedom of expression vary widely among different countries. Similarly, control of the Internet varies widely. Most countries employ some degree of filtering of messages that are sent through the Internet. The filtering differs in kind, with the most frequent categories of filtered messages being concerned with politics and power, social norms and morals, security concerns, or messages to or from sites providing network tools for social interaction and the sharing of information.

- In the United States, filtering by the federal government occurs with respect to child pornography and terrorism.

- One form of expression that is restricted in the United States and most other countries is obscene expression. In the United States, a common test for obscenity is the Miller test, which has three criteria: 1) the expression must appeal to prurient interest, 2) the expression must present sexual conduct in a patently offensive way, and 3) the expression must lack serious literary, artistic, political, or scientific value.

- States are not the only source of censorship and restriction of free speech. Restrictions on free speech can potentially be levied by private concerns.

- Five significant doctrines pertain to the affirmative interpretation of the First Amendment: 1) the public forum doctrine, 2) the state action doctrine, 3) the fairness doctrine, 4) the must carry doctrine, and 5) the common carriage doctrine.

- Internet service providers were originally treated as common carriers. However, after the *Brand X v. Federal Communications Commission* case, broadband providers have been treated as providing an information service that is free of common carrier restrictions.

- The principle of net neutrality has been challenged in several incidents in which interruption or reduction of service occurred for apparent political or economic reasons directly related to the content of the messages that were impeded.

## CHAPTER EXERCISES

1. REVIEW Explain why the Fourteenth Amendment is usually tied to the First Amendment when we refer to our freedom of expression.

2. REVIEW Describe the significance of the *Sullivan* case concerning our current ability to criticize our government.

3. POSITION Did Julian Assange act morally when he published United States classified documents on the WikiLeaks site? Explain.

4. REVIEW Suppose the problem that Thomas Jefferson's bookseller, Mr. Monticello, encountered when purchasing Becourt's book had occurred this year. According to the case law you know, would it be constitutional to sell the book in this country? Which cases that we have discussed would apply?

5. RESEARCH It is ironic that Justice Holmes gave his famous "clear and present danger" as the criterion in the first of three cases in which he wrote for the majority in upholding convictions for seditious speech. In a fourth case, in which the court upheld a conviction, he developed the criterion further when writing the minority opinion. Look up the cases *Schenk v. United States*, *Frohwerk v. United States*, *Debs v. United States*, and *Abrams v. United States*. In which of these cases, if any, do you think the "clear and present danger" principle was applied correctly?

6. RESEARCH This chapter presented only the basic facts of the case involving Yahoo! and the French courts. A number of aspects of the case were omitted for simplicity. Research the case and examine the additional legal and ethical principles that are involved with that case. In particular, make the strongest

case you can, after reviewing the details, that Yahoo! did or did not behave in a morally permissible way.

7. POSITION Did Yahoo! behave in a morally permissible way when it revealed the identity of the Chinese journalist, Shi Tao? Explain.

8. POSITION Suppose a network services company from another country was doing business in the United States. Suppose, further, that the United States discovered that a person using that company's e-mail service was involved in a suspected terrorist plot against the United States. Would the United States government be justified in demanding that the company reveal that person's identity? If the company refused, what would be a justifiable response by the United States? Explain your reasoning.

9. CONTEXT Suppose you were a professional software engineer working for Yahoo! and that you were the person asked to determine the identity of the individual who sent the offending e-mail with the leaked memo. Would it be ethical for you to comply with that request? Explain. Would it matter whether you were working in China or in the United States at the time you received the order? Explain.

10. REVIEW It is legal to both sell and possess Nazi memorabilia in the United States. Why?

11. REVIEW State the three criteria of the Miller test.

12. POSITION Does the Miller test do a satisfactory job of determining whether a particular work is pornographic? Explain your reasoning.

13. APPLICATION Suppose you accept the premise that it is necessary to have a school board that monitors which text books and library books are appropriate for the schools in your state. Suppose, further, that you are leading a committee charged with developing a code of ethics for school board members. List the three most important items that should be included in such a code. Explain your reasoning.

14. POSITION Using the partial code of ethics you developed in Question 13, explain why the members of the Texas School Board, who banned *Brown Bear, Brown Bear, What Do You See?*, did or did not act ethically.

15. APPLICATION Suppose you are required to judge whether a particular book is obscene and you wish to try to use the Miller test. How could you know whether the book met the third criteria of the test?

16. REVIEW Is John Stuart Mill correct in his reasoning concerning protection of free speech? Justify your answer.

17. REVIEW What is net neutrality?

18. POSITION Is net neutrality, in your view, something that should be maintained? Explain your reasoning.

19. REVIEW What is the fairness doctrine? What, if anything, is its significance with respect to the Internet?

20. REVIEW What is the common carriage doctrine? What, if anything, is its significance with respect to the Internet?

21. REVIEW How does the viewpoint of Judge Oliver Wendell Holmes compare with that of John Stuart Mill with regard to free speech? List the points, if any, where they agree and also the points, if any, where they differ.

22. APPLICATION Hate speech, for which there is no clear and present danger, is not illegal in the United States. However, it is illegal in some countries. Give the strongest argument you can in favor of the American position and the strongest argument you can for making hate speech illegal.

23. APPLICATION One of the problems created by the Internet with respect to protection of children is that it is very difficult for a Web site to reasonably verify the age of the individual signing onto that site. Some have argued that, because it is almost impossible to verify age on the Internet, all sites should be policed as though a child might visit them, and that any site unsuitable for children should be blocked for everybody. Give the strongest argument you can in favor of that proposal. Then give the strongest argument you can against that proposal.

24. POSITION Suppose Yale University Press had published the cartoons and that, as a result, violent demonstrations had erupted, resulting in many deaths. Would Yale University Press be morally responsible for those deaths? Explain.

25. POSITION Make the strongest case you can that Yale University Press made the correct decision when it expunged all of the images of Muhammed from Jytte Klausen's book.

## WORKS CITED

Coetzee, J. M. *Giving Offense: Essays on Censorship*. Chicago: The University of Chicago Press, 1996. Print.

Heins, Marjorie. *Not in Front of the Children: "Indecency," Censorship, and the Innocence of Youth*. New Brunswick: 2007. Print.

Hull, Gary. *Mohammad: The Banned Images*. Gilbert: Voltaire Press. 2009. e-book.

Jackson, David. "Obama aides condemn WikiLeaks; Obama orders review," *USA Today* November 2010. Web. May25, 2011. <http://content.usatoday.com/communities/theoval/post/2010/11/obamas-team-faces-sensitive-diplomacy-over-wikileaks/1>.

Joyce, Robert A. "Pornography and the Internet," *IEEE Internet Computing* July/August 2008. Print.

Klausen, Jytte. *The Cartoons that Shook the World*. New Haven: Yale University Press, 2009. e-book.

LaRue, James. *The New Inquisition: Understanding and Managing Intellectual Freedom Challenges*. Westport: Libraries Unlimited, 2007. Print.

Legal Information Institute, Cornell University Law School. *New York Times v. Sullivan*, Concurring Opinion by Justice Hugo Black. Web. September 1, 2011. <http://www.law.cornell.edu/supct/html/historics/USSC_CR_0376_0254_ZC.html>.

Legal Information Institute, Cornell University Law School. *New York Times v. Sullivan,* Opinion by Justice William Brennan. Web. September 1, 2011. <http://www.law. cornell.edu/supct/html/historics/USSC_CR_0376_0254_ZO.html>.

Legal Information Institute, Cornell University Law School. *Jacobellis v. Ohio,* Concurring Opinion by Justice Potter Stewart. Web. September 1, 2011. <http://www.law. cornell.edu/supct/html/historics/USSC_CR_0378_0184_ZC1.html>.

Lewis, Anthony. *Freedom for the Thought That We Hate: A Biography of the First Amendment.* New York: Basic Books, 2007. Print.

Martin, Bill. *Ethical Marxism: The Categorial Imperative of Liberation (Creative Marxism).* Chicago: Open Court, 2008. Print.

Martin, Bill Jr. and Eric Carle. *Brown Bear, Brown Bear, What Do You See?* New York: Henry Hold & Co., 1996. Print.

Mill, John Stuart. *The Basic Writings of John Stuart Mill: On Liberty, the Subjection of Women, & Utilitarianism.* New York: The Modern Library, 2008. Print.

Morozov, Evgeny. *The Net Delusion: The Dark Side of Internet Freedom.* New York: PublicAffairs, 2011. Print.

Moss, Stephen. "Julian Assange, the Whistleblower," *The Guardian* July 14, 2010. Web. May 25, 2011. <http://www.guardian.co.uk/media/2010/jul/14/julian-assange-whistleblower-wikileaks>.

Nunziato, Dawn C. *Virtual Freedom: Net Neutrality and Free Speech in the Internet Age.* Stanford: Stanford Law Books, 2009. Print.

Rushdie, Salman. *The Satanic Verses.* New York: Random House, 2008. Print.

Stone, Geoffrey R. *Perilous Times: Free Speech in Wartime.* New York: W. W. Norton and Company. 2004. Print.

Trager, Robert and Donna L. Dickerson. *Freedom of Expression in the 21$^{st}$ Century.* Thousand Oaks: Pine Forge Press, Inc., 1999. Print.

Wittern-Keller, Laura and Raymond J. Haberski Jr. *The Miracle Case: Film Censorship and the Supreme Court.* Lawrence: University of Kansas Press. 2008. Print.

## RELATED READINGS

### Nonfiction Books

Barry, Bruce. *Speechless: The Erosion of Free Expression in the American Workplace.* San Francisco: Berett-Koehler Publishers, Inc., 2007. Print. (Addresses the issue of suppression of expression by employers rather than by the state. Barry has a clear point of view and he presents it well.)

Bode, Carl, ed. *The Editor, the Bluenose, and the Prostitute: History of the "Hatrack" Censorship Case.* Boulder: Roberts Rinehart Inc. 1988. Print. (Bode provides an explanation and source book for H. L. Menken's account of the "Hatrack" case. The story "Hatrack" was a fictional story of a prostitute by the same name published in the *American Mercury* in 1926. The magazine was published by H. L. Menken, who intended to get himself prosecuted under the obscenity laws in Massachusetts. He further wished to test the postal censorship laws. Bode includes his own account of the context of the legal battles, the article itself, and Menken's account of the complete sequence of events. The editor of the title was Menken. The bluenose was the Reverend J. Frank Chase, who was the leader of the Watch and Ward Society, a watchdog group who pushed for prosecution of people responsible for material it found obscene. The Prostitute was, of course, the protagonist of the article. That article was really only one of three items in the magazine that potentially violated Massachusetts's obscenity law, but it was the most significant.)

Cornell, Drucilla, ed. *Feminism & Pornography*. New York:  Oxford University Press, 2000. Print. (A collection of readings by feminist writers concerning pornography. Includes articles that make the argument that pornography—or at least a large portion of pornography—is inherently harmful to women.)

Ingelhart, Louis Edward, ed. *Press and Speech Freedoms in the World, from Antiquity until 1998: A Chronology*. Westport:  Greenwood Press, 1998. Print. (Ingelhart has compiled, in chronological order, a long sequence of events relating to freedom of expression from around the world. Each entry is short—sometimes a single sentence—but it is interesting to browse for events that might be worthy of further investigation in other sources and for some that are just interesting trivia regarding freedom of expression.)

Lidsky, Lyrissa Barnett and R. George Wright. *Freedom of the Press: A Reference Guide to the United States Constitution*. Westport:  Praeger Publishers, 2004. Print. (As the title suggests, this is a reference, and as such, is not always easy reading. It is, however, a very good reference, organized around major issues of the press.)

Robbins, Louise S. *The Dismissal of Miss Ruth Brown: Civil Rights, Censorship, and the American Library*. Norman:  University of Oklahoma Press, 2000. Print. (A story about an attempt to use prevention of subversive speech as pretext for political purposes. Ruth H. Brown was a librarian who was fired supposedly for distributing subversive materials, but in reality it was because she was a member of the Congress of Racial Equality.)

Strossen, Nadine. *Defending Pornography: Free Speech, Sex, and the Fight for Women's Rights*. New York:  New York University Press, 2000. Print. (Nadine Strossen, feminist who, unlike many other feminists, argues that pornography should be not banned as harmful to women.)

Taylor, Max and Ethel Quayle. *Child Pornography: An Internet Crime*. New York, New York:  Brunner-Routlege, 2003. Print. (A scholarly investigation into the nature of child pornography, its offenders, and its victims. The focus is on child pornography on the Internet and what might reasonably done about it. It does not address sites that use virtual photos of nonexistent children.)

## Film and TV

Truffau, Francois. *Farenheit 451*. Universal Pictures, 1966. (This science fiction film is based on the novel of the same name by Ray Bradbury. The film depicts a future American society where books are banned and firemen are dedicated to finding and burning all books. The story is not really about censorship, but rather about the diminishing of books at the expense of other media. In today's world of the Internet and the World Wide Web, the issues are even more worthy of consideration.)

Welles, Orson. *Citizen Kane*. RKO Pictures, 1941. Film. (Orson Welles produced, directed, and starred in this story of a fictitious newspaper magnate Charles

Foster Kane. It has been almost universally acclaimed and is considered by some movie critics to be the greatest film of all time. The protagonist, Charles Kane, appeared to be based rather closely on the real life of newspaper magnate William Randolph Hearst. Mr. Hearst took great offense at the movie and would not allow it to be advertised or reviewed in any of his papers. Both the plot of the movie and its real-life history are heavily connected to freedom of expression.)

# Chapter 8

# Computing and Vulnerable Groups

When you bump into someone, while walking down the street, what do you do? Most people would just say, "Oops, sorry!" and keep on walking. But what if you bumped into a very small child? In that case you would probably stop and check if the child was injured and then find the child's parent or guardian and apologize before continuing.

We pay special attention to children because children are much more vulnerable than adults. They are more likely to be injured, and when injured they are less likely to be able to take care of themselves. We pay a greater degree of attention to children because there is a greater chance that our actions could inflict significant harm.

This distinction between children and the general population is an important ethical concern for computer professionals. As a general rule, computer professionals have a duty to pay special attention to all vulnerable people who might be harmed by their work. For example, Rule 1.07 of the *ACM/IEEE Software Engineering Code of Ethics and Professional Practice* says that a software engineer should "[c]onsider issues of physical disabilities, allocation of resources, economic disadvantage, and other factors that can diminish access to the benefits of software."

The goal of this chapter is to make you aware of how the work of computer professionals can harm vulnerable people in society. This chapter provides examples of past harm inflicted on these groups by computing technology and illustrates the many ways that computing professionals could potentially have a negative effect on society as a whole.

This chapter is organized around five major categories of vulnerable populations: people controlled by institutions, people with limited autonomy, people with physical limitations or frailties, people with insufficient resources, and people at risk of being the victims of hate-motivated behaviors. Each section includes one or two case studies to illustrate each group's special relationship to computer technology. Before we turn our attention to the case studies, however, we review the main arguments from ethical theory, introduced in Chapter 1, that justify paying special attention to vulnerable groups.

## 8.1   WHY PAY SPECIAL ATTENTION TO VULNERABLE GROUPS?

The introduction to this chapter takes for granted the idea that the rich and powerful are less deserving of attention, in ethical analysis, than the poor, weak, and sick. Is this fair? From an ethical standpoint, can we justify paying special attention to society's most vulnerable?

The most direct argument in support of this position comes from Rawls's theory of justice. According to Rawls, we would not want to live in a society unless it conforms to the difference principle, which can be summarized as follows: Differences in socio-economic status should be allowed if, and only if, they benefit the least advantaged. The terms "vulnerable" and "least advantaged" are not synonyms, but they both generally refer to the people in society who have the hardest time taking advantage of society's benefits. Rawls's theory requires us to analyze how any proposed changes to society would affect the least advantaged, and to show that such changes would benefit them.

Recall (from Chapter 1) that Rawls does not argue that his difference principle is correct because it is "more fair" or because it would be accepted by altruistic people. Instead, he argues that because even selfish people would choose this type of society, it must be a just society. According to Rawls's "veil of ignorance" argument, if we didn't know whether or not we were a member of a vulnerable group, we would want to hedge our bets by making sure that society takes care of vulnerable people.

The other ethical theories presented in Chapter 1 do not specifically address the problems of vulnerable people. In fact, you could argue that some of those theories, if implemented as public policy, would make life more difficult for vulnerable people. Utilitarianism, in particular, can be criticized because its focus on total overall utility can sometimes lead to exploitation of vulnerable groups.

Recall from Chapter 1 that the utilitarian calculus is the process of trying to calculate how much a particular decision will affect the overall amount of happiness in the world. When doing the utilitarian calculus, you need to account for all of the affected parties. It is easy, however, to overlook vulnerable groups in these calculations, because such groups are often small or lacking in political power. This, in turn, could mean that your calculation of the net change in utility is incorrect. Thus, any careful person using a utilitarian analysis must pause and ask, "Have I included all the vulnerable groups in my calculation?" This is especially important because any action can have a disproportionate effect on the happiness of vulnerable people and hence a disproportionate effect on the overall utility. In other words, because utilitarian analyses tend to focus on how a decision affects the majority, a careful utilitarian has a special duty to counteract this by paying special attention to vulnerable groups.

Another theory that's relevant here is Nel Noddings's ethics of caring. As you learned in Chapter 1, Noddings argues that the only inherent moral good is caring for another person. You might expect that this theory would directly support the idea that vulnerable groups should be given special consideration, but that's not necessarily the case. After all, according to Noddings, we are not morally obligated to be concerned about everyone. We are only morally obligated, in her view, to be concerned with people with whom we have natural or formal relationships. This would seem to imply that if we have no relationships with people in vulnerable groups, then we are not obligated to care for them. Other philosophers who have taken up the study of the ethics of caring disagree with Noddings on this point, but that debate is beyond the scope of this book.

With these ethical theories in mind, we are ready to explore an essential question: What makes a person vulnerable? Starting with Section 8.3, we will explore five major categories of vulnerable populations. These categories are certainly not exhaustive, but they provide a sampling of the kinds of vulnerable populations we ought to be concerned with today. Indeed, as society changes, some groups become more vulnerable while others become less vulnerable, so the list of important vulnerable groups will change over time.

### Reflection Questions

1. [APPLICATION] In this section we provided arguments only in support of paying special attention to vulnerable groups. Using one of the ethical theories from Chapter 1, write an argument *against* paying special attention to vulnerable groups in ethical decision-making. Which side do you find to be more convincing? Why?

2. [RESEARCH] What types of assistance does your school provide to students from vulnerable groups? Do some research, and make a list of your key findings. Note that in most cases there will be so many things to choose from that you won't be able to list them all. In that case, try to focus on examples that involve computer technology in some significant way.

## 8.2 THE THREAT ANALYSIS METHOD

Throughout this book we have applied ideas from philosophy and social criticism to the world of computer technology. In this section, we will do the opposite, applying a technique from the field of computer security to issues related to vulnerable people.

In computer security, a **threat analysis** is an attempt (usually in the form of a document or diagram) to systematically identify the ways that a technology might be vulnerable to a malicious attack. The first job of a threat analysis is to identify any **threats**, which are potential attackers, along with their motivations for attacking. Thus, a threat analysis should address these questions:

- Who might want to abuse this system?
- Why would they want to do so? (That is: What will they do with the system that they should not?)

A threat analysis also usually includes a description of the **vulnerabilities**, or potential avenues of attack, that could allow the system to be exploited.

One of the main jobs of computer security researchers is to try to design strategies to mitigate (that is, to lessen the danger of) the risks that are identified in a threat analysis. In most cases this involves addressing the vulnerabilities in the system. The assumption in this approach is that threats will always exist because there will always be bad people who are looking to exploit others. Attacking threats (through the law) can decrease the number of threats, but never completely eliminate them. Vulnerabilities, on the other hand, are often under our control. Thus, the best way to protect a system is to remove as many vulnerabilities as possible.

As a society, we can take a similar approach to protect vulnerable populations. In this case, our threat analysis should try to identify those who might exploit a vulnerable person and then explain why. To protect against these threats, we could then implement new laws or policies that attack the threat, usually through law enforcement or the courts. We can also look at the source of the vulnerability and try to take action to reduce it. This often takes the form of social programs of one type or another.

### Reflection Questions

1. APPLICATION In Section 3.9 you read about a school district that distributed to students laptop computers with software that allowed school officials to remotely operate each the computer's Web camera. Write a threat analysis that: a) lists the types of people or groups of people who might want to abuse the Web cams on the laptops; b) explains why they might want to abuse the Web cams; and c) lists the vulnerabilities that make such abuse possible. Base your threat analysis on Section 3.9; extra research is not required.

2. APPLICATION In your answer to the previous question, did you include the fact that the students were minors, and are therefore members of a vulnerable population, in your list of vulnerabilities? Explain why or why not.

## 8.3  PERSONS SUBJECT TO INSTITUTIONAL CONTROL

Many people live in institutions that take away some of their liberties. This includes prisoners, permanent hospital residents, members of the military, and citizens living under repressive governments.

Most people would agree that in some cases it is ethically justifiable for society to take away some of an individual's liberties. For example, imprisoning criminals to protect the general population is something most people would consider ethically justifiable. In the case of infectious diseases, the situation is a little murkier. For example, some countries imprison patients with drug-resistant tuberculosis to prevent it from spreading, while other countries consider such imprisonment unjust. In the case of military personnel, some liberties are taken away because it is necessary for the proper functioning of the army. Freedom of association and freedom of expression are often curtailed to prevent the leaking of sensitive information about military operations.

Persons in such situations are very vulnerable to decisions made by those who command or oversee them. Prisoners (both in penitentiaries and hospitals) have often been abused by guards or (supposed) caregivers. Military personnel have often been subjected to abuse by superiors. Even when there is no intentional abuse, these groups are incredibly vulnerable to bad decisions made by the institution, because they have very few effective tools for resisting or protesting their treatment.

Computer technology is having a huge impact on the ability of institutions to control people. On the one hand, many computer technologies increase personal liberty by creating new outlets for organizing and communication. On the other hand, as more and more of our daily lives are spent online, whoever controls the online sphere has an ever greater degree of control over individual lives.

### 8.3.1 Case: Should Gun Camera Videos be Public?

Many military vehicles include gun cameras that shoot footage of whatever the gun is aimed at. This gun camera footage allows military commanders to review soldiers' actions during a firefight. The footage can be used to evaluate and refine tactics, to verify whether or not a particular target was killed, and to identify friendly fire incidents, among other things.

WikiLeaks, an organization that collects and reveals secret information (primarily from governments and large corporations), has posted some gun camera footage on its Web site. The footage seems to show gunners in a U.S. assault helicopter killing two journalists after mistaking the photographer's camera for a rocket-propelled grenade. The video also shows the helicopter firing on a minivan. When ground forces arrived, they discovered two children in the van who had been wounded in the attack.

Some commentators on the Internet have concluded, based on the gun camera video, that the attack was a "war crime" and that the soldiers involved are morally blameworthy. The military holds that the attack was lawful and was based on a reasonable interpretation of the facts that the soldiers observed.

Gun camera footage is classified and is not usually released to the public. One of the main reasons for this is that soldiers are required, by their profession, to do things that are not ordinarily considered moral. In the Reflection Questions we explore whether this policy should be revised.

**Reflection Questions**

1. [POSITION] Does the existence of gun cameras make soldiers vulnerable to harm that they otherwise would not experience? Support your answer by listing some ways that leaking the gun camera footage could harm the soldiers.

2. [APPLICATION] Should the U.S. military release all gun camera footage publicly, online? Support your answer by listing both positive and negative consequences of doing so. You may wish to refer back to Solove's taxonomy of privacy problems, in Chapter 3, to help clarify your thinking.

3. [POSITION] Should the U.S. military stop using gun cameras altogether? After all, if the gun camera footage does not exist, it cannot be leaked. Explain your answer.

4. [CONTEXT] Many police departments also use gun or vehicle cameras to gather evidence and monitor police officers. Should the police make all footage from these cameras publicly available online? Does this situation differ in morally significant ways from the case of military gun cameras? Why or why not?

## 8.3.2  Case: Enabling Government Suppression on the Internet

The growth of the Internet has posed significant challenges for law enforcement agencies. Consider, for example, the difference between tapping a phone line and tapping a conversation carried out though voice chat software. With a traditional phone line, you attach a device to the physical telephone wire that is connected to a phone and record the continuous signal transmitted over the wire.

With voice chat software, however, there is no continuous signal. Instead, speech is converted into data, which is then broken into smaller chunks (called packets). These packets of speech data are intermixed with all of the other packets of data that the computer is constantly sending and receiving. Thus, with voice chat, it's not possible to directly listen in on a conversation simply by tapping a wire. Instead, you need software to collect all of the packets of data, sieve out the ones that correspond to the voice conversation, and reassemble them into an intelligible stream of sound.

Numerous companies have designed software that allows law enforcement to analyze, record, or block Internet traffic. Many countries now use these systems to block the transmission over the Internet of child pornography and hate material. Many countries also use this software to eavesdrop on voice chat conversations as part of criminal investigations. American colleges and corporations use such software to monitor their networks for unauthorized use, or to block undesirable traffic (like video games). Some countries use this software to suppress freedom of speech, freedom of the press, or the organization of antigovernment groups.

Similar technology is used to tap cellular phone calls, although the situation is slightly different than with Internet voice chat because, with cellular phone calls, the communication device can move around from place to place. As the phone moves, it connects to the nearest cellular tower, sometimes connecting to multiple towers within a single phone call. These multiple connections make tapping cellular phone calls difficult because there is no single data transmission to zero in on. Instead, to implement a phone tap, you need special software and access to the phone company's internal network.

In Iran, during the unrest after the 2009 election, the government blocked much of the Internet, and in some cases rounded up and imprisoned antigovernment bloggers. The Iranian regime also used phone taps, surveillance videos, and other investigative methods to track down protestors. This led some commentators to wonder whether or not any American companies were selling technology to Iran that helped the Iranian government suppress the protests. Declan McCullagh of CNET News reported that:

> The source of the surveillance technology used by Iran's Internet service providers remains an unresolved political question that could prove an embarrassment for any Western company linked to Tehran's censorial regime. Few technology executives have forgotten the spectacle of Washington politicians calling Yahoo! CEO Jerry Yang to a hearing and denouncing him as "spineless" for doing business in China, or Cisco being dubbed as "collaborating with the Chinese government" for supplying Internet switches and routers.

Though it is unclear what companies sold Iran its Internet technology, we do know who sold them mobile phone technology: Nokia Siemens Networks. The systems that Nokia Siemens sold the Iranian government included software for intercepting cellular phone calls. This feature is required in both the U.S. and Europe in order to support intercept orders for law enforcement. Nokia Siemens decided that the same version should be made available to any government buying its systems.

As reported by McCullagh, Nokia Siemens's spokesman Ben Roome argued that the company made the right choice:

> Mobile networks in Iran, and the subsequent widespread adoption of mobile phones, have allowed Iranians to communicate what they are seeing and hearing with the outside world. The proof of this is in the widespread awareness of the current situation.

This argument could be converted into a utilitarian argument in favor of Nokia Siemens selling their intercept-enabled cell phone systems to Iran. We could argue that if Nokia Siemens refused to enable this intercept capability, then Iran would have chosen not to build a wireless infrastructure in the country. The result, Roome argues, would have been less total happiness.

It is not completely clear, based on currently available evidence, whether or not this argument is correct. It is true that after the election, the Iranian government suppressed the traditional press to a large degree. However, thanks to camera phones and the cell phone network, Iranian citizens were able to take matters into their own hands and report what was going on inside the country. On the other hand, unlike several other oppressive regimes that fell during the "Arab Spring" of 2011, Iran's regime remains firmly in power. We do not know how big a role cell phone intercept capabilities played in this outcome.

### Reflection Questions

1. RESEARCH In your view, are the citizens of Iran more vulnerable than citizens of the United States? Support your answer with concrete examples.

2. APPLICATION Was it morally permissible for Nokia Siemens to sell intercept-enabled cell phone technology to the government of Iran? Explain your reasoning and support your argument using one of the ethical theories from Chapter 1.

3. APPLICATION Was selling wiretap-ready cell phone technology to the government of Iran acceptable under the *ACM/IEEE Software Engineering Code of Ethics and Professional Practice*? Explain your reasoning and cite the *Code* to support your argument.

4. POSITION For the sake of argument, assume (whether you agree or not) that the citizens of Iran are a vulnerable population, much more vulnerable than citizens of the United States. Should Nokia Siemens have factored the vulnerability of the Iranian people into its decision to sell wiretap-ready technology to Iran? You may wish to refer back to your answers to the previous two questions.

5. POSITION On August 11, 2011, the Bay Area Rapid Transit District (which provides subway and light rail service in San Francisco) turned off cellular phone service inside its subway tunnels. This was allegedly an attempt to quell protests that were taking place in BART stations by making it more difficult for protestors to organize. Was this action morally permissible?

6. POSITION Would it be morally permissible for a third party to set up a cellular phone network inside the BART tunnels, so that BART would no longer be able to cut off its riders from cellular phone service?

7. CONTEXT Would it be morally permissible for a third party to setup a cellular phone network inside Iran, so that the Iranian government would no longer be able to cut off or intercept its citizens' cellular phone calls? List any morally significant differences between this case and the one in the previous question.

### 8.3.3  Case: E-Mail and Pen Pals for Prisoners

People who are convicted of crimes and sentenced to prison lose much of their autonomy. Their daily schedule is highly regimented by prison officials, and they often spend long periods of time locked in a single cell. One right that they do not lose, however, is their right to communicate with people on the outside via mail. In addition to corresponding with friends and family, many prisoners have pen pals—people whom they did not know before being incarcerated.

Why would anyone want to become a prisoner's pen pal? There are many reasons. Many religious figures and social activists choose to correspond with a prisoner in order to help in the prisoner's rehabilitation and to act as watchdogs to ensure that prison conditions are humane. In some cases, people correspond with inmates because of a romanticized view of crime and criminals; they view criminals (especially famous ones) as celebrities. This well-known phenomenon has been the subject of many television shows and movies, including several episodes of *The Simpsons*. In real life, there are many examples of prison pen pals getting married, including former Louisiana Governor Edwin Edwards who, when released from prison at 83 years old, married his 32-year-old pen pal. (McGill)

The rise of e-mail has created serious new problems for prison officials in overseeing these pen pal relationships. To prevent prisoners from getting involved in new crimes, prison officials are expected to screen all mail to and from prisoners. Prisoners have been known to use the mail (and pen pals, specifically) to organize jailbreaks and to arrange retribution against law enforcement officials and jurors involved in their incarceration. In the past (according to an article by Mark Thompson in the *Online Journalism Review*), most inmates only had a few pen pals, so checking the mail did not cost prisons much time or money. Even with the introduction of e-mail, this did not change much, at first. Since most prisons did not provide prisoners with computer access, screening e-mails was not a major concern.

Recently, however, several entrepreneurs realized that many people wanted to have prison pen pals, but did not know how to get them. Furthermore, many people who want prison pen pals were unwilling to go to the effort of writing and mailing physical letters, but would be willing to correspond with prisoners via e-mail. Several Web sites sprang up that allowed prisoners to advertise for pen pals. They also provided an extra service: The pen pal could communicate with the pen pal service via e-mail, and then the service would convert these e-mails into physical letters for a small fee. When the prisoner responded (via a physical letter), the service could type or scan the letter, and send it back to the pen pal via e-mail. This also provided a safety barrier between the pen pal and the prisoner, because it was not necessary for the pen pal to give the prisoner his or her address.

As reported by Thompson, this innovation caused the popularity of prison pen pals to skyrocket, especially for the most notorious prisoners, such as mobsters and serial killers. He quotes one prison official as saying that the number of pen pals an inmate might have has increased from "two or three" to "hundreds." Naturally, this means more work for prison mailrooms. In fact, many can no longer keep up with the flow of mail. In response, some prisons have chosen to increase prisoner access to e-mail and to the Internet. As reported by the Associated Press, in 2009 the Kansas Department of Corrections started offering e-mail to its inmates. The inmates are charged for each e-mail a fee that is the same as the cost of first-class postage (43 cents at the time the Associated Press article was written).

Allowing prisoners access to e-mail means the Kansas Department of Corrections can take advantage of software to scan both the incoming and outgoing communications of prisoners. Software, similar to the spam filter that you probably use every day, scans each message for keywords or suspicious patterns. Those that pass the test are sent on to their destinations automatically. Those that throw up red flags are held so that a prison official can review them before they are forwarded.

Advocates of allowing prisoners access to e-mail say that the Kansas Department of Corrections e-mail policy not only cuts costs for prison managers, but also improves the lives of prisoners by giving them more freedom and more access to the Internet. Prison officials claim that it does not cost taxpayers anything, because the costs for computers and network service are completely paid for by the fees charged to prisoners and their correspondents.

### Reflection Questions

1. POSITION What are some possible negative consequences of giving prisoners access to e-mail? Compare these potential negative consequences to the negative consequences of *not* giving prisoners access to email.

2. POSITION In one case reported by Thompson, a death row prisoner who was convicted of rape and murder and who claimed to have committed several similar crimes, used a Web-based pen pal service to post short stories and drawings describing his crimes on the Web. He would send them via regular mail to a pen pal, who would then digitize and upload them. These items were also posted for sale on the Internet. Some (for example, the Arizona state legislature) have argued that prisoners should be denied Internet access, even mediated through pen pal services, because it will lead to an increase in this type of activity. Do you agree? Explain your reasoning.

## 8.4   PEOPLE WITH IMPAIRED, OR LEGALLY LIMITED, DECISION-MAKING ABILITIES

In Chapter 9 we discuss, at length, the problem of autonomy. An entity has **autonomy** if it is free to make decisions without outside constraints or interference. (Here we say "an entity" instead of "a person" because, in Chapter 9, we will apply this definition to computer programs and corporations as well.) Children have little legal autonomy, with all significant decisions being made by a parent or guardian. People with mental illnesses or disabilities may have limited autonomy if they are ruled to be legally incompetent. In that case the court may appoint a legal guardian to make many decisions for them. Also, the elderly often lose their legal autonomy due to the onset of dementia.

People with limited legal autonomy are vulnerable because they depend on the good will and attention of their guardians. Such people are disproportionately targeted by wrongdoers because they are seen as less likely to be able to protect themselves. When computer systems fail, people with limited autonomy have a higher likelihood of being harmed because they cannot act directly on their own behalf to correct errors or seek redress.

In the following cases, we consider the effects of some forms of technology on people with limited autonomy.

### 8.4.1 Case: Cell Phones and Family Locator Services

Many cellular telephone companies now provide family locator services. **Family locator services** allow the owner of a cellular phone account to keep track of the phone's location, thereby keeping track of the phone's user. For the purposes of this case, keep in mind these significant facts about family locator services:

1. Cell phones can be located using GPS, but they can also be located by cell phone signal and whenever they access the Internet over Wi-Fi. In other words, simply turning off the GPS feature does not stop the locator from working (though it does decrease the precision of the location measurement).

2. A family locator service works only for cell phones that are all on a single family cell phone plan.

3. A **locator** is anyone who has permission to see the locations of others using the family locator service. The owner of the cellular plan is always a locator, but she can designate other members of the family to also be locators.

4. A **locatee** is anyone whose cellular phone is being tracked. The account owner decides which members of the family will be locatees.

5. A person can be both a locator and a locatee. For example, the account owner might want her spouse to be able to see where she is.

6. The family locator service can also be set to send text messages based on time and location conditions. For example, if a child leaves school during school hours, a text message can be automatically sent to a parent.

7. The family locator service can also restrict cell phone service based on location and time of day. For example, a phone can be restricted so that it cannot send text messages on school grounds during school hours, or that it cannot be used to make phone calls except to 911 or to a parent's phone.

Our central question is: How should this system be used? In particular, in what situations should it be used contrary to a child's wishes or without a child's knowledge?

### Reflection Questions

1. APPLICATION Recall the concept of a chilling effect, described in Chapter 3. List some possible chilling effects that this system could have, especially on the behavior of teenage children. That is, what are some things that teenagers might technically be allowed to do, but which they might choose not to do if they think parents are watching?

2. POSITION Write an argument either supporting or refuting the following claim: "The most moral way to use this technology is for *all* members of the family to be both locators and locatees. That is perfectly fair."

3. CONTEXT Most families make all adults locators and all children locatees. What are some potential chilling effects on the adult members of the family if all family members are both locators and locatees?

4. POSITION Considering only the *harms* of being a locatee, are children more vulnerable than adults? You may want to refer back to your answers to Questions 1 and 3.

5. POSITION List some ways that using a family locator service actually decreases the vulnerability of children. Do these benefits outweigh the potential harms?

6. POSITION Let us assume that we accept the premise that adult family members (parents, grandparents, adult children) should be locators, and young children should be locatees. At what age should a child no longer be a locatee? Explain your reasoning. In particular, should college students who are still on their parents' cell phone plans be locatees?

7. POSITION Should the phones of locatees display an icon or message, so that the users knows they are being tracked? Explain your reasoning.

8. POSITION Should it be possible for locatees to turn off the location feature whenever they want? Explain your reasoning.

### 8.4.2 Case: Monitoring Dementia Patients

Most people, as they age, become increasingly vulnerable to accident and injury. Lack of mobility or loss of memory can cause a person to leave a hot stove unattended, for example. After a fall, an elderly person might be too injured to call for help. Dementia, in particular, can make it impossible for elderly people to care for themselves safely. For this reason, many elderly people choose to move into group retirement homes where the staff provide assistance and regularly check on residents to make sure they are safe and healthy.

Some people, however, prefer to stay in their own homes as long as possible. It is now possible to buy systems that allow round-the-clock monitoring of people in their own homes. The *New York Times* (Taub) describes several systems that allow a remote user (usually an adult daughter or son) to keep tabs on an elderly parent. Some systems provide video feeds from the house, allowing the user to literally look in and make sure everything is okay. Other systems will send an automatic text message if certain conditions are met. If, for example, the elderly person left the house in the middle of the night, or did not get out of bed by 9 A.M., a caregiver would be notified about this unusual behavior.

### Reflection Questions

1. APPLICATION Do a threat analysis of the monitoring systems described here, listing ways that you think the system is likely to be abused.

2. CONTEXT Some parents of college students purchase a house for their child to live in while attending college. Would it be morally acceptable for a parent to require a monitoring system be installed in the house? What are the morally significant ways that this use of home monitoring technology differs from the use with elderly parents?

3. POSITION Are the elderly more vulnerable, or less vulnerable, than college students? Explain your reasoning.

# 8.5 PEOPLE WITH PHYSICAL LIMITATIONS OR FRAILTIES

People with physical disabilities often face challenges using new technology, because the developers don't necessarily think about making their technology accessible. The term **accessibility** refers to the degree to which people with disabilities can use the technology. Some examples of technologies that promote accessibility include:

- Screen-readers: Software that reads the text on the screen audibly, for people with vision or reading impairments.

- Predictive typing: Software that can tell which word you are trying to type based on the first few letters. This is good for people with motor control problems that make typing difficult.

- Subtitles: Software that displays the text of any audible dialog, useful for hearing-impaired users.

- High contrast displays: Software that changes the colors of the screen to make text easier to read by vision-impaired users.

- Haptic feedback: User interfaces that make cell phones vibrate. (Haptic means "touch-based.") Often used to help a vision-impaired user know when he has clicked a button and to help hearing-impaired users know when the phone is ringing.

- Text alternatives for images: On a Web page, provides a text description of an image so that a screen-reader can describe the image to a vision-impaired user.

Even if technology developers fully intend to add accessibility features, these features are usually not available in the first few versions of a product.

People with physical frailties or chronic diseases tend to be much more dependent on technology than other people. This makes them more vulnerable to technological failures or attacks. In addition to the cases presented here, you may also wish to read Section 9.7.2, which addresses the effects of touch-screen interfaces on blind users, and Section 5.5.3, which discusses the case of a defective medical radiation machine that led to the death of some patients.

## 8.5.1 Case: Hackers and Implantable Medical Devices

Computer attacks such as Trojan horses or viruses are the bane of every computer user. But imagine how you would feel if a computer hacker sitting near you could, with the press of a button, stop your heart. For the more than three million people worldwide with implantable cardiac defibrillators (ICDs), this is a true concern. (Wood) In 2008, a group of researchers from University of Washington and University of Massachusetts Amherst demonstrated just such serious security flaws in ICDs sold in the United States in 2003. (Halperin)

The main purpose of an ICD is to automatically detect ventricular fibrillation (V-Fib, a rapid or irregular heartbeat), and "administer an electrical shock to restore a normal heart rhythm, then later report this event to a health care practitioner." (Halperin 129) The ICD's reports can be read, and the ICD re-programmed, using a special console that communicates with the ICD via 175-kilohertz radio signals. In addition to the ability to stop V-Fib, the ICD also has the ability to cause V-Fib. This is an important feature because it allows the doctor implanting the ICD to verify that the ICD can accurately detect and stop ventricular fibrillation. The doctor must intentionally cause V-Fib in order to test the device.

This means that, without an effective security system, it is possible to cause a heart attack remotely using an ICD's programming console. Halperin and the other researchers from the University of Washington and the University of Massachusetts Amherst found the security features on the device they tested to be ineffective. The group's critiques of the three main security features are as follows:

1. The system is designed so that the ICD will not broadcast information unless a powerful magnet is nearby, usually placed on the patient's chest. However, the ICD still accepts commands even when the magnet is not present, so this does not prevent an attacker from causing V-Fib.

2. Radio signals have limited range. Because the ICD is inside the patient's body, it is hard to reprogram the ICD without a wireless console that is very close to the patient. An attacker could overcome this by modifying the programming console's hardware to boost the signal.

3. The ICD manufacturers keep the communication protocols of their devices secret, so that attackers will not be able to figure out how to send the command to start ventricular fibrillation. (Security researchers often call this strategy of trying to provide security by keeping the protocol secret, "security through obscurity." The phrase is meant to be pejorative.) This provides no protection, however, if the attacker has access to a genuine programming console.

Halperin et al. showed that it is possible to trigger V-Fib, even without a programming console, by recording and replaying the message that initiates the intentional V-Fib. The key weakness in these systems is that anyone who has access to the programming console can cause great harm. Keeping the programming consoles under control is hard, because there are thousands of them. More than half a million ICDs are implanted each year.

Most patients benefit from the use of ICDs. There has never been a case of an attacker maliciously accessing an ICD. Nevertheless, the use of a (mostly) unsecured ICD that is wirelessly programmable creates a new vulnerability for the patient.

### Reflection Questions

1. APPLICATION In response to Halperin et al., a paper presented by Denning et al. at the International Conference on Human Factors in Computing Systems proposed several possible security systems for ICDs, which are listed below. (See the Works Cited list for a complete reference to this paper.) Rank the possible security systems in order from most preferable to least preferable, and explain your reasoning. Your answer should include consideration of human values as well as technical issues.

   a. Do nothing and continue to use the current system.
   b. Remove the feature that makes it possible to intentionally cause V-fib. Even with this feature disabled, however, it would still be

possible for an attacker to access the ICD to get personal information or to turn off the ICD.

c.  Require the patient to memorize a password or PIN that must be
entered in the programming console to gain access to the ICD.

d.  Tattoo a password or PIN on the patient that must be entered in
the programming console to gain access to the ICD. The tattoo
would be placed on an area of skin that is not seen in public, to
prevent the password from being stolen.

e.  Require the patient to wear a bracelet continuously that sends out a
radio signal. As long as this signal is present, the ICD ignores the
programming console. When the ICD needs to be accessed or
programmed, the patient removes or turns off the bracelet.

2.  RESEARCH Read Denning et al.'s arguments for and against the options
listed in the previous question. What did you miss in your answer to the
previous question? Are there any problems with their arguments?

3.  APPLICATION Given the security vulnerabilities of the ICDs studied by
Halperin et al., was it ethically permissible for the ICD manufacturer
to create and sell the devices? Use one of the ethical theories from
Chapter 1, or the *ACM/IEEE Software Engineering Code of Ethics and
Professional Practice*, to support your argument.

## 8.5.2  Case: A Right to Gaming?

Most Americans play video or computer games, at least occasionally. Popular games
like Tetris and Pac-Man have become part of our shared cultural experience, with
allusions to them appearing in t-shirts, television shows, and popular music. The
designs of many video games, however, make them unplayable for people with
color blindness.

Figure 8.1 shows two versions of a puzzle game. (The game was designed to
illustrate the challenges of living with Type-1 diabetes, but that is not relevant to

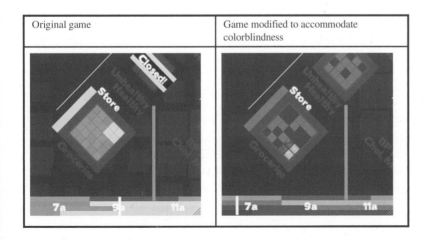

**FIGURE 8.1** Two versions of
a game as seen by a color-blind
person

this discussion.) The game's designer chose to use two shades of lime green to represent money and two shades of canary yellow to represent time. Although it's not possible to show the full-color images in this one-color book, the left-hand image in Figure 8.1 gives you a sense of how the screen would look to someone with red-green color blindness, which affects more than 5% of males in the United States. (Note: A full-color version of this figure is available at *http://EthicsInAComputingCulture.com/figure-8-1/.*) Instead of four different colors in the puzzle, a color-blind person would see only two colors (light and dark yellow). The designer's color choices made the game unplayable for people with red-green color blindness.

The right-hand image in Figure 8.1 shows changes made to accommodate various forms of color blindness. In the new version, the green color was darkened significantly, to distinguish it from the yellow color, and texturing was used to distinguish between incomplete parts of the puzzle and completed parts of the puzzle.

Many user interface designers rely on color to communicate ideas. For example, red often communicates danger or failure, whereas green communicates success. This is true in business applications as well as in games. In accounting, for example, it is quite common to use a black font for positive numbers, and red for negative numbers. In fact, it is quite common to leave off the negative sign completely, leaving a person who cannot distinguish between red and black unable to tell the difference between a negative and positive number. For a bookkeeper, this could lead to disastrous mistakes.

## Reflection Questions

1. APPLICATION Suppose a software company is designing a spreadsheet program. The program designers are considering using red to indicate negative numbers and do not plan to provide any other formatting options. Is it *morally* permissible to create such software? Explain your answer using one of the ethical theories from Chapter 1. Would it be *ethically* permissible for a software engineer to create this software? Explain your reasoning.

2. CONTEXT Suppose a software company is designing a video game. The game designers are considering using yellow and green puzzle pieces and do not plan to provide any accommodations for color blind users. Is it morally permissible to create such software? Is this more or less permissible than the software proposed in the previous question? Explain your reasoning.

3. CONTEXT Is it morally significant for either of the previous two questions that roughly 5% of men in the U.S. suffer from red-green color blindness? Would your answer to either of the questions be different if it was only 0.5%, or only 0.05%? What if it was 50%? Explain your reasoning.

### 8.5.3 Is Accessibility Good Business?

In the previous section, we treated accessibility as a moral and ethical problem related to a vulnerable group. Our argument could be viewed as supporting the position that software creators should, out of altruistic motives, spend some extra time and effort to make sure that their products are accessible.

Dennis Scimeca, in a feature in the online gaming magazine *Gamasutra*, argues that this approach is the result of a false dichotomy. In spite of the fact that adding accessibility to a product adds time to the development process and increases the cost of development, Scimeca argues that technologies designed with accessibility in mind are usually more useful to everyone. Hence, by focusing on accessibility during the design process, a company will naturally create products that do better in the marketplace because consumers—not only those with disabilities—will prefer them.

One instructive example is video game maker Valve Software. Mike Ambinder, of Valve, told Scimeca that:

> "Most of the accommodations we make for disabled gamers (closed captioning/subtitles, color-blind mode, in-game pausing in single player, easier difficulty levels, re-mappable keys/buttons, open-microphones, mouse sensitivity settings, use of both mouse and keyboard and gamepads, etc.) stem from functionality added to improve the experience of both able and disabled gamers."

He also gave the example of the use of glowing halos around fallen teammates, which help you find and rescue them. Originally there were no glowing halos, and you could find teammates only if they verbally called for help. This would obviously be unworkable for a deaf player. Adding the halos made the game much more enjoyable for everyone, not just hearing-impaired players. Armbinder said that the visual location cues made the game more cohesive, allowing teammates to locate each other much more quickly and precisely.

There are many other examples outside of games. Zoom technology built into Web browsers helps people with vision impairments, but it also allows college professors to zoom in on Web pages on classroom projectors. Voice dialing makes it easier for vision-impaired people to use cell phones, and it also makes cell phone use safer and easier for everyone else. Speech-to-text allows hearing-impaired people to receive voice mail, but it has also become a very popular feature with business professionals who need to read and answer voice mail without disturbing those around them, or in high-noise environments. Redesigning a word processor so that the most commonly used commands take only one mouse-click benefits everyone. The fact that it makes the program much more usable for people with motor-control problems is not the only reason to do it.

### Reflection Questions

1. [RESEARCH] Most public buildings built in the United States are now required to be wheelchair accessible. List some of the benefits of this policy for people who do *not* use wheelchairs.

2.   RESEARCH Another argument in favor of accessibility is that the number of people who currently have disabilities is actually fairly high, and the number of people who will eventually have disabilities is projected to be even higher. Adding accessibility features could increase your market share enough to pay for itself. Do some research to find out the most common disabilities in the United States, and the numbers of people with these disabilities, and then evaluate the claim.

## 8.6   PEOPLE WITH INSUFFICIENT RESOURCES

The poor, whether urban or rural, and whether global or local, are another vulnerable population. The poor often lack access to the computing and communications infrastructure that others take for granted. In economically depressed locations it can be hard to get nutritious food or clean water, much less a functional Internet connection. Access to high-quality education can be limited, further reducing a person's ability to benefit from computer technology. Professional help for legal problems is often too expensive to be a real option.

In general, the poor seem to receive less benefit from computing technology than do the upper and middle classes. For example, according to a research study by Jim Jansen of the Pew Research Center, American households with income above the median are almost twice as likely to have broadband Internet as poor households, 50% more likely to use the Internet regularly, and 25% more likely to have a cellular phone. This gap between technology haves and have-nots is called the **digital divide**. Case 8.6.2 addresses the gap between rural and urban dwellers. Two additional cases demonstrate how computing affects the poor.

### 8.6.1   Case: Computer Donations and Recycling

According to the United Nations Environment Programme (UNEP), about 40 million tons of electronic devices such as cell phones, computers, TVs, and batteries are created each year. (Schluep 1) When discarded, these devices are referred to as **e-waste**. Due to the short life-span of these devices, the amount of e-waste generated per year is estimated to be in the dozens of millions of tons. These devices contain significant amounts of valuable metals. According to UNEP, the manufacturing of computers "adds up to 3% of the world mine supply of [gold] and [silver], to 13% of [palladium] and to 15% of [cobalt]." Recycling e-waste can be very lucrative, but it is also labor intensive and dangerous. Electronic devices contain toxins such as lead, arsenic, and mercury in significant amounts, and it can be difficult to process electronics for recycling without exposing workers to these chemicals.

As with many labor-intensive industries, most e-waste recycling occurs in developing countries like China, Ghana, Nigeria, and India. A recent episode of the PBS show, *Frontline,* showed the terrible health risks faced by e-waste recyclers. (Klein) The series showed women in China cooking circuit boards on griddles to remove lead solder, breathing in the vapor while they worked.

In another scene, a teenager in a walled courtyard in India used huge vats of sulfuric acid to extract metal from circuit boards. He wore no gloves, no goggles, and no respirator. In yet another scene, orphan boys in Ghana burned circuit boards to extract the metal, breathing in harmful smoke that contained dioxins. The toxic ash, and the pieces of trash that cannot be sold, collect in piles around the city and in the field where the boys play soccer.

Because of the risks associated with e-waste recycling, many countries have banned both the import and export of hazardous waste, including broken computers, TVs, cell phones, and used-up batteries. Reporter Peter Klein and his team, reporting for *Frontline*, demonstrate the difficulty of enforcing these rules. Many well-meaning people in developed countries want to help narrow the digital divide between developed and developing countries by donating their old, but working, computers to schools in developing countries. However, disreputable traders use these charity shipments to mask shipments of e-waste. One Ghanaian computer vendor, interviewed by Klein, said that only about 50% of the computers that he receives as "donations" are actually working. The rest are e-waste which he either dumps or sells to e-waste recyclers.

### Reflection Questions

1. RESEARCH How would you go about recycling an electronic device, while ensuring that it did not end up polluting a developing country? Do some online research to identify recyclers that do not use outsourcing. As Klein's reporting showed, you cannot necessarily take the company at its word.

2. POSITION If people in developing countries understood the harm they were doing to themselves and their children by participating in e-waste recycling, do you think that they would stop? Explain your reasoning.

### 8.6.2 Case: Internet Access as a Human Right

Tim Berners-Lee, the inventor of the World Wide Web, recently proposed that access to the Web should be considered a fundamental human right. As reported by Jon Brodkin in *Network World*, he said:

> "Access to the Web is now a human right…It's possible to live without the Web. It's not possible to live without water. But if you've got water, then the difference between somebody who is connected to the Web and is part of the information society, and someone who (is not) is growing bigger and bigger."

Building the infrastructure needed to provide usable access to the Web is very expensive. As a result, there are many places in the world, even in the United States, where high-speed access is either unavailable or prohibitively expensive. If Web access is a human right, then those of us who have enough money to pay for fast Web access would have to help pay for access for those who cannot. This is what ethicists call a **claim right**, a right that one cannot obtain without the help of other people. By contrast, a **liberty**, is a right that you have as long as you are left alone. Freedom of religion, for example, is a liberty, while the right to an education is a claim right. In order to provide every child with an affordable education, we raise money through taxes.

In rural areas in the United States, high-speed Internet access is often hard to come by. Some people have proposed using tax money to build high-speed Internet infrastructure in these areas. The idea is that everyone who has high-speed access would pay the same amount of tax, and the money raised via this tax would be used to install high-speed data lines in parts of the country where private companies have chosen not to build their own. Once they begin to use their new Internet access, people in rural areas would pay the same taxes as everyone else.

## Reflection Questions

1. APPLICATION Is freedom of speech a liberty or a claim right? Explain your reasoning.

2. APPLICATION Is the right to life a liberty or a claim right? Explain your reasoning.

3. POSITION Whether you agree with him or not, make the strongest case you can that supports Berners-Lee's claim. In particular, are there any other key human liberties or claim rights that one cannot exercise without the Web?

4. POSITION Whether you agree with him or not, make the strongest case you can that contradicts Berners-Lee's claim. You might find it useful to consider your answer to the previous question and provide counter-arguments.

5. APPLICATION Select one of the ethical theories from Chapter 1 and use it to analyze the following two questions:

   a. Is it morally permissible to use a tax on all U.S. Internet users to pay for Internet infrastructure in rural areas of the United States?

   b. Is it morally obligatory to use a tax on all U.S. Internet users to pay for Internet infrastructure in rural areas of the United States?

6. CONTEXT Use one of the ethical theories from Chapter 1 to analyze the following three questions:

   a. Is it morally permissible for the U.S. government to use tax money to provide Internet access to groups that are rebelling against a totalitarian regime, such as the pro-democracy rebellion in Libya in 2011?

   b. Is it morally obligatory for the U.S. government to use tax money to provide Internet access to groups that are rebelling against a totalitarian regime, such as the pro-democracy rebellion in Libya in 2011?

   c. What are the significant moral differences between the situation described in this question and in Question 5?

7. POSITION Are people who live in rural places more or less vulnerable than people who live in cities? Explain your reasoning.

### 8.6.3    Workers as a Vulnerable Group

New technologies often face a popular backlash when they are first introduced because of fears that they will lead to massive unemployment. Here are just some examples:

- In the early nineteenth century, skilled textile makers attacked and destroyed factories that used new mechanized looms. These protesters were called **Luddites**.

- In the United States, in the 1980s, automobile workers worried that the introduction of robots into factories would result in job losses and in poor working conditions for remaining workers. Consumer and labor activist Ralph Nader wrote about one plan proposed by autoworkers in which the productivity gains from robot workers would be passed on to human workers in the form of early retirement incentives.

- Computer programs that make a job easier (such as tax preparation programs) are sometimes seen as **deskilling** that job.

These fears come from the perception that new technologies will automate tasks that were previously done by humans. **Automation** means taking a task that used to require human control and oversight, and removing or reducing the amount of oversight required. Automation has long been seen as the primary purpose of computing. Thanks to an increasing reliance on automation, jobs that were done by skilled workers now either require less skill (and hence command less pay), or they require no workers at all. One of the most well-known modern critics of automation is author Kirkpatrick Sale. In a 1995 interview with Kevin Kelly, published in *Wired* magazine, they discussed the impacts of automation on workers:

> KELLY: I find it instructive that most of this Neo-Luddite sentiment is arising not from people who are out of jobs because of computers, but from over-educated academic or author types. I don't detect much dissatisfaction among the unemployed regarding computers, per se.

> SALE: You're quite right that in these last 20 or 25 years, the immense effects of automation on the labor force have not been met by resistance other than the most trivial kind. What happened was that unions caved in and accepted strategies of the corporations to give workers lifetime pay in return for having their jobs automated. However, that luxury of lifetime pay is now no longer being offered, so we have an estimated 6 million people who have lost their jobs to automation, or to overseas shops, since 1988.

The **neo-Luddites** that Kelly and Sale are speaking of here are the modern-day opponents of computer automation, who use the original Luddites as a symbol and inspiration. They believe that automation is always antiworker, and that workers are a vulnerable group. Sale claims that the purpose of automation is to increase the quantity of goods and the amount of consumption in society. He believes this mostly benefits those at the very top of society; increased productivity has led to increased profits for those who own and run big corporations, but less jobs for ordinary workers.

In the same interview, Kelly (a technology writer) comes to the defense of automation. He claims that the primary purpose of automation is to let humans do jobs that are more humanizing, more fit to our skills. He says,

> The Luddite cottagers thought it was inhuman to be put out of work by machines. But what's really inhuman is to have cloth made by human labor at all. Cloth should be made by machines, because machines make much better cloth than humans. Making cloth is not a good job for humans, unless they want to make a few pieces for art.

He claims that, even as technology deskills some jobs, it creates new jobs that require greater skill. For example, before e-mail, many companies had huge internal mailrooms that sorted and delivered inter-office mail. The introduction of e-mail has allowed companies to drastically cut the number of staff they employ for handling mail. At the same time, however, they now must employ many skilled information technology workers to setup and maintain their e-mail systems, to purchase and maintain computers for employees, and so on. One could argue that the overall standard of living is going up. Because automation is making us more productive and efficient, there are more goods and services being produced that ever before. Though a particular individual may lose a job and have to retrain for a new one, on average we each receive an increasing amount of goods and services, and are better off, due to automation.

### Reflection Questions

1. RESEARCH Consider the claim that "computing has led to increased unemployment due to automation." Look at the United States Bureau of Labor Statistics' Web site, *www.bls.gov*, to see how the unemployment rate has fluctuated over the past sixty years. Does this evidence tend to support or refute the claim?

2. POSITION Are workers more vulnerable to changes in technology than managers or executives? Explain your reasoning.

### 8.6.4    Case: The PTA Newsletter

Throughout this chapter we have focused mainly on big cases, things that affect public policy or society in big ways. But it is important to remember also that we interact with vulnerable groups in our ordinary lives. Our everyday decisions can either help or harm vulnerable people. This case, though fictional, is based on a real decision faced by an elementary school's parent teacher association (PTA).

The PTA is a community group made up of the parents and teachers (and sometimes staff members) of a particular school. They work together to improve the school experience in various ways. PTA groups often organize fundraisers, get-out-the-vote efforts for school bond issues, volunteers for field trips and after-school activities, and so on.

The school in this case is an elementary school, with children in kindergarten through sixth grade. The school has about 100 students in each grade, for a total of 700 students. Each month the president of the PTA sends all parents a newsletter, letting them know about upcoming volunteer opportunities and other important information. The school provided her with the mailing addresses of all parents in the school, so that all parents would receive the newsletters, whether or not they had ever attended a PTA meeting.

After a recent downturn in the economy, the PTA's fundraisers were less successful than in the past. The PTA president looked for ways to cut costs, so that more of the organization's money could go to the school. She realized that the monthly newsletters were actually fairly expensive. Each newsletter was double-sided, printed in color, and sent via regular mail. This cost about $1 each for printing and mailing, for a total of about $6300 per school year.

The PTA president decided that, instead, she would send the monthly newsletter by e-mail. It would still be a two-page color newsletter, as in the past, but now it would be virtually free to produce and send out. She just needed to collect e-mail addresses for all parents in the school. The school district did not have this information, so unlike the mailing addresses, the PTA would have to collect this information through meetings. The school's teachers also agreed to help collect e-mail addresses for each child's parents. Even so, the PTA president was able to get e-mail addresses for only about 90% of families.

It quickly became apparent that there were some patterns to which families were left off the list. Some parents in the district did not own cars, or they worked night shift jobs, and as a result did not attend PTA meetings. These families tended to be left out when the e-mail newsletters were sent. Some students' families did not own a computer, and did not have an e-mail address to give. Some students were living in a homeless shelter, and others in a shelter for victims of domestic abuse where these facilities did not have computers that allowed e-mail access. In other words, a digital divide separated the families who had regular access to e-mail from the families headed by nightshift workers, people who didn't own cars, the homeless, and people who had left their homes due to domestic violence.

The PTA president now had a problem: How should she respond to ensure that no one was left out? One option would be to mail physical copies to the 70 families she couldn't reach by email, at a cost of $1800 per year. When the PTA was sending 700 newsletters at a time, they received big volume discounts on both copying and postage, so sending 70 instead of 700 only cuts the price by a factor of 3.5, not 10.

Another option would be to print newsletters for the 70 families, at a cost of $900 per year, but then have teachers hand them out at school. Several teachers objected to this, however, because they don't want to single out the vulnerable children in each class. The teachers feared that the two to three students in each class who received a paper copy of the newsletter would be labeled "poor kids" and teased by the other students. Because those particular children were already vulnerable, the teachers did not want to single them out, preferring instead to treat all students the same, as much as possible.

## Reflection Questions

1. **POSITION** Assume that these two plans are the only options for solving the problem. Which of the two plans should the PTA president choose? Explain your reasoning.

2. POSITION List some other options available to the PTA president not mentioned here. Of these alternatives, pick the one you think is the best, and explain how it is better (or worse) than the two options we presented.

3. POSITION Someone might argue that this case, when compared with the others in this section, is somewhat frivolous. These people might argue that the decision faced by the PTA's president isn't really important, so all of these options are morally permissible. Do you agree or disagree? Explain your reasoning.

## 8.7  MEMBERS OF MINORITY GROUPS

Systems of discrimination against members of minority groups can make it more difficult for them to benefit from technology and to seek legal redress for harms caused by technology. Members of minority groups are sometimes intentionally targeted by hate groups who use the anonymity of the Internet to hide their actions. Although authorities have attempted to limit hate speech online, many of these attempts have backfired, as we will see.

Note that we have already written about some of the effects of computing on minority groups like the elderly (Section 8.4.2), people with disabilities (Section 8.5), and racial or ethnic minorities (Section 6.6). You may wish to refer back to those cases. In our case studies here we will investigate the impact of technology on some other groups that we have not yet considered.

### 8.7.1  Case: Protecting Gay Gamers From Harassment

Because of the apparent anonymity of online interactions, harassment and incivility are a common part of the Internet experience. This is particularly true in online games, where players from across the world log in to compete against each other. It is very common to hear players taunt their opponents with slurs based on race, religion, or sexual orientation.

Preventing hate speech and harassment within games has turned out to be one of the main challenges for computer game developers. Some games, such as Disney's *ToonTown*, allow users to select chat messages only from a very small list of prewritten phrases. In this case, possible phrases include "Hi there," "Later," and "Have fun." Though it is possible to use a normal text-based chat in the game, children cannot see chat messages generated that way unless they get parental permission. Other games employ human moderators who respond to complaints filed by users. In Blizzard's *World of Warcraft*, users can report harassment through an online form. A game master follows up on each complaint and punishes wrongdoers if warranted.

In many online games, players are encouraged to form teams, or guilds, which allow players to work together to accomplish goals that a solo player could not accomplish alone. Game companies often want to make sure that these guilds do not become breeding grounds for harassing behavior. (As we saw in Chapter 6, many players, called griefers, see harassing others as part of the fun of the game.) For this reason, game companies generally prohibit the formation of guilds that explicitly promote antisemitism, racial hatred, religious hatred, or harassment of other groups. Implementing such policies can be very tricky, as Blizzard discovered in the spring of 2006.

Jose Vargas reported in the *Washington Post* that a *World of Warcraft* (WoW) player, Sara Andrews, fell afoul of Blizzard's antiharassment policy when she attempted to start a guild that was welcoming to GLBT people (that is, gay, lesbian, bisexual, and transgender people), as well as open to anyone who was comfortable, or friendly, with GLBT people. In other words, the guild would be GLBT-friendly. According to the Washington Post:

> In late January, Andrews was trying to recruit new members to her GLBT-friendly guild…Repeatedly, she wrote in general chats within the game: "We are not 'GLBT only,' but we are 'GLBT friendly!' "Then one of the game's moderators, interpreting the game's "terms of use," cited her for "Harassment-Sexual Orientation." "Advertising sexual orientation" was inappropriate, said a spokesman for Blizzard, the California-based company that owns "WoW." Many people are offended at the mere sight of the word "homosexual," the company noted. Furthermore, "we do feel that the advertisement of a 'GLBT friendly' guild is very likely to result in harassment for players that may not have existed otherwise," Blizzard wrote Andrews. (Vargas)

Blizzard later clarified its policies, and stated that Andrews should not have been cited. Their rules were meant to prevent the formation of hate groups, not to prevent the formation of GLBT-friendly groups.

What went wrong? The wording of Blizzard's original policy statement is very interesting. As reported by Lambda Legal (Chase), Blizzard's original policy, published on the company's public message boards, was as follows:

> To promote a positive game environment for everyone and help prevent such harassment from taking place as best we can, we prohibit mention of topics related to sensitive real-world subjects….This includes openly advertising a guild friendly to players based on a particular political, sexual or religious preference, to list a few examples.

It is not hard to see the appeal of this policy. It would allow Blizzard to stop hate groups inside the game, but at the same time avoid taking sides on controversial issues. As a result, however, the policy banned not just hate groups, but also any group that had preferences that other players objected to, something that they probably did not intend.

## Reflection Questions

1.  POSITION Is it possible to write a policy that would ban hate groups, while not banning other innocent groups? Note the key difficulty here: How can you tell which groups are hate groups and which are not? Part

of Blizzard's principle was that a group should not "openly advertise a guild friendly to players based on a particular political, sexual or religious preference," but most people seem to think this definition is too broad. Do one of the following:

a. If you think it *is* possible, then write a policy you think would work. Your policy must lay out some principles for determining whether or not a particular group is a hate group based on the group's activities in the game. Make sure your policy passes the publicity test. That is, would you be willing to publish this policy on the front page of the newspaper, with your name listed as the author? If not, it is probably not an acceptable policy, because policies cannot be kept secret.

b. If you think it is *not* possible, then explain your reasoning. Also explain what should be done, instead, to stop hate groups from harassing other players in the game.

2. POSITION Blizzard's antiharassment policies seem to go above and beyond what the law ordinarily requires. Should private companies like Blizzard create and enforce policies that are different from the law? Or should the police handle all harassment complaints? Explain your reasoning.

### 8.7.2 Case: Sex Selection in India

A 2006 article in the medical journal *The Lancet* states, "There are fewer girls than boys in India, and this sex ratio has become more skewed towards boys in recent decades." (Jha et al.) According to the authors, the ratio was 927 female births per 1000 male births in 2001. They list many factors that could have contributed to this imbalance: diet, hormonal factors, misreporting of female birth rates, and so on. The authors conclude, however, that the real culprit is the wide availability of prenatal sonograms and the resulting increase of abortions of females.

Dan McDougall, a reporter for *The Times*, explained that, in India, "male offspring are typically regarded as a blessing—future breadwinners who will look after parents in old age—but many parents still see girls as a financial burden." The *Lancet* study suggests that large numbers of expectant parents are using prenatal sonograms to determine the sex of the fetus and then having it aborted if it is female. They claim that this "practice accounts for about 0.5 million missing female births yearly, translating over the past 2 decades into the abortion of some 10 million female fetuses." It is not completely clear whether Jha et al. are correct in their hypothesis. For the purposes of this case, we will put that issue aside, and see what ethical questions arise if it does turn out to be true.

First of all, can the group of female fetuses be considered a vulnerable population? Are fetuses, at the point that it is possible to determine sex via ultrasound, people, and hence entitled to certain rights? Or are they merely a part of the mother's body, and not entitled to rights? We don't expect to be able to shed any useful new light on this much-debated question, but we think it is important to acknowledge the question and the consequences of each of the two positions. If female fetuses are people, with inherent rights, then this use of sonogram technology to selectively abort female fetuses is a significant ethical problem.

But female fetuses are not the only vulnerable population involved in this case. Indian women, in general, are also at risk. The most obvious is that, according to McDougall, women can come under serious pressure to abort a female baby, even if they don't wish to do so. Because Indian women are often financially dependent on men, they can be subject to coercion. Giving in to this coercion incurs risks for the mother. For one thing, having an ultrasound for the purposes of identifying a fetus's sex is illegal in India, so women who choose to have one for this purpose risk prosecution. Also, abortions carry a risk of medical complications (though, of course, so does carrying a baby to term and delivering it).

The law prohibiting the use of sonograms to determine sex is very difficult to enforce, because there are many legal reasons to obtain a sonogram. In order to catch doctors or clinics violating the law, law enforcement officials send in fake patients who indicate that they want the sonogram for a sex test.

### Reflection Questions

1. APPLICATION Use a rule utilitarian analysis to explain why the Indian government might ban sex selection of babies. In particular, what are the consequences for a society if a serious imbalance arises between the number of boys and number of girls born each year?

2. POSITION Indian officials could, if they wanted, ban ultrasound sonograms altogether. Should they? Overall, would this benefit female fetuses? Who would it harm?

3. POSITION Defend or refute the following claim: "It is possible to build an ultrasound machine without computers, using only electric circuits. Therefore, the widespread use of sonograms to determine the sex of a fetus is not a consequence of computing."

## 8.7.3   Case: Assumptions Behind Demographic Questions

In a 2011 *New York Times* article by Susan Saulny and Jacques Steinberg, a student applying for college posed a moral question about the demographic questions on college applications:

> "I just realized that my race is something I have to think about," she wrote, describing herself as having an Asian mother and a black father. "It pains me to say this, but putting down black might help my admissions chances and putting down Asian might hurt it."

> "My mother urges me to put down black to use AA"—African-American—"to get in to the colleges I'm applying to. I sort of want to do this but I'm wondering if this is morally right."

| Traditional radio button design forces a multiracial person to make an inaccurate statement | Checkbox design allows greater accuracy |
|---|---|
| 1. What is your race?<br><br>◉ White, not of Spanish or Hispanic origin<br>◉ Spanish or Hispanic origin<br>◉ Black<br>◉ American Indian or Alaskan Native<br>◉ Asian<br>◉ Pacific Islander | 1. Are you of Spanish or Hispanic origin?<br><br>◉ Yes<br>◉ No<br><br>2. What is your race? Mark all boxes that apply.<br><br>☑ White<br>☑ Black<br>☑ American Indian or Alaskan Native<br>☑ Asian<br>☑ Pacific Islander |

**FIGURE 8.2** Two possible survey designs

The student is facing a moral dilemma. In many of the forms we fill out online, poor design assumptions can make it impossible to answer honestly. Figure 8.2 shows two possible designs for a Web-based fill-in form that allows the user to specify her ethnicity. The survey design on the left forces multiracial people to make an inaccurate statement

Neither form is particularly complete: Both leave off an "other" option, and neither contains all of the racial categories that are recognized by the U.S. census. The form on the right, however, is preferable to the one on the left. The form on the left uses an interface called "radio buttons." A **radio button** interface allows the user to select only one choice at a time, just like a radio allows you to tune in to just one station at a time. If the user selects both "Black" and "Asian," only the last option selected will stick; the previously selected option will be automatically cleared. With the check box option in the second survey, the user can select none of the options, or all of them.

Specific assumptions in their data model lead many software developers to prefer the radio button option. A **data model** is a description of the type of data to be collected, and an explanation of how the pieces of data relate to each other. For example, the creator of the radio-button-based form probably envisioned a data model with one database record for each individual, with multiple pieces of data (such as first name, last name, gender, race, age, and so on) in each record. The mistake was in thinking that "race" is a simple category like "age" that can be represented by a single value. Instead, a person's "race" can be too complicated to be entered in a single data field. This misunderstanding about the definition of "race" can lead to an incorrect form design.

The "gender" settings in popular social media sites like Facebook and Google+ are also controversial. Most sites present gender as a strictly binary (two choices) decision, male or female. Health officials and advocates point out that neither sex nor gender is so simple. The World Health Organization gives the following definitions:

**"Sex"** refers to the biological and physiological characteristics that define men and women.

**"Gender"** refers to the socially constructed roles, behaviours, activities, and attributes that a given society considers appropriate for men and women.

Sex is surprisingly problematic. The biological characteristics of many people mean they do not fit precisely into either "male" or "female." Gender is even more controversial. Many people feel that each person should be free to define their gender as they see fit, even if it does not match their biological sex. Others feel that this is unnatural and morally wrong.

We will not take a position on this question. Our goal is simply to point out the moral, social, and ethical implications behind seemingly simple choices when designing Web forms. As of September 2011, Facebook's solution to this problem is to include "sex" as an option on its profiles instead of "gender." The options are "male" or "female," but you also have the option to hide this information from others. Google+, which chooses to use gender instead of sex, provides three choices: male, female, and other.

## Reference Questions

1.  APPLICATION Which approach to sex/gender on social networks is morally preferable, Facebook's approach or the Google+ approach? Explain your reasoning. Use one of the ethical theories from Chapter 1 in your explanation if you think that would be helpful.

2.  CONTEXT Facebook currently allows users to use a pseudonym (a fake name), while Google+ requires users to use their real names. Does this change your answer to the previous question? Explain your reasoning.

3.  APPLICATION According to the *ACM/IEEE Software Engineering Code of Ethics and Professional Practice,* should software engineers use the check box method for representing race or the radio button method? Explain your answer, being sure to reference the appropriate principles or rules from the code.

## SUMMARY

- The *ACM/IEEE Software Engineering Code of Ethics and Professional Practice* explicitly requires software engineers to give consideration to certain vulnerable groups.

- The difference principle, as defined in Rawls's theory of justice, provides some support for the idea that vulnerable groups are special.

- Even if you do not consider vulnerable groups deserving of special treatment for reasons of justice, they may still need special consideration, especially in the utilitarian calculus. This is because they tend to be easily overlooked or forgotten, which leads to incorrect calculations of utility.

- A threat analysis is a method of documenting the vulnerabilities of a system, often used in computer security research. It documents threats (attackers and their motivations), vulnerabilities (the openings in a system that allow misuse), and mitigations (strategies for preventing attacks). This method can also be used to analyze society, and mitigate threats to vulnerable groups.
- Some vulnerable groups in modern society include:
    - People subject to institutional coercion
        - Prisoners
        - Military personnel
        - Persons living under oppressive governments
    - People at risk of coercion due to lack of autonomy or life choices
        - Mentally disabled persons
        - Children, particularly orphans
    - People with increased risks due to physical frailty or limitation
        - The elderly
        - Physically disabled persons
        - Pregnant women
        - Dying patients
    - People with limited recourse due to lack of resources
        - The poor
        - Workers with obsolete skills or those who are not permitted to organize in unions
    - People at risk of hate-motivated behaviors
        - Racial or ethnic minorities
        - Religious minorities
        - Minorities of gender identity or sexual preference

## CHAPTER EXERCISES

1. REVIEW Summarize the argument, based on Rawls's theory of justice, that vulnerable groups deserve special consideration.
2. REVIEW Summarize the argument that utilitarians need to pay special attention to vulnerable groups.
3. REVIEW Define "threat," "vulnerability," and "mitigation" in the context of threat analysis in computer security.
4. REVIEW Define "institution," as it is used in this chapter, and give several examples.
5. REVIEW Describe the purpose of a Web-based prison pen pal service.

6. REVIEW Define "autonomy."

7. REVIEW Describe the main functions of a "family locator service." Also define "locator" and "locatee" in this context.

8. REVIEW List some examples of "accessibility" technologies or features in the technologies you use every day.

9. REVIEW Define "digital divide."

10. REVIEW Define "e-waste."

11. REVIEW Define "claim right" and "liberty," and explain the difference between them.

12. REVIEW Define "Luddite" and "neo-Luddite."

13. REVIEW Explain, in your own words, what it means for technology to "deskill" a job, and give an example.

14. REVIEW Define "automation" and explain how this relates to "autonomy."

15. REVIEW Define "data model" and explain how a bad data model can lead to an unethical user interface.

16. REVIEW Give the WHO's definitions of "sex" and "gender," and explain the difference between them.

17. POSITION It is currently not clear whether it is legal for ordinary citizens to videotape police officers while they are on the job. In some states this practice is prohibited by anti-wiretapping laws. Several state legislatures have considered making it explicitly legal; the proposed laws would say that it is always legal to make video and audio recordings of uniformed officers while they are on the job. How would such a law affect vulnerable populations? Be sure you consider whether or not police officers are, themselves, a vulnerable population.

18. POSITION This chapter makes the following claim: "Computer professionals ought to pay special attention to how their actions will affect vulnerable populations." Write three different arguments supporting this claim using the following three ethical theories.

    a. Utilitarianism (you may select either Act or Rule)
    b. Virtue Ethics
    c. Rawls's Theory of Justice

19. RESEARCH Keeping in mind Case 8.6.1, which discusses e-waste, do you think the United States should prohibit bulk exports of used electronics? Who would such a prohibition harm? Who would it help? You may need to look up more stories about the trade in used electronics to inform your answer.

20. POSITION Consider the following claim: "The existence of a digital divide is inherently unethical, and computer professionals should strive to narrow it." Write an argument either supporting or refuting this claim. You may wish to support your argument using ethical theories from Chapter 1 or by referring to the *ACM/IEEE Software Engineering Code of Ethics and Professional Practice.*

21. [POSITION] Section 8.7.1 discusses a woman who was disciplined, by the video game company Blizzard, for advertising a "GLBT-friendly" players group. In the United States, a person arrested by the police and charged with harassment (or with a hate crime), is guaranteed the right to defend himself against the charges in court. However, Blizzard, a corporation, is not required to give players a chance to defend themselves, and can ban players for any reason or no reason at all. Should video game companies be legally required to allow customers to appeal a ban to an impartial third party? Explain your reasoning.

22. [POSITION] Do prisoners have a right to Internet access, as long as it is supervised by prison officials? Keep in mind that while prisoners lose some rights (like the right to go where they wish), they retain some rights (like the rights to food, shelter, and medical care). In particular, should prison inmates be allowed to access online training or college courses, online job search sites, online substance abuse treatment sites, and so on?

## WORKS CITED

Brodkin, Jon. "Berners-Lee: Web access is a 'human right'." *Network World*, 12 Apr. 2011. Web. 23 May 2011.

Chase, Brian. "When the Pen Is Mightier Than the (Magic) Sword." *LambdaLegal.org*, 11 Jun 2009. Web. 31 May 2011.

Denning, Tamara et al. "Patients, pacemakers, and implantable defibrillators: human values and security for wireless implantable medical devices." Proceedings of the 28th international conference on Human factors in computing systems. New York, NY, USA: ACM, 2010. 917-926. Web. 3 Sept 2011.

Halperin, D. et al. "Pacemakers and Implantable Cardiac Defibrillators: Software Radio Attacks and Zero-Power Defenses." IEEE Symposium on Security and Privacy. 2008. 129-142. Web. 3 Sept 2011.

"Is Kansas correct to give inmates limited e-mail access?" *Topeka Capitol Journal*, 14 May 2009. Web. 11 Sept. 2011.

Jansen, Jim. "Use of Internet in Higher-income Households." *Pew Internet & American Life Project*, 24 Nov 2010. Web. 4 Sept 2011.

Jha, Prabhat et al. "Low male-to-female sex ratio of children born in India: national survey of 1.1 million households." *The Lancet* 367.9506 (2006): 211-218. Web. 8 Sept. 2011. [Note: The title in the printed version of this article was incorrect. It should have read "Low female-to-male sex ratio." The *Lancet* printed a correction in the next issue.]

Kelly, Kevin. "Interview with the Luddite." *Wired*, June 1995. Web. 5 Sept 2011.

Klein, Peter. *Ghana: Digital Dumping Ground*. 2009. Film.

McCullagh, Declan. "Tech giants deny helping Iran eavesdrop." *CNET News*, 22 June 2009. Web. 25 May 2011.

McDougall, Dan. "The ten million baby girls lost to the ultrasound generation." *Times Online*, 10 Jan. 2006. Web. 8 Sept. 2011.

McGill, Kevin. "Ex-La. gov, 83, marries 32-year-old prison pen pal." *Huffington Post*, 29 July 2011. Web. 11 Sept. 2011.

Nader, Ralph. "Robots Coming Fast." *nader.org,* 21 Nov 1981. Web. 4 Sept 2011.

Saulny, Susan, and Jacques Steinberg. "Multiracial Students Face Quandary on College Application." *The New York Times* 13 June 2011. Web. 4 Oct. 2011.

Schluep, Mathias. *Recycling—From E-waste to Resources,* 2009. United Nations Environment Programme. Web. 5 Sept 2011.

Scimeca, Dennis. "Resetting Accessibility in Games." *Gamasutra,* 23 Dec. 2010. Web. 10 Sept. 2011.

Taub, Eric A. "The Technology for Monitoring Elderly Relatives." *nytimes.com,* 28 July 2010. Web. 23 May 2011.

Thompson, Mark. "Internet Access Turns Prisons Into Free Speech Battlegrounds." *Online Journalism Review.* 24 Apr. 2004. USC Annenberg School for Communication, Web. 11 Sept. 2011.

Vargas, Jose. "For Gay Gamers, A Virtual Reality Check." *Washingtonpost.com* 11 Mar. 2006. Web. 31 May 2011.

Wood, Mark A., and Kenneth A. Ellenbogen. *American Heart Association.* "Cardiac Pacemakers From the Patient's Perspective." Circulation 105.18 (2002): 2136-2138. Web. 26 May 2011.

World Health Organization. "What do we mean by 'sex' and 'gender'?" *WHO.int.* Web. 12 Sept. 2011.

## RELATED READINGS

### Novels

Moon, Elizabeth. *The Speed of Dark.* Del Rey, 2003. Print. (In this novel, which won the Nebula award for the best science fiction novel of the year in 2003, Moon explores the special vulnerability of autistic workers. The mother of an autistic son, Moon questions the very idea that autism is a "defect" that needs to be "cured." The protagonist, an autistic computer programmer, faces pressure from his boss to undergo an experimental "cure" for autism. His struggle to decide whether to go along, or to resist, highlights the problematic nature of "normalcy.")

Vonnegut, Kurt, Jr. *Player Piano.* First edition. Macmillan Pub Co, 1952. Print. (Vonnegut's novel envisions a world in which automation has completely eliminated the working class. The only valuable members of society are engineers, who design mechanical devices. Skilled labor is a thing of the past, and those people who were traditionally employed as skilled workers are given busywork to keep them occupied. Is this vision ever likely to become a reality, or will there always be jobs that require skilled laborers, regardless of how far technology advances?)

### Short Fiction

Vonnegut, Kurt. "Harrison Bergeron." *Welcome to the Monkey House: Stories.* New York: Dial Press Trade Paperback, 1998. 7-14. Print. (Vonnegut's classic short story, which questions the idea that all people can have equal abilities. In this dystopian story, the solution is to pull down the strong, rather than to help up the vulnerable.)

## Essays and Articles

Brooks, David. "The Limits of Empathy." *The New York Times* 29 Sept. 2011. Web. 4 Oct. 2011. (Columnist David Brooks discusses the limits of empathy in moving us to moral action. He summarizes some recent psychology results that show that empathy is a poor motivator to help others, but happiness is a strong one. That is, if you feel happy, you are very likely to help others, whether you feel empathy for them or not.)

Manjoo, Farhad. "Robot Invasion." *Slate Magazine*. Web. 4 Oct. 2011. (In this series of articles written for *Slate Magazine*, Farhad Manjoo examines six jobs that are being eliminated by robots. They include jobs you might not expect, like lawyer and radiologist.)

Stanton, Elizabeth Cady. "The Solitude of Self." *The Struggle for women's rights: theoretical and historical sources*. Upper Saddle River, NJ: Prentice Hall, 1999. 118-121. Print. (Stanton presented this speech to the Judiciary committee of the U.S. Congress in 1892. In it she argues that women have a fundamental right to a college education, and that such education should include the same topics that men study, not topics designed to make them better wives, mothers, or homemakers. Her argument is grounded in ideas of self-reliance. According to Stanton, denying women access to a college education stops them from caring for themselves and others. She says "To throw obstacle in the way of a complete education is like putting out the eyes; to deny the rights of property, like cutting off the hands.")

## Other Media

Zimbardo, Phillip. <*http://www.prisonexp.org/*> (This Web site presents a multimedia slide show explaining the Stanford Prison Experiment. Zimbardo, a psychology professor, was interested in understanding how relatively normal people can become part of abusive and inhumanly oppressive systems. In 1971 he recruited twenty-four college-aged men to role-play a prison, with twelve taking the roles of guards and twelve taking the roles of prisoners. The experiment, which was meant to last two weeks, quickly devolved into real abuse and violence and had to be canceled after six days. In addition to being a classic experiment in social psychology and morality, this experiment demonstrates the special vulnerability of students, prisoners, and members of military-like groups.)

## Film and TV

Sargent, Joseph. *Miss Evers' Boys*. HBO Home Video, 2002. Film. (*Miss Evers' Boys*, a made-for-TV movie from HBO, tells the story of the Tuskegee syphilis study. Between 1932 and 1972, the United States government studied the progress of untreated syphilis in poor black men living in rural parts of Tuskegee, Alabama. The subjects of the experiment believed they were receiving free treatment from the government. Instead, they were prevented from receiving penicillin, which would have cured the disease. This case demonstrates the special vulnerability of poor African Americans during that time period. Moral outrage over the experiment, once it became public, was one of the major forces that led to the establishment of medical ethics and research ethics laws.)

# Chapter 9

# Autonomous and Pervasive Technology

In this book you've learned how modern technologies force us to make serious and complicated ethical decisions. In this chapter we zero in on two qualities of modern technology that are especially problematic: pervasiveness and autonomy. When we say a technology is **pervasive**, we mean that it has spread widely throughout society. By **autonomy**, we mean the freedom to make decisions without outside constraints or interference.

As you will see, pervasiveness and autonomy work together in new technologies, changing society in potentially significant ways, and also taking away some of the autonomy of human beings. After all, autonomous computer systems are intentionally designed to make decisions without direct human control or supervision. This built-in autonomy makes these computer systems easier to use and cheaper to operate and maintain. As a technology gets easier and cheaper to use, people use it more often and in new situations (other than the one for which it was originally designed). This in turn increases the technology's pervasiveness throughout society. Our first case investigates a clear example of this interplay between pervasiveness and autonomy—cell phone cameras.

## 9.1 CASE: PERVASIVENESS OF CAMERA PHONES

In Case 3.7 we considered a bill by Representative Peter King of New York that proposed a new Camera Phone Predator Alert Act. In that section, we asked you to think about why such a law might be necessary:

In the past it was not deemed necessary to require cameras to make a sound so that people would know photographs were being taken. What, if anything, has changed?

There are many good answers to this question, but two key differences distinguish the role of cameras today, from the role they played in society thirty years ago.

First, cameras today are much more pervasive than in the past. An ordinary student today might be carrying seven cameras with him at all times in the following forms:

- Nintendo 3DS, with three cameras—two forward-facing cameras for taking 3D pictures and one facing the user.
- Smart phone, with two cameras—a forward-facing camera for taking pictures and one facing the user for video chatting and self-portraits.
- Laptop computer, with one user-facing Web-camera for video chatting.
- High-quality digital camera, for situations when the cell phone camera isn't sufficient.

In the past, cameras were bulky, expensive to buy, and, because of the cost of film and developing, expensive to operate. Most people carried a camera only when they were planning to take pictures. Today, due to the pervasiveness of cell phones, most people have a camera on them at all times. This is true in developing countries and developed countries alike; according to the International Telecommunication Union, 67.6% of people living in developing countries have cell phones.

The second important shift in the way cameras are used has to do with autonomy. These days, camera owners have considerably more autonomy in deciding what pictures to take. In the past, most cameras took pictures using film, and these rolls of film had to be taken to a lab to be developed. Because there was a potential for workers at the film lab to see, steal, or copy photographs, most people avoided taking obscene or damaging photographs. Furthermore, both film and film developing were expensive, so many people were careful not to waste pictures on unimportant subjects. With modern cameras, however, none of these issues matter anymore.

So Representative King's bill is an attempt to respond to these changes in the role of cameras in society. In the past, the low availability of cameras and the supervision of film developing labs served to discourage child predators from taking inappropriate pictures. Today, with the increasing pervasiveness of cameras, and the increasing autonomy of camera users, new laws may be necessary to punish and discourage these behaviors.

## Reflection Questions

1. RESEARCH What are some of the other effects of the pervasiveness of cameras, and especially camera phones? List some of the ways people use cameras differently now than they did 20 years ago. Are these changes good, bad, or neutral? Explain your reasoning.

2.  POSITION Several researchers and artists have experimented with an idea called lifelogging. A lifelogger wears a computer that records every moment of his life, usually in both audio and video. The camera and audio recording devices are never turned off, no matter what, but the recorded data is not necessarily publicly posted. What are the potential dangers, and benefits, of lifelogging? Is lifelogging morally permissible? Explain your reasoning.

## 9.2 CASE: INJURED BY GPS

Who is at fault when a human and a computer program work together to make a decision, and the outcome is bad? On January 19, 2010, Lauren Rosenberg was trying to walk from one place to another in Park City, Utah, using Google Maps on her Blackberry cell phone to compute walking directions. Following the directions provided by Google Maps, Rosenberg walked along Utah State Route 224, a highway with no sidewalks and a relatively high speed limit. Ms. Rosenberg was hit and injured by a car. Ms. Rosenberg has sued Google for negligently providing unsafe directions, as well as the driver of the car for negligent driving. See the screenshot in Figure 9.1 for an example of walking directions computed by Google Maps.

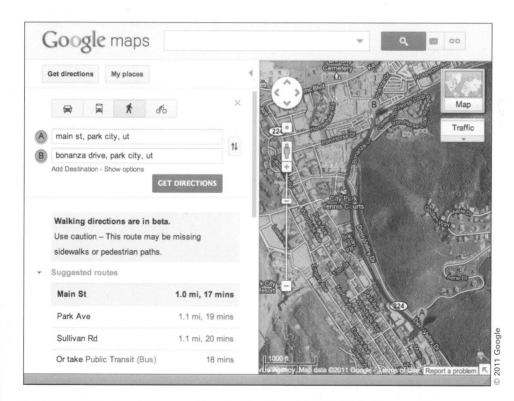

**FIGURE 9.1** Google Maps walking directions from Main Street to Bonanza Drive in Park City, Utah

Note that, in the screenshot, generated in October, 2011, Google maps does not recommend Deer Valley Drive as a suggested route, as it allegedly did in Ms. Rosenberg's case. Deer Valley Drive is also State Route 224.

Two important issues in this case are the pervasiveness of hand-held **GPS (Global Positioning System)** devices (such as Lauren Rosenberg's Blackberry) and the great trust we put in them. The heart of GPS is a network of more than 30 earth-orbiting satellites that can calculate a device's location anywhere on Earth. Each satellite continuously sends out messages that include the precise time each signal was sent. Using this information, a GPS device on the ground can calculate its distance to each satellite. As long as the GPS unit can detect the signal from at least four satellites, it can then calculate its precise location, including latitude, longitude, and elevation. Many cell phones now include GPS receivers, but consumers can also choose from many standalone GPS devices designed for giving directions for driving or for outdoor activities.

This widespread pervasiveness of GPS devices has serious implications because, as we saw in Chapter 5, humans have a tendency to trust computers such as GPS receivers to do certain kinds of tasks. The task of getting directions from one place to another appears to be one of those tasks. The computer-generated directions are usually superior to human-generated ones for a variety of reasons:

- Online maps can be updated any time roads change, which means the online map is usually more accurate than a paper map.

- A computer can precisely calculate the length of every possible route from one place to another, guaranteeing the directions generated really are the best possible.

- A computer can factor in extra information, besides length, to help generate better routes. For example, the computer can factor in speed limit, to get the fastest route even if it is not the shortest. The computer can also try to minimize left turns, which often take much more time than right turns.

- A computer uses consistent and precise terminology and is very good at estimating when it should tell the driver about the next turn. With GPS, unlike with a human navigator, it is rare to be told, "I think that was the turn, back there."

The effectiveness and convenience of GPS devices makes people depend on them in situations when they would be better off making their own decisions. Recently, while visiting the Poynter Center for the Study of Ethics and American Institutions at Indiana University, one of the authors of this book nearly drove up onto a pedestrian sidewalk. The sidewalk used to be a road, and the map in his GPS had not yet been updated to reflect the change. The device insisted that the best way to get to the destination was to drive across campus on the sidewalk, and there was no easy way to inform the device that this route was impassable and get an alternate route. Because he had not packed a physical map, he had to find his way the rest of the way by trial and error, and eventually he even had to stop to ask for directions!

In the case of Ms. Rosenberg's injury, who was at fault? Many commentators on the Internet, including *PC World*'s Sarah Jacobsson, seem to blame Ms. Rosenberg for the accident. They argue that she had a responsibility to use common sense when following the computer's directions, and that she should have known not to follow Google's directions when it directed her onto a highway. In other words, these critics argue that Ms. Rosenberg should not have ceded her decision-making autonomy to Google Maps.

### Reflection Questions

1. [POSITION] Consider the three main parties in the case: 1) Ms. Rosenberg, 2) Google, and 3) the driver of the car. What percentage of the blame does each deserve for what happened? Explain your reasoning.

2. [CONTEXT] Using Google Street View, you can view the route that Ms. Rosenberg most likely followed. She was walking along Utah State Highway 224 from Daly Avenue to Prospector Avenue in Park City, Utah. Use Google Street View to examine the stretch of Utah State Highway 224 in that area. Does this road look like it is too dangerous to follow when walking? Does this change your answer to the previous question? Explain your reasoning.

3. [CONTEXT] Jacobsson's article about the lawsuit only briefly mentions the driver of the car. Why do you think that the article focuses on the Rosenberg vs. Google part of the case, instead of Rosenberg vs. the driver?

## 9.3 CASE: MORE GPS, MORE RISKS

In the previous case we looked at the effects of GPS technology on autonomy. Now let's examine another result of the pervasiveness of that technology. In an interview with National Public Radio's Melissa Block, Matt Scharper, the search and rescue coordinator for the state of California, described one unintended consequence of GPS devices—an increase in the number of emergency search and rescue operations.

The problem stems from the increasing popularity of a device called a personal locator beacon. This device, which typically takes the form of a small yellow box about the size of walkie talkie, contains a button the user can press if he or she is in trouble and needs to be rescued. The device uses GPS to calculate the user's location, and then directly uploads this information to the Search and Rescue Satellite Aided Tracking system (SARSAT). Search and rescue teams are then notified and given the person's precise location. Because SARSAT uses satellite communication instead of cellular communication, it works anywhere outdoors, regardless of whether or not cellular service is an option.

The original name of the devices—"distress radio beacons" or "emergency beacons"—reflects the fact that they were only meant to be used in emergencies. The SARSAT system was first designed to provide homing beacons for airplanes, and then, later, for ships as well. However, improvements in computer technology, battery technology, and GPS have made it economically feasible for hikers, skiers, and other individuals to have personal locator beacons. The beacons, which are now called by the much less formidable name—personal locator beacon—cost about $250 and are therefore becoming increasingly popular.

Armed with these devices, many hikers and boaters are no longer planning ahead to avoid getting into trouble. Instead, according to Scharper, they assume that, if they do get into trouble, they can summon help using a beacon. Scharper described one case in which a hiker, due to inclement weather, pitched his tent and decided to stay an extra night on the trail. He knew that people were expecting him back, so he went ahead and pushed the button on the beacon, so that people would know where he was. As a result, search and rescue teams were sent out to find him, even though he was perfectly safe and did not need rescue.

These unnecessary searches can be very expensive. For example, based on numbers given in an article for *TheDay.com* by Steven Fagin, the average cost of a Coast Guard search and rescue is around $15,000. To defray the costs of search and rescue operations, and to discourage frivolous distress calls, several search and rescue agencies have started charging rescued people the cost of the rescue operation. For example, one Massachusetts teen was charged $25,000 by the state of New Hampshire after being rescued from a hiking trail in 2009. However, in this case the distress call was not frivolous, the teen had injured his ankle and was not able to hike back on his own.

### Reflection Questions

1. POSITION Overall, do you think that emergency locator beacon technology is a good thing, or a bad thing? Explain your reasoning.

2. POSITION How should the authorities handle false alarms? Should people who send false alarms be fined, charged for the cost of their rescue, or otherwise penalized?

3. APPLICATION Scharper argues that increases in the pervasiveness and availability of safety technology can lead to riskier behavior. What are some other examples of this phenomenon? For each example, explain how the pervasiveness of the technology has resulted in riskier behavior.

4. POSITION Is it morally permissible to charge people to be rescued when they really are in danger?

## 9.4   MORE ON THE DEFINITION OF "AUTONOMOUS"

Later in this chapter we focus on three related concepts: autonomous technology, robots, and artificial intelligence. Although these concepts are closely related, they are not identical. Autonomous technology does not have to be intelligent, nor does it have to reside in something that we would ordinarily think of as a robot body.

We have already explained the concept of autonomous technology. To clarify the discussion that follows, we take a moment here to define the other two terms. But keep in mind that these definitions are contested, and many respected researchers would not be completely satisfied with the definitions provided here.

For the purposes of this discussion, a **robot** is an electro-mechanical device capable of movement or action. **Artificial intelligence** is a human-made artifact's ability to learn and reason. (The term **artifact** means any object made by humans.)

Note that we speak very generally here of "intelligence" as the ability to learn and reason. Many sub-disciplines of artificial intelligence research focus on very specific aspects of the topic. In this case, though, a general definition of "intelligence" is more useful than a very technical one.

It is easy to see why one might confuse these three concepts. When you hear the word "robot," the first image that pops into your mind is probably a character from science fiction, like R2-D2 from the *Star Wars* movies, or WALL-E from the Pixar movie. These characters are robots with a very advanced artificial intelligence and a high degree of autonomy. Though such robots, with human-like intelligence, do not yet exist, our lives are already being affected by autonomous technologies. Some of these autonomous systems use robots, and some include rudimentary artificial intelligence.

Table 9.1 provides some examples that illustrate the distinctions between autonomy, intelligence, and robotics.

**TABLE 9.1    Comparison of the autonomy, intelligence and robotic capabilities of various technologies**

|  | Autonomous | Intelligent | Robotic |
|---|---|---|---|
| **Roomba, vacuum cleaner robot sold by iRobot** | Yes. Traverses the room automatically, without human supervision. | No. The robot simply rolls back and forth, turning when it bounces off the wall. It does not learn or reason. | Yes. |
| **Bomb-defusing robots** | No. Remotely operated by a human operator. | No. | Yes. |
| **Stock-trading software used in algorithmic trading** | Yes. Automatically chooses what shares to buy or sell, much faster than a human could. | Varies. Some follow simple pre-defined rules for when to buy or sell, others learn from experience. | No. Purely a piece of software, without any mechanical or physical components. |
| **TD-Gammon algorithm for playing backgammon** | Yes. Learned how to play backgammon by playing against itself, no human supervision needed. | Yes. Invented a more conservative play style that has changed the way humans play backgammon. | No. Purely a piece of software, without any mechanical or physical components. |
| **A marble rolling down a hill** | No. Although it is unsupervised, the marble is not making any decisions. | No. | No. |

The last example, of a marble rolling down a hill (proposed by Noel Sharkey, a University of Sheffield robotics professor), may seem silly, but it highlights the difficulty in providing precise and universally accepted definitions for these terms. The Reflection Questions investigate this idea in more detail.

### Reflection Questions

1.  APPLICATION For each of the following technologies, state whether or not it is autonomous, intelligent, or robotic. Explain your reasoning for each. If you are already familiar with these technologies, you should not need to do any research, and you may base your answer on your current understanding.
    a.  Google's Web search
    b.  Security cameras that can "recognize" wanted criminals and alert authorities if a match is seen
    c.  The control mechanism of a traffic light, which causes it to cycle through its signals appropriately

2.  RESEARCH Look up some other definitions of "autonomous" that are used by computer science and robotics researchers. How do these differ from the definition provided in this chapter?

3.  RESEARCH Some might argue that the Roomba robotic vacuum cleaner and a marble rolling down hill are the same, with respect to autonomy. Both objects follow a set of pre-defined rules. Do some research on the latest model of the Roomba. Do you agree or disagree with the argument that a Roomba is just as autonomous as a marble rolling down hill? Explain your reasoning.

4.  RESEARCH Do some online research about the TD-Gammon algorithm (mentioned in Table 9.1), and then answer the following: Is TD-Gammon's new approach to playing backgammon an example of intelligence, an example of creativity, or neither? Explain your reasoning.

5.  RESEARCH Find some other examples of technologies that have become pervasive as a direct result of automation. Explain why the technology could not be as pervasive as it is without automation.

## 9.5  THE SYNERGY OF AUTONOMY AND PERVASIVENESS

We have made the argument that autonomy and pervasiveness go hand in hand. This works in two ways. The first is that greater autonomy makes technology cheaper to use, which in turn allows it to become pervasive. The other is that as a technology becomes pervasive, the financial incentives for automating it increase. In this section we present several examples and cases that illustrate this phenomenon, and that also have significant ethical impacts.

### 9.5.1 Automated Security Cameras

Automated security cameras are one pervasive technology that has drawn a lot of attention recently. The City of London has one hundred closed-circuit security cameras, plus eighty Automatic Number Plate Recognition (ANPR) cameras in its 1.2 square mile area. (The greater London area, of course, is much larger than this. The "City of London" is only the traditional heart of London, with boundaries that are mostly unchanged since the year 1300.) The ANPR cameras automatically read license plates as cars drive by. This can be used to track down stolen cars, to automatically charge tolls on toll roads, or to automatically issue tickets for speeding or running red lights. In the past, before automated plate reading, there were already quite a few security cameras in public places, but they were not used for tracking stolen cars. Having human beings monitor the cameras and read all the license plates would not have been cost effective. Automating the process of reading and looking up license plate numbers greatly reduced the cost associated with monitoring the cameras. This in turn created an incentive to buy more cameras, and the cameras gradually became pervasive.

This is an example of automation helping to make a technology more pervasive because the automation reduces the ongoing costs of running the system. The pervasiveness of the technology leads, in turn, to new ethical challenges and new types of automation.

As a technology becomes pervasive, it tends to find new uses. For example, now that the borough of London has so many surveillance cameras, authorities could try to use other forms of automatic recognition to identify wanted criminals. Two technologies, in particular, have been tested as means of crime prevention and investigation:

- Face recognition technology—A computer with access to a large database of images can identify people as they walk past a security camera. Face recognition has been used as a security measure at the Super Bowl, and Borders Books considered using it to identify shoplifters. In 2011, Professor Alessandro Acquisti of Carnegie Mellon demonstrated an iPhone app that can identify a person and even provide his or her Social Security number, based on a picture of the person's face and information published on the Internet. After the London riots of 2011, Internet vigilantes attempted to combine face recognition technology with Facebook photographs to identify looters; however, these attempts appear to have been unsuccessful.

- Gait recognition technology—Face recognition technology does not work if the subject is hiding his face, as criminals often do. Several university research labs, including a group at the Georgia Institute of Technology, are working on technology that can identify individuals by how they walk—that is, by their gait.

The widespread deployment of cameras, by police, traffic authorities, and businesses, is creating a demand for new types of automation to increase the usefulness of the cameras. Ethically speaking, this proliferation is leading to significant new privacy problems. There have already been many cases of misuse of surveillance cameras reported in the news. Some examples include:

- In 2009, two FBI employees were charged with using surveillance cameras to spy on teenage girls trying on prom dresses at a charity event.

- In London, following a violent protest at the Israeli embassy, several people were charged based on video evidence from surveillance cameras. In one case the government dropped charges against a protestor named Jake Smith after it was revealed that the videos provided by the police omitted key evidence. Smith had been charged with throwing a stick at police officers, and then running away, but the video appears to show him still in the crowd after the attacker ran away. This section of video and another section showing police beating Smith were initially omitted. Whether these omissions were intentional or not is under investigation.

- Transport for London (TfL), the government agency in charge of transportation in London, provides live traffic videos that allow commuters to check on traffic conditions. As reported by the *Sun* newspaper, a TfL camera turned and pointed into a woman's bedroom, in Richmond, Surrey. As a result, high quality video of her bedroom was broadcast live over the Internet for 90 minutes. TfL blamed a camera failure, and denied intentional misuse.

It is easy to see, from these examples, why privacy advocates might be concerned about the increasing use of automated surveillance cameras. Even if such cameras are not intentionally misused, they create the opportunity for accidental but harmful security breaches.

Finally, we should also note that many of the surveillance cameras used today are robotic in the sense that they have built-in motors that allow the camera to zoom in on a subject, to rotate left and right to pan an area, and to tilt up and down. These features, which are remotely controlled over a computer network, increase the pervasiveness of the cameras because they allow a greater area to be covered by a smaller number of video cameras. They make it possible to cover a larger area for the same price.

### Reflection Questions

1. POSITION One way to minimize the possibility for abuse of surveillance cameras is to remove the robotic tilt and pan, so that the cameras cannot be redirected to spy on people. What are the possible negative consequences of this policy? Should the policy be adopted? Explain your reasoning.

2. POSITION We have argued that automation is one of the forces that is causing increased use of video surveillance cameras. List some of the other social issues or technologies that have also contributed to this increase.

### 9.5.2  Web Search Quality: Google vs. Yahoo

The World Wide Web was launched in 1991 by Tim Berners-Lee. It rapidly gained popularity and users, and by 1993-1994 it was so big that it was hard to find what you were looking for. You might know, for example, that all of

Plato's writings were posted on the Web, but there was not yet any way to search for and find them. If you did not know the exact Web address, you were out of luck.

To solve this problem, many different groups simultaneously invented a type of Web search engine known as a **Web crawler**. A Web crawler is a program whose job is to autonomously surf the Web and remember the content and location of everything it encounters. So if you need to find Plato's *Republic* online, you would simply give the Web crawler the search phrase "Plato's Republic," and, if it had ever seen that phrase online, it would give you the matching Web address.

Web crawlers that work in this way are sometimes called **spiders**, because they "crawl the Web." Even though they are computer programs only, with no electro-mechanical body, Web crawlers are often called robots, or bots. This is because they work autonomously and because of the "crawling the Web" metaphor. Even though they do not crawl around a real, physical web, the way they work is easily visualized as a physical process.

While these early Web crawlers seemed like a great idea at first, they had a major flaw: they simply searched for keyword matches. For example, if you searched for "Plato's Republic" you would get more than one address, many of them not containing the actual text of the *Republic*. The search engine would also return pages that talked *about* Plato's Republic, or an advertisement for "Plato's Republic Bar and Grille," or anything that used the phrase "Plato's Republic." Thus, this first generation of search engines was better than nothing, but the quality of the search results was still low. Search engine companies began to look for ways to improve their results.

In 1994, two Stanford Ph.D. students, Jerry Yang and David Filo, hit on a very simple idea: have humans actually evaluate the quality of Web pages and keep a directory of the best Web pages on every subject. This became the Yahoo! Directory, a modernized version of which is still available at *dir.yahoo.com*. Searching for "Plato's Republic" in the Yahoo! Directory leads you to online library Web sites which have been vetted for quality by a human operator. For many years this approach to improving the quality of Web search results was one of the most successful. Although many other search engines existed, the Yahoo! Directory was the best place to find items of broad public interest.

This all changed in 1996, when a second pair of Stanford Ph.D. students, Larry Page and Sergey Brin, started the research project that would eventually become Google. They asked a very simple question: Can we teach a Web crawler algorithm the difference between a good Web page and an inferior one? Can we take the humans, which Yahoo! used for this purpose, out of the equation? Their solution to the problem is the PageRank algorithm.

The **PageRank algorithm** looks at the links between Web pages to figure out which Web pages are most important. The basic idea behind this algorithm is that a Web page that 100 other Web pages link to is probably better than a page that only three other Web pages link to. In a sense, by linking to a Web page, other Web pages vote for that Web page, or vouch for its quality.

The second major idea behind the PageRank algorithm is that not everyone's vote is equal. A link from a good Web page is better than a link from an inferior one. This is important, because it stops someone from tricking the algorithm by creating millions of worthless Web pages that all link to each other.

The founders of Google had two important insights about the Web: 1) A link to a page is a vote of confidence for that page; and 2) The votes from good Web pages should count more than votes from inferior Web pages. The PageRank algorithm automates the process of ranking Web pages based on their quality using these two insights. When you do a Google search, it compiles a list of results that match your search terms, but then it sorts them using PageRank.

This automation helped Google beat Yahoo! in the race to be the best search service. While the quality of Yahoo!'s results was very high, they simply could not keep up with the huge number of Web pages being created every day. It was also very difficult to search the Yahoo! Directory for topics that appealed to only a small group of people, because there might not be any editor at Yahoo! who cared enough (or had the necessary expertise) to add those topics to the directory. Google, by automating the quality ranking of Web pages, was able to search the entire Web, not just a carefully chosen subset. As a result, Google's results were more thorough, while being of comparable quality to Yahoo!'s. Not surprisingly, Google quickly became pervasive.

Today, the verb "to google" (to search for information about something on the Internet) is listed in most major dictionaries, including the *Oxford English Dictionary* and *Merriam-Webster*. This example demonstrates, again, the way that autonomy leads to pervasiveness, and pervasiveness necessitates autonomy, in computer technologies. The pervasiveness of Google, and its crowding out of the other search engines of the 1990s, is due entirely to the ability to automate the process of evaluating the quality of Web pages. At the same time, the pervasiveness of the Web necessitated the creation of Web crawlers in the first place.

## Reflection Questions

1. RESEARCH Many services, such as *Quora.com* and *ChaCha.com*, use crowdsourcing, instead of automation, to answer queries from users. When you submit a query such as "When was Google founded?" the system forwards it to a human being, who finds the answer and sends it to you. This all happens very rapidly, so you won't be waiting long. Look at the ChaCha and Quora Web sites, and then give an example of a question where they are likely to be better choices than Google for finding the answer.

2. RESEARCH Some people are unaware that many libraries employ reference librarians, whose job is to help patrons with difficult to answer questions. Find out whether or not your school or local library employs reference librarians. If so, visit one, and ask them for some examples of questions that they have helped answer that are not easy to answer through Google, ChaCha, and Quora. Write a summary of your findings.

### 9.5.3  Case: Grading Essays by Computer

In Section 2.3.5, Question 2, we asked whether or not teachers are professionals. Many students, in answering the question, point out that most teachers have significant amounts of autonomy in their work. Though the subjects they teach are usually set by state curriculum guidelines, teachers often have significant autonomy in designing lesson plans, allocating time spent in the classroom, and in grading. Many people view this as beneficial, because it allows the teacher to tailor the classroom experience to the particular students in their class, customizing classes to best fit the needs of the students.

As with everything, this autonomy also has some drawbacks. Many people have noticed that autonomy, especially in grading, can lead to inconsistency. For example, in some high school classes students may learn a lot, but get low grades, where in another class they learn less, but get better grades. This makes it very hard for colleges to tell which students are the best ones to admit. Students cannot be selected based on grades alone if some high schools routinely give higher grades than others. For this reason, almost every college in the United States uses standardized testing in admissions decisions. The grades in standardized tests are totally consistent; students who give the same set of answers will receive the same grade. This does not necessarily mean the test is fair (the questions themselves might be biased in favor of one group or another), but it at least means that the grading and scoring process is fair.

Most standardized tests consist of multiple-choice questions, with five possible answers for each question, only one of which is correct. Students mark their answers on computer-readable forms. The scoring process, which does not require any thought or decision-making, is then done by computers.

As a result, standardized testing is very economical and is pervasive throughout our society. For instance, early in their lives, most American students encounter the standardized tests used to evaluate students' progress throughout their school career. In aggregate, these test scores are used to evaluate the effectiveness of individual schools and school districts and can have enormous effects on school funding and educational policy decisions. Most American school students take some form of a standardized test at least once a year. (For example, the state of Missouri tests math and communication arts skills every year in grades 3-8 and science skills in grades 5, 8 and 11.)

Standardized testing of this type is highly controversial, for a variety of reasons. We will not address all of the arguments for and against testing, but instead focus on one particular issue. Multiple-choice tests cannot test one of the key skills that we want students to learn, which is the ability to communicate through writing. For this reason, human graders are still used for many types of examinations. Most of the College Board's Advanced Placement tests (the exams in the subjects of literature and history, in particular) have substantial essay-based sections that are scored by human graders. Similarly, most colleges require students to submit essays as part of their application packets, in part to help the schools rate each student's writing ability.

The GMAT (Graduate Management Admissions Test), a required standardized test for students applying to many MBA programs in the United States, is different. Since the year 2000, the GMAT has used a program called e-rater to evaluate everything from student answers to essay questions. The e-rater program was developed by the Educational Testing Service (ETS); GMAT pays ETS for access to e-rater.

When grading an essay, e-rater expects essays to follow the standard five-paragraph form, as follows:

- First paragraph—Background information, an introduction, and a thesis or main idea
- Middle three paragraphs—One supporting idea per paragraph
- Fifth paragraph—Conclusion

The e-rater evaluates each essay on twelve criteria, the most important ones being grammar, usage, mechanics, and style. Development of ideas is ranked fifth. A very simple version of machine-learning is used to turn e-rater's ratings on the twelve criteria into a score on a scale of 1 to 6. First, humans grade a small subset of the essays, giving each one a score from 1 to 6. These are then used as training data for e-rater, which looks at how the human graders rated the essays and tries to grade accordingly. Grammar, usage, mechanics, and style are the top criteria used by human graders in the training data; thus, they are also e-rater's top four criteria.

In addition to GMAT, several other businesses and educational institutions are considering using computers to score essays. *TurnItIn.com*, one of the most commercially successful plagiarism prevention and detection services, has licensed e-rater for use in its GradeMark product. GradeMark is a suite of software tools, provided through TurnItIn's Web site, that helps instructors grade essays. A student can also submit her paper to e-rater to be scored, and then revise the essay to improve it. Several state and local school boards have also considered adopting e-rater, or other similar products, for scoring student essays in middle school and high school.

Scoring essays by computer is understandably controversial. For example, reporter Shirley Jinkins interviewed several experts on writing and testing. She summarizes an argument of Les Perelman, director of writing at Massachusetts Institute of Technology, as follows:

> The programs can be fooled because of their overemphasis on grammar, structure and word length, critics say. Good sentences, organization and clear transitions score well even if the essay makes no logical sense.

Jinkins also cites Bob Schaeffer, of the National Center for Fair and Open Testing.

> The scoring "doesn't take into account all the different ways something can be written well," he said. "The writing styles of Hemingway and James Joyce would be judged as unacceptable."

Indeed many, if not most, college instructors would be inclined to focus primarily on more in-depth issues and less on the top four criteria used by e-rater. For example, in the supplementary materials for this textbook, the authors encourage instructors to focus not on grammar, usage, mechanics, and style, but rather on the quality of the student's thesis. In the sample rubrics provided for paper assignments, the interestingness and importance of a thesis are the first, and most important, criteria for judging the quality of a paper. In the future, computers may be able to judge papers on these types of criteria, but they are not yet up to the task. Nevertheless, computer grading of essays will likely grow in popularity over the next few years.

What does the future hold for standardized testing? Over the past 20-30 years, standardized testing of students has continuously grown in popularity and importance, and that trend is likely to continue. As automation has cut the cost of evaluating student learning, the amount of evaluation done has increased, and standardized testing has become pervasive. The need to standardize the grading of essay tests, as well as multiple-choice tests, has led to a demand for computer programs that can score writing. This automation may, in turn, lead school systems and governments to collect more and more samples of student work, and to do more and more routine and standardized assessment. Again, pervasiveness and automation reinforce each other.

## Reflection Questions

1.   POSITION  Based on your experience in school, do you think that a computer could do as good a job of grading essays as an average teacher? Could it do a better job than the worst teacher you have had? Than the best teacher you had? Explain your reasoning.

2.   POSITION  Should students have the right to challenge their grades and demand that a human grade their papers if they disagree with a computer-generated grade? Explain your reasoning.

3.   CONTEXT  Should students have the right to challenge their grades and demand that a computer grade their papers if they disagree with a human-generated grade? Explain your reasoning.

4.   POSITION  Is it morally permissible for a college instructor to use e-rater and assign grades to student essays based on its output, without actually looking at the essays? Explain your reasoning.

5.   POSITION  Assuming that college instructors continued to grade papers in the way that they always have, would it be beneficial for them to also use e-rater, to get a second opinion? Explain your reasoning.

6.   POSITION  Imagine a situation in which a student applies to an MBA program, but is rejected due to a low GMAT score. Suppose also that this low GMAT score was an error: The student's essays were actually quite good, but e-rater scored them incorrectly because the student had an unusual writing style. Who, if anyone, is morally responsible for the student's unfortunate situation? Explain your reasoning.

## 9.6   WHO IS RESPONSIBLE FOR AUTONOMOUS SYSTEMS?

As you read in Chapter 5, assigning moral blame for software failures can be difficult. In some cases, the end-user makes inappropriate use of the system, causing the failure. In other cases, the system designers deserve the blame because they produced an unsafe design. The introduction of autonomy adds another wrinkle to this problem, because, in autonomous systems, the end-user is essentially a bystander in the decision-making process.

Ethicists who study technology are concerned that autonomous systems may become scapegoats that shield corporations and individuals from taking responsibility for their decisions. The cases in the following sections explore this issue.

### 9.6.1   Case: Remote Parking

Several car companies produce models with a remote parking assistance feature that allows a driver to pull a car close to a parking space, and then get out. After exiting the vehicle, the driver presses a button on his keychain that tells the car to park itself automatically. This feature is very useful for parking in a narrow space and for parallel parking. The car uses a system of sensors that emit ultrasonic sounds to detect cars, the curb, and pedestrians. Many versions also include video cameras to monitor the location of the curb and any painted parking-space lines. A computer in the car uses this information to automatically pull the car into the space, while avoiding collisions.

Imagine the following scenario: A driver pulls up next to a parking space, checks to make sure the space is clear, presses the button to start the automatic parking, and then walks away. After the driver's back is turned, a small child runs into the space and is seriously injured. Who has moral responsibility for the child's injury? Note that, as always, moral responsibility may be different from legal or financial responsibility.

### Reflection Questions

1. [POSITION] Who is primarily morally responsible for the child's injury? The most obvious choices are: 1. the driver; 2. the car company; 3. the child; 4. the adult in charge of the child; 5. no one. State your position and explain your reasoning. You can choose from the choices presented here, or argue for a different choice. You can also assign blame to more than one party if you think that is appropriate.

2. [CONTEXT] Imagine that, instead of using a computerized parking assistant, the driver had used valet parking (that is, a human parking assistant), and a child was injured. In this case, who would be morally responsible?

3. [CONTEXT] Imagine that, instead of using a computerized parking assistant, the driver had used valet parking (that is, a human parking

assistant), and a child was injured. What if the valet was noticeably dizzy and smelled strongly of alcohol, and the driver still chose to give his keys to the valet? In this scenario, which party or parties deserve moral blame? Why?

### 9.6.2 Software with Emergent Behaviors

One common misconception about computer software is that, for any particular piece of software, somewhere there is a human programmer who wrote and understands that software. If this were true it would make it very easy to blame human programmers any time their software malfunctions.

Unfortunately, this simplistic scenario does not apply to most software in wide use today. Consider TD-Gammon, the backgammon-playing software mentioned earlier in Table 9.1. TD-Gammon was not programmed to be good at playing backgammon. Instead, TD-Gammon was programmed with the legal moves of the game and designed to autonomously learn from experience. It played against itself 1,500,000 times, eventually learning to play at a level competitive with human master players. The technology that made this possible is called temporal difference learning (hence, the "TD" in TD-Gammon).

The temporal difference learning algorithm is an example of machine learning, which is one type of artificial intelligence. **Machine learning** algorithms allow computers to take in data and automatically learn to recognize patterns and make predictions about them. For example, by playing backgammon over and over, TD-Gammon was able to learn to predict how its moves would affect its chances of winning the game. Even though TD-Gammon saw only some of the many possible moves and game play styles, it was able to learn to recognize the difference between a good strategy and a bad one. Machine learning algorithms are in wide use in voice recognition, handwriting recognition, and military applications.

Like students in school, machine learning algorithms require supervision, to some extent, by a human teacher. With TD-Gammon, this supervision was very limited. The human trainer programmed a system with the rules of backgammon. This prevented TD-Gammon from making illegal moves and allowed TD-Gammon to determine which player won or lost. TD-Gammon was then allowed to experiment and learn on its own, without human supervision. TD-Gammon did not play against humans at all until after it had finished its training. It only played against itself, over and over, 1.5 million times. Unlike a human player, TD-Gammon did not have the benefit of playing against, and learning from, experienced players.

These same techniques are used in software systems with significant safety implications. For example, machine learning systems are used in the **Unmanned Aerial Vehicles (UAVs)** that are being widely adopted by both militaries and police forces. UAVs (which are often called **drones** in the news media) are small airplanes that fly autonomously. Instead of a human pilot onboard, a human at a ground control station (GCS) controls the UAV using a point-and-click interface. The human in charge can click an object to target; the UAV then autonomously plans and follows a flight path that keeps the target in view.

UAVs of this type serve a variety of purposes. In addition to performing surveillance, they can also be used to provide targeting information for artillery or manned aircraft. In some cases the drones themselves have rockets and can attack an enemy target directly.

Designers of UAVs are trying to increase the autonomy of UAVs through machine learning. Because the drones often operate in rugged and remote areas, they sometimes lose contact with the ground control station. This means that the drone has to have a built-in autopilot. At a minimum, the drone's autopilot should be able to bring the drone to a place where it can reestablish contact with the ground control station, and it should do so without crashing the drone. Creating a computer program that achieves these goals is not too difficult.

For drones used in combat operations, however, such a minimally functioning autopilot is not sufficient. If the drone is spying on someone, it needs to avoid detection, not just take the shortest path to get back into communication. Furthermore, if the drone is involved in combat operations, it should be able to automatically recognize and avoid threats on the ground, such as anti-aircraft weapons. The computer systems used to automatically recognize threats, based on visual input, are usually created through machine learning. In the reflection questions we will ask you to consider the ethical implications of using algorithms created by machine learning in these sorts of military applications.

## Reflection Questions

1. **POSITION** List some possible negative effects of a UAV failing to recognize a threat.

2. **POSITION** List some possible negative effects of an over-sensitive UAV that mistakes something harmless for a threat.

3. **POSITION** In a short paragraph, defend or refute the following statement: "An erroneous decision made by the UAV is a fault in the UAV, and not directly attributable to any person or group of persons."

4. **APPLICATION** In the United States, children are usually not held to the same moral standards as adults, because they are not as competent to make decisions. In cases of property destruction, a child's legal guardian is often held financially responsible. Should the laws governing software created by machine apply similar rules? In other words, should the human who oversaw the training of the software be held responsible for its actions? Explain your reasoning.

### 9.6.3  Moral Responsibility for Computing Artifacts: Five Rules

Computer ethicists are concerned that the complexity and autonomy of modern computer systems allow people to duck responsibility for the problems they cause by releasing unsafe or unpredictable software. If a system is so complicated that even technically literate people can't easily understand why a system behaves as it does, how can we decide who (or what) is to blame?

To help formulate a solution to this problem, a committee of ethicists and computer science researchers known as the **Ad Hoc Committee for Responsible Computing** formulated a set of principles, known as the Five Rules, for apportioning blame for harm caused by complicated computer systems. The committee's membership includes many of the leading figures of computer ethics, among them:

- All three members of the executive committee that created the *Software Engineering Code of Ethics and Professional Practice*: Donald Gotterbarn, Keith Miller, and Simon Rogerson.

- Several winners of the Jon Barwise prize for contributions to philosophy and computing: Terrell Ward Bynum, James H. Moor, and Deborah Johnson.

- Michael Davis, whose definition of "profession" we discussed extensively in Chapter 2.

- University of Washington security expert Tadayoshi Kohno (one of the co-authors of the paper on implanted defibrillators discussed in Chapter 8).

The rules themselves, which are available online at *https://edocs.uis.edu/kmill2/www/TheRules/*, are complex and require many definitions. The following is a paraphrase:

1. People who make computing artifacts are morally responsible for the foreseeable effects of those artifacts. (Recall that the term "artifact" means any object made by humans.)

2. The amount of blame assigned to a person does not depend on the number of people involved, but on whether or not that person should have been able to foresee the consequences. In other words, blame is not something that can be divided among multiple people, like a pie, with the portions getting smaller depending on the number of people involved. If three people working together make a bad decision, then each of the three people deserve 100% of the blame for the results of that decision.

3. The user of a computing artifact is morally responsible for the consequences of that use.

4. People must always make a reasonable effort to foresee the societal effects of a technology they design or use.

5. People who design computing artifacts must provide enough information about them so that others can foresee the consequences of using them.

Of course, once you create a set of rules, people will immediately begin to think up exceptions. Thus, the committee included the following caveat:

> No matter how sophisticated computing artifacts become, the rules still apply. For example, if an artifact uses a neural net, and the designers subsequently are surprised by the artifact's effects, the rules hold. If a computing artifact is self-modifying, and eventually becomes quite different from the original artifact, the rules still hold.... If a person

launches a computing artifact A in order to launch a second artifact B that is designed to launch a third artifact C, then the rules apply to all three artifacts. (That is, if you are not willing to accept moral responsibility for A, B, and C, then you should not launch A.)

The Five Rules imply that if you cannot accurately predict what a system will do, then you should not allow it to be used. They are generally applicable, and might just as well have been included in the discussion on safety in Chapter 5. We include them here because they directly address the problem of autonomous systems.

### Reflection Questions

1. POSITION Rules 1 and 3, taken together, mean that the user of an artifact cannot shift the blame to the creator, and the creator cannot shift the blame to the user. In your view, is it accurate to claim that both the creator and the user are to blame for the negative consequences of using computing artifacts? Explain your reasoning.

2. APPLICATION Recall that in Chapter 6 we presented Marshall McLuhan's claim that it is the technology itself, not the use to which it is put, that remakes society. If McLuhan rejected Rule 3 on these grounds, would you support or oppose him? Explain your reasoning.

3. POSITION Write an argument either critiquing or defending Rule 2.

4. APPLICATION In Reflection Question 1 for Case 9.2, we asked you to consider a car accident and apportion blame among the three key moral entities involved (Ms. Rosenberg, Google, and the driver). When you answered that question, did you make sure that your "percentages of blame" added up to 100%? Based on Rule 2, revise your answer. Whether or not you change your answer to the earlier question, explain your reasoning.

5. APPLICATION The Five Rules are connected to the privacy concerns raised in Chapter 3. In particular, which of Solove's privacy concerns, presented in Figure 3.1, are likely to be caused by a failure to follow Rule 4? Which are likely to be caused by a failure to follow Rule 5?

## 9.7 DIVERSE AND MULTICULTURAL PERSPECTIVES

As we have seen throughout this book, different cultures react to new technologies in different ways. In this section we address two examples of diversity affecting the acceptance of a technology. In the first example, we consider the different ways that American and Japanese culture accept or do not accept autonomous robots. The second example examines the impact of pervasive touch-screen technology on people with vision impairments.

### 9.7.1   I, Roommate

The title of this section is an allusion to Isaac Asimov's famous collection of science fiction short stories about robots, *I, Robot*. Published in 1950, the book was the basis for a successful movie starring Will Smith. Many of the stories in *I, Robot* focus on the interaction between humans and the robots that live and work among them.

Robots have long been used in industry to automate tasks, but we are only now starting to see robots appearing in the home. The most popular home robot is the Roomba vacuum cleaner made by the iRobot Corporation. The use of autonomous robots like Roomba to perform simple household tasks is not controversial. In Japan, however, people are considering using robots for tasks that, some might argue, should only be performed by humans. For example, some Japanese corporations have proposed using robots as companions and caregivers for the elderly. Robots, they argue, can help Japan manage its great challenges in caring for the country's expanding population of elderly citizens.

In a 2003 article, *Wired* magazine reported that, by 2015, 26% of Japan's population would be over 65. According to the Machine Industry Memorial Foundation, using robots to care for the elderly could save Japan $21 billion per year. It is hoped that the robots will be able carry or guide mobility-impaired people from place to place, clean up messes, remind patients to take medication, alert authorities in case of an injury, and so on. According to *Wired*, Toyota believes that "partner robots" will be one of their core businesses by 2020. Similarly, National Geographic reports that the government of South Korea intends to have a robot in every home by 2020.

Daniel Bartz titled his piece in *Wired*, "Toyota Sees Robotic Nurses in Your Lonely Final Years." His use of one particular word, lonely, is revealing. It is well understood that the elderly, both in the United States and in Japan, sometimes suffer from extreme loneliness. Elder-care institutions often use visits by young people and dogs as part of the therapeutic strategy to address this loneliness. While it seems clear that robots can help senior citizens with tasks (remembering to take pills, notifying emergency services if the person is injured), can they also help reduce loneliness and isolation?

The answer might be yes. A growing body of research indicates, somewhat counter-intuitively, that robot companions do indeed decrease loneliness. In a recent study, researchers found that AIBO (short for Artificial Intelligence roBOt) robot dogs (made by Sony) were very similar to real dogs in their ability to stimulate conversation and attention in long-term care residents with dementia. In a 2007 study, researchers at the St. Louis University School of Medicine (Banks et al.) measured the effects of an AIBO on loneliness. They found that the AIBO dogs do decrease loneliness and that there was no significant difference between real dogs and robot dogs in decreasing loneliness. They also found that nursing home residents formed emotional attachments to the AIBO robots, just as they did with real dogs. As a therapy for reducing loneliness and stimulating interaction, AIBO dogs seem to work just as well as real dogs. The robots have several up sides compared to real dogs; they do not need to eat, nor do they make messes or excessive noise. Researchers have recommended that nursing home patients who cannot have pets should be encouraged to adopt robot pets.

The media often portray a love of robots as a cultural phenomenon unique to Japan. Lisa Thomas, in a *Time* magazine article, suggests that Americans tend to see robots as threatening or evil, and often blame robots for taking away manufacturing jobs. In contrast, she claims that Japanese people tend to see robots as benevolent. She quotes University of Michigan anthropology professor Jennifer Robertson: "Robots have a long and friendly history in Japan, and humanoid robots are considered to be living things and even desirable members of families." According to Thomas, anthropologists speculate that this acceptance of inanimate friends into the home may be based in the Shinto religion, which holds that all things, even inanimate objects, have a spirit (in Japanese, kami). Other anthropologists quoted in the article see robots as the natural synthesis of two other major Japanese passions: Animated cartoons and technology. Whatever the cause, it is sometimes implied that robots may solve serious social and economic problems in places like Japan or South Korea, but that they will never be accepted into the home in the United States.

On the other hand, the success of Roomba, and of virtual pets like Tamagotchi and the Sony EyePet, cast some doubt on this position. Tamagotchi is a little egg-shaped device with an LCD screen and a small number of buttons, first introduced by the Bandai corporation in the mid-1990s. When first activated, a picture of an egg appears on the Tamagotchi's display. The user's job is to raise the egg to adulthood. The user interacts with the Tamagotchi by pressing buttons. The user must press a button to feed the Tamagotchi and a different button to clean up after it; users can press buttons to reward or punish the Tamagotchi for certain behaviors. All of this is on a schedule determined by the Tamagotchi, just like with a real pet. Failure to attend to these duties results in the "death" of the Tamagotchi.

The Sony EyePet (for the Playstation video game system) and Nintendogs (for the Nintendo DS hand-held game system) are modern iterations of the same concept. In these more modern versions, the virtual pet can be taught tricks and can interact with the user in very realistic ways. In the case of the Sony EyePet, the virtual pet can actually see the user, using a camera plugged into the Playstation game console. It can understand hand gestures and spoken commands, and it can recognize common household objects, like toys, and react to them appropriately. The popularity of virtual pets and of the Roomba in the United States may signal a shift in American perceptions of robots from negative to more positive.

## Reflection Questions

1.  APPLICATION One thing that makes many people uncomfortable with companion robots is that they are not capable of "loving you back"—that is, of feeling attachment or affection for a human. Is it ethical to encourage senior citizens to form emotional bonds with robots, simply because it makes them feel happier? Explain your reasoning. You may wish to use either a Kantian or a Utilitarian analysis in your answer.

2.   POSITION  In *I, Robot*, Isaac Asimov proposed three rules that would provide the basic moral guidelines for a robot. These rules, which are commonly called the "three laws of robotics," state that:

   a.   A robot may not injure a human being or, through inaction, allow a human being to come to harm.

   b.   A robot must obey orders given it by human beings except where such orders would conflict with the First Law.

   c.   A robot must protect its own existence as long as such protection does not conflict with the First or Second Law.

   Should rules a and c apply to humans as well? Explain the implications of accepting rules a and c as moral imperatives, and explain why they should (or should not) be applied to humans.

3.   POSITION  In general, do you think most people your age have a positive or negative view of robots? In particular, do you think that having a robotic pet or companion could be considered normal during your lifetime? Explain your position, and give evidence where possible.

## 9.7.2   Touch Screens and Visual Disabilities

As new technologies become pervasive, the old way of doing things often dies out. For example, many colleges no longer accept paper applications or letters of recommendation, and instead ask applicants and their recommendation-writers to fill out online forms. For anyone who does not have access to the Internet (according to the Census Bureau, 30% of American households), this can make applying to college a serious challenge.

The sudden growth in market-share of touch-screen devices, led by the iPhone, iPod Touch, and iPad, has had a similar negative effect on the blind. With older types of user interfaces, which had physical buttons, it was easy for vision-impaired users to learn the positions of buttons and to navigate by feel.

The lack of tactile feedback is a problem with modern touch-screen interfaces, but not the only problem. On modern devices, each time you press a button, the screen layout can change. This means that the user cannot even memorize the screen layout. Figure 9.2 shows how a screen can change when a user is trying to check her voicemail. The user starts by using the dialpad, in the left-hand image, to dial her voicemail number. After the call connects, the dialpad on the screen is replaced with buttons designed to be useful when a person is having a voice conversation (right image). In order to enter her voicemail password, the user has to locate and press the Dialpad button in the lower-right corner of the display.

Despite the problems with touch-screen interfaces, ultra-portable computing devices (like the iPhone and Android phones) can be very useful tools for vision-impaired people. Google has hired a famous blind researcher, T.V. Raman, to develop technologies to make it possible to use an Android even if you can't see the screen (or perhaps aren't free to look at it). In other words, Google wants to make the Android "eyes-free."

| The user starts by using the dialpad to dial her voicemail number. | After the call connects, the dialpad on the screen is replaced with buttons designed to be useful when a person is having a voice conversation. |
|---|---|

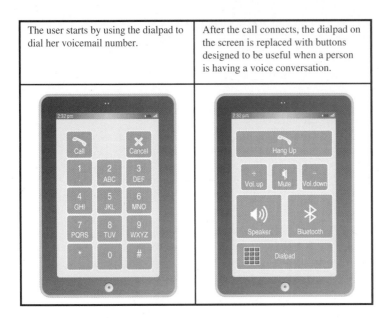

**FIGURE 9.2** Calling voicemail on a touch-screen phone

Many of the techniques used by Raman's team boil down to two key ideas:

- Provide tactile and auditory feedback
- Use relative position, not absolute position, for controls

The second idea, using relative position, is particularly interesting. In his series of YouTube videos (collected in the YouTube channel EyesFreeAndroid), Raman describes the difference between absolute and relative position. In a normal dialpad interface, which is designed using absolute position, the buttons are located at a particular place on the screen. You have to tap that exact spot in order to dial the number. With relative position, you tap, and then drag your finger. The number dialed is based on the direction of the motion, not on the place you tapped. So, if you make an upward motion, the phone dials a 2. If you make a down-and-left motion, it dials a 7. This means the user no longer needs to rely on sight to determine where to tap the screen. You can tap anywhere, and then indicate which number to dial by making a movement relative to that starting position.

Advocates for people with disabilities argue that companies should invest more money in making simple and accessible interfaces. They point out that many technologies originally designed for accessibility are, or should be, widely used by others. For example:

- Eyes-free dialing is most likely safer than traditional dialing, so widespread adoption could reduce phone-related accidents.
- Large-text font options on electronic book readers, in part intended for the elderly, make it easier to read while running on a treadmill.

- Haptic/tactile feedback has been incorporated in many phones that have touch screens, to make it easier to tell when a button has been pressed successfully. (Recall from Chapter 8 that "haptic" means touch-based.)

- National Public Radio (NPR), with the help of Harris Corporation and Towson University, has begun to stream text captions of their most popular shows simultaneously with the audio. This enables captioned radio (for the hearing-impaired) and braille radio (for those with both hearing and vision impairments). As a side benefit, however, these transcripts will make it very easy to search NPR shows, and to incorporate NPR stories into live data feeds on the Internet.

### Reflection Questions

1. POSITION In Chapter 2 we discussed the *ACM/IEEE Software Engineering Code of Ethics and Professional Practice*, which describes how software engineers ought to behave. In your view, should software and hardware developers be required, by the Code of Professional Ethics, to take vision impairments into account when designing new technologies?

2. POSITION Was it morally praiseworthy for Google to hire T.V. Raman to work on accessibility features for their products? Explain why or why not.

## 9.8   INTER-DISCIPLINARY TOPICS

Many disciplines are being revolutionized by pervasive and autonomous technologies. This in turn leads to new ethical and social challenges. In this section we examine the role that autonomous systems are playing in financial markets and the future of marketing platforms that make use of pervasive computing technology.

### 9.8.1   Case: The Flash Crash

One of the most potent uses of autonomous machines is in the trading of stocks and commodities. **Algorithmic trading** is the practice of allowing a computer program to make decisions about what shares to buy and sell. Trading algorithms often uses complicated statistical models along with machine learning to find investments that will soon rise in price. Such systems can make a profit when a human trader would not be able to, because an algorithm can use statistical models and decision processes that are too complex for a human to fully comprehend.

The other reason such systems are more efficient than human traders is their speed, which makes high-frequency trading possible. **High-frequency trading** is the practice of using computers to trade investments back and forth much more quickly than humans can. Some systems can react to news in the market in as little as 30 milliseconds. By comparison, it takes 72 milliseconds for a message to travel from New York to London via the Internet. This means that high-frequency trading computers based in New York City can potentially squeeze all of the profit out of a change in the market before computers at the London stock exchange even know about the change.

With increased speed comes increased danger. Think about the difference between driving around a racetrack at 60 miles per hour and at 229 miles per hour (the fastest lap speed at the Indianapolis 500). Small mistakes that one might not even notice at 60 mph can result in a deadly crash at race speeds. Many people are concerned about a similar increased risk of market crashes caused by high-frequency trading.

Around 2:30 p.m. on May 6, 2010, the Dow Jones Industrial Average (a financial index that is used to summarize the performance of the U.S. stock market) dropped 900 points (9%) in the span of about 15 minutes. It then recovered almost as quickly, returning nearly to its original price by 3 p.m. Because of the speed at which it occurred, this event came to be known as the **flash crash**.

As reported by Graham Bowley of the *New York Times*, the crash was caused by the interaction of several automated trading systems. First, a large mutual fund told a computer program to sell about $4.1 billion worth of assets. Normally such a large sale would be executed over 5 hours, but the program doing the selling ended up selling all the assets in less than 20 minutes, causing prices to drop rapidly. High-frequency trading intensified the problem. Computers running high-frequency trading software bought the assets the mutual fund was selling. They (the algorithms) quickly realized that something was going wrong in the market, and tried to sell back the items they had just purchased, causing prices to drop even further. Finally, the algorithms pulled out of the market altogether.

This was a big problem, because the algorithms control nearly 70% of the actual cash in the market. It is very hard to trade stocks when the algorithms are staying out of the market, because the parties swap stocks for cash. If the computers that control all the cash are staying away, even those that want to do trades cannot, because there is no cash available. As a result, during the flash crash, many stocks offered for sale were not purchased because the high-frequency trading algorithms hoarded cash instead of making purchases. The sellers assumed (incorrectly) that the reason the stocks were not selling was because their asking prices were too high, and they automatically started to slash prices, causing the stock market to drop. One investor lost $17,000, or one third of his portfolio, because he had the bad luck of selling shares at 2:46 p.m. (LaCapra 2010). Had his stock sale gone through 10 minutes earlier or later, he would not have been affected.

It appears that no one person or system was to blame for the flash crash. Each link in the chain involved software that was either malfunctioning, used incorrectly, or based on incorrect assumptions. These malfunctions include the following:

- The software the mutual fund used to sell its assets sold them too quickly, perhaps due to user error.
- The high-frequency trading software used by many different companies bought these assets too aggressively, because they were not designed to react correctly to such mistakes by large firms.

- The programs used by normal brokerages (ones not using high-frequency trading) to set buy and sell prices for stocks were not designed to handle cases in which there are buyers and sellers in the market, but no cash available to facilitate their transactions.

From an ethical standpoint, this case is troubling because, all else being equal, we want financial markets to be fair and efficient. The flash crash directly harmed many investors and also caused many people to doubt the fairness, safety, and efficiency of the stock market. Based on what you read in Chapters 2 and 5, you can probably guess that one way to reassure the public about safety issues is to make sure that the people trading stocks are properly trained and certified. And in fact, that has long been the case in the United States. Stock trading is a profession; people are allowed to trade on a stock exchange only after doing an apprenticeship, taking a government exam (among other things), and finally earning a professional license. However, algorithmic trading has created a loophole in these rules and regulations. Currently, neither the programmers who create trading programs, nor the programs themselves, are required to be licensed or examined.

### Reflection Questions

1. POSITION Should developers who create algorithmic trading programs be regulated by the government and be required to obtain some kind of license? Explain your reasoning.

2. POSITION Instead of requiring software developers to obtain licenses to develop stock trading software, would it make more sense to test and then license individual pieces of trading software? Explain your reasoning.

3. APPLICATION Most experts believe that high-frequency trading has significantly increased the efficiency of the stock market. This results in everyone, not just the high-frequency traders, being better off. Is the risk of periodic flash crashes worth the benefits of high-frequency trading? Which ethical theory (from Chapter 1) is best suited to analyzing this question, and why? Also, what additional information would you need to answer this question more fully?

### 9.8.2 Augmented Reality Marketing

**Augmented reality** is a computer graphics technology that draws virtual objects laid over the real world. In augmented reality, virtual objects appear to inhabit the real world, and the user cannot always easily tell which objects are real and which are virtual. For most people, the most familiar commercial use of augmented reality is the yellow "first down" line in telecasts of NFL football games. The yellow line marks a particular place on the field. As the camera moves, the line stays in place on the field, looking as if it is actually painted on the field in real life. In fact, the yellow line is drawn by computers and does not exist on the field.

Although augmented reality has been studied for more than twenty years, it is only recently that computers (in the form of smart phones) have gotten portable enough and powerful enough to put augmented reality into everyday use. So far, commercial uses of augmented reality are primarily limited to advertising. In this section, we introduce one potential application of augmented reality for advertising: skirting public decency laws.

Advertisers often try to push the limits of public propriety. The clothing brand Calvin Klein, in particular, is known for sexy billboards and TV ads that stir up controversy. In fact, Australia recently banned one of Calvin Klein's billboards because it appeared to portray violence against women.

In New York City, Calvin Klein has experimented with a new type of advertising using QR codes. A **QR code** is a sort of 2-dimensional bar code that can be read by camera phones and computers. Once you install a piece of software called a "QR code reader" on your phone, you can take a picture of a QR code, and the software will automatically decode it and take you to the Web page encoded by the code. The QR code shown in Figure 9.3 contains a link to the Twitter feed for this textbook, *http://twitter.com/eiacc.*

Calvin Klein bought several billboards around New York City, but did not place the racy advertisement on the billboard. Instead, the ad consisted of a gigantic QR code, with the words "Get it uncensored" above. When you view the billboard through a QR-code-reading application, it takes you to a Web site where you can view the actual advertisement. It would not be hard to create an augmented reality application for cell phones that would graft the racy ad into the billboard, so that it looks as if it is actually there, just as the yellow "first down" line looks like it is really part of the field. Right now there is not much incentive to do this, because most people do not walk around town looking at the world through a cell phone.

**F I G U R E   9.3** QR Code that contains a link to the *Ethics in a Computing Culture* Twitter feed, *http://twitter.com/eiacc*

In the future, however, all of the abilities that currently exist in smart phones (cameras, high resolution screens, network access, motion and direction sensors, GPS, and so on) will be built into eyeglasses and sunglasses. (Such systems already exist, but they are still too expensive for ordinary people to afford and are too heavy to be practical.) Once this happens, the nature of advertising in public places (such as on billboards) will change dramatically.

If such augmented reality glasses become pervasive, it will be possible to make billboards and advertisements in public places that target each person individually. Whenever you look at a billboard with these augmented reality glasses on, they will be able to replace the billboard's real world advertisement with a different, virtual ad. Advertisers will be able to use this technology to make sure that they do not waste money advertising products to people who are unlikely to buy them.

This is similar to a scene in *Minority Report*, a 2002 film starring Tom Cruise and based on a short story by Philip K. Dick. At one point, Cruise's character is walking through a mall. After surveillance cameras on the walls identify him, the advertisements in the mall begin to speak directly to him. They call him by name and advertise items that are likely to appeal to him. Such ads, which change based on the viewer, are already beginning to appear. For example, Amnesty International has bus kiosk ads that can tell if anyone is looking at them. The ad shows a scene of domestic violence, but as soon as someone looks towards the ad, it changes to a more harmonious scene, with the caption "It happens when nobody is watching."

So advertising that adapts to the viewer already exists. What is new about augmented reality is that the advertising you see will not only adapt to you, but it will also be private to you, and it may be very hard for you to tell when it is real, and when it is not. It is not clear how public advertising laws will apply to this situation. Currently, local governments make the rules about what is, and is not, acceptable for the content of a public advertisement, like a billboard or bus kiosk. Widespread adoption of augmented reality goggles could take this decision out of the hands of the government, and make the decision up to individuals. You might set the parental controls or content filters on your glasses to match your own personal preferences. Because these ads create a private viewing experience, instead of the public experience of a billboard, other people are less likely to be offended.

On the other hand, this also means that it will be harder for parents to monitor what children are seeing, because each person will have their own private view of the world that is not necessarily visible to others. While parental content controls will likely be available, this is not a complete substitute for parental supervision. Many children are able to eventually learn to work around parental controls. Also, parental control software is not perfect; sometimes it blocks good content and lets objectionable content through. Governments will have to decide how to respond to this. Should they extend advertising laws into the augmented world, to punish advertisers when parental controls fail?

## Reflection Questions

1.   POSITION  If augmented reality is widely adopted, the government could make regulations about what types of ads can be associated with public billboards (for example, banning ads for cigarettes or ads with obscene sexual content). Should the government regulate these ads? If so, how? Explain your reasoning.

2.   POSITION  Should the public posting of QR codes that lead the viewer to racy ads be banned? Explain your reasoning.

3.   CONTEXT  Shock images are incredibly graphic images posted on the Internet that are designed to shock or sicken ordinary people. Examples include pictures of real deaths and violence, obscene or illegal pornography, and the like. Should the public posting of QR codes leading to shock images be banned? Explain your reasoning.

## SUMMARY

- **Autonomous** technologies are technologies that make decisions with little or no human oversight.

- **Pervasive** technologies are technologies that are present everywhere throughout society.

- Autonomy is linked to **robotics** and **artificial intelligence**. Artificial intelligence is used to make a technology smarter, and more able to be autonomous. People are using autonomous robots to do work on the job and in the home. It is very important to understand the distinctions among autonomy, robotics, and artificial intelligence; otherwise your ethical analysis of these issues is likely to be flawed.

- In computer technology, autonomy and pervasiveness are interrelated. Autonomy reduces the cost of using a technology, which allows it to become more pervasive. At the same time, the fact that a technology is already pervasive creates incentives to make the technology more autonomous. We presented three examples of this: Automatic Number Plate Recognition, Google's PageRank algorithm, and e-rater.

- It can be confusing to assign moral or legal blame when an autonomous system causes a problem. The Five Rules say that both the creator and the user are fully responsible for whatever goes wrong, and that individual responsibility does not decrease as the number of people involved increases.

- Technologies become pervasive at different rates in different cultures. Japan and South Korea expect helper robots to become pervasive, due to the aging populations of those countries.

- The flash crash, a massive stock market crash that lasted only a few minutes, was caused by the interactions of several different pieces of automated stock trading software.

- Augmented reality is a technology that, if it becomes pervasive, will create many new ethical and social challenges.

## CHAPTER EXERCISES

1. REVIEW Define "pervasive" as it applies to a technology.
2. REVIEW Define the term "autonomy" as it pertains to people or computers making decisions.
3. REVIEW Explain how autonomy leads to pervasiveness, and how pervasiveness leads to autonomy, in technology.
4. REVIEW Define "lifelogging."
5. REVIEW Define "GPS" and briefly explain how it works.
6. REVIEW What is a "personal locator beacon," and why are they problematic?
7. REVIEW Restate the definition of "robot" given in this chapter. Do you agree with this definition? If not, provide your own.
8. REVIEW Restate the definition of "artificial intelligence" given in this chapter. Do you agree with this definition? If not, provide your own.
9. REVIEW What is "Automatic Number Plate Recognition?" Explain its uses and list the other technologies that must be pervasive before Automatic Number Plate Recognition can be useful.
10. REVIEW Explain what is meant by a robotic surveillance camera. Explain why such a camera is both more useful, and more ethically troubling, than a nonrobotic camera.
11. REVIEW Explain what a Web crawler or spider is, in the context of Web search engines.
12. REVIEW List and briefly explain the Five Rules for moral responsibility for computing artifacts. What does the word "artifact" mean in this context?
13. REVIEW List Asimov's three laws of robotics.
14. REVIEW Define "algorithmic trading" and explain why some people think it might be dangerous.
15. REVIEW Define "high-frequency trading" and explain why some people think it might be dangerous.
16. REVIEW What was the flash crash of May 6, 2010? Explain what happened and what caused it.

17. REVIEW Define "augmented reality" and give two or three examples of augmented reality technologies that are already used in everyday life.

18. RESEARCH Pick a technology that is now pervasive (such as e-mail, cell phones, GPS, or the Web). Interview someone who went to college at least twenty years ago in order to discover how your selected technology has affected college life. Write a brief summary of your findings.

19. RESEARCH During the first half of 2011, a wave of popular uprisings swept the Middle East, toppling several autocratic rulers. Some commentators believe that the pervasiveness of social networks like Facebook and Twitter was crucial to the success of these revolutions. Others, most notably author Malcolm Gladwell, believe that Facebook and Twitter were not important at all. Research first-hand accounts and news reporting from this time period, and answer this question: How crucial were Facebook and Twitter in the Middle Eastern revolutions of 2011? Be sure to explain your reasoning, and support it with evidence.

20. APPLICATION In Case 9.8.1, which discussed the flash crash, we identified three types of software programs that, because of the way they interacted, made the crash possible. According to the Five Rules from Section 9.6.3, who should receive the most blame for the crash? Explain your reasoning.

21. POSITION Do you agree with the conclusion you reached in the previous question? Explain your reasoning. If you disagree, explain which part of the rules you disagree with and why.

## WORKS CITED

Ad Hoc Committee for Responsible Computing. Moral Responsibility for Computing Artifacts: Five Rules, Version 27. 30 Oct. 2010. Web. 6 Oct. 2011. <https://edocs.uis.edu/kmill2/www/TheRules/>.

Banks, Marian R., Lisa M. Willoughby, and William A. Banks. "Animal-Assisted Therapy and Loneliness in Nursing Homes: Use of Robotic versus Living Dogs." *Journal of the American Medical Directors Association* 9.3 (2008): 173-177. Print.

Bartz, Daniel. "Toyota Sees Robotic Nurses in Your Lonely Final Years." *Wired.com*, 19 Jan. 2010. Web. 14 Feb. 2011.

Batista, Elisa. "Wakamaru Bot at Your Service." *Wired.com*, 24 Apr. 2003. Web. 14 Feb. 2011.

Block, Melissa. "With New GPS Devices, Hikers Taking More Risks." *All Things Considered*, 26 Oct. 2009. Web. 7 Jan. 2011.

Bowley, Graham. "Lone Sale of $4.1 Billion in Contracts Led to 'Flash Crash' in May." *The New York Times*, 1 Oct. 2010. Web. 18 Feb. 2011.

Chopra, Samir. "Rights for autonomous artificial agents?" *Communications of the ACM* Aug. 2010: 38-40. Print.

Fagin, Steve. "Lessons of the Mount Hood Tragedy: Who Pays for Search and Rescue?" *TheDay.com*, 19 Dec. 2009. Web. 16 Oct. 2011.

Internation Telecommunications Union. "Key Global Telecom Indicators for the World Telecommunication Service Sector." *www.itu.int*, 21 Oct. 2010. Web. 16 Oct. 2011.

Jacobsson, Sarah. "Woman Sues Google for Bad Directions." *Today @ PC World Blog*, 31 May 2010. Web. 5 Jan. 2011.

Jinkins, Shirley. "Computer grading of student essays is tested at Colleyville Heritage High." *Star-Telegram.com*, 2 July 2011. Web. 14 Oct. 2011.

LaCapra, Lauren. "How P&G Plunge Derailed One Investor." *TheStreet.com*, 17 May 2010. Web. 18 Feb. 2011.

Lovgren, Stefan. "Robot Code of Ethics to Prevent Android Abuse, Protect Humans." *National Geographic*, 16 Mar. 2007. Web. 14 Feb. 2011.

Raman, T.V. "Stroke Dialer For Eyes-Free Keypad Input." *YouTube.com*, 31 Mar. 2009. Web. 6 Oct. 2011.

Thomas, Lisa. "What's Behind Japan's Love Affair with Robots?" *Time.com*, 3 Aug. 2009. Web. 14 Feb. 2011.

## RELATED READINGS

### Novels

Orwell, George. *Nineteen Eighty-Four*. New York: Plume, 2003. Print. (Orwell's famous novel is a hugely influential tale of the perils of pervasive surveillance technology. The concept of two-way telescreens might seem to be a more natural fit for Chapter 3, which focused on privacy, but the pervasiveness of telescreens is key to understanding their power. You might also want to think about this book in relation to panopticism, as discussed in Chapter 3.)

### Short Fiction

Asimov, Isaac. "Runaround." *I, Robot*. New York: Gnome Press, 1950. Print. (Asimov's "three laws of robotics" are one of the earliest and most influential attempts to define a type of moral code for autonomous machines. For example, Motorola recently purchased Three Laws Mobility (3LM), a company that makes mobile-phone security software. Their design philosophy is based on a version of Asimov's three laws.)

### Nonfiction Books

Wallach, Wendell, and Colin Allen. *Moral Machines: Teaching Robots Right from Wrong*. New York: Oxford University Press, 2010. Print. (Yale ethicist Wendell Wallach and Indiana University cognitive scientist Colin Allen explore the possibility of engineering morality and creating moral autonomous agents.)

### Essays and Articles

Bowley, Graham. "Lone Sale of $4.1 Billion in Contracts Led to 'Flash Crash' in May." *The New York Times*, 1 Oct. 2010. (Bowley's summary of the joint CFTC/SEC report on the flash crash makes an excellent case; it starts about halfway down the article. For a more in-depth history of the events of the flash crash, see the original report, which is called "Finding Regarding the Market Events of May 6, 2010" and can be found at *www.sec.gov*.)

## Film and TV

Bicks, Michael. "Smartest Machine on Earth." Nova, 9 Feb. 2011. (A computer named Watson plays the popular game show Jeopardy! against the game's greatest human champions, Ken Jennings and Brad Rutter. This episode of Nova explores the development of Watson's technology, which allows him to understand riddles, puns, colloquialisms, and natural-language questions much better than computers of the past.)

# Appendix A

# ACM Code of Ethics and Professional Conduct

*Adopted by ACM Council 10/16/92.*

## PREAMBLE

Commitment to ethical professional conduct is expected of every member (voting members, associate members, and student members) of the Association for Computing Machinery (ACM).

This Code, consisting of 24 imperatives formulated as statements of personal responsibility, identifies the elements of such a commitment. It contains many, but not all, issues professionals are likely to face. Section 1 outlines fundamental ethical considerations, while Section 2 addresses additional, more specific considerations of professional conduct. Statements in Section 3 pertain more specifically to individuals who have a leadership role, whether in the workplace or in a volunteer capacity such as with organizations like ACM. Principles involving compliance with this Code are given in Section 4.

The Code shall be supplemented by a set of Guidelines, which provide explanation to assist members in dealing with the various issues contained in the Code. It is expected that the Guidelines will be changed more frequently than the Code.

The Code and its supplemented Guidelines are intended to serve as a basis for ethical decision making in the conduct of professional work. Secondarily, they may serve as a basis for judging the merit of a formal complaint pertaining to violation of professional ethical standards.

It should be noted that although computing is not mentioned in the imperatives of Section 1, the Code is concerned with how these fundamental imperatives apply to one's conduct as a computing professional. These imperatives are expressed in a general form to emphasize that ethical principles which apply to computer ethics are derived from more general ethical principles.

It is understood that some words and phrases in a code of ethics are subject to varying interpretations, and that any ethical principle may conflict with other ethical principles in specific situations. Questions related to ethical conflicts can best be answered by thoughtful consideration of fundamental principles, rather than reliance on detailed regulations.

## CONTENTS & GUIDELINES

1.   **General Moral Imperatives.**
2.   **More Specific Professional Responsibilities**.
3.   **Organizational Leadership Imperatives**.
4.   **Compliance with the Code**.
5.   **Acknowledgments.**

## 1. GENERAL MORAL IMPERATIVES.

*As an ACM member I will....*

### 1.1 Contribute to society and human well-being.

This principle concerning the quality of life of all people affirms an obligation to protect fundamental human rights and to respect the diversity of all cultures. An essential aim of computing professionals is to minimize negative consequences of computing systems, including threats to health and safety. When designing or implementing systems, computing professionals must attempt to ensure that the products of their efforts will be used in socially responsible ways, will meet social needs, and will avoid harmful effects to health and welfare.

In addition to a safe social environment, human well-being includes a safe natural environment. Therefore, computing professionals who design and develop systems must be alert to, and make others aware of, any potential damage to the local or global environment.

### 1.2 Avoid harm to others.

"Harm" means injury or negative consequences, such as undesirable loss of information, loss of property, property damage, or unwanted environmental impacts. This principle prohibits use of computing technology in ways that result in harm to any of the following: users, the general public, employees, employers. Harmful actions include intentional destruction or modification of files and programs leading to serious loss of resources or unnecessary expenditure of human resources such as the time and effort required to purge systems of "computer viruses."

Well-intended actions, including those that accomplish assigned duties, may lead to harm unexpectedly. In such an event the responsible person or persons are obligated to undo or mitigate the negative consequences as much as possible. One way to avoid unintentional harm is to carefully consider potential impacts on all those affected by decisions made during design and implementation.

To minimize the possibility of indirectly harming others, computing professionals must minimize malfunctions by following generally accepted standards for system design and testing. Furthermore, it is often necessary to assess the social consequences of systems to project the likelihood of any serious harm to others. If system features are misrepresented to users, coworkers, or supervisors, the individual computing professional is responsible for any resulting injury.

In the work environment the computing professional has the additional obligation to report any signs of system dangers that might result in serious personal or social damage. If one's superiors do not act to curtail or mitigate such dangers, it may be necessary to "blow the whistle" to help correct the problem or reduce the risk. However, capricious or misguided reporting of violations can, itself, be harmful. Before reporting violations, all relevant aspects of the incident must be thoroughly assessed. In particular, the assessment of risk and responsibility must be credible. It is suggested that advice be sought from other computing professionals. See principle 2.5 regarding thorough evaluations.

## 1.3 Be honest and trustworthy.

Honesty is an essential component of trust. Without trust an organization cannot function effectively. The honest computing professional will not make deliberately false or deceptive claims about a system or system design, but will instead provide full disclosure of all pertinent system limitations and problems.

A computer professional has a duty to be honest about his or her own qualifications, and about any circumstances that might lead to conflicts of interest.

Membership in volunteer organizations such as ACM may at times place individuals in situations where their statements or actions could be interpreted as carrying the "weight" of a larger group of professionals. An ACM member will exercise care to not misrepresent ACM or positions and policies of ACM or any ACM units.

## 1.4 Be fair and take action not to discriminate.

The values of equality, tolerance, respect for others, and the principles of equal justice govern this imperative. Discrimination on the basis of race, sex, religion, age, disability, national origin, or other such factors is an explicit violation of ACM policy and will not be tolerated.

Inequities between different groups of people may result from the use or misuse of information and technology. In a fair society, all individuals would have equal opportunity to participate in, or benefit from, the use of computer resources regardless of race, sex, religion, age, disability, national origin or other such similar factors. However, these ideals do not justify unauthorized use of computer resources nor do they provide an adequate basis for violation of any other ethical imperatives of this code.

## 1.5 Honor property rights including copyrights and patent.

Violation of copyrights, patents, trade secrets and the terms of license agreements is prohibited by law in most circumstances. Even when software is not so protected, such violations are contrary to professional behavior. Copies of software should be made only with proper authorization. Unauthorized duplication of materials must not be condoned.

## 1.6 Give proper credit for intellectual property.

Computing professionals are obligated to protect the integrity of intellectual property. Specifically, one must not take credit for other's ideas or work, even in cases where the work has not been explicitly protected by copyright, patent, etc.

## 1.7 Respect the privacy of others.

Computing and communication technology enables the collection and exchange of personal information on a scale unprecedented in the history of civilization. Thus there is increased potential for violating the privacy of individuals and groups. It is the responsibility of professionals to maintain the privacy and integrity of data describing individuals. This includes taking precautions to ensure the accuracy of data, as well as protecting it from unauthorized access or accidental disclosure to inappropriate individuals. Furthermore, procedures must be established to allow individuals to review their records and correct inaccuracies.

This imperative implies that only the necessary amount of personal information be collected in a system, that retention and disposal periods for that information be clearly defined and enforced, and that personal information gathered for a specific purpose not be used for other purposes without consent of the individual(s). These principles apply to electronic communications, including electronic mail, and prohibit procedures that capture or monitor electronic user data, including messages, without the permission of users or bona fide authorization related to system operation and maintenance. User data observed during the normal duties of system operation and maintenance must be treated with strictest confidentiality, except in cases where it is evidence for the violation of law, organizational regulations, or this Code. In these cases, the nature or contents of that information must be disclosed only to proper authorities.

## 1.8 Honor confidentiality.

The principle of honesty extends to issues of confidentiality of information whenever one has made an explicit promise to honor confidentiality or, implicitly, when private information not directly related to the performance of one's duties becomes available. The ethical concern is to respect all obligations of confidentiality to employers, clients, and users unless discharged from such obligations by requirements of the law or other principles of this Code.

# 2. MORE SPECIFIC PROFESSIONAL RESPONSIBILITIES.

*As an ACM computing professional I will....*

## 2.1 Strive to achieve the highest quality, effectiveness and dignity in both the process and products of professional work.

Excellence is perhaps the most important obligation of a professional. The computing professional must strive to achieve quality and to be cognizant of the serious negative consequences that may result from poor quality in a system.

## 2.2 Acquire and maintain professional competence.

Excellence depends on individuals who take responsibility for acquiring and maintaining professional competence. A professional must participate in setting standards for appropriate levels of competence, and strive to achieve those standards. Upgrading technical knowledge and competence can be achieved in several ways: doing independent study; attending seminars, conferences, or courses; and being involved in professional organizations.

## 2.3 Know and respect existing laws pertaining to professional work.

ACM members must obey existing local, state, province, national, and international laws unless there is a compelling ethical basis not to do so. Policies and procedures of the organizations in which one participates must also be obeyed. But compliance must be balanced with the recognition that sometimes existing laws and rules may be immoral or inappropriate and, therefore, must be challenged. Violation of a law or regulation may be ethical when that law or rule has inadequate moral basis or when it conflicts with another law judged to be more important. If one decides to violate a law or rule because it is viewed as unethical, or for any other reason, one must fully accept responsibility for one's actions and for the consequences.

## 2.4 Accept and provide appropriate professional review.

Quality professional work, especially in the computing profession, depends on professional reviewing and critiquing. Whenever appropriate, individual members should seek and utilize peer review as well as provide critical review of the work of others.

## 2.5 Give comprehensive and thorough evaluations of computer systems and their impacts, including analysis of possible risks.

Computer professionals must strive to be perceptive, thorough, and objective when evaluating, recommending, and presenting system descriptions and alternatives. Computer professionals are in a position of special trust, and therefore have a special responsibility to provide objective, credible evaluations to employers, clients, users, and the public. When providing evaluations the professional must also identify any relevant conflicts of interest, as stated in imperative 1.3.

As noted in the discussion of principle 1.2 on avoiding harm, any signs of danger from systems must be reported to those who have opportunity and/or responsibility to resolve them. See the guidelines for imperative 1.2 for more details concerning harm, including the reporting of professional violations.

## 2.6 Honor contracts, agreements, and assigned responsibilities.

Honoring one's commitments is a matter of integrity and honesty. For the computer professional this includes ensuring that system elements perform as intended. Also, when one contracts for work with another party, one has an obligation to keep that party properly informed about progress toward completing that work.

A computing professional has a responsibility to request a change in any assignment that he or she feels cannot be completed as defined. Only after serious consideration and with full disclosure of risks and concerns to the employer or client, should one accept the assignment. The major underlying principle here is the obligation to accept personal accountability for professional work. On some occasions other ethical principles may take greater priority.

A judgment that a specific assignment should not be performed may not be accepted. Having clearly identified one's concerns and reasons for that judgment, but failing to procure a change in that assignment, one may yet be obligated, by contract or by law, to proceed as directed. The computing professional's ethical judgment should be the final guide in deciding whether or not to proceed. Regardless of the decision, one must accept the responsibility for the consequences.

However, performing assignments "against one's own judgment" does not relieve the professional of responsibility for any negative consequences.

## 2.7 Improve public understanding of computing and its consequences.

Computing professionals have a responsibility to share technical knowledge with the public by encouraging understanding of computing, including the impacts of computer systems and their limitations. This imperative implies an obligation to counter any false views related to computing.

## 2.8 Access computing and communication resources only when authorized to do so.

Theft or destruction of tangible and electronic property is prohibited by imperative 1.2 - "Avoid harm to others." Trespassing and unauthorized use of a computer or communication system is addressed by this imperative. Trespassing includes accessing communication networks and computer systems, or accounts and/or files associated with those systems, without explicit authorization to do so. Individuals and organizations have the right to restrict access to their systems so long as they do not violate the discrimination principle (see 1.4). No one should enter or use another's computer system, software, or data files without permission. One must always have appropriate approval before using system resources, including communication ports, file space, other system peripherals, and computer time.

# 3. ORGANIZATIONAL LEADERSHIP IMPERATIVES.

*As an ACM member and an organizational leader, I will....*

**BACKGROUND NOTE**: This section draws extensively from the draft IFIP Code of Ethics, especially its sections on organizational ethics and international concerns. The ethical obligations of organizations tend to be neglected in most codes of professional conduct, perhaps because these codes are written from the perspective of the individual member. This dilemma is addressed by stating these imperatives from the perspective of the organizational leader. In this context "leader" is viewed as any organizational member who has leadership or educational responsibilities. These imperatives generally may apply to organizations as well as their leaders. In this context "organizations" are corporations, government agencies, and other "employers," as well as volunteer professional organizations.

## 3.1 Articulate social responsibilities of members of an organizational unit and encourage full acceptance of those responsibilities.

Because organizations of all kinds have impacts on the public, they must accept responsibilities to society. Organizational procedures and attitudes oriented toward quality and the welfare of society will reduce harm to members of the public, thereby serving public interest and fulfilling social responsibility. Therefore, organizational leaders must encourage full participation in meeting social responsibilities as well as quality performance.

## 3.2 Manage personnel and resources to design and build information systems that enhance the quality of working life.

Organizational leaders are responsible for ensuring that computer systems enhance, not degrade, the quality of working life. When implementing a computer system, organizations must consider the personal and professional development, physical safety, and human dignity of all workers. Appropriate human-computer ergonomic standards should be considered in system design and in the workplace.

## 3.3 Acknowledge and support proper and authorized uses of an organization's computing and communication resources.

Because computer systems can become tools to harm as well as to benefit an organization, the leadership has the responsibility to clearly define appropriate and inappropriate uses of organizational computing resources. While the number and scope of such rules should be minimal, they should be fully enforced when established.

## 3.4 Ensure that users and those who will be affected by a system have their needs clearly articulated during the assessment and design of requirements; later the system must be validated to meet requirements.

Current system users, potential users and other persons whose lives may be affected by a system must have their needs assessed and incorporated in the statement of requirements. System validation should ensure compliance with those requirements.

## 3.5 Articulate and support policies that protect the dignity of users and others affected by a computing system.

Designing or implementing systems that deliberately or inadvertently demean individuals or groups is ethically unacceptable. Computer professionals who are in decision making positions should verify that systems are designed and implemented to protect personal privacy and enhance personal dignity.

## 3.6 Create opportunities for members of the organization to learn the principles and limitations of computer systems.

This complements the imperative on public understanding (2.7). Educational opportunities are essential to facilitate optimal participation of all organizational members. Opportunities must be available to all members to help them improve their knowledge and skills in computing, including courses that familiarize them with the consequences and limitations of particular types of systems. In particular, professionals must be made aware of the dangers of building systems around oversimplified models, the improbability of anticipating and designing for every possible operating condition, and other issues related to the complexity of this profession.

# 4. COMPLIANCE WITH THE CODE.

*As an ACM member I will....*

## 4.1 Uphold and promote the principles of this Code.

The future of the computing profession depends on both technical and ethical excellence. Not only is it important for ACM computing professionals to adhere to the principles expressed in this Code, each member should encourage and support adherence by other members.

## 4.2 Treat violations of this code as inconsistent with membership in the ACM.

Adherence of professionals to a code of ethics is largely a voluntary matter. However, if a member does not follow this code by engaging in gross misconduct, membership in ACM may be terminated.

This Code and the supplemental Guidelines were developed by the Task Force for the Revision of the ACM Code of Ethics and Professional Conduct: Ronald E. Anderson, Chair, Gerald Engel, Donald Gotterbarn, Grace C. Hertlein, Alex Hoffman, Bruce Jawer, Deborah G. Johnson, Doris K. Lidtke, Joyce Currie Little, Dianne Martin, Donn B. Parker, Judith A. Perrolle, and Richard S. Rosenberg. The Task Force was organized by ACM/SIGCAS and funding was provided by the ACM SIG Discretionary Fund. This Code and the supplemental Guidelines were adopted by the ACM Council on October 16, 1992.

This Code may be published without permission as long as it is not changed in any way and it carries the copyright notice. Copyright (c) 1992 by the Association for Computing Machinery, Inc.

# Appendix B

# ACM/IEEE Software Engineering Code of Ethics and Professional Practice

Software Engineering Code of Ethics and Professional Practice (Version 5.2) as recommended by the ACM/IEEE-CS Joint Task Force on Software Engineering Ethics and Professional Practices and jointly approved by the ACM and the IEEE-CS as the standard for teaching and practicing software engineering.

## Software Engineering Code of Ethics and Professional Practice (Short Version)

### PREAMBLE

The short version of the code summarizes aspirations at a high level of the abstraction; the clauses that are included in the full version give examples and details of how these aspirations change the way we act as software engineering professionals. Without the aspirations, the details can become legalistic and tedious; without the details, the aspirations can become high sounding but empty; together, the aspirations and the details form a cohesive code.

Software engineers shall commit themselves to making the analysis, specification, design, development, testing and maintenance of software a beneficial and respected profession. In accordance with their commitment to the health, safety and welfare of the public, software engineers shall adhere to the following Eight Principles:

1. PUBLIC - Software engineers shall act consistently with the public interest.
2. CLIENT AND EMPLOYER - Software engineers shall act in a manner that is in the best interests of their client and employer consistent with the public interest.

3.  PRODUCT – Software engineers shall ensure that their products and related modifications meet the highest professional standards possible.

4.  JUDGMENT – Software engineers shall maintain integrity and independence in their professional judgment.

5.  MANAGEMENT – Software engineering managers and leaders shall subscribe to and promote an ethical approach to the management of software development and maintenance.

6.  PROFESSION – Software engineers shall advance the integrity and reputation of the profession consistent with the public interest.

7.  COLLEAGUES – Software engineers shall be fair to and supportive of their colleagues.

8.  SELF – Software engineers shall participate in lifelong learning regarding the practice of their profession and shall promote an ethical approach to the practice of the profession.

## Software Engineering Code of Ethics and Professional Practice (Full Version)

### PREAMBLE

Computers have a central and growing role in commerce, industry, government, medicine, education, entertainment and society at large. Software engineers are those who contribute by direct participation or by teaching, to the analysis, specification, design, development, certification, maintenance and testing of software systems. Because of their roles in developing software systems, software engineers have significant opportunities to do good or cause harm, to enable others to do good or cause harm, or to influence others to do good or cause harm. To ensure, as much as possible, that their efforts will be used for good, software engineers must commit themselves to making software engineering a beneficial and respected profession. In accordance with that commitment, software engineers shall adhere to the following Code of Ethics and Professional Practice.

The Code contains eight Principles related to the behavior of and decisions made by professional software engineers, including practitioners, educators, managers, supervisors and policy makers, as well as trainees and students of the profession. The Principles identify the ethically responsible relationships in which individuals, groups, and organizations participate and the primary obligations within these relationships. The Clauses of each Principle are illustrations of some of the obligations included in these relationships. These obligations are founded in the software engineer's humanity, in special care owed to people affected by the work of software engineers, and the unique elements of the practice of software engineering. The Code prescribes these as obligations of anyone claiming to be or aspiring to be a software engineer.

It is not intended that the individual parts of the Code be used in isolation to justify errors of omission or commission. The list of Principles and Clauses is not exhaustive. The Clauses should not be read as separating the acceptable from the unacceptable in professional conduct in all practical situations. The Code is not a simple ethical algorithm that generates ethical decisions. In some situations standards may be in tension with each other or with standards from other sources. These situations require the software engineer to use ethical judgment to act in a manner which is most consistent with the spirit of the Code of Ethics and Professional Practice, given the circumstances.

Ethical tensions can best be addressed by thoughtful consideration of fundamental principles, rather than blind reliance on detailed regulations. These Principles should influence software engineers to consider broadly who is affected by their work; to examine if they and their colleagues are treating other human beings with due respect; to consider how the public, if reasonably well informed, would view their decisions; to analyze how the least empowered will be affected by their decisions; and to consider whether their acts would be judged worthy of the ideal professional working as a software engineer. In all these judgments concern for the health, safety and welfare of the public is primary; that is, the "Public Interest" is central to this Code.

The dynamic and demanding context of software engineering requires a code that is adaptable and relevant to new situations as they occur. However, even in this generality, the Code provides support for software engineers and managers of software engineers who need to take positive action in a specific case by documenting the ethical stance of the profession. The Code provides an ethical foundation to which individuals within teams and the team as a whole can appeal. The Code helps to define those actions that are ethically improper to request of a software engineer or teams of software engineers.

The Code is not simply for adjudicating the nature of questionable acts; it also has an important educational function. As this Code expresses the consensus of the profession on ethical issues, it is a means to educate both the public and aspiring professionals about the ethical obligations of all software engineers.

## PRINCIPLES

### Principle 1: PUBLIC

Software engineers shall act consistently with the public interest. In particular, software engineers shall, as appropriate:

1.01.   Accept full responsibility for their own work.

1.02.   Moderate the interests of the software engineer, the employer, the client and the users with the public good.

1.03.   Approve software only if they have a well-founded belief that it is safe, meets specifications, passes appropriate tests, and does not diminish quality of life, diminish privacy or harm the environment. The ultimate effect of the work should be to the public good.

1.04.   Disclose to appropriate persons or authorities any actual or potential danger to the user, the public, or the environment, that they reasonably believe to be associated with software or related documents.

1.05.   Cooperate in efforts to address matters of grave public concern caused by software, its installation, maintenance, support or documentation.

1.06.   Be fair and avoid deception in all statements, particularly public ones, concerning software or related documents, methods and tools.

1.07.   Consider issues of physical disabilities, allocation of resources, economic disadvantage and other factors that can diminish access to the benefits of software.

1.08.   Be encouraged to volunteer professional skills to good causes and contribute to public education concerning the discipline.

## Principle 2: CLIENT AND EMPLOYER

Software engineers shall act in a manner that is in the best interests of their client and employer, consistent with the public interest. In particular, software engineers shall, as appropriate:

2.01.   Provide service in their areas of competence, being honest and forthright about any limitations of their experience and education.

2.02.   Not knowingly use software that is obtained or retained either illegally or unethically.

2.03.   Use the property of a client or employer only in ways properly authorized, and with the client's or employer's knowledge and consent.

2.04.   Ensure that any document upon which they rely has been approved, when required, by someone authorized to approve it.

2.05.   Keep private any confidential information gained in their professional work, where such confidentiality is consistent with the public interest and consistent with the law.

2.06.   Identify, document, collect evidence and report to the client or the employer promptly if, in their opinion, a project is likely to fail, to prove too expensive, to violate intellectual property law, or otherwise to be problematic.

2.07.   Identify, document, and report significant issues of social concern, of which they are aware, in software or related documents, to the employer or the client.

2.08.   Accept no outside work detrimental to the work they perform for their primary employer.

2.09.   Promote no interest adverse to their employer or client, unless a higher ethical concern is being compromised; in that case, inform the employer or another appropriate authority of the ethical concern.

## Principle 3: PRODUCT

Software engineers shall ensure that their products and related modifications meet the highest professional standards possible. In particular, software engineers shall, as appropriate:

3.01.    Strive for high quality, acceptable cost and a reasonable schedule, ensuring significant tradeoffs are clear to and accepted by the employer and the client, and are available for consideration by the user and the public.

3.02.    Ensure proper and achievable goals and objectives for any project on which they work or propose.

3.03.    Identify, define and address ethical, economic, cultural, legal and environmental issues related to work projects.

3.04.    Ensure that they are qualified for any project on which they work or propose to work by an appropriate combination of education and training, and experience.

3.05.    Ensure an appropriate method is used for any project on which they work or propose to work.

3.06.    Work to follow professional standards, when available, that are most appropriate for the task at hand, departing from these only when ethically or technically justified.

3.07.    Strive to fully understand the specifications for software on which they work.

3.08.    Ensure that specifications for software on which they work have been well documented, satisfy the users' requirements and have the appropriate approvals.

3.09.    Ensure realistic quantitative estimates of cost, scheduling, personnel, quality and outcomes on any project on which they work or propose to work and provide an uncertainty assessment of these estimates.

3.10.    Ensure adequate testing, debugging, and review of software and related documents on which they work.

3.11.    Ensure adequate documentation, including significant problems discovered and solutions adopted, for any project on which they work.

3.12.    Work to develop software and related documents that respect the privacy of those who will be affected by that software.

3.13.    Be careful to use only accurate data derived by ethical and lawful means, and use it only in ways properly authorized.

3.14.    Maintain the integrity of data, being sensitive to outdated or flawed occurrences.

3.15.    Treat all forms of software maintenance with the same professionalism as new development.

## Principle 4: JUDGMENT

Software engineers shall maintain integrity and independence in their professional judgment. In particular, software engineers shall, as appropriate:

4.01.    Temper all technical judgments by the need to support and maintain human values.

4.02.    Only endorse documents either prepared under their supervision or within their areas of competence and with which they are in agreement.

4.03.    Maintain professional objectivity with respect to any software or related documents they are asked to evaluate.

4.04.    Not engage in deceptive financial practices such as bribery, double billing, or other improper financial practices.

4.05.    Disclose to all concerned parties those conflicts of interest that cannot reasonably be avoided or escaped.

4.06.    Refuse to participate, as members or advisors, in a private, governmental or professional body concerned with software related issues, in which they, their employers or their clients have undisclosed potential conflicts of interest.

## Principle 5: MANAGEMENT

Software engineering managers and leaders shall subscribe to and promote an ethical approach to the management of software development and maintenance. In particular, those managing or leading software engineers shall, as appropriate:

5.01.    Ensure good management for any project on which they work, including effective procedures for promotion of quality and reduction of risk.

5.02.    Ensure that software engineers are informed of standards before being held to them.

5.03.    Ensure that software engineers know the employer's policies and procedures for protecting passwords, files and information that is confidential to the employer or confidential to others.

5.04.    Assign work only after taking into account appropriate contributions of education and experience tempered with a desire to further that education and experience.

5.05.    Ensure realistic quantitative estimates of cost, scheduling, personnel, quality and outcomes on any project on which they work or propose to work, and provide an uncertainty assessment of these estimates.

5.06.    Attract potential software engineers only by full and accurate description of the conditions of employment.

5.07.    Offer fair and just remuneration.

5.08.    Not unjustly prevent someone from taking a position for which that person is suitably qualified.

5.09.    Ensure that there is a fair agreement concerning ownership of any software, processes, research, writing, or other intellectual property to which a software engineer has contributed.

5.10.    Provide for due process in hearing charges of violation of an employer's policy or of this Code.

5.11.    Not ask a software engineer to do anything inconsistent with this Code.

5.12.    Not punish anyone for expressing ethical concerns about a project.

## Principle 6: PROFESSION

Software engineers shall advance the integrity and reputation of the profession consistent with the public interest. In particular, software engineers shall, as appropriate:

6.01.   Help develop an organizational environment favorable to acting ethically.

6.02.   Promote public knowledge of software engineering.

6.03.   Extend software engineering knowledge by appropriate participation in professional organizations, meetings and publications.

6.04.   Support, as members of a profession, other software engineers striving to follow this Code.

6.05.   Not promote their own interest at the expense of the profession, client or employer.

6.06.   Obey all laws governing their work, unless, in exceptional circumstances, such compliance is inconsistent with the public interest.

6.07.   Be accurate in stating the characteristics of software on which they work, avoiding not only false claims but also claims that might reasonably be supposed to be speculative, vacuous, deceptive, misleading, or doubtful.

6.08.   Take responsibility for detecting, correcting, and reporting errors in software and associated documents on which they work.

6.09.   Ensure that clients, employers, and supervisors know of the software engineer's commitment to this Code of ethics, and the subsequent ramifications of such commitment.

6.10.   Avoid associations with businesses and organizations which are in conflict with this code.

6.11.   Recognize that violations of this Code are inconsistent with being a professional software engineer.

6.12.   Express concerns to the people involved when significant violations of this Code are detected unless this is impossible, counter-productive, or dangerous.

6.13.   Report significant violations of this Code to appropriate authorities when it is clear that consultation with people involved in these significant violations is impossible, counter-productive or dangerous.

## Principle 7: COLLEAGUES

Software engineers shall be fair to and supportive of their colleagues. In particular, software engineers shall, as appropriate:

7.01.   Encourage colleagues to adhere to this Code.

7.02.   Assist colleagues in professional development.

7.03.   Credit fully the work of others and refrain from taking undue credit.

7.04.   Review the work of others in an objective, candid, and properly-documented way.

7.05.   Give a fair hearing to the opinions, concerns, or complaints of a colleague.

7.06.   Assist colleagues in being fully aware of current standard work practices including policies and procedures for protecting passwords, files and other confidential information, and security measures in general.

7.07.   Not unfairly intervene in the career of any colleague; however, concern for the employer, the client or public interest may compel software engineers, in good faith, to question the competence of a colleague.

7.08.   In situations outside of their own areas of competence, call upon the opinions of other professionals who have competence in that area.

## Principle 8: SELF

Software engineers shall participate in lifelong learning regarding the practice of their profession and shall promote an ethical approach to the practice of the profession. In particular, software engineers shall continually endeavor to:

8.01.   Further their knowledge of developments in the analysis, specification, design, development, maintenance and testing of software and related documents, together with the management of the development process.

8.02.   Improve their ability to create safe, reliable, and useful quality software at reasonable cost and within a reasonable time.

8.03.   Improve their ability to produce accurate, informative, and well-written documentation.

8.04.   Improve their understanding of the software and related documents on which they work and of the environment in which they will be used.

8.05.   Improve their knowledge of relevant standards and the law governing the software and related documents on which they work.

8.06.   Improve their knowledge of this Code, its interpretation, and its application to their work.

8.07.   Not give unfair treatment to anyone because of any irrelevant prejudices.

8.08.   Not influence others to undertake any action that involves a breach of this Code.

8.09.   Recognize that personal violations of this Code are inconsistent with being a professional software engineer.

This Code was developed by the ACM/IEEE-CS joint task force on Software Engineering Ethics and Professional Practices (SEEPP):

Executive Committee: Donald Gotterbarn (Chair), Keith Miller and Simon Rogerson;

Members: Steve Barber, Peter Barnes, Ilene Burnstein, Michael Davis, Amr El-Kadi, N. Ben Fairweather, Milton Fulghum, N. Jayaram, Tom Jewett, Mark Kanko, Ernie Kallman, Duncan Langford, Joyce Currie Little, Ed Mechler, Manuel J. Norman, Douglas Phillips, Peter Ron Prinzivalli, Patrick Sullivan, John Weckert, Vivian Weil, S. Weisband and Laurie Honour Werth.

# Index